Organization and Administration in Higher Education

Efficiency, focus, and accountability have become the defining standards for contemporary higher educational leaders. Situating strategic planning and budgeting within the organization and administration of higher education institutions, *Organization and Administration in Higher Education* provides effective and proven strategies for today's change-oriented leaders. Bringing together distinguished administrators from two-year, four-year, public, and private colleges and universities, this volume provides both practical and effective guidance on the intricacies of the institutional structure, its functional activities, and contingency planning. Coverage includes:

- Key leadership positions and expectations
- Faculty and student governance
- Accreditation and assessment
- Budget processes
- Curriculum alignment
- Philanthropic efforts
- Human resource development
- Legal considerations
- Strategic planning
- Crisis management

Effective planning and administration can elevate an institution in critical ways, by enhancing recruitment and retention, strengthening student life, increasing outside support and private giving, and advancing a reputation for excellence. This practical and authoritative guide orients future and current administrators to the major areas of an academic institution and will assist higher education administrators in leading their institutions to excellence.

Patrick J. Schloss, Ph.D., is Assistant Executive Vice Chancellor for Retention, Progression, and Graduation for the University System of Georgia and former President of Valdosta State University, USA.

Kristina M. Cragg, Ph.D., is Associate Vice President of Institutional Research at Ashford University, USA.

Organization and Administration in Higher Education

Edited by
Patrick J. Schloss and Kristina M. Cragg

Routledge
Taylor & Francis Group

NEW YORK AND LONDON

First published 2013
by Routledge
711 Third Avenue, New York, NY 10017

Simultaneously published in the UK
by Routledge
2 Park Square, Milton Park, Abingdon, Oxon OX14 4RN

Routledge is an imprint of the Taylor & Francis Group, an informa business

Library of Congress Cataloging in Publication Data
Organization and administration in higher education / edited by Patrick J. Schloss and Kristina M. Cragg.
p. cm.
Includes bibliographical references and index.
1. Universities and colleges—United States—Administration. 2. Universities and colleges—United States—Planning. 3. Education, Higher—United States—Administration. 4. Education, Higher—United States—Planning. I. Schloss, Patrick J. II. Cragg, Kristina Marie
LB2341.C7234 2004
378.1'01—dc23
2012019155

ISBN: 978-0-415-89269-8 (hbk)
ISBN: 978-0-415-89270-4 (pbk)
ISBN: 978-0-203-81762-9 (ebk)

Typeset in Minion
by Book Now Ltd, London

Printed and bound in the United States of America by
Edwards Brothers Malloy on sustainably sourced paper

Dedication
To my mom (Julia A. Goodwin), for a
lifetime of love, support, and encouragement
—Kristina M. Cragg

CONTENTS

FIGURES

TABLES

FOREWORD

Whether one chooses to serve in public, private not-for-profit, private for-profit, community/technical, liberal arts or research institutions, there are certain tools every administrator should have in order to be successful in a career in higher education leadership. These generally include adequate academic preparation usually in the form of an advanced degree, an adequate and varied number of professional experiences within the academy, a strong support system outside of the institution, and an understanding of every complex aspect of the institution they're going to lead. Now, an invaluable addition to that tool box is this publication.

Most administrators in higher education rise through the ranks of faculty to mid-manager, Vice President, and then President and have no official training in academic leadership. Additionally, most begin their administrative careers with a limited understanding of how the entire organization works. They may be familiar with how faculty work together, at least in their own division, but not necessarily with the role faculty play in the overall governance of the institution. Or they may have had to develop and manage a budget for their division but have never seen, let alone been involved in, the development of the entire institutional budget. As they serve in their first administrative position, they probably also experience a great deal of angst in moving from "us" to "them" as they lose support from the group with which they had been most familiar.

Often times, when initially confronted with building a budget that evolves from a strategic planning process, first-time administrators spend many hours in a fog trying to develop objectives that are directed by the plan and that support the budget. Or when faced with the prospect of evaluating employees, have no idea how to document their performance and, when needed, suggesting training opportunities to increase their effectiveness. This publication explains the intricacies of each area in a language that is simple to follow yet concise and well documented.

As administrators, we are often so focused upon the issues for which we are directly responsible that we fail to see the "big picture" until we are sitting in the chair of the Vice

President or President. By then, there is often a steep learning curve related to putting everything together and understanding how it all flows together. All along the way, we learned by trial and error how to respond to each issue and process that faced us each day. The authors of this publication have taken all of the mystery out of the very issues that surface on a day-to-day basis for academic leaders, and provided the proverbial road map to success.

From strategic planning and budgeting, governance and human resource development, curriculum and assessment, and crisis management and legal issues, this publication explains the intricacies of each, offers suggestions as to how each area impacts everything else within the institution, and then provides a brief summary that can be used later to reinforce what was read. It is truly a practical guide to orienting administrators to the major areas of an academic institution and to assisting them in becoming effective leaders. Whether as a textbook or as a reference source, this book will serve current and future leaders well in their quest for excellence as they lead our institutions of higher education in the 21st century.

Belle S. Wheelan, Ph.D., President
Southern Association of Colleges and Schools, Commission on Colleges

PREFACE

Successful technical schools, community colleges, liberal arts colleges, and comprehensive universities can be defined by the quality of their leadership teams. Effective planning and administration, regardless of strategic advantages, can elevate a school beyond its peers in a vast array of critical dimensions. All can enhance recruitment and retention, strengthen student life opportunities, increase extramural support and private giving, and advance the institution's reputation for excellence.

Irrespective of level, leaders who effectively utilize governance groups, planning tools, and budgeting techniques make a difference in the prospects of the institution. More important, they make a difference in the prospects of graduates and other stakeholders. Our primary goal in writing *Organization and Administration in Higher Education* was to offer guidance to change-oriented higher education leaders. Its contents are also valuable to pre-service administrators taking courses in higher education administration and finance. The book seeks to provide guidance in the best and worst of times, though it is during the hard times that outstanding leadership is most desperately needed.

We refer liberally to "postsecondary" and "higher education" institutions. These terms apply to any institution that builds upon a high school education, including technical schools, liberal arts colleges, specialty institutions, community colleges, and comprehensive universities. Relevant institutions may be private, requiring substantial tuition income, or public, receiving governmental support. They may be operated for profit or not for profit. We also reference institutions that provide Web-based programs or other distance learning options.

This book may be useful to anyone working at or toward the "cabinet" or "senior leadership" level. These individuals may be currently employed in a leadership position, using the contents to expand their perspective and skill, or they may be preparing for advancement into such a position, as would be the case with students in graduate leadership programs.

The contents cut across a wide range of disciplines and areas of expertise. Resource management, finance, law, human capital, and political action all form the basis of effective administration. No single author is likely to be as capable of addressing all these subjects as a team of specialized individuals. For this reason, we called upon a number of chapter authors. Each is a recognized expert in a critical area of higher education administration. These authors followed a common format and style so that while the expertise underlying the text is diverse, the voice is relatively uniform. We appreciate the authors' flexibility in working within a preset template. While challenging for the authors, this consistency will benefit the reader.

The book is structured around functional themes in the management of postsecondary institutions. Not intended to be a "cookbook" or operations manual, the content strikes a balance between philosophical underpinnings and basic operations. The goal was to make the philosophical foundation clear to the reader while fully developing approaches consistent with that foundation.

The first broad theme is the structure of higher education. Related chapters range from a broad overview of institutions by style and a characterization of personnel by responsibility and expertise, to discussions of institutional and student governance. The second broad theme examines the functional activities that characterize effective institutions. We combine the complex areas of strategic planning and budgeting within the context of organization and administration of higher education institutions. Relevant chapters focus on planning and budgeting as well as the evaluation of outcomes. The final theme includes contingency planning, with chapters addressing crisis management and the legal foundations for decision-making. The approach described in the text is comprehensive, including all levels of decision-makers and a full range of objectives. Similarly, the planning and budgeting constructs are applied to all typical postsecondary institutions.

Regardless of the specific focus of a chapter, certain content is woven throughout the text. Special attention is given to the importance of directing institutional resources to areas of strategic advantage, diminishing spending in areas of marginal distinction, cultivating alternative revenue sources, obtaining broad-based support for strategic decisions, and creating a culture of accountability and excellence. Traditional challenges of crisis management, communication, curriculum development, and institutional communication are also addressed.

We often focus on the challenge of declining state appropriations for state institutions and diminishing discretionary dollars from families for private institutions. Efficiency, focus, and accountability have become the defining standards for contemporary educational leaders in all sectors. Regardless of the chapter, there is continual reference to approaches that allow institutions to do more with less.

Legal issues and governmental intervention have become an increasing part of the landscape in higher education, particularly with respect to personnel issues. For this reason, we have devoted a chapter each to higher education law and human resources. Moreover, related content appears in chapters on resource allocation, crisis management, governance, and performance expectations.

Best practices that have been reported in the literature and for which certain institutions have become renowned serve as a foundation for concepts and techniques described in the text. The content is also shaped by "lessons learned" by the authors, most of whom have held high-level administrative positions in postsecondary institutions. We believe these lessons, combined with the authors' deep knowledge of the professional literature, will make this work both practical and authoritative for current and future administrators.

ACKNOWLEDGMENTS

We would like to express our heartfelt appreciation to those who have made this book possible. First, we would like to acknowledge all of the chapter authors. Their collective expertise resulted in a resource of breadth and depth for current and future administrators. We thank Belle Wheelan, President of the Southern Association of Colleges and Schools, Commission on Colleges, for writing the foreword and eloquently capturing the book's purpose and value to the field of higher education. We deeply admire the editing expertise of Tracy Kendrick. Her attention to detail, combined with passion for her profession, was the patina on this collective effort. Finally, an honorable mention goes to the family and friends of all contributors to this book; it is with their support that we are able to complete the research that we are so passionate about.

Part I

Structure of Institutions

1

UNDERSTANDING THE RANGE OF POSTSECONDARY INSTITUTIONS AND PROGRAMS

Kristina M. Cragg and Angela E. Henderson

INTRODUCTION

When traveling, be it for business or pleasure, we tend to compare and contrast our new location with more familiar surroundings. The new location may be bigger or smaller, more or less diverse, or warmer or colder than our current home. Having a common set of criteria for evaluation allows us to make comparisons and acclimate. The same is true for higher education institutions, for which a national database provides a common set of definitions and variables for each institution, making it possible to compare more than 7,000 institutions that submit federal data to the National Center for Education Statistics (NCES) each year.

Current and future administrators try to better understand the higher education landscape; they will benefit from this chapter's detailed descriptions of types of institutions and quality indicators that key external stakeholders such as parents, prospective students, legislators, and media focus on when evaluating an institution. Key internal stakeholders such as the president, vice presidents, deans, and directors also focus on key indicators, but do so with unique management challenges described herein.

PRIVATE, PUBLIC, AND PROPRIETARY

Within the general structure of higher education, there are two main categories of postsecondary institutions: public and private. Private institutions are further divided into two types: not-for-profit and for-profit (proprietary).

Public Institutions

The NCES defines a public institution as "an educational institution whose programs and activities are operated by publicly elected or appointed school officials and which is supported primarily by public funds" (IPEDS, n.d.b, para. 44). Public institutions include institutions of all levels and program offerings, from two-year community colleges to doctorate-granting research-level universities. In 2008-09, public institutions constituted 41% of the accredited postsecondary institutions in the United States that submitted data to NCES, with a total enrollment of over 14 million students (IPEDS, n.d.a). The key commonality among these institutions is that they all receive some form of public funding.

The number of public institutions in the United States has increased in the last 30 years. In fall 1980, there were a total of 1,497 public degree-granting institutions, the majority of which were two-year institutions (NCES, 2009). Public four-year degree-granting institutions were less plentiful, comprising less than 40% of all public degree-granting institutions (NCES, 2009). Enrollment at degree-granting public institutions totaled nearly 9.5 million; which represented more than three-quarters (78%) of all students attending postsecondary institutions in 1980 (NCES, 2009).

By fall 2008, the number of public degree-granting institutions had increased by 12% (NCES, 2009). Despite this gain, the distribution between two-year and four-year public degree-granting institutions remained virtually unchanged; from 1980 to 2008, approximately 60% of all public degree-granting institutions were two-year colleges (NCES, 2009). Figure 1.2, which shows the distribution of public degree-granting institutions by type as of 2008, clearly illustrates the predominance of two-year colleges (NCES, 2009).

As the number of public degree-granting institutions has grown, so too has their total enrollment, from nearly 9.5 million in 1980 to nearly 14 million in fall 2008, a 48% increase (NCES, 2009). Public degree-granting two-year institutions experienced a greater enrollment increase than public degree-granting four-year institutions, with gains of 53% in comparison to the latter's 43% (NCES, 2009).

Private Institutions

While public institutions receive some public funding, private institutions are "usually supported primarily by other than public funds, and operated by other than publicly elected or appointed officials" (IPEDS, n.d.b, para. 33). They must therefore fund all costs through private means such as tuition. There are two financial structures utilized by private institutions: not-for-profit and for-profit (or proprietary). Not-for-profit institutions operate like not-for-profit organizations in that surplus revenue must all be directed to institutional goals. For-profit institutions have no restrictions with surplus revenue, but are arguably subject to greater accountability than their counterparts.

Because private institutions do not receive public funding, they have the flexibility to provide educational experiences not available in public institutions, such as faith-based programs. Like their public counterparts, private institutions include two- and four-year postsecondary schools with various degree programs and specialties. In 2008-09, private institutions constituted 59% of the accredited postsecondary institutions in the United States that submitted data to NCES, with a total enrollment of over 5 million, or 27% of all students enrolled (IPEDS, n.d.a). The 38% of these private institutions classified as private not-for-profit enrolled 3.7 million students and the 20% classified as private for-profit enrolled over 1.5 million (IPEDS, n.d.a). Similar to the trend shown by public institutions, the number of private institutions increased during the period 1980-2008; however, the increase was much greater, as the number of private for-profit institutions rose by 58% (NCES, 2009).

Private Not-for-Profit Institutions

Despite this growth, the total number of degree-granting private not-for-profit institutions increased by less than 5% in the same timeframe. The number of two-year private not-for-profit degree-granting institutions experienced a substantial decrease, dropping 49%, from fall 1980 to fall 2008, while the number of four-year private not-for-profit degree-granting institutions increased by more than 10% (NCES, 2009). Figure 1.2 illustrates the distribution of private not-for-profit degree-granting institutions by type as of 2008 (NCES, 2009). With the gain in the number of four-year private not-for-profit degree-granting institutions, total enrollment at private not-for-profit degree-granting institutions grew to more than 3.6 million students, an increase of 45% over fall 1980 (NCES, 2009). Enrollment at four-year private not-for-profit degree-granting institutions grew by 50%, while enrollment at private not-for-profit two-year degree-granting institutions dropped by nearly 70% during the same time (NCES, 2009).

Private For-Profit Institutions

The slight growth in private not-for-profit degree-granting institutions is overshadowed by the considerable growth in private for-profit institutions. While only 165 private for-profit degree-granting institutions existed in fall 1980, by fall 2008 there were over 1,100, a more than 500% increase. The number of four-year private for-profit degree-granting institutions rose most dramatically, from 20 to 530, an increase of over 2,800% (NCES, 2009). The number of two-year private for-profit degree-granting institutions also grew,

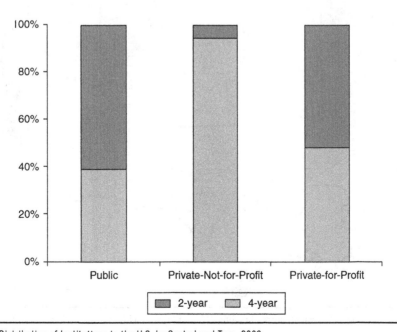

Figure 1.1 Distribution of Institutions in the U.S. by Control and Type, 2008

from 147 to 574, or 290% (NCES, 2009). As illustrated in Figure 1.1, the distribution of two- and four-year private for-profit degree-granting institutions was nearly even, at 52% and 48% respectively, by fall 2008 (NCES, 2009).

As would be expected with such a substantial increase in the number of institutions, enrollment at private for-profit degree-granting institutions rose sharply. In fall 1980, just over 110,000 students were enrolled at private for-profit degree-granting institutions—less than 1% of all students attending postsecondary schools (NCES, 2009). By fall 2008, that number had increased by more than 1,200% to 1.4 million, or nearly 8% of all postsecondary students (NCES, 2009). Four-year degree-granting institutions account for much of this overall growth; their enrollment totaled nearly 1.2 million students in fall 2008, an increase of over 4,000% from 1980 (NCES, 2009). While two-year degree-granting institutions also experienced enrollment growth, the gain (254%) was not as substantial (NCES, 2009).

Overall Geographical Distribution of Institutions and Enrollment

In 2008, over 4,000 degree-granting colleges and universities in the United States with a collective enrollment of over 20 million students provided data to the National Center for Education Statistics (NCES), a division of the U.S. Department of Education responsible for collecting and analyzing data related to education (IPEDS, n.d.a). Public degree-granting institutions represented 41% of the respondents and enrolled nearly

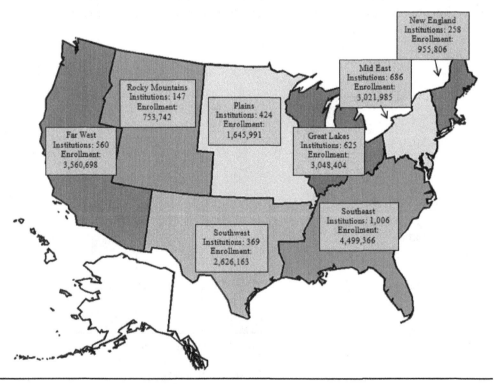

Figure 1.2 Distribution of Accredited, Degree-Granting, U.S. Institutions and Enrollment by Region, 2009

three-quarters of all students (approximately 15 million), while private degree-granting institutions enrolled 5.3 million students (IPEDS, n.d.a).

Figure 1.2 shows the total number of accredited, degree-granting institutions and students enrolled in each of eight regions of the United States as of 2009 (IPEDS, n.d.a). The Southeast region, which includes 12 states (Alabama, Arkansas, Florida, Georgia, Kentucky, Louisiana, Mississippi, North Carolina, South Carolina, Tennessee, Virginia, and West Virginia), constituted the largest percentage of institutions and student enrollment: 29% of all institutions and 24% of total enrollment. Overall, the Southeast region contains the highest number of private for-profit and public institutions. The Mid East is the only region containing more private not-for-profit institutions than the Southeast; however, it has fewer students. More institutions lie within the Southeast than in the New England, Rocky Mountains, and Southwest regions combined.

CLASSIFICATION OF INSTITUTIONS

Since the 1970s, degree-granting postsecondary institutions in the United States that have attained accreditation and that report data to the NCES have been classified using the Carnegie Classification system (Carnegie, n.d.a). The Carnegie Commission's efforts to organize "a classification of colleges and universities to support its program of research and policy analysis" prompted development and implementation of the categorization process (Carnegie, n.d.a, para.1). Since its implementation in 1973, and subsequent revisions and enhancements, the system has become the definitive source of institutional comparison categorization data. This has become increasingly important, as more than 4,000 institutions participate in the Carnegie Classification system as of 2010. McCormick and Zhao commented on the 2005 revised Carnegie Classifications, "One goal of the new system was to call attention to—and emphasize the importance of—the considerable institutional diversity of U.S. higher education" (2005, p. 52). The Carnegie Classifications allow institutions and researchers to make informed decisions regarding the selection of peer institutions based on analytical groupings of institutions using consistent standards.

Since 1973, the Carnegie Classifications have been revised periodically to reflect changes in higher education, most recently in 2010 (Carnegie, n.d.a). Institutions are categorized using data they submit to the Department of Education, the College Board, and the National Science Foundation (McCormick & Zhao, 2005). Carnegie researchers compile the data and classify the institutions based on location, enrollment, programs, and degrees conferred (McCormick & Zhao, 2005).

The most substantial update to the classification system, which occurred in 2005, revised its structure, offering more categories so that institutions can more easily identify potential peer institutions (Carnegie, n.d.c).

The 2005 (and the subsequent 2010) Carnegie Classifications are structured around the core aspects of institutions: programs offered, students enrolled, degrees conferred, and size and setting (Carnegie, n.d.a). They thus allow researchers to "represent and control for institutional differences, and … to ensure adequate representation of sampled institutions, students, or faculty" (Carnegie, n.d.a, para. 1).

More specific than its predecessors, the 2005 system offers a total of 33 classifications, 15 more than the 2000 version (Carnegie, 2001, n.d.d). The classification of Associate's Colleges experienced the most substantial shift, from a single classification in 2000 to 14 classifications in the 2005 system (Carnegie, 2001, n.d.d). Doctoral and Master's institutions each gained one additional classification level in the 2005 structure (Carnegie, 2001, n.d.d).

In addition to providing a more granular structure, the 2005 system reflects a change in methodology, drawing on the most recent data provided by institutions to NCES "to maximize the timeliness of the classifications" (Carnegie, n.d.c, para. 18). This approach categorizes institutions based on "time-specific snapshots of institutional attributes and behavior" (Carnegie, n.d.b, para. 1) rather than on three-year averages of variables, as in previous Carnegie Classification systems.

The structure established with the 2005 revisions form the basis of the most current set of classifications, the 2010 Carnegie Classifications. These classifications utilize the structure of the 2005 classifications and incorporate more recent data points to provide updated institutional snapshots. Changes to the existing 2005 structure were minimal in order to facilitate multi-year comparisons (Carnegie, n.d.c, para. 3).

The 2010 (and the preceding 2005) structure includes six areas of classification, as shown in Table 1.1.

Table 1.1 2010 Carnegie Classifications and Descriptions

Classification	Description
Basic Classification	An update of the traditional classification framework developed by the Carnegie Commission on Higher Education in 1970
Size and Setting Classification	Describes institutions' size and residential character
Undergraduate Instructional Program Classification	Based on three pieces of information: the level of undergraduate degrees awarded (associate's or bachelor's), the proportion of bachelor's degree majors in the arts and sciences and in professional fields, and the extent to which an institution awards graduate degrees in the same fields in which it awards undergraduate degrees
Graduate Instructional Program Classification	Based on the level of graduate degrees awarded (master's degrees, and doctoral degrees categorized as either research, professional practice, or other doctorate), the number of fields represented by the degrees awarded, and the mix or concentration of degrees by broad disciplinary domain
Enrollment Profile Classification	Groups institutions according to the mix of students enrolled at the undergraduate and graduate/professional levels
Undergraduate Profile Classifications	Describes the undergraduate population with respect to three characteristics: the proportion of undergraduate students who attend part- or full-time; achievement characteristics of first-year, first-time students; and the proportion of entering students who transfer in from another institution

Source: Carnegie (n.d.d, n.d.e, n.d.f, n.d.g, n.d.h, n.d.i).

Table 1.2 2010 Basic Carnegie Classification and Descriptions

Classification	Description
Doctorate-Granting Universities	Award a minimum of 20 doctoral degrees annually (excluding professional doctorates)
Master's Colleges and Universities	Award a minimum of 50 master's degrees and fewer than 20 doctoral degrees annually
Baccalaureate Colleges	Award at least 10% of all undergraduate degrees as baccalaureate degrees; fewer than 50 master's degrees or 20 doctoral degrees awarded annually
Associate's Colleges	Award only associate's degrees or bachelor's degrees; account for less than 10% of all undergraduate degrees
Special Focus Institutions	Award baccalaureate or higher degrees in a single field or set of related fields
Tribal Colleges	Award levels vary. Include all colleges and universities within the American Indian Higher Education Consortium

Source: Carnegie (n.d.d).

The Basic Classification, the one most commonly used, categorizes institutions into six levels: Doctorate-Granting Universities, Master's Colleges and Universities, Baccalaureate Colleges, Associate's Colleges, and Special Focus Institutions (theological, medical, law,

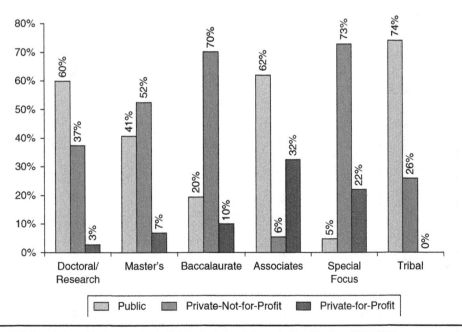

Figure 1.3 Distribution of Institutions in the U.S. by Control and Carnegie Classification, 2008–2009

Source: IPEDS, n.d.a.

Table 1.3 Distribution of U.S. Carnegie Institutions and Students by Institution Control and Carnegie Classification, 2009

Classification Level	Total Number of Institutions	Total Number of Students	Public Institutions				Private Not-for-Profit Institutions				Private for-Profit Institutions			
			Number of Institutions	Percent of Institutions	Number of Students	Percent of Students	Number of Institutions	Percent of Institutions	Number of Students	Percent of Students	Number of Institutions	Percent of Institutions	Number of Students	Percent of Students
RU/VH: Research Universities (Very high research activity)	99	2,549,735	66	67%	2,048,560	80%	33	33%	501,175	20%	0	0%	0	0%
RU/H: Research Universities (high research activity)	102	1,813,329	75	74%	1,493,987	82%	27	26%	319,342	18%	0	0%	0	0%
DRU: Doctoral/ Research Universities	80	1,212,967	27	34%	407,190	34%	45	56%	338,731	28%	8	10%	467,046	39%
Master's/L: Master's Colleges and Universities (larger programs)	336	3,033,937	164	49%	2,034,091	67%	155	46%	819,869	27%	17	5%	179,977	6%
Master's/M: Master's Colleges and Universities (medium programs)	184	806,089	67	36%	442,146	55%	103	56%	336,381	42%	14	8%	27,562	3%

Master's/S: Master's Colleges and Universities (smaller programs)	123	375,255	25%	31	152,411	41%	79	64%	199,448	53%	13	11%	23,396	6%
Bac/A&S: Baccalaureate Colleges—Arts & Sciences	280	572,110	14%	38	153,656	27%	240	86%	417,584	73%	2	1%	870	0.2%
Bac/Divers: Baccalaureate Colleges—Diverse Fields	326	626,491	21%	70	211,112	34%	236	72%	353,893	56%	20	6%	61,486	10%
Bac/Assoc: Baccalaureate/Associate's Colleges	109	393,675	29%	32	156,371	40%	27	25%	74,734	19%	50	46%	162,570	41%
Assoc: Associate's Colleges	1684	8,089,112	62%	1,041	7,602,069	94%	96	6%	52,070	1%	547	32%	434,973	5%
Special Focus Institutions (all)	729	638,227	5%	38	77,952	12%	532	73%	331,713	52%	159	22%	228,562	36%
Tribal: Tribal Colleges	31	19,460	74%	23	14,365	74%	8	26%	5,095	26%	0	0%	0	0%

Source: IPEDS (n.d.a).

etc.), and Tribal Colleges. The descriptions for each level are shown in Table 1.2 and addressed in detail in the following section.

Table 1.3 shows the total number of institutions and students enrolled at each type of institution by Carnegie Classification as of 2009; Figure 1.3, the distribution of institutions by control and Carnegie Classification.

Doctorate-Granting Universities

Doctorate-Granting Universities, referred to as Doctoral/Research I and Doctoral/Research II institutions prior to 1994, were renamed Doctoral/Research Extensive and Doctoral/Research Intensive institutions in the 2000 Carnegie Classification "to avoid the inference that the categories signify quality differences" (Carnegie, n.d.c, para. 4). The 2005 version separated these institutions into three categories based on level of research activity: RU/VH: Research Universities (very high research activity), RU/H: Research Universities (high research activity), and DRU: Doctoral/Research Universities (Carnegie, n.d.c, para. 5). Research activity was determined based upon analysis of

> research & development (R&D) expenditures in science and engineering; R&D expenditures in non-S&E fields; S&E research staff (postdoctoral appointees and other non-faculty research staff with doctorates); doctoral conferrals in humanities fields, in social science fields, in STEM (science, technology, engineering, and mathematics) fields, and in other fields (e.g., business, education, public policy, social work).
>
> (Carnegie, n.d.b, sec. 2)

The revisions "created two indices of research activity reflecting the total variation across these measures" (Carnegie, n.d.b, sec. 2). These indices, based on "aggregate level of research activity and per-capita research activity using the expenditure and staffing measures divided by the number of full-time faculty whose primary responsibilities were identified as research, instruction, or a combination of instruction, research, and public service," were used to determine an institution's "distance from a common reference point" (Carnegie, n.d.b, sec. 2). This distance in turn determined the institution's placement in one of the three Doctoral/Research classifications (Carnegie, n.d.b, sec. 2). As the two indices were considered equal, institutions rating very high or high on either item were classified as RU/VH: Research Universities (very high research activity) or RU/H: Research Universities (high research activity) respectively (Carnegie, n.d.b, sec. 2). Institutions not meeting the criteria for either index or not included in the data were assigned to the DRU: Doctoral/Research Universities classification (Carnegie, n.d.b, sec. 2).

As of fall 2009, 281 institutions—less than 7% of the total number considered—fell under one of the three Doctoral/Research classifications (IPEDS, n.d.a). Of these, 35% were classified as Research Universities with very high research activity, 36% as Research Universities with high research activity, and 29% as Doctoral/Research universities (IPEDS, n.d.a). The majority of Doctorate-granting Universities (60%) were public, over a third (37%) were private not-for-profit, and the remaining 3% were private

Table 1.4 Examples of Doctorate-Granting Institutions by Carnegie Classification

Carnegie Classification	Example Institutions
Public RU/VH: Research Universities (very high research activity)	University of Virginia, Washington State University, Georgia Institute of Technology
Private-not-for-profit RU/VH: Research Universities (very high research activity)	Cornell University, Duke University, University of Notre Dame
Public RU/H: Research Universities (high research activity)	Clemson University, Rutgers University, Texas Tech University
Private-not-for-profit RU/H: Research Universities (high research activity)	Baylor University, Nova Southeastern University, Wake Forest University
Public DRU: Doctoral/Research Universities	Bowie State University, Florida A&M University, South Carolina State University
Private-not-for-profit DRU: Doctoral/Research Universities	Brigham Young University, Pepperdine University, St. John's University
Private-for-profit DRU: Doctoral/Research Universities	Argosy University, Capella University, University of Phoenix

Source: Carnegie (n.d.j).

for-profit (IPEDS, n.d.a). Enrollment at Doctorate-granting Universities totaled nearly 6 million in fall 2009, with over 70% of these students attending public institutions (IPEDS, n.d.a). Despite accounting for less than 3% of the Doctoral/Research total, private for-profit institutions enrolled 8% of all students attending Doctoral/Research institutions (IPEDS, n.d.a). This disparity is most obvious in institutions classified as DRU: Doctoral/Research Universities. Table 1.4 illustrates the types of institutions within the doctorate-granting category and provides examples of each.

Master's Colleges and Universities

Designation as a Master's College or University is dependent upon the number of master's degrees an institution awards per year. In general, institutions classified as Master's-level must award a minimum of 50 master's degrees per year and fewer than 20 research doctoral degrees (Carnegie, n.d.b). Master's Colleges and Universities are categorized into three groups, as shown in Table 1.5.

Colleges and universities awarding fewer than 50 master's degrees per year are eligible for inclusion in the Master's S category if their Enrollment Profile classification indicates they are "Exclusively Graduate/Professional" or "Majority Graduate/Professional" institutions

Table 1.5 Carnegie 2005/2010 Master's Colleges and Universities Classifications

Carnegie Classification	Description
Master's L (larger programs)	Awards 200 or more master's degrees
Master's M (medium programs)	Awards 100 to 199 master's degrees
Master's S (smaller programs)	Awards 50 to 99 master's degrees

Source: Carnegie (n.d.b, sec. 3).

Table 1.6 Examples of Master's Colleges and Universities by Carnegie Classification

Carnegie Classification	Example Institutions
Public Master's L: Master's Colleges and Universities (larger programs)	Alabama State University, Marshall University, University of North Florida
Private not-for-profit Master's L: Master's Colleges and Universities (programs)	Concordia University, Liberty University, Mercer University
Private for-profit Master's L: Master's Colleges and Universities (programs)	DeVry University—California, Full Sail University, University of Phoenix—Atlanta Campus
Public Master's M: Master's Colleges and Universities (programs)	College of Charleston, SUNY at Fredonia, Western Oregon University
Private not-for-profit Master's M: Master's Colleges and Universities (programs)	Bethel University, Excelsior College, Park University
Private for-profit Master's M: Master's Colleges and Universities (programs)	American InterContinental University, Aspen University, Western International University
Public Master's S: Master's Colleges and Universities (programs)	Coastal Carolina University, University of Guam, Virginia State University
Private not-for-profit Master's S: Master's Colleges and Universities (programs)	Elon University, Lourdes College, Warner University
Private for-profit Master's S: Master's Colleges and Universities (programs)	Argosy University—Tampa, ITT Technical Institute—Indianapolis, University of Phoenix—Tulsa Campus

Source: Carnegie (n.d.j).

which award more graduate/professional degrees than undergraduate degrees (Carnegie, n.d.b, sec. 3).

As of fall 2009, 643 institutions in the United States, or 16% of the total number considered, were classified as Master's Colleges and Universities (IPEDS, n.d.a). Of these, over half were classified as Master's/L: Master's Colleges and Universities and over half were private not-for-profit institutions (IPEDS, n.d.a). Enrollment in Master's Colleges and Universities

Table 1.7 Carnegie Baccalaureate Colleges Classifications

Classification	Description
Bac/A&S: Baccalaureate Colleges—Arts & Sciences	Of institutions that award at least half of their undergraduate degrees as bachelor's degrees—those with at least half of bachelor's degree majors in arts and sciences fields
Bac/Diverse: Baccalaureate Colleges—Diverse Fields	Of institutions that award at least half of their undergraduate degrees as bachelor's degrees—those not included in the Arts & Sciences group
Bac/Assoc: Baccalaureate/ Associate's Colleges	Bachelor's degrees represent at least 10 percent, but less than half, of undergraduate degrees

Source: Carnegie (n.d.b, sec. 4).

Table 1.8 Examples of Baccalaureate Colleges by Carnegie Classification

Carnegie Classification	Example Institutions
Public Bac/A&S: Baccalaureate Colleges—Arts & Sciences	Kentucky State University, New College of Florida, Virginia Military Institute
Private-not-for-profit Bac/A&S: Baccalaureate Colleges—Arts & Sciences	Beloit College, Furman University, Occidental College, Thomas Aquinas College
Private-for-profit Bac/A&S: Baccalaureate Colleges—Arts & Sciences	Argosy University-Denver, Argosy University—Los Angeles, Argosy University—Phoenix Online Division
Public Bac/Diverse: Baccalaureate Colleges—Diverse Fields	California Maritime Academy, Nevada State College, University of South Carolina—Aiken
Private-not-for-profit Bac/Diverse: Baccalaureate Colleges—Diverse Fields	Atlanta Christian College, Huntingdon College, Texas Lutheran University
Private-for-profit Bac/Diverse: Baccalaureate Colleges—Diverse Fields	Daniel Webster College, Post University, University of Phoenix—Louisville Campus
Public Bac/Assoc: Baccalaureate/Associate's Colleges	Great Basin College, St Petersburg College, Vermont Technical College
Private-not-for-profit Bac/Assoc: Baccalaureate/Associate's Colleges	Arkansas Baptist College, Lincoln College, New England Institute of Technology
Private-for-profit Bac/Assoc: Baccalaureate/Associate's Colleges	DeVry University—Michigan, Keiser University—Ft. Lauderdale, Platt College—Los Angeles

Source: Carnegie (n.d.j).

totaled over 4 million, with the majority of students attending public institutions (IPEDS, n.d.a). Of students enrolled at Master's Colleges and Universities, 72% attended Master's/L: Master's Colleges and Universities (larger programs) (IPEDS, n.d.a). Table 1.6 provides examples of master's institutions for each of the Carnegie Classification categories.

Baccalaureate Colleges

Institutions that award at least 10% of their total undergraduate degrees as bachelor's degrees and award fewer than 50 master's degrees or 20 doctoral degrees per year are designated as Baccalaureate Colleges (Carnegie, n.d.b). These are categorized into three distinct classifications based upon distribution of bachelor's degrees, as shown in Table 1.7.

As of fall 2009, Carnegie Baccalaureate Colleges totaled 715 in number, representing nearly 18% of all institutions considered (IPEDS, n.d.a). Over 70% of Baccalaureate Colleges were private not-for-profit institutions (IPEDS, n.d.a). Enrollment at Baccalaureate Colleges totaled nearly 1.6 million students, with over half of students attending private not-for-profit institutions (IPEDS, n.d.a). Of students enrolled at Baccalaureate Colleges, 39% attended institutions classified as Bac/Diverse: Baccalaureate Colleges—Diverse Fields (IPEDS, n.d.a). Table 1.8 shows examples of Baccalaureate Colleges for each of the 2005/2010 Carnegie Classification categories.

Associate's Colleges

Institutions classified as Associate's Colleges award less than 10% of all undergraduate degrees as bachelor's degrees or award no higher degree than the associate's degree (Carnegie, n.d.b.). Many community colleges fall into this category. Associate's Colleges are divided into 14 classes, the majority of which further define public institutions; only 4 address private institutions (Carnegie, n.d.b).

Public colleges are further classified based on control of institution (public, private, or proprietary), size (small, medium, or large), location (rural-serving, suburban-serving, or urban-serving), and number of campuses (single or multi-campus) (Carnegie, n.d.b, sec. 1). Public colleges located within Primary Metropolitan Statistical Areas (PMSAs) or Metropolitan Statistical Areas (MSAs) with populations of at least 500,000 are classified as urban-serving or suburban-serving, while those located outside of PMSAs/MSAs or in PMSAs/MSAs with fewer than 500,000 residents are classified as rural-serving institutions (Carnegie, n.d.b, sec. 1). Colleges enrolling fewer than 2,500 students are classified as small, those enrolling 2,500 to 7,500 as medium, and those enrolling more than 7,500 as large (Carnegie, n.d.b).

The classification of single or multi-campus is based on whether the college has one or more than one "primary physical campus under the institution's exclusive control and governance, at which the institution provides all courses required to complete an associate's degree" (Carnegie, n.d.b, sec. 1). Colleges classified as multi-campus

> have more than one primary physical campus under the institution's exclusive control and governance, each of which provides all courses required to complete an associate's degree, or (b) they are part of a district or system comprising multiple institutions, at any of which students can complete all requirements for an associate's degree, and that are organized under one governance structure or body.
>
> (Carnegie, n.d.b, sec. 1)

While the majority of Associate's Colleges fit into the classifications described above, there are several additional classifications. Public 2-year Colleges under Universities include "public 2-year institutions under the governance of a 4-year university or system"; Primarily Associate's, colleges are "baccalaureate-granting institutions where bachelor's degrees account for fewer than 10 percent of undergraduate degrees"; and Special Use Colleges are institutions whose "curricular focus is narrowly drawn" and that "are not a part of a more comprehensive two-year college, district, or system" (Carnegie, n.d.b, sec. 1).

Totaling 1,684 in number as of 2009, Associate's Colleges represented over 40% of all Carnegie institutions (IPEDS, n.d.a). While the majority were public, a third were classified as private for-profit (IPEDS, n.d.a). Enrollment at Associate's Colleges totaled over 8 million, or 40% of all students attending Carnegie institutions (IPEDS, n.d.a). Over 90% of students attending Associate's Colleges were enrolled at public institutions (IPEDS, n.d.a).

Special Focus Institutions

Special Focus Institutions offer specialized degree programs, such as a "concentration of degrees in a single field or set of related fields, at both the undergraduate and

graduate levels" (Carnegie, n.d.b, sec. 5). The institution must confer at least 75% of all degrees in a single field of concentration (Carnegie, n.d.b, sec. 5). Exceptions to the 75% cutoff may be made if an institution has declared "a special focus on the College Board's Annual Survey of Colleges, or if an institution's only recognized accreditation was from an accrediting body related to the special focus categories" (Carnegie, n.d.b, sec. 5).

In 2009, 729 institutions received the Special Focus designation; nearly three-quarters of those were classified as private not-for-profit (IPEDS, n.d.a). Enrollment at Special Focus Institutions totaled over 600,000, representing 3% of all students attending Carnegie institutions (IPEDS, n.d.a).

Tribal Colleges

Tribal Colleges constitute less than 1% of all Carnegie institutions and are classified based on institutional reporting status as a Tribal College to NCES and membership in the American Indian Higher Education Consortium (Carnegie, n.d.b, sec. 6). In 2009, there were 31 Tribal Colleges with a total enrollment of just under 20,000, 0.1% of all students attending Carnegie institutions (IPEDS, n.d.a).

Carnegie Overall

The detailed descriptions above illustrate just one facet of the Carnegie system: the Basic Classification. The other classifications, while not as commonly employed, provide consistent means for grouping and comparing institutions based on a variety of variables. As the definitive system of institutional classification in the United States, Carnegie Classifications are used by administrators, education researchers, educational systems, and a host of others.

KEY INSTITUTIONAL QUALITY INDICATORS

Despite the numerous categories of indicators that theoretically enable key stakeholders (prospective students, parents, administrators, researchers, legislators, media, etc.) to compare institutions, there is variation within each category. The remainder of this chapter focuses on quality indicators that key stakeholders use to better understand institutions, as well as on unique management challenges related to improving those indicators.

Each year more than two million new freshmen enter college (NCES, 2009) after exploring a variety of options to select the institution that best meets their academic and personal needs. There are common institutional quality indicators that influence prospective students and their parents in this search; they are also utilized by local, state, and federal governments, boards of regents/trustees, independent watch organizations, think-tanks, and others. These indicators include academic selectivity (e.g., high-school grade point average, SAT/ACT test scores), retention and graduation rates, and employment and job placement rates. An additional indicator, less often used by prospective students and parents but tracked by other aforementioned constituent groups, is the alumni giving rate. Each of these indicators is discussed below with regard to the various types of institutions.

College Entry Indicators

Colleges and universities utilize specific admissions criteria to determine if a prospective student has the potential to be successful at the institution. Typical quantitative entry criteria include high-school grade point average (HS GPA) and standardized test scores (i.e., SAT or ACT). Qualitative indicators such as high-school curriculum rigor and quality may also factor into admissions decisions. Each of these admission entry indicators has an administrative and financial impact on higher education institutions. Research (Braxton, 2000; Camara & Kimmel, 2005; Heller, 2002) has shown that students who are more academically qualified are more likely to achieve academic success. Graduation is an important indicator of institutional success and is further addressed below.

Administrative and Financial Impact

While the number of applications for admission is one indicator of interest, more important is the number of accepted students, as it reflects the number of interested students who have met an institution's admissions requirements. The final indicator of interest, and arguably the only one that matters, is the actual enrollment of students in the institution. The more precise that an institution can be in admitting students who are likely to graduate, the fewer administrative and financial resources that the institution expends unnecessarily. Concentrating their financial and administrative resources on assisting students in obtaining a degree allows institutions to invest in student success rather than in replacing students who have transferred or dropped out.

Retention and Graduation Rates

Retention and graduation rates are corollaries of college entry indicators. According to federal definitions, retention is defined as:

> A measure of the rate at which students persist in their educational program at an institution, expressed as a percentage. For four-year institutions, this is the percentage of first-time bachelor's (or equivalent) degree-seeking undergraduates from the previous fall who are again enrolled in the current fall. For all other institutions this is the percentage of first-time degree/certificate-seeking students from the previous fall who either re-enrolled or successfully completed their program by the current fall.
>
> (IPEDS, n.d.b, para. 17)

Graduation rates are calculated from "the number of full-time first-time degree-seeking students in a particular year (cohort) and their status after six years at four-year institutions or after three years at less than four-year institutions" (NCES, 1997, p. II-1). The "rate is calculated as the total number of completers within 150% of normal time divided by the revised cohort minus any allowable exclusions" (IPEDS, n.d., para. 14).

More than 40 years of research (Braxton, 2000; Heller, 2002; Tinto, 1993) have established a linkage between college entry indictors, retention rates, and graduation rates. As retention and graduation rates are measures of institutional efficiency and effectiveness, they are often monitored by prospective students and their parents, boards of regents/ trustees, state legislators, federal legislators, think-tanks, and interest groups.

Administrative and Financial Impact

Institutions are held accountable for offering students an opportunity to complete a program of study of their choosing in a timely manner and with qualified faculty that prepares them for the job market. The question remains whether retention and graduation rates are valid measures of gauging an institution's success in providing students with a quality education and preparing them for employment, as the rates do not count or reflect the success of all students. Per federal definitions, retention and graduation rates are based solely on the success of entering traditional freshmen, which can present a challenge for institutions where this cohort accounts for only a small percentage of the students on campus; however, for institutions where a large proportion (75%+) of enrollment comprises first-time, full-time students, these rates are a good measure of quality. As many as "20 percent of the bachelor's degree recipients who start in a four-year school earn the degree from a different four-year school" (Adelman, 2007, para. 7) and are not included in institutional retention and graduation rates. According to the Department of Education, "roughly half of traditional-age undergraduates are excluded from the Education Department's calculation of graduation rates" (Adelman, 2006, p. 57).

With such variance among institutions, it is unlikely that retention and graduation rates are universally appropriate measures of efficiency and effectiveness. Institutions that have higher retention and graduation rates, which are highly correlated with more academically qualified students, are viewed as being more efficient and effective than community colleges that educate students who would not qualify for admission to a selective institution. As a result, administrators at lower tiered institutions who focus on increasing retention and graduation rates may be working against stacked odds, and may be better off channeling efforts and resources in another direction.

Impact on Doctoral Institutions

Doctoral-granting universities, the most selective of all postsecondary institutions, are large institutions that offer a wide array of degree programs and opportunities that appeal to new students. As a result, these institutions tend to receive considerably more applications for admission than they can accommodate. This allows the universities to be selective and offer admission only to the most academically qualified applicants, who tend to graduate at higher rates than students at lower tiered higher education institution counterparts.

Administrative and Financial Impact on Doctoral Institutions

While doctoral institutions typically enjoy above average retention and graduation rates due to their ability to attract and recruit the most academically qualified students, their ability to predict, and in some cases cap, the number of entering students enables them to select the best applicants for the slots available. On its face, this ability to select a limited number of the most highly qualified applicants may seem ideal; however, if the number of students entering the institution is restricted, so too is the revenue stream generated by tuition, and in the case of state institutions, state appropriations.

Impact on Master's and Bachelor's Institutions

While master's and bachelor's institutions are often less selective than doctoral institutions, they offer a wide array of degree programs. Master's and bachelor's institutions often offer degree programs in specific areas such as education, liberal arts, or nursing, as well as clubs, sports, and other non-academic activities, but often on a more limited scale than at doctoral universities. Since these institutions often tend to focus their recruitment efforts on a specific region, they generally receive fewer applications than doctoral institutions; however, their acceptance rates are usually higher due to lower admissions requirements.

Administrative and Financial Impact on Master's and Bachelor's Institutions

Master's and bachelor's institutions face a different set of administrative and financial impacts than doctoral universities. One issue unique to these institutions is the challenge of retaining students who enrolled with the intention of transferring to a doctoral university. Students unable to meet the admissions criteria at a doctoral university will enroll at a master's or bachelor's institution with the goal of transferring to their first-choice school. This has a domino effect on the institution's indicators of success, as a student who transfers is not included in its retention and graduation rates. Additionally, there is a financial impact on the institution, which must increase its recruiting efforts. For an institution to realize an increase in the incoming cohort, it must replace the number of students lost to transfer and increase enrollment beyond that number.

Impact on Community Colleges and Technical Institutions

Community colleges and technical institutions educate students in liberal arts and technical/trade areas. They are often referred to as "access institutions" because their graduates gain access to bachelor's (or higher) degree-granting institutions that they would not have been able to attend otherwise. Admission and entry indicators are virtually non-existent for these colleges, which do not require standardized test scores and generally have an open admissions policy whereby all students are accepted. Additionally, many of their students do not fit the cohort definition, and thus are not counted in retention and graduation rates. Community colleges and technical institutions also measure their success by focusing on the rate at which students transfer to a four-year institution and obtain a bachelor's degree.

Administrative and Financial Impact on Community Colleges and Technical Institutions

While individual student entry indicators are not evaluated for admissions due to the open admissions policy, community colleges and technical institutions are still accountable for their retention and graduation rates. Typically, these rates capture approximately 20% of their student population (Adelman, 2007), making it difficult to measure institutional and student success accurately. While community colleges receive "credit for students who transfer ... the four-year colleges to which they transfer get no credit when these transfer students earn a bachelor's degree, as 60 percent of traditional-age community college transfers do" (Adelman, 2007, para. 7).

UNIQUE MANAGEMENT CHALLENGES

While the various types of institutions share many commonalities, each has its own unique management challenges. The remainder of this chapter focuses on these challenges, some of which are discussed in greater detail throughout the book.

Variation in Tuition-Setting Policies

Public and private institutions rely on tuition and fees as a primary source of revenue, and suffered a new low in 2010. According to the State Higher Education Executive Officers, "educational appropriations per FTE [full-time equivalent student] (defined to

Table 1.9 Entity with Primary Authority for Establishing Public Tuition, by State

State	Governor	Legislature	Statewide Coordinating or Governing Agency for Multiple Systems	Coordinating or Governing Board(s) for Individual Systems	Local District Governing Board(s)	Individual Institutions
Alabama						X
Alaska				X		
Arizona				X		
Arkansas						X
California		X				
Colorado			X			
Connecticut				X		
Delaware						X
Florida		X				
Georgia				X		
Hawaii			X			
Idaho			X			
Illinois				X		
Indiana						X
Iowa			X			
Kansas				X		
Kentucky			X			
Louisiana		X				

(Continued)

Table 1.9 (Continued)

State	Governor	Legislature	Statewide Coordinating or Governing Agency for Multiple Systems	Coordinating or Governing Board(s) for Individual Systems	Local District Governing Board(s)	Individual Institutions
Maine				X		
Maryland				X		
Massachusetts						X
Minnesota				X		
Mississippi				X		
Missouri						X
Montana			X			
Nebraska				X		
New Hampshire				X		
New Mexico					X	
New York				X		
North Carolina			X			
North Dakota			X			
Ohio						X
Oklahoma			X			
Oregon					X	
Pennsylvania				X		
South Carolina						X
South Dakota			X			
Tennessee				X		
Texas				X		
Utah			X			
Vermont				X		
Virginia						X
West Virginia				X		
Wisconsin				X		
Wyoming						X
Total	0	3	11	19	2	10

Source: SHEEO (2011).

include state and local support for general higher education operations) fell to $6,454 in 2010, a 25-year low in inflation-adjusted terms" (SHEEO, 2011, p. 9).

Typically, at private institutions, boards of trustees are primarily responsible for changing tuition and fees. The authority for increasing tuition and fees at public institutions varies by state, such that SHEEO has conducted *The Survey of State Tuition, Fees, and Financial Assistance Policies* six times since 1988. Table 1.9 shows the 2010-2011 survey results of the entity with the primary authority for establishing public tuition by state.

The group most commonly responsible for establishing tuition costs for public institutions is the coordinating or governing board(s) for individual systems, followed by state coordinating or governing agencies for multiple systems, individual institutions, the legislature, and local district governing board(s). Contrary to popular belief, the governor of a state does not set tuition. With the exception of the 10 states that allow individual institutions to determine tuition (shown in Table 1.9), all states appoint individuals indirectly connected to higher education to determine the price of tuition. Awareness of the authority that sets tuition, as well as the procedures for determining tuition rates, is vital to institutional administrators, as these factors play a significant role in balancing the institutional budget.

Unionized vs. Non-Unionized Institutions

Unions and the role they play in higher education vary from state to state. Some institutions are heavily influenced by unions, which may have an important hand in their administration and internal and external financing, while in other states, unions do not exist. Unions can include faculty as well as staff (e.g., police, physical plant employees). This section outlines the advantages and disadvantages of unionization. One advantage is that unions adhere to a thoroughly vetted set of rules and policies, which university administrators can utilize to govern the institution. In the absence of unions, university administrators must negotiate policy changes and implementation with faculty and staff, spending a substantial amount of time obtaining their input and meeting with administrators to discuss options.

Alternatively, the rules and policies governing unions may be inflexible and minimize an institution's ability to quickly take advantage of, or respond to, economic or environmental changes. While a non-unionized institution that allows for quick action may sound appealing, flexibility brings its own challenges. Administrators who implement changes too quickly are often criticized for not fully vetting the consequences and may be asked to step down (e.g., Carlson, 2011; Fain, 2008a; 2008b; 2010; Stripling, 2011).

Location

Institutional location has significant administrative and financial implications. Colleges and universities in poorer, rural, low-technical areas may lack the philanthropic resources that many other institutions rely on. An urban campus can quickly become land-locked, requiring the purchase of new property and buildings. It is important to note that institutions located within smaller cities can also be land-locked. Land-locked difficulty, for these purposes, is defined as the degree to which an institution is able to obtain land contiguous to its campus at fair market value.

Student Body Composition

The composition of the student body greatly impacts the administration and financing of institutional operations. Colleges and universities with high retention and graduation rates typically have a relatively stable and predictable freshman cohort. These institutions are thus able to plan for the number of courses and seats freshmen will need, increasing or decreasing programs and services based on the size of the incoming class.

More commonly, institutions admit transfer students, which complicates administrative and financial operations. For example, transfer students usually have completed some general education courses toward their degrees, which can be more costly to an institution, as those courses are the cheapest to offer. Transfer students who need upper division courses, which tend to be more expensive because of the need for smaller classes, end up requiring a greater investment on the part of the institution.

Housing and Students Living on Campus

Residential housing presents unique financial challenges, be they related to new construction in response to increased demand or the need to ensure sufficient facilities for the existing student body. There is a positive correlation between on-campus living and higher retention and graduation rates (Pascarella & Terenzini, 2005). With the increased enrollment experienced by many institutions, it should come as no surprise that on-campus housing capacity has risen from 2.3 million to 2.9 million (26.6%) over a 10-year period (IPEDS, n.d.a). The Carnegie size and setting classification includes three residential classifications:

- *Primarily residential:* "25-49 percent of degree-seeking undergraduates live on campus and at least 50 percent attend full time" (Carnegie, n.d.k, sec. 4).
- *Highly residential:* "At least half of degree-seeking undergraduates live on campus and at least 80 percent attend full time" (Carnegie, n.d.k, sec. 4).
- *Primarily non-residential:* "Fewer than 25 percent of degree-seeking undergraduates live on campus and/or fewer than 50 percent attend full time (includes exclusively distance education institutions)" (Carnegie, n.d.k, sec. 4).

While retention and graduation rates may be increased through on-campus housing, so too are liability and administrative challenges. Campuses without housing facilities close each day when the last class concludes, whereas residential campuses remain open throughout the year and around the clock.

CONCLUSION

The large number of higher education institutions necessitates the collection of multiple variables, hence the creation of Carnegie Classifications for comparison purposes. Analysis of annual data allows us to identify patterns and trends at higher education institutions and for the students they serve. As when traveling to a location for the second or third time, we find that the destination is familiar but never exactly the same.

REFERENCES

Adelman, C. (2006). The propaganda of numbers. *Chronicle of Higher Education, 53*(8), 57.

Adelman, C. (2007). Making graduation rates matter. *Inside Higher Ed.* Retrieved March 30, 2011 from http://www.insidehighered.com/views/2007/03/12/adelman

Braxton, J. M. (Ed.). (2000). *Reworking the student departure puzzle.* Nashville, TN: Vanderbilt University Press.

Camara, W. J., & Kimmel, E. W. (Eds.). (2005). *Choosing students: Higher education admissions tools for the 21st century.* Mahwah, NJ: Lawrence Erlbaum Associates.

Carlson, S. (2011). Provost at Southern Illinois U. at Carbondale resigns after just a month. [Electronic version]. *The Chronicle of Higher Education.* Retrieved March 17, 2011 from http://chronicle.com

Carnegie Foundation for the Advancement of Teaching. (2001). *The Carnegie classification of institutions of higher education: 2000 edition.* Retrieved March 30, 2011 from http://classifications.carnegiefoundation.org/resources/

Carnegie Foundation for the Advancement of Teaching. (n.d.a). *About the Carnegie classifications.* Retrieved January 2, 2011 from http://classifications.carnegiefoundation.org

Carnegie Foundation for the Advancement of Teaching. (n.d.b). *Basic classification methodology.* Retrieved January 27, 2011 from http://classifications.carnegiefoundation.org/methodology/basic.php

Carnegie Foundation for the Advancement of Teaching. (n.d.c). *Carnegie classification FAQs.* Retrieved January 27, 2011 from http://classifications.carnegiefoundation.org/resources/faqs.php

Carnegie Foundation for the Advancement of Teaching. (n.d.d). *Classification description: Basic classification.* Retrieved January 27, 2011 from http://classifications.carnegiefoundation.org/descriptions/basic.php

Carnegie Foundation for the Advancement of Teaching. (n.d.e). *Classification description: Enrollment profile classification.* Retrieved January 27, 2011 from http://classifications.carnegiefoundation.org/descriptions/enrollment_profile.php

Carnegie Foundation for the Advancement of Teaching. (n.d.f). *Classification description: Graduate instructional program classification.* Retrieved January 27, 2011 from http://classifications.carnegiefoundation.org/descriptions/grad_program.php

Carnegie Foundation for the Advancement of Teaching. (n.d.g). *Classification description: Size and setting classification.* Retrieved January 27, 2011 from http://classifications.carnegiefoundation.org/descriptions/size_setting.php

Carnegie Foundation for the Advancement of Teaching. (n.d.h). *Classification description: Undergraduate instructional program classification.* Retrieved January 27, 2011 from http://classifications.carnegiefoundation.org/descriptions/ugrad_program.php

Carnegie Foundation for the Advancement of Teaching. (n.d.i). *Classification description: Undergraduate profile classification.* Retrieved January 27, 2011 from http://classifications.carnegiefoundation.org/descriptions/undergraduate_profile.php

Carnegie Foundation for the Advancement of Teaching. (n.d.j). *Lookup and listings.* Retrieved March 17, 2011 from http://classifications.carnegiefoundation.org/lookup_listings/standard.php

Carnegie Foundation for the Advancement of Teaching. (n.d.k). *Size and setting classification methodology.* Retrieved January 27, 2011 from http://classifications.carnegiefoundation.org/methodology/size_setting.php

Fain, P. (2008a). Baylor U. fires president, citing failure to unite campus. [Electronic version]. *The Chronicle of Higher Education.* Retrieved March 17, 2011 from http://chronicle.com

Fain, P. (2008b). President of Southwestern Oregon Community College resigns hastily. [Electronic version]. *The Chronicle of Higher Education.* Retrieved March 17, 2011 from http://chronicle.com

Fain, P. (2010). Birmingham-Southern's president resigns while trustees explain college's financial meltdown. [Electronic version]. *The Chronicle of Higher Education.* Retrieved March 17, 2011 from http://chronicle.com

Heller, D. E. (Ed.). (2002). *Condition of access: Higher education for lower income students.* Westport, CT: Praeger.

Integrated Postsecondary Education Data System. (n.d.a). *IPEDS data center.* [Data file]. Retrieved March 19, 2011 from http://nces.ed.gov/ipeds/datacenter/

Integrated Postsecondary Education Data System. (n.d.b). *IPEDS glossary.* Retrieved January 2, 2011 from http://nces.ed.gov/IPEDS/glossary

McCormick, A. C., & Zhao, C. (2005). Rethinking and reframing the Carnegie classification. *Change,* September/October, 50–57.

National Center for Education Statistics. (1997). *IPEDS graduation rate survey guidelines for survey respondents.* Retrieved from http://nces.ed.gov/ipeds/surveys/1997/pdf/grsguide.pdf

National Center for Education Statistics. (2009). *Digest of education statistics.* [Data files]. Retrieved January 26, 2011 from http://nces.ed.gov/programs/digest/d09/tables_3.asp

Pascarella, E. T., & Terenzini, P. T. (2005). *How college affects students.* San Francisco: Jossey-Bass.

SHEEO (State Higher Education Executive Officers) (2011). *State higher education finance FY 2010.* Retrieved from http://www.sheeo.org/finance/shef/SHEF_FY10.pdf

Stripling, J. (2011). Resigning chief of Huntsville campus had turbulent relations with faculty. [Electronic version]. *The Chronicle of Higher Education.* Retrieved March 17, 2011 from http://chronicle.com

Tinto, V. (1993). *Leaving college: Rethinking the cause and cures of student attrition* (2nd ed.). Chicago: The University of Chicago Press.

2

KEY LEADERSHIP POSITIONS AND PERFORMANCE EXPECTATIONS

Julie Carpenter-Hubin and Lydia Snover

INTRODUCTION

American colleges and universities are like snowflakes, with structures that appear similar to the casual observer, though in fact no two have been found to be exactly alike. Degree-granting institutions can be tiny; the Byzantine Catholic Seminary reported a total enrollment of 11 for fall 2009, and the Southwest Institute of Technology enrolled 21. At the upper end of the scale is The Ohio State University; with over 55,000 students on its main campus alone, the school is larger than 36 of Ohio's 50 largest cities (maps-n-stats.com). Research universities, technical and community colleges, religious institutes, liberal-arts colleges, and trade schools all have unique facets that require different organizations of administrators and leaders. Even within a particular sector and among institutions of similar sizes, administrative authority may be maintained centrally or decentralized to the academic units. Higher education institutions are complex structures that branch and connect, each forming a distinctive administrative pattern. This chapter examines these unique structures that make up the landscape of American higher education.

GOVERNING BOARDS

The enormous diversity among American colleges and universities is reflected in their disparate governance structures and functions. Although the culture and process of governance varies widely among institutions, the presence of lay citizen governing boards distinguishes American higher education from most of the rest of the world, where universities ultimately are dependencies of the state.

(Association of Governing Boards of
Universities and Colleges, 2010, Foreword)

Institutions of higher education are led by independent governing boards using a variety of names (e.g., board of trustees, corporation board, or board of overseers). The New England Association of Schools and Colleges Commission on Institutions of Higher Education Standards for Accreditation clearly outlines the role of governing boards:

> The governing board is the legally constituted body ultimately responsible for the institution's quality and integrity. The board demonstrates sufficient independence to ensure it can act in the institution's best interest. The composition of the board includes representation of the public interest and reflects the areas of competence needed to fulfill its responsibilities. Fewer than one-half of the board members have any financial interest in the institution, including as employee, stock-holder, or corporate director. Members of the governing board understand, accept, and fulfill their responsibilities as fiduciaries to act honestly and in good faith in the best interest of the institution toward the achievement of its purposes in a manner free from conflicts of interest.
>
> (New England Association of Schools and Colleges, n.d., Section 3.2)

Governing boards of public institutions are often appointed by public officials such as governors, while boards of private institutions are self-perpetuating. Governing boards of private institutions recruit members using a variety of criteria. Depending upon the mission of the institution, members might represent alumni, the local community, business, or academic disciplines.

In a private college or university, the governing board has fiduciary responsibility for preserving the long-term viability and health of the institution and adhering to the purposes for which the institution was established. It is generally the responsibility of the board to select the president or chief operating officer of the institution. The board must work closely with the senior officers of the institution to ensure that operating practices are consistent with long-term goals and the mission of the college or university. Boards of trustees are often required to approve changes in degree offerings, investment policies, budget and expenditure policies, and appointment of faculty. The following are examples of responsibilities that various private institutions charge to their governing boards.

- Massachusetts Institute of Technology:

> The Corporation – the board of trustees of the Massachusetts Institute of Technology – holds a public trust: to see that the Institute adheres to the purposes for which it was chartered and that its integrity and financial resources are preserved for future generations as well as for current purposes. The Corporation and its committees have responsibility for reviewing and providing guidance on strategic directions, approving annual budgets, exercising long-term fiduciary responsibility, approving the establishment of new degree programs or courses of study, approving degrees, electing the President (as well as the other Corporation officers), and being available (individually as well as collectively) to advise the President on issues that he/she may wish to raise with them.

It is also understood that trustees are expected to represent the interests of MIT to outside constituencies as appropriate and help provide financial support for the Institute.

(http://web.mit.edu/corporation/about.html)

- Reed College:

Legal authority for the operation of the college, under the charter granted by the State of Oregon, rests with the board of trustees .... In practice, it is generally recognized as a chief responsibility of the board of trustees to select the president of the college .... The board also approves faculty appointments, which are recommended by the president and approved by an academic affairs committee of the board. Other specific and important responsibilities of the board include approval of the college budget, including the general salary schedules; management of investment and other financial and property considerations, with the assistance of an investment counsel; approval of new buildings and general planning and upkeep of the campus; and assistance in fund raising.

(http://web.reed.edu/academic/gbook/coll_org/governance.html)

- Washington University in St. Louis:

The Board of Trustees is legally responsible for the institution whose assets it holds in TRUST. Trustees must assure themselves that the institution is heading in the right direction and is well-managed. In short, they must fulfill their responsibilities, legal and moral, as TRUSTEES. The Trustees of Washington University: appoint the Chancellor; review and approve or disapprove annual budgets; review and approve or disapprove major capital expenditures; make final decision on awards of tenure and degrees, and on new degree programs; oversee the management of the endowment; oversee and participate in development programs; take an interest in and are supportive of the University's people and its programs.

Board members exercise a policy and oversight role in contrast to the implementation and operational role of the administration, staff and faculty.

(http://boardoftrustees.wustl.edu/composition.html)

- Emory University:

The Board of Trustees governs the University by establishing policy and exercising fiduciary responsibility for the long-term well-being of the institution. The Board and its Executive Committee act on recommendations from board committees, University officers, and the University Senate.

(http://www.emory.edu/secretary/board_of_trustees/index.html)

- New York University:

As directors of a nonprofit and as leaders of an institution responsible for educating the next generation of world leaders and for creating new knowledge, trustees are the keepers of the mission of NYU: Educating qualified individuals from all walks of life to become the leaders of the local, national, and, now, international community. They must pay particularly close attention to the mission and the obligations to society that are unique to the academic enterprise. NYU's Board of Trustees is the overall fiduciaries for the University. As such it is responsible for, among other things, creating policy, setting mission and purpose, strategic planning, reviewing programs, and relating campus to community and community to campus. Chief among its roles is fund-raising for the University, as well as engaging our alumni, parent, and student communities.

(http://www.nyu.edu/about/leadership-university-administration/
board-of-trustees.html)

Adherence to mission, fiduciary responsibility, setting policy, strategic planning, advising, selecting the senior officer, and fund-raising are themes that run through most such statements. The need to balance longer-term issues with day-to-day operations creates tension between governing boards and senior administration. While the board oversees the operation of the institution, it is not responsible for running the institution.

States have developed multiple approaches to the governance of public colleges and universities, with state boards of postsecondary education described by three principal models:

1) *Governing boards*, with governing or line responsibility for institutions. This responsibility may include strategic planning and allocating resources among institutions within their jurisdiction; developing institutional and faculty/personnel policies; appointing, setting the compensation for, and evaluating system and institutional chief executives; awarding degrees; advocating for the institutions to the legislature and governor.

2) *Coordinating boards*, with coordinating responsibility for institutions. This responsibility does not include appointing, determining compensation for, or evaluating institutional chief executives, nor does it include developing institutional and personnel policies. The focus of coordinating boards is more on state and system needs and priorities, and planning efforts may include both public and private institutions, and in some states extend to for-profits as well.

3) *Planning, regulatory, and/or service agency* with either limited or no formal governing nor coordinating authority, and which carry out regulatory and service functions.

(McGuinness, 2002, 2003)

In addition to the state boards, public colleges and universities may also have their own institutional boards of trustees. For example, the Ohio Board of Regents (OBOR) serves as the state coordinating board for Ohio's public colleges and universities, each of which is governed by its own board of trustees. OBOR develops policies and strategies that support statewide needs; a recent example is the creation of a set of transfer articulation agreements that make it easier for students to move from one Ohio institution to another. Institutional boards of trustees focus on issues of immediate concern to their particular college or university—the salary of the president, the strategic plan, development campaigns, and the like.

Very often, members of college and university boards of trustees serve without financial compensation. State boards may have quite a large staff, with several senior-level administrators. Boards of trustees are often supported by a secretary, and median compensation for this position ranges from $61,000 for the two-year sector to $153,000 for doctoral universities. Members of governing boards usually receive no compensation for their time and are often called upon to provide financial support to the institution through gifts and bequests.

SYSTEM LEADERSHIP

Public colleges and universities may be grouped together as a system led by a chief executive officer (CEO). Some states, such as Ohio, have a single system that oversees all public institutions, including universities, community colleges, and technical colleges. The chancellor of Ohio's state governing board also serves as the chancellor of the University System of Ohio. Other states group postsecondary institutions by sector, with separate systems for technical colleges, community colleges, and universities. The California Postsecondary Education Commission serves as a coordinating board for California's three higher education systems (the University of California System, the California State University System, and the California Community College System), each of which is headed by its own chancellor or president. Nearly every combination between these two extremes can be found as well.

Much of the system CEO's time is spent demonstrating higher education's value to the state legislature, advocating for resources, and creating fair, equitable strategies for distributing those resources to advance the missions of the various system institutions. Institutions may well resist subjugating their own goals for the good of their system, and system CEOs must work to demonstrate the value in collective action. This may take a very practical form; in many states, systems have encouraged greater collaboration between member institutions with regard to business practice, including sharing services such as payroll and instituting collective purchasing programs. Collective planning processes can ensure that students can easily transfer from one state institution to another, that institutions do not unnecessarily duplicate academic programs, and that information about effective and efficient practices at one institution can be made known to other member institutions.

Depending upon the structure of the governing board, a system CEO may well have the authority to mandate such policies. Yet even when this is the case, persuasion is often a more effective means to achieving desired ends. Successful system CEOs demonstrate moral authority; they understand that intelligent leaders act in the best interest of their organization, and they persuade their college and university presidents that the shared goals of the system will best serve the individual institutions. Successful system CEOs help their institutions to garner necessary resources, assure the quality of the academic programs, and provide greater access to higher education (Fingerhut, 2011).

The CEO of a system, whatever his or her title, earns a median salary of between $210,000 and $438,000, depending on the sector to which institutions in the system belong.

ACADEMIC LEADERSHIP

The academic leadership structures of colleges and universities are fairly standard across all types of institutions, though institutional size plays a significant role in the number and scope of positions involved. The organization charts in Figures 2.1 and 2.2 show two very different types of institutions. As is typical, both have a provost who reports to the president, and deans who report to the provost. Other reporting lines are less standard. For example, the associate vice president for student services reports to the provost at the institution shown in Figure 2.1, but not at the one shown in Figure 2.2.

Presidents

College and university presidents are the public faces of their institutions, and good presidents interact regularly and often with students, parents, and alumni; with boards of trustees, faculty, and staff; with representatives of the media and with legislators; and with donors and prospective donors. Presidents are properly seen as accountable to all of these constituents through their boards of trustees and other governing bodies, and they are accountable for achieving institutional goals in accordance with institutional values.

The scope of topics that constituent groups expect presidents to address ranges from the very narrow to the broadest possible; from individual student concerns to

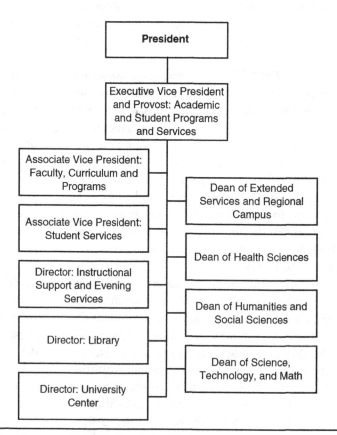

Figure 2.1 Columbia State Community College Organization Chart

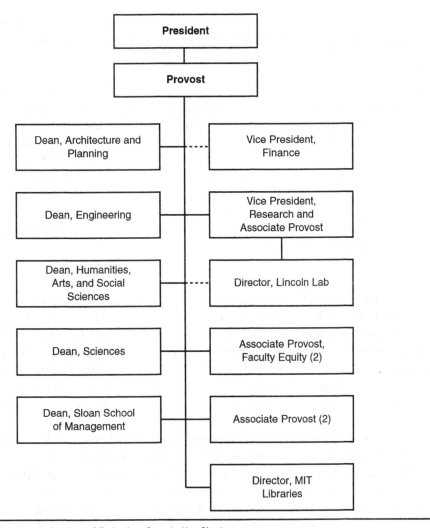

Figure 2.2 Massachusetts Institute of Technology Organization Chart

institutional policy matters, from individual cases of employee or student misconduct to larger questions about institutional accountability, from the value of a particular degree program to the value of higher education in general. Because presidents cannot themselves have first-hand knowledge and understanding of every issue and activity on their campuses, their most important role is to assemble and guide the senior leadership team for their institution. Fundamental to this role are the abilities to appropriately interpret constituent goals and to create a vision, potentially transformational for long-term goals, to achieve them; to build support for that vision among the senior leadership, throughout the organization, and among constituents; and to hold senior leaders accountable for fulfilling the vision in accordance with institutional values. Presidents who have mastered these abilities can confidently address the full scope of their constituents' concerns.

Presidents do not, of course, envision the path forward in solitude, nor is there but a single path that will advance their institutions. Colleges and universities are made up of academic and administrative units, each of which has specific interests that it hopes to promote, and that it sees as contributing to the goals of the institution. Within those units are subunits, and within those subunits are individual faculty, students, and staff; each level reveals competing ideas and interests, many of which could reasonably be seen as furthering the institution's goals and values. External constituents as well advocate on behalf of aspects of higher education ranging from career training to basic research, and their support for a president's vision may be largely shaped by their own values. Presidents are challenged to hear the voices of individuals and small groups, to move those voices from cacophony to conversation, and to lead, informed by the multiple perspectives represented in the conversation.

The median salary for a president of a doctoral university is $375,000; for a president of a two-year institution, $166,000.

Provosts

Provosts serve as the chief academic officers of their institutions and are often given the additional title of Vice President for Academic Affairs. At most institutions, they are considered first among equals with regard to other vice presidents, as they oversee those activities at the very core of higher education: teaching, learning, research, and innovation. Provosts report to the president of their institution, but typically interact as well with trustees and other governing bodies. Depending on the size of their college or university, provosts may delegate high levels of authority to vice provosts or associate provosts.

The level of authority vested in a provost and his or her senior staff varies in accordance with the level of centralization or decentralization of the academic structure of the institution. Some institutions devolve nearly all of the academic decision-making to college deans, with the provost serving primarily to coordinate and promote the work of the colleges. More typically, however, deans of colleges report to the provost, and the provost, along with his or her senior staff, ensures that resources are distributed to academic units consistent with the goals and values of the institution; that qualified faculty are hired, promoted, tenured, and compensated through processes that are fair and equitable; and that students receive a quality education through exposure to a challenging and vibrant curriculum. Provosts play a central role in strategic planning for their institutions.

Like presidents, provosts face the difficulty of competing interests and limited resources. It is incumbent upon the provost to encourage and support creativity and innovation throughout the academic community; it is essential as well that the institution live within its means. The challenge for today's provosts goes beyond making difficult resource allocation decisions, however. Provosts must engage the campus community in developing new models of teaching and learning that use resources more efficiently, fostering innovation not only among individuals, but also collectively as an organization. And they must ensure that their institutions demonstrate value, effectiveness, and efficiency, for without this evidence, resources will be ever more difficult to garner.

A provost's success is best judged by the success of the students and the faculty. Successful provosts are those who recruit and retain students and faculty whose own goals are well supported by the mission of the institution and whose endeavors in turn advance institutional priorities; enable students to complete their desired programs of study in a reasonable time frame and serve their communities as educated citizens; and support and honor faculty success as outstanding teachers and innovators.

Median salaries for provosts range from $115,000 in the two-year sector to $265,000 at doctoral universities. The range of median salaries for assistant provosts, associate provosts, and vice provosts extends from $83,000 for an assistant provost at a two-year college to $180,000 for a vice provost at a doctoral university.

Academic Dean/Associate Deans

Large colleges and universities group similar academic departments into colleges or schools headed by academic deans. Academic deans typically report to the provost and are expected to provide active leadership in the promotion, direction, and support of the educational and research activities of the institution (The Ohio State University, 2009). The deans are thus, in a very real sense, the chief academic officers of the academic colleges or schools they oversee.

While the array of responsibilities delegated to deans varies by institution, academic deans and their staff usually have oversight of the curricula and instruction offered by their departments and centers, and they are often responsible for student academic advising and career services. They ensure support for faculty teaching and research, which may include sabbatical leave, computer and technical support, and provision of administrative services. In many institutions, academic deans and their staff decide which departments may hire faculty and also review hiring, tenure, and promotion decisions regarding faculty in their colleges and schools, primarily to ensure fair and equitable processes. While these are their official responsibilities, in large part, the job of an academic dean is to develop a community of scholars, to facilitate collaborations between teachers and researchers with similar interests, to promote the intellectual experience of their faculty and students, and to further knowledge in the disciplines of their organization.

Salaries for academic deans and associate deans depend both on the sector of the institution in which they work and their discipline. Deans of colleges of medicine earn the highest median salary, at $428,000. They are followed by deans of dentistry, public health, and law, whose median salaries range from $284,000 to $303,000 in the doctoral university sector. Deans of business schools have the greatest disparity between sectors, with deans at two-year institutions earning a median salary of $88,000, and those at doctoral universities $260,000. Deans who oversee colleges made up of some or all of the arts and sciences disciplines draw median salaries of between $85,000 and $224,000, depending on the disciplines under their jurisdiction.

Salaries for associate and assistant deans follow the same pattern, with medicine heading the median salary list at $183,000. Associate and assistant deans of arts and sciences have median salaries ranging between $132,000 and $88,000.

Department Chairs

Academic departments are the unit of the institution most directly responsible for teaching, research, and outreach, and they are led by department chairs. At most institutions, these chairs are appointed by academic deans in consultation with members of the department, and they generally serve for an agreed-upon number of years. Department chairs have two main spheres of responsibility; they are both the business manager and the academic leader for their units.

As few department chairs (outside of colleges of business!) have backgrounds in accounting or other business practices, most delegate the associated tasks to professional staff. Nonetheless, department chairs are accountable to their deans for accomplishing the expected teaching, research, and service within their allotted budgets, and for assuring that their department's business practices conform to the rules of the institution.

As the academic leaders of their departments, chairs are accountable both to their faculty and to their deans for allocating resources to best support the missions of their departments. Thus, the department chair has multiple "bosses," serving both the dean and, collectively, the members of the department faculty. Chairs are in no way, however, subordinate to individual faculty members. Chairs make decisions about such issues as which courses faculty will teach, the salary increases they will receive, and whether or not research leaves may be granted.

The nature of this position is all the more complicated because the chair does not leave the faculty to become an administrator, but remains a teacher and scholar, and so a peer of his or her faculty. The best chairs develop good relationships with their colleagues and make decisions through consensus-building. The wise chair keeps in mind that the next department chair will surely be chosen from among the colleagues affected by his or her decisions, and sets fairness and the good of the department as a whole as the standard.

In general, department chairs receive some amount of pay in addition to their faculty salary, but practices for determining the additional compensation are not standardized across institutions and may vary even within a single college or university.

Other Academic Unit/Department Heads

Many institutions have created interdisciplinary centers, which bring together faculty from different departments to collaborate on scholarship, that benefit from the perspectives of multiple disciplines. These centers are generally headed by faculty members appointed as directors. Much of the description of the department chair position holds true for center directors, but the center director may find it still more challenging to build consensus and collegiality among faculty with different disciplinary backgrounds. The development of innovative courses and scholarship that integrate methods and ideas across disciplinary boundaries are the hallmark of a successful center and center director.

Academic library directors commonly report to the provost. Depending on the size of the college or university library, its director may be considered a peer of the deans or of the department chairs. Academic librarians, including the library director, often have faculty status, and the Association of College and Research Libraries has promulgated guidelines for the promotion and tenure of library faculty (Association, 2010).

Academic libraries have as their principal purpose the provision of trustworthy, authoritative knowledge (Campbell, 2006, p. 16). As more and more information becomes available online, and as online information becomes more and more trustworthy and authoritative, libraries are revising their missions in order to remain relevant. Academic libraries have an opportunity to re-envision their purpose, perhaps with greater focus on offering virtual reference services, teaching information literacy, choosing resources and managing resource licenses, collecting and digitizing archival materials, and maintaining digital repositories (p. 20).

Median salaries for directors of academic libraries range from $69,000 to $155,000.

Faculty

While they do not appear on most administrative organization charts, faculty are the core of every higher education institution. Members of the faculty have multiple responsibilities, including teaching, scholarship and research, public service, and administration. Many institutions operate using a model of shared governance between the faculty, the governing board, and the senior administration. Faculty participation in administration includes service on institutional and departmental committees; and development of junior faculty, staff, and students.

Higher education administration traditionally draws from the ranks of the faculty for many important positions, including president, provost, deans, and department heads. In the case of deans and department heads, these positions are usually for a defined term, after which individuals often return to the regular faculty to teach and do scholarly research. One of the challenges for faculty assuming these roles is a lack of preparation and administrative training when they are thrust into positions of authority above their once and future colleagues.

Regardless of whether the institution is a community college, private liberal arts college, public university, or research university, its faculty are responsible for turning its educational mission into an appropriate curriculum and pedagogy. These educational duties include student advising and institutional and departmental service. Members of the faculty at research universities must secure funding for research and supervise how that money is spent (pre- and post-award management). At research intensive universities, the administrative responsibilities of the faculty, comprising fiscal management, compliance with government regulations, and supervision of research and clerical staff, may dwarf other obligations. No clear division between administrative and educational responsibilities exists with regard to the supervision of graduate students; faculty supervise both their educational and funded research, which, in the best of all worlds, are highly related.

There are myriad challenges in the interaction of faculty with administration. Because members of the faculty perceive that they have the overall responsibility for the educational mission, they often regard management changes as challenges to that role. For example, budget constraints often result in changes in class sizes or the hiring of non-tenure-track faculty to supplement the regular faculty. In large research universities, the ever-present need for resources (people, money, and space) creates constant strains between faculty and administration.

In some universities, each member of the faculty is able to negotiate with the administration with regard to compensation, workload, and resources. In others, the faculty is represented by a union. Each of these models presents its own challenges. In the former case, individual faculty negotiations can be inordinately time-consuming for the administration (department chairs, academic deans, and chief academic administrators). In the latter, negotiations with faculty unions may inhibit rapid response to economic pressures or changes in pedagogical requirements.

Evaluation of faculty performance is very much dependent upon the type of educational institution and the specific academic discipline. In large research universities, faculty productivity metrics in science, technology, engineering, and mathematics (STEM) fields include the number and quality of publications, citations, and honors and awards; the amount of research funding; and successful graduation of doctoral students. Other types of institutions rely more heavily on metrics such as teaching evaluations, number of courses taught, and advising performance.

Faculty salaries vary widely by institution and discipline. The American Association of University Professors' annual survey of faculty compensation is a useful guide (http://www.aaup.org/aaup).

STUDENT LIFE LEADERSHIP

Students' higher education experiences extend beyond the classroom. Whether they live on a residential campus, commute to their schools, or connect primarily online, students are supported in their success and development by a network of student life professionals. Figure 2.3 provides an overview of the complex organization overseen by the Vice President of Student Life at The Ohio State University, illustrating the myriad activities for which student life leadership may be responsible.

Vice President/Dean

Vice presidents or deans of student life promote student success and enrich the student experience through a multitude of services that address all aspects of the student's life outside the classroom. Depending on the degree to which student life is viewed as being aligned with and supporting the academic side of the institution, the vice president may report to the provost or to the president. Regardless of where student life lands on the organization chart, the vice president must connect with every major organization of the institution, because each one touches the lives of students.

Perhaps the best way to understand the responsibilities of vice presidents of student life is to examine the various functions over which they preside. As with most college and university senior administrative positions, responsibilities vary depending on the size and type of institution. As one might expect, technical colleges that primarily serve adult learners offer services very different from those provided by universities that serve a large, traditional-aged undergraduate population, especially those with a large number of students who reside on campus.

The residence and dining halls unit is one of the largest within student life on most residential campuses, and is overseen by an associate or assistant vice president or director, depending in part upon the size of the operation. The director of residence and dining halls is usually responsible for residential management, social and educational programming in the residence halls, facilities improvements, leases and assignments, fiscal management, building services, and campus dining services. Today's director of residence and dining halls faces many of the same challenges directors have

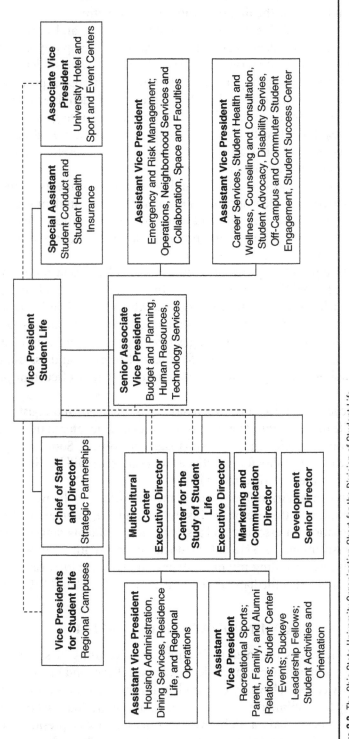

Figure 2.3 The Ohio State University Organization Chart for the Division of Student Life

always faced —providing safe and enriching environments in which young adults living away from home for the first time can grow and mature.

Student life's programming to enhance student learning and enrich student lives reaches far beyond the residence halls. Student life staff develop opportunities for students to engage in community service, to participate in clubs and student organizations, and to experience leadership opportunities. On many campuses, spirituality and religious life are supported by a student life office, and most student life organizations have staff devoted to meeting the needs of particular groups, including commuter students, minority students, students with disabilities, and lesbian, gay, bisexual, and transgender (LGBT) students. Student life staff are also responsible for developing and upholding the institution's code of student conduct.

Student life offices address the health and wellbeing of students in multiple ways, reducing the barriers to student success. At some institutions, student health centers are part of the student life organization, and many student life offices offer psychological counseling services. Recreational sports programs support students' fitness goals, providing social opportunities at the same time.

Student life vice presidents operate multi-million dollar organizations and must be adept managers of people and other resources. In addition to the student life offices that most directly touch the lives of students, vice presidents of student life in large institutions rely upon a cadre of senior staff who manage their unit's administration, human resources, communications and marketing, strategic planning, development, and information technology operations. Student life offices of research and assessment support functions throughout the organization through their analysis of current practices and methods.

At some colleges and universities, admissions, financial aid, and registration are part of the student life organization. These units will be discussed later in this chapter, as part of the portfolio of the chief enrollment management officer. Some vice presidents of student life have responsibility for athletics as well (athletics will be discussed as a separate unit headed by the athletic director).

The chief student affairs officer earns a median salary of between $102,000 and $183,000, depending on the size of the institution and the complexity of the position. Median compensation for associate and assistant vice presidents ranges from $63,000 at baccalaureate institutions to $118,000 at doctoral universities. Directors of student affairs organizations, including minority affairs, student activities, campus recreation, and student housing, earn median salaries of between $39,000 and $89,000.

ADMINISTRATIVE LEADERSHIP

Colleges and universities organize their administrative units in some ways that are fairly predictable and in others that are less so. Most colleges and universities, including some community colleges, have a vice president for research, a position that at research universities may be combined with that of dean of the graduate school. In the main, colleges and universities have a high-level person, often a vice president, in charge of human resources. The chief information officer is generally a position equivalent to vice president. In recent years, the position of director of enrollment management has at many institutions been elevated to the vice presidential level. Colleges and universities may have one or more vice presidents devoted to administrative, financial, and other business affairs. Vice presidents of communications, government relations, and development, along with the chief legal counsel, a vice presidential-level position, round out the list of usual vice presidents in higher education. The following sections briefly describe the positions mentioned above and note the major director positions that report to each.

Vice President for Research

The position of vice president for research is typically found in research universities. In most institutions, the vice president for research is a member of the senior officer cabinet or team. Duties will vary according to the breadth and depth of research activities, but typically include responsibilities related to government relationships, compliance, conflict of interest, negation of employee benefit, and indirect cost recovery rates. Vice presidents for research have ultimate responsibility for the pre- and post-award activities of the institution, and they are often involved in negotiating a wide range of research grants and contracts. Some have responsibility for the negotiation and implementation of affiliation agreements when there is relationship between the institution and an independent entity.

Technology transfer is usually part of the portfolio of this position. It is through the licensing of technology that discoveries made at universities are transferred to the public sector and move to applied uses. Technology transfer includes disclosure of research results, applying for patents and copyrights, and licensing. The U.S. government, which provides the bulk of external funding for research at universities and colleges, promotes commercialization of the results of research for the public good. Licensing also provides needed revenue to institutions and the inventors.

Most vice presidents for research spend a large amount of their time working with government agencies, either independently or in concert with organizations such as the Association of Public and Land-grant Universities (https://www.aplu.org/), Association of American Universities (http://www.aau.edu/), National Council of University Research Administrators (http://www.ncura.edu/content/), or Association of University Technology Managers (http://www.autm.net/Home.htm), as well as state and local agencies.

Evaluation of the performance of the vice president for research ultimately includes the success of an institution at attracting and sustaining externally sponsored research and the minimization of issues related to the conduct of the research. At doctoral universities, the median salary for the vice president for research is $218,400. The median salary for this position is lowest at two-year institutions, at $93,000.

At many doctoral and master's institutions, the vice president for research is supported by one or more associate or assistant vice presidents, who may or may not be members of the faculty. Associate and assistant vice presidents for research earn median salaries of $163,000 at doctoral institutions and $111,000 at master's institutions. Chief technology transfer and senior technology licensing officers may report to the vice president for research. Such positions are found almost exclusively at doctoral institutions. The median salary for chief technology officers is $157,000; for senior technology licensing officers,

$99,000. Directors of sponsored research and programs are found in all sectors, with median salaries ranging from $71,500 to $112,600.

Vice President for Human Resources

The vice president for human resources is responsible for supporting the recruitment and hiring of faculty and staff; providing quality compensation and benefits programs for employees; and providing education and training to support faculty and staff development. In addition, this vice president attends to the climate and quality of work life.

Because the hiring of faculty is primarily conducted by search committees, human resources staff generally play the smallest of roles in faculty hires. Nonetheless, the human resources vice president is responsible for developing and promulgating policies that ensure fair and equitable hiring practices for faculty and staff alike. Directors of affirmative action and equal employment, disability services, and labor relations are among the human resources staff who support the vice president in developing and implementing such policies. At smaller institutions, these functions may be clustered under an employment services director.

Determining and providing appropriate compensation and benefits for both faculty and staff are among the responsibilities of human resources vice presidents. College and university offices of human resources exchange information about salaries through their professional associations, and institutions draw on this information as they compete for talent. At large colleges and universities, this responsibility is often delegated to a director or assistant vice president.

Human resources staff offer new employee orientations, ongoing professional development, support for performance management, and organizational development training—vital support for a high-performance organization. Human resources information systems staff provide data and analysis to inform the entire campus about staffing-related trends and outcomes.

Vice presidents of human resources clearly demonstrate success through high levels of employee retention and satisfaction. The capacity to control the cost of employee benefits while ensuring access to quality health care is another hallmark of an outstanding human resources leader.

Median salaries for vice presidents of human resources range from $82,000 to $145,000, depending on the sector. Median salaries for assistant vice presidents and directors range from $53,000 to $99,500.

Vice Presidents for Business, Administration, and Finance

Ivory towers are neither cost-free nor maintenance-free, and the business of higher education is complex. Every college and university has one or more senior officers who are responsible for the business, administrative, and financial operations of the institution. Where these roles are split among multiple senior officers, institutions— even those similar in size and belonging to the same sector—have developed different reporting schemas. At some institutions, the chief financial officer and the chief business or administration officer both report to the president. At others, the chief business officer reports to the chief administration officer—or vice versa. Still another model has the chief budget officer or the chief administration officer reporting to the chief financial officer. While no organizational pattern emerges as typical, what is clear is that numerous operations support, but are quite distinct from, the academic enterprise. These operations include facilities planning, operation, maintenance, and development; parking and transportation; campus security; accounting and budgeting; risk management; purchasing; and printing and mail services.

One might argue that colleges and universities are no different from any other large organization with regard to business, administrative, and financial services. That similar services are needed in both non-academic and academic organizations is certainly true; the culture of academia, however, requires a different approach to business decision-making. For example, at most colleges and universities, governance structures give faculty a significant voice in determining institutional priorities, and this affects all aspects of planning and budgeting. Faculty committees do not generally make final decisions on the subject, but wise administrators take their advice and recommendations seriously. Furthermore, faculty at most institutions act with a great deal of autonomy. As experts in their fields, they know best the types of equipment and facilities they need to accomplish their teaching and research. It may be necessary for faculty to deviate from a preferred vendor list to purchase the equipment and materials that best suit their needs; they may have a better understanding of laboratory design than facility planners. The challenge for vice presidents with responsibility for business and administrative operations is to involve faculty in decision-making in a way that harnesses and respects their expertise, and to help faculty understand the fiscal, political, and legal constraints within which the institution must operate.

Median salaries for vice presidents for business, administrative, financial, planning, and budget operations range from $93,000 to $228,000, depending upon the individual's portfolio, the reporting line, and the sector and size of the institution. Salaries for staff reporting to these vice presidents vary along similar lines, and also with regard to educational requirements. University architects' median compensation ranges between $83,000 and $111,000, and directors of real estate and space management receive similar remuneration, ranging between $75,000 and $113,000. Median salaries are somewhat lower for directors of accounting and purchasing, at $64,000 to $95,000 and $67,000 to $94,000 respectively.

Chief Investment Officer

The chief investment officer is responsible for managing the institution's investment pool, including selecting investment managers, developing and implementing investment policy, and providing leadership on asset allocation. Chief investment officers often report both to the board of trustees' investment committee and to the institution's president or chief financial officer. Return on the investment pool is the clear success metric for this position, and chief investment officers are often rewarded for such success with bonuses. According to College and University Personnel Association data, 15% of chief investment officers at reporting institutions received bonuses for performance, and the average bonus exceeded the median salary for these positions. Depending on the size and sector of the institution, median salaries, not including bonuses, range between $109,000 and $200,000 for chief investment officers.

Chief Legal Officer

Not surprisingly, the National Association of College and University Attorneys (NACUA) provides the best description of the college and university chief legal officer position. The organization's website (www.nacua.org) explains that these attorneys are

> involved with issues such as governance, employment and human resources, student affairs, campus security, athletics, financial and business affairs, risk management, government and community relations, contracts, intellectual property, and various forms of dispute resolution. Higher education law attorneys are involved with virtually every part of the institution since legal matters can affect each and every function of the college or university.

The NACUA website further explains the structure of higher education legal offices:

> Some colleges employ a single attorney or rely solely on outside counsel for their institutional representation. Other institutions, typically larger or more complex ones, have multiple attorneys serving as in-house counsel, with as many as 10-15 attorneys at a large research university. In-house counsel are often supplemented with external counsel who have particular expertise. Higher education attorneys manage institutional compliance with federal, state, and local laws to determine methods to avoid potential legal liability. They practice preventive law to educate clients on campus about legal issues so that conflicts can be handled in a civil and collegial manner before the legal issues even arise or can be mediated before they become serious. They often participate in the representation of clients in formal dispute resolution, including litigation, arbitration, grievances, administrative hearings, and other adversarial proceedings.

Median salaries for chief legal affairs officers range from $130,000 to $193,000.

Chief Information Officer

The chief information officer at a college or university provides services to help faculty, students, and staff use technologies in learning, teaching, research, and administrative settings. The CIO does not, however, simply provide the services requested, but rather seeks to innovate, inform, and lead the campus community toward new and better ways of accomplishing their work supported by technology. Criteria listed for the Chief Information Officer Innovation Leadership Award, given annually at the Massachusetts Institute of Technology Sloan CIO Symposium, describe the key characteristics of great CIOs:

- Trusted Advisor—to the CEO, CFO, and other senior executives. Incorporates IT into business decision-making by educating business executives on IT potential, managing risk and participating in key operational and executive committees.
- Business Leader—intimately aware of business challenges, competitive landscape, and the organization's core strengths. Able to identify opportunities to improve business performance and deliver business value through the innovative use of IT and business processes.

- Strong Communicator—articulates a vision for IT-enabled innovation and works across the organization and with external stakeholders to gain support for this vision. Collaborates to identify, secure resources for, and achieve organizational alignment to enable innovations.
- Proven Manager—delivers core IT services, using internal staff and external services, within budget and staff constraints. Measures and reports IT performance against business-oriented metrics. Recognized among peers as an effective manager.

(MIT Sloan Alumni Club of Boston, n.d.)

Median salaries for chief information officers range between $98,000 and $192,000. Senior-level staff reporting to the chief information officer include directors of academic computing, enterprise information systems, instructional technology, and telecommunications and networking. Salaries for these professionals range from $66,000 to $137,000.

Chief External Affairs Officer

External affairs may comprise governmental and legislative relations, communications and marketing, and at some institutions, development and fund-raising. A single vice president may be charged with all of these components, as at the University of Georgia (University of Georgia Division of External Affairs, 2010), or each component may be led by a separate vice president, as at the University of Michigan (University of Michigan, 2011). Because development is most commonly a separate organization, the vice president for development will be discussed in the section following this one.

Vice presidents whose portfolios include government relations pursue policy outcomes that benefit their institutions and higher education more broadly. They and their staff monitor legislation of interest to universities, identifying emerging federal and state issues affecting students, faculty, and staff. Large institutions may have offices in Washington, D.C., enabling government relations staff to facilitate meetings between senior personnel and legislators and policy makers. At both the state and federal level, government relations staff endeavor to build and maintain good working relationships with public officials. In addition, government relations staff respond to public officials' requests for data and information about the institution.

Not every college and university has staff devoted to government relations, but it is inconceivable that an institution of higher education would not have communications and marketing staff. Vice presidents of communications and marketing may be responsible for media relations, advertising, and public relations for the institution as a whole, or, especially at smaller institutions, for units within the university. Their portfolio may or may not include media relations for their athletic department and sports teams, or production of marketing materials for admissions and recruitment. Where communications responsibilities are distributed, with academic units, athletics, and other departments responsible for their own marketing and media relations, successful vice presidents develop ways to collaborate with their campus colleagues.

Communications offices are finding innovative ways to take advantage of new media, and nearly every institution has links to Twitter, Facebook, and YouTube on its home page. With today's volume of information and the multiple delivery channels, the challenge for communications offices is to be heard—to provide timely information in a way that captures the attention of the intended audience.

Median salaries for chief external affairs officers range between $124,000 and $211,000, depending on the sector of the institution and the scope of the position. Directors of federal relations, positions primarily found at doctoral universities, have a median salary of $121,000, and directors of state government relations at doctoral universities earn slightly less, with a median income of $103,000. Salaries for directors of marketing, publications, and news services range between $58,000 and $89,000.

Vice President for Development

The goal of the vice president for development is to attain private philanthropic funding from alumni, friends, corporations, and foundations. The vice president typically reports to the college or university president. Development offices and foundations organize and coordinate fund-raising programs for colleges and universities to support the academic missions and objectives determined by the academic leadership of the institution. Many schools have adopted structures for development that include both a centralized office that coordinates efforts across the institution and decentralized development staff who work closely with specific units, such as the office of student life or the school of social work.

Vice presidents of development at public institutions may also serve as the president or executive director of a separate college or university foundation, organized as a not-for-profit 501(c)(3) corporation. Governed by a board of directors, these fund-raising foundations allow for confidentiality of donors' personal documents, greater flexibility with regard to expenditures, and opportunities for greater investment returns than can be attained under low-risk, low-return strategies required by many states.

Vice presidents for development at large institutions are usually supported by associate/assistant vice presidents or directors with responsibility for annual giving, planned giving, and corporate and foundation relations. Median salaries for the vice president for development range between $99,000 and $224,000; associate/assistant vice presidents and directors earn median salaries of between $57,000 and $153,000.

Vice President for Enrollment Management

Chief enrollment management officers most commonly report to their president, provost, or vice president of student life. The vice president for enrollment management brings together the offices that recruit, fund, track, and retain students, facilitating the coordination of staff, flow of information, and integration of decisions to coordinate and improve the following processes (Kurz, 2006):

- research, planning, recruitment, and communication;
- admissions marketing that attracts appropriate students in sufficient numbers;
- implementing pricing and financial aid strategies that optimize the institution's ability to generate net tuition revenue and attract and retain the desired mix of students through;

- anticipating immediate and long-term student demand and improving the institution's ability to respond to these interests;
- identifying reasons for attrition, minimizing it to the extent desirable, and enrolling qualified transfer students as replacements.

Offices of enrollment management evolved to help institutions better target the shrinking population of traditional-age college students and, at many colleges and universities, to attract more highly qualified students. These challenges persist, and those involved with enrollment management must continually create new strategies to meet the goals of their institution. Chief enrollment management officers earn median salaries of between $82,000 and $149,000, depending on the sector in which they are employed and the size of their institution. Among the senior staff who report to vice presidents for enrollment management are registrars, with median salary ranges of $62,000 to $99,000, and directors of admissions and financial aid, with median salary ranges of $70,000 to $114,000.

Chief Diversity Officer

Over the last decade, increasing numbers of colleges and universities have appointed a chief diversity officer to develop and drive their diversity agenda. Many institutions have historically had senior staff responsible for promoting access to higher education for minority students and to employment opportunities for minority faculty and staff. But as Damon A. Williams and Katrina C. Wade-Golden explain,

> What distinguishes the current executive diversity officer from its historical predecessors is the functional definition of diversity as a resource that can be leveraged to enhance the learning of all students and is fundamental to institutional excellence, in addition to its historic definition as the presence of individuals that differ by race, gender, or some other social identity characteristic.
>
> (Williams, 2006)

Most college and university strategic plans for diversity emphasize recruitment and retention of diverse students, faculty, and staff not only as an issue of fairness and equity, but also in recognition of the benefit of diverse perspectives for the growth and learning of the entire community. Effective chief diversity officers promote a campus climate that embraces and celebrates diversity and inclusion throughout their institution, and this is reflected not only in the size and success of the minority population, but also in the enhanced cultural competencies of the entire campus community.

The chief diversity officer may report to the president, to the provost or an associate provost, or to the vice president for student life, depending upon the focus of the position. Median salaries for this position range from $70,000 to $129,000, depending upon the size and sector of the institution.

STUDENT LEADERSHIP

Student leaders provide colleges and universities with valuable perspectives and insights. Undergraduate and graduate students serve at various levels throughout their colleges and universities, and their opportunities for leadership and input are as varied as the institutions they attend. The most visible role is as a member or officer of a student government or other official student body. Members and officers of these organizations are usually elected by their peers, and at most institutions there is a process to ensure that those elected are representative of the student body in terms of major or discipline. Generally, at master's and doctoral institutions, there are separate such organizations for undergraduate and graduate students. These organizations advocate on behalf of students with regard to issues as diverse as the information institutions should provide on diplomas to expenditures of student fees. In recent years, student leadership organizations have campaigned for more affordable textbooks and against college and university apparel manufactured in sweatshops. Undergraduate and graduate student organizations have joined forces both within and across institutions to support sustainability efforts at colleges and universities.

Students may also serve on their institution's board of trustees, and in leadership roles within their college, school, or department. In this capacity, students can provide reflections on their academic experience that can be invaluable in the shaping of curricula and advising. It can be tempting for those outside of the academy to describe such feedback as "customer input." This temptation to think of students as "customers" of the faculty with whom they study must be resisted. The student–faculty relationship, in which both parties commit to the student's learning and development, is time-honored, and is diminished rather than enhanced by the "customer" designation. Nonetheless, the student perspective on the quality and benefits of the student–faculty relationship within a particular department is immensely valuable for improving the educational experience.

A particular challenge for student leaders is time management. Jason Marion, who served as student government president as an undergraduate at Morehead State University, as Council of Graduate Students president as a doctoral student at The Ohio State University, and as a student trustee at both institutions, notes that

> the time period to learn the leadership role and then actually exhibit effective leadership is very short, and it all occurs while one is engaging in a rigorous time-intensive academic program, thereby creating a serious challenge for even the most effective time manager.
>
> (Marion, 2011)

A further challenge is creating continuity in student organizations, whose membership and constituencies are constantly changing. Marion sees continuity as a critical measure of success for student organizations: "I watch the organization after me and see how effective the organization is for the next leader. If the organization is still successful one academic year after I have left, then I deem that as a big success" (Marion, 2011).

Members of student government organizations, and especially officers, may receive a stipend for their services. Most, however, serve without financial compensation.

CONCLUSION

It should be clear from this review of higher education leadership positions that there is no single administrative pattern for colleges and universities, nor is there even a best pattern. Administrative configurations within colleges and universities largely evolve over time, according to the needs of the institution, and, in part, according to the competencies of talented institutional leaders. The higher education world is a learning community, and academic leaders learn about the administrative structures of units with goals similar to their own through professional organizations and networks. Many structures can be successful, and institutions striving to become more effective have multiple models to examine and evaluate.

REFERENCES

Association of College and Research Libraries. (2010). Retrieved April 2011, from http://www.ala.org/acrl/standards/promotiontenure

Association of Governing Boards of Universities and Colleges. (2010). Statement on Board Responsibility for Institutional Governance, http://www.agb.org/news/2010-03/statement-board-responsibility-institutional-governance

Campbell, J. D. (2006). Changing a cultural icon: The academic library as a virtual destination. *Educause Review,* *41*(1), 16–31.

Columbia State Community College Organization Chart. Retrieved December 15, 2011, from http://forms.columbiastate.edu/policies-procedures/01-01-00_Appendix_A_CSCC_Organizational_Chart.pdf

Kurz, K. A. (2006). *Enrollment Management Grows Up,* May. Retrieved April 2011, from University Business: http://www.universitybusiness.com/viewarticle.aspx?articleid=23&p=1#0

McGuinness, A. C. (2002). *The authority of state boards of postsecondary education.* Denver, CO: Education Commission of the States.

McGuinness, A. C. (2003). *Models of postsecondary education coordination and governance in the States.* Denver, CO: Education Commission of the States.

MIT Organization Chart. Retrieved December 15, 2011, from http://web.mit.edu/orgchart/

MIT Sloan Alumni Club of Boston. (n.d.). *MIT Sloan CIO Symposium Award;* © *2003–2011 All Rights Reserved.* Retrieved April 9, 2011, from http://www.mitcio.com/award/signup.php

New England Association of Schools and Colleges. (n.d.). Standards for Accreditation, Section 3.2, http://cihe.neasc.org/standards_policies/standards/standards_html_version/#standard_three

The Ohio State University. (2009). *Bylaws of the Board of Trustees of The Ohio State University,* April 3. Columbus, OH.

University of Georgia Division of External Affairs. (2010). *UGA Division of External Affairs,* Copyright © 2010. Retrieved April 9, 2011, from http://www.alumni.uga.edu/ea/index.php/site/

University of Michigan. (2011). *University of Michigan Administration.* Retrieved April 9, 2011, from http://www.umich.edu/admin.php

Williams, D. A.-G. (2006). What is a Chief Diversity Officer. *Inside Higher Ed.,* April 18. Retrieved from http://www.workforcediversitynetwork.com/docs/Article_goldemwilliams_WhatisaChief%20DiversityOfficer.pdf

3

THE ROLE OF INTERNAL GOVERNANCE, COMMITTEES, AND ADVISORY GROUPS

Kerry Brian Melear

INTRODUCTION

While institutions of higher education must operate by integrating the directives articulated by many external constituents, including state legislatures, boards of trustees, and various accrediting agencies, they also function through a system of shared governance on the internal institutional level, which has "significant consequences for the health of institutions" (Minor, 2004b, p. 361). The American system of higher education is largely characterized by this participatory governance model in both the public and private sectors, through which operations are facilitated by a central administration in concert with input from faculty, staff, and students. Myriad committees, advisory groups, task forces, and panels form the threads that are woven into the tapestry of internal governance, from community colleges to liberal arts colleges to research universities. Concerning campus-level operations, Salter and Tapper (2002) posit:

> The internal governance of universities is shaped by a political environment which encourages, chastises or is indifferent to the various forms that governance may take. To the extent that institutions adopt a form of governance which can readily engage with the pressures generated by their environment, they are then able to compete effectively in the political game for resources. To the extent that they do not, they will fall behind and, ultimately, succumb.
>
> (p. 245)

The for-profit sector of higher education operates in a wholly more corporate fashion, not even remotely akin to the not-for-profit sector. In the for-profit context, institutional decision-making is deliberate and largely flows from executive authority. The results of these decisions are quickly implemented, a rarity in the not-for-profit sector, where various parties, especially the faculty, insist upon shared governance as part of the sound function of a college or university. Indeed, Gayle, Tewarie, and White (2003) reason that "the extent to which campus stakeholders perceive institutional governance to be shared can enhance or constrain the role of a college or university as a vehicle for teaching and learning" (p. 73).

This chapter explores the role of some of the basic advisory bodies inherent in most colleges and universities in the not-for-profit sector, as well as the influence of campus-wide forums and university foundations in internal governance questions. Specifically, the chapter addresses the faculty's role in shared governance through the lens of the faculty senate and the curriculum committees, and then transitions into a discussion of other functional groups, such as space and facilities committees, planning and budget committees, and athletics committees, along with the impact of personal and professional decision processes within those contexts. The chapter then examines the internal role played by external university foundations, legally separate entities, yet integral to internal operations, and briefly discusses the benefit of campus-wide forums in terms of the dissemination of information to the campus community and the opportunity for robust discourse and discussion. Because of the variance in institutional types and internal governance models across the broad range of higher education institutions, these functions are addressed in generally applicable terms.

FACULTY SENATE

The faculty senate is a primary vehicle through which members of the professorate exercise the shared governance that characterizes higher education. Such bodies provide a forum for faculty and administrators to deliberate a range of issues associated with academic administration (Pope & Miller, 2005). As noted by Bess and Dee (2008), a faculty senate bears primary responsibility for academic concerns, "but it shares responsibility with the administrative structure for others. The responsibilities of and relationships between these two entities are inherently somewhat ambiguous, and important institutional policy decisions must often be negotiated" (p. 176). Faculty senates exist on campuses across the spectrum of higher education, from the community college to the university, although some scholars contend that faculty governance issues are less problematic at the community college level because of more clearly articulated faculty expectations (Miller, 2003; Miller & Miles, 2008).

The role of the faculty in sharing academic governance was emphasized when the American Association of University Professors (AAUP), founded in 1915, promoted the concept in one of its early committees. The AAUP urged that faculties should share in the process of administration and should be the controlling voice concerning academic matters. This philosophy did not manifest until after World War II, when faculties began to enjoy a more powerful role, controlling appointments, academic calendars, and work schedules, either by delegation of authority from governing boards or approval of trustees (Brubacher & Rudy, 1976). The AAUP affirmed its position in 1966 in its *Statement on Government of Colleges and Universities*, which calls for faculty primacy over the curriculum and faculty involvement with internal administrative matters (AAUP, 1966). By the 1970s, senates of the faculty "had evolved into influential policy-making bodies on many campuses" (Brubacher & Rudy, 1976, p. 375), thus formalizing increased faculty power and input on campus (Kezar & Eckel, 2004).

It has been long recognized, however, that the faculty senate is but one participant in shared campus governance, along with administration and students (Lizzio & Wilson, 2009). Faculty senates on campuses that permit faculty unionization share governance over faculty-related matters, with senates focusing on academic concerns and faculty unions working on employment-related matters such as salaries and benefits (Aronowitz, 2006). In 1973, Bornheimer, Burns, and Dumke noted:

> Thus, while we feel that the faculty should have primacy in curricular matters, it should be no means be exclusive. When other responsible voices are heard along with the faculty, in determining the courses that shall be taught, the final product is well balanced and even the faculty is better served than if it alone made all the decisions in this sensitive area.
>
> (p. 83)

For the most part, contemporary faculty senates do not wield great power beyond their advisory capacities, particularly with regard to non-academic matters. Since the 1960s and 1970s, their relative power on campuses has waxed and waned according to economic pressures and accountability initiatives emanating from state legislatures (Lee, 1979). Further, faculty senates face new internal governance challenges as higher education continues to rely on external funding sources, such as curricular regulation of special-interest centers funded by outside parties (Burgan, 2009). Barbara Lee's 1979 assessment rings true today: "The faculty role in academic governance at institutions of higher education remains a topic of controversy, ambiguity, and misunderstanding among faculty themselves, administrators and, more recently, state legislators" (p. 565).

Indeed, faculty senates have faced criticism for being weak and exerting little influence beyond their advisory roles (Birnbaum, 1989). With regard to budget matters, for example, Sufka (2009) found that senates are challenged by lack of understanding of budget processes, short response times required by state-level leadership, apathy on the part of some faculty members about financial issues and their role in addressing them, and inability to respond quickly because of internal structures and processes. He suggested senates could play a positive role in budget matters if they improved response times, identified strong leaders, and developed a statement of values to follow during times of fiscal crisis. Through survey research, Minor (2004a) found that faculty senates are challenged because they are understudied, exist in multiple governance environments, and suffer from a lack of faculty interest and the incongruence between the philosophy of shared governance and its function.

Although faculty governance bodies such as senates are quite common in higher education, research into their efficacy is scant (Kezar & Eckel, 2004). Miller and Pope (2003) note the ambiguity surrounding faculty senates and their roles on campuses, recognizing that multiple factors affect the influence of senates, which makes it difficult to generalize about them:

> The push and pull environment that has arisen in faculty governance is often one of adversarial relationships that either produce hostility or inhibit effective decision making. In other instances, the converse is true, as senates serve as healthy instruments of communication between and among faculty and administrators.
>
> (p. 121)

Miller and Pope did state, however, that consistent themes demonstrated the ambiguous nature of faculty senates. The structure of senates has not been fundamentally altered, but respect afforded senates and perceptions of their usefulness on campus has been eroded by delays in decision-making and lack of internal cooperation. For example, the governing board of Rensselaer Polytechnic University suspended the faculty senate in 2007 for refusing to include non-tenure track faculty in membership. The administration cited the senate's interference in the review of faculty governance as one part of the rationale for its suspension and created an interim faculty governance structure in its place (Olson, 2011).

Minor (2004b) proposes four useful and distinct models of faculty senate composition: functional, influential, ceremonial, and subverted (Figure 3.1). In the functional model, the most traditional rendering of the structure of faculty senates, a senate primarily represents and protects the faculty interest in academic decisions. Members are elected from the faculty, the group is led by a chair or president, and various committees undertake the duties of the senate. By-laws or other governing documents guide the work, and advisory statements are issued through deliberation and formalized voting processes.

An influential faculty senate has status within a college or university as a legitimate governing body; rather than focusing solely on curricular matters, it makes significant contributions to decisions across a broader cross-section of the institution. Such senates are powerful, and Minor underscores that they traditionally exist on campuses where "the power center shifts between constituencies as the contextual circumstances change" (Minor, 2004b, p. 350). Administrators recognize their legitimacy as a viable governing body on campus.

Ceremonial faculty senates "exist in name only and operate as symbolic artifacts" (Minor, 2004b, p. 351), meeting infrequently and contributing little to campus governance. Presidential and administrative power in institutions with such a faculty senate is strong, and decision-making with regard to academic issues is delegated to individual colleges and departments. While not powerful, such senates can serve useful latent functions (Birnbaum, 1989). "By providing opportunities for socialization, congregation, discussion, professional screening, and the like, senates can contribute to institutional stability in the potentially contentious, volatile environment of higher education" (Helms, 2005, p. 35).

Finally, a subverted faculty senate's role in institutional governance is diminished by alternative methods of faculty input. Administrators consider such bodies to be obstacles rather than viable sources of assistance. Minor notes that subverted senates "usually

- Functional: Powerful and elected
- Influential: Significant contribution
- Ceremonial: Symbolic
- Subverted: Not recognized as contributory

Figure 3.1 Minor's Faculty Senate Governance Model

suffer from negative cultural and communicative aspects that affect their role in campus decision-making" (Minor, 2004b, p. 353), and campus leaders and other members of the community lack confidence in decisions rendered by such groups. As a result, these senates are avoided in the decision-making process.

CURRICULUM COMMITTEE

The centrality of the curriculum committee on college campuses clearly illustrates the primary role that the faculty plays in academic governance. The primary function of curriculum committees is to maintain an institution's curricular offerings through approval of proposals for new courses of study, oversight of current offerings, course discontinuances, program reviews, determination of course articulation, and recommendations about the curriculum to the appropriate governing body, provost, or faculty. Such committees have long been integral to faculty oversight of academics in liberal arts colleges and universities, but their importance on the community college campus is also now greatly emphasized because of the increasing role faculty members play in community college governance (Miller & Miles, 2008).

Institutions commonly employ numerous curriculum committees, particularly on campuses with both undergraduate and graduate programs. Because of the diversity of institutional types, governance models, and programs, curriculum committees operate at numerous levels on college and university campuses. Individual colleges and schools may house a curriculum committee composed of members of the faculty and responsible for overseeing the academic programs offered within that unit. Administrators such as provosts, deans, and registrars are often ex-officio members. A campus might be home to both an undergraduate curriculum committee that oversees the institution's baccalaureate courses of study and a graduate curriculum committee responsible for a graduate school's academic programs. The process of marshaling a particular institution's curriculum is specific and appropriate to a given campus and its programs, and Muffo (2001) cautions that curriculum committees should not lose sight of the general education, or core curriculum, by focusing attention on other functions, such as new course approvals.

Curriculum committees must be responsive to the evolution of the collegiate course of study over time. As noted by Clark Kerr (1977, as cited in Rudolph, 1977):

> In the final analysis, the curriculum is nothing less than the statement a college makes about what, out of the totality of man's constantly growing knowledge and experience, is considered useful, appropriate, or relevant to the lives of educated men and women at a certain point of time.
>
> (p. xxi)

The curriculum in American higher education has changed dramatically since the inception of our system of higher learning, and now reflects an amazing spectrum of courses of study ranging from the liberal arts to professional preparation programs, for which curriculum committees bear primary responsibility. "The specific needs of the students, society, and the sector should be addressed in the curriculum" (Collins, 2006, p. 53).

Not only must members of curriculum committees remain responsive to the curriculum itself, they must also be mindful of accreditation, particularly for professional programs for which outside bodies set standards that must be met to maintain programmatic recognition. Accrediting bodies are influential and play a critical role in the administration of an institution's curriculum. Loss of accreditation, particularly regional accreditation, can lead to severe penalties that can adversely affect a college or university's function or even solvency.

Increasingly, external funding sources have also begun to exert influence on collegiate curricula in the United States. As noted by Burgan (2009), special-interest research and teaching centers sponsored by outside parties have proliferated in recent years, and those sponsoring benefactors often "expect to be involved in the content and management of programs they pay for" (p. 15). She further argues that while such centers may provide tangible benefits and enrich a campus environment, they can also distort the priorities associated with regulation of the curriculum. Curriculum committees must remain flexible and responsive to the needs of external constituents, but mindful of protecting academic integrity.

Figure 3.2 highlights key characteristics of curriculum committees.

SPACE AND FACILITIES COMMITTEE

Allocation of space and facilities on postsecondary campuses is a function of balancing needs across various constituencies, and is a process that is becoming increasingly complex as colleges and universities evolve and the demand for available space grows. One major challenge involves the unique requirements of Millennial college students, born between 1982 and 2002, who "influence space planning, design, and construction and will continue to transform higher education as they return to campus as faculty and staff" (Rickes, 2009, p. 7). These students are inveterate users of technology and have different spatial needs than their predecessors, necessitating careful space administration and planning. As Romano and Hanish (2003) note, meeting the needs of a diverse and consistently shifting student population is becoming more complex an endeavor for many reasons, "not the least of which is financial" (p. 3).

In addition to accommodating students, institutions must also be sensitive to the needs of faculty, staff, and external constituencies who all compete for a finite pool of

---

Curriculum committees are:

- Broadly constructed or related to specific programs, majors, departments, or fields
- Composed of faculty and some administrators, such as provosts and deans
- Focused on general requirements on the undergraduate and graduate levels
- Sensitive to field-specific and accreditation concerns, such as law and medicine

Figure 3.2 Curriculum Committees

spatial resources based on their particular needs; faculty members, for example, may require substantial research space. A college or university must therefore develop space management methods that coalesce with its research missions, priorities, and culture (Fink, 2004). Classroom space is always at a premium, especially as enrollments increase.

Colleges and universities establish space and facilities committees to evaluate and allocate space; these committees are known by various names on different campuses. It is also not uncommon for institutions to establish committees that are responsible for campus planning as well as space allocation, but planning committees will be discussed in the following section.

The primary function of space and facilities committees is to facilitate the equitable and most efficient, cost-effective allocation of campus space in order to maximize the learning environment for students, faculty, staff, and external constituents. These committees must evaluate requests for use of space or reallocation of unused space. If they do not also embody a planning component, they must work in concert with university planning committees to reduce redundancy and marshal resources effectively while allowing for future needs or challenges.

Membership on space and facilities committees is campus-specific, but is typically composed of senior administrators, such as provosts; vice presidents for finance, administration, student affairs, and planning; various deans; representatives from the faculty; physical plant directors; and occasionally students. The committees typically report in an advisory capacity to the institution's president or to a vice president charged with campus facilities, or they issue decisions about space requests to the campus community at large. These committees meet regularly, usually monthly and on an ad hoc basis to respond to the constantly changing space requests on campuses.

Some institutions have adopted guiding principles to facilitate the distribution of campus space. For example, the University of California has adopted a set of "Space Management Principles" that establish seven goals for allocating facilities and space: functionality (meets functional requirements), equity (fair distribution across all divisions), consistency (all practices are identifiable and user-friendly), efficiency (space is utilized to the greatest extent possible), flexibility (current needs are met while being mindful of the future), cost-effectiveness (fiscally responsible allocations), and proximity (facilitates coordination of university business matters) (University of California, 2005, p. 3).

Likewise, Sacramento State University has established guidelines to assist its "Space Planning Advisory Group." As shown in Figure 3.3, these guidelines contain detailed information regarding the types of decisions that may face the committee, as well as regulations to provide a framework for decision-making, in order to address growth and "the changing needs of the University and those whom it serves" (Sacramento State University, 2011, p. 1). The University of Dayton has also adopted space management guidelines that provide guiding principles for space allocation decisions, outline operating procedures, detailed information about the space and facilities allocation process on that campus in order to "facilitate an effective and efficient utilization of University space resources resulting in a quality learning and working environment for students, faculty, and staff" (University of Dayton, 2008, p. 3).

Campus Space Planning

The Space Planning Advisory Group (SPAG) has been formed to assist University officers in making sound judgments regarding the allocation and utilization of space. SPAG has primary oversight for all space use considerations, and is established to impartially serve the needs of all campus constituencies in assigning the primary use of space. The group will also assist in more routine matters such as adjudicating controversial use requests and developing policy and procedure for space use.

Responsibilities

The Space Planning Advisory Group's activities will typically address such questions as: Who should occupy new or vacated space? What types of space should be emphasized in facilities planning? The group will address such policy and procedural issues as: How should faculty and staff offices be allocated? How should space use priorities be set? What rules should govern the use of space for non-instructional purposes? In addition, all space issues that are anticipated to result in expenditure greater than $25k will be forwarded to the University Budget Advisory Committee for financial consideration prior to submission to the Vice President for Administration.

The work of SPAG is in the form of recommendations to the Vice President for Administration, who will consult with the affected Vice Presidents and/or the Provost prior to submission to the President for consideration and decision.

Scope

This policy applies to the allocation/utilization of all California State University, Sacramento owned, controlled, and operated space. Auxiliary owned, controlled, and operated space is not covered by this policy.

Figure 3.3 Sacramento State University Campus Space Planning Policy

PLANNING AND BUDGET COMMITTEE

Planning and budget committees on college and university campuses are critical elements of internal governance. Where space and facilities committees focus on maximizing available resources, planning and budget committees seek to maximize future resources including facilities and beyond. These committees are charged with a broad, complex, and difficult task that requires environmental scanning and predictions of future resource availability, or lack thereof, in a constantly changing world:

> Every day, college and university campuses change—usually imperceptibly and occasionally dramatically. Programs change, people change, financial resources change, buildings change, land and landscapes change, environs change. The way campuses look today is the result of all the minor and significant, casual and formal, rational and irrational decisions that are made in the day-to-day dynamic interaction of a living institution responding to such changes.
>
> (Lidsky, 2002, p. 69)

Strategic planning has become increasingly prominent in higher education as a more nuanced approach to long-term planning. In general terms, Bess and Dee (2008) find the concept of aligning organizational resources and goals to be congruent with the organization's environment. Dooris, Kelley, and Trainer (2004) define strategic planning in the postsecondary context as follows:

> In higher education, bettering one's condition includes hiring better faculty, recruiting stronger students, upgrading facilities, strengthening academic programs and student services, and acquiring the resources needed to accomplish these things. Since most institutions of higher education share a similar mission and compete for these same objectives, an essential part of strategic planning involves shaping the institution in ways that ensure mission attainment by capturing and maintaining a market niche in the quest for resources, faculty, and students. Thus, strategic planning has both external and internal faces.
>
> (p. 6)

Planning and budget exist in a state of symbiosis; one concept remains dependent upon the other as they cycle together, and problems associated with one with certainly affect the other. For this reason, planning and budget committees are integral to the overall health of a college or university, as the decisions they reach and recommend to upper administration can have far-reaching consequences. This requires deliberate and judicious planning processes that are "woven tightly into the day-to-day operations and interactions of the institution, whatever its type" (Lidsky, 2002, p. 70). Sound planning is essential to good budgetary practices, particularly because higher education faces "increasingly complex facilities, shortening time lines, proliferating code and regulatory requirements, emerging technologies, and growing concerns for indoor air quality and environmental sustainability" (Guckert & King, 2003-2004, p. 24).

Planning and budget committees are thus typically designed to provide an institution's chief executive officer with guidance and input regarding the evolution of the environs and the effect of that evolution on the academic experience and institutional tenets. They often work in concert with other committees, such as long-range planning committees or academic planning committees. The institution's budgetary and academic priorities are considered, as well as the context of institutional mission.

Faculty senates may have planning and budget subcommittees, but these are composed and governed only by members of the faculty. Broader administrative planning and budget committees also include faculty representation, as well as upper-level administrators such as provosts; vice presidents for finance, administration, and student affairs; deans; staff representatives; and students.

It is noteworthy that some institutions have expanded the role of the planning committee into separate planning departments with staff members responsible for numerous facets of institutional forecasting, master planning, or space allocation. Such campuses include Carnegie Mellon University; the University of California, Los Angeles; and Massachusetts Institute of Technology (Fink, 2004). This trend will likely continue, as institutions recognize the importance of judicious planning and the volume of effort associated with that endeavor.

ATHLETICS COMMITTEE

The intent of intercollegiate athletics is to provide an extracurricular developmental outlet for college students to enrich their learning experience and campus life on the whole. Athletics, while certainly not without its criticisms, provides this experience for students and affords institutions a valuable framework to increase alumni connections and philanthropy. The financial impact of college athletics is tremendous and undeniable across the spectrum of higher education, as the revenue generated through intercollegiate athletics reaches new levels. According to the National Collegiate Athletic Association (NCAA), the Football Championship Subdivision of Division I alone, which is composed of only 120 institutional members, generated revenues of $45,698,000 in 2009 (NCAA, 2010).

Intercollegiate athletics has long been under the lens of scrutiny for many reasons, including questions of academic quality and student engagement with campus life. Athletics committees must police these issues on college campuses. For example, one study indicated that many faculty members felt disconnected from campus athletics, found the salaries paid to coaches excessive, and felt that decisions regarding campus sports were driven by external entities without regard to academic mission (Sander, 2007). This perceived tension between commercial values and institutional mission was addressed by a 2010 report by the Knight Commission on Intercollegiate Athletics, which urged institutions to bring athletics and academics back into balance through greater transparency of financial reporting, placing incentives on prioritizing student-athlete academics, and emphasizing the notion that student athletes are students, not professional athletes (Knight Commission on Intercollegiate Athletics, 2010).

As with the committees previously discussed, the structure of the athletics committee as a form of internal governance will vary according to the institution in which it is housed, and will reflect the nature of that college or university's athletic program. The NCAA permits institutions to participate as members of one of three divisions, each with differing requirements regarding the number of sports offered. Regardless of divisional association, the NCAA regulates intercollegiate athletics, and postsecondary institutions must comply with these regulations closely or risk costly sanctions. Assisting with that compliance process is one of the key roles of the athletics committee.

Athletics committees have numerous duties, according to the size and extent of an institutional athletics program. In general, athletics committees are responsible for overseeing the athletics programs, with particular regard to compliance with NCAA regulations, as mentioned above. Such committees also typically render recommendations for practice regarding athletic policy and programming on campus, as well as regulate academic requirements for student athletes.

As with the committees previously discussed, the composition of the athletics committee on most campuses illustrates key principles of shared governance. Membership of postsecondary athletics committees is typically drawn from a broad cross-section of the campus community, with representation from upper-level administration, the faculty, the student body, and the institution's athletic foundation, a separate legal entity that supports campus athletic programs through philanthropy and development.

RESPONSIBILITY FOR COMMITTEE DECISION-MAKING

Service on various departmental and institutional committees sometimes requires a balance of personal responsibility with responsibility to committee function. Committees formed within individual colleges housing multiple departments may find that individual department perspectives dominate the discussion. Bright and Richards (2001) argue that "...departmental barriers frequently seem insurmountable to those inside them. This silo mentality impedes progress both internal and external" (p. 84). Likewise, Buller (2006) encourages administrators, particularly department chairs, to cultivate relationships outside of the department, arguing that to meet with success, "you will need to know how you can best serve these external constituents, where to draw the line with them, under which circumstances to turn to them as allies, and when it is desirable to maintain a distance" (p. 237).

Service may also require a balance of what is best for an individual against the collective interest of the academic department. Wheeler et al. (2008) refer to this phenomenon, particularly among faculty members, as "distributed loyalties," and caution that administrators must find the delicate balance that satisfies both personal aspiration and the needs of a department or unit (p. 38). The concept of distributed loyalty is woven into the fabric of higher education for faculty members, who are not only individual scholars requiring autonomy but also members of programs, departments, colleges, and ultimately, the college or university, as well as outside professional and personal associations. Wheeler et al. suggest charting individual progress toward shared goals as a method to overcome the effect of distributed loyalties. Figure 3.4 highlights key components of committee service.

FOUNDATIONS

Although college and university foundations are separate legal entities and not part of the system of shared governance that typifies higher education, they play an integral role in campus operations that bears discussion in this context. Publicly funded colleges and universities are typically supported by foundations responsible for developing private gifts to the institution and maintaining those gifts in endowments. While this has long been true for universities, community colleges have only recently begun to establish separate foundations for their support (Gose, 2006). The role of private giving for all of public higher education continues to increase in importance as state funding steadily decreases (Kelderman, 2011).

Service on committees requires:

- Balance of self-interest with department or programmatic concerns
- Significant investment of time and intellectual resources
- Cultivation of relationships and shared decision processes

Figure 3.4 Committee Service

Foundations are not operational units of a college or university. Rather, they are separate, not-for-profit educational corporations under Section 501(c)(3) of the United States Internal Revenue Code and established to support institutions of higher learning under the laws of each respective state. The intent of establishing a separate legal entity to seek private external funding and manage these funds once they are endowed is the removal of the endowment and other private funds from direct control and influence of college and university administration (Mississippi Legislature, 2007). Also, public funds can remain under the purview of state legislatures, so removing private gifts from the public domain insulates the institution's endowments from governmental intrusion and provides more privacy for the donor. A foundation is directed by a chief executive officer who is advised by a board of trustees, and a college or university is associated with a foundation through a contractual affiliation agreement.

Because foundations are separate entities, they are more insulated from state open-meetings and open-records laws than the public institution itself. However, while foundations are separate legal entities, the very rationale for their existence is to support the college or university with which they are affiliated. As a result, foundations do come to bear in a discussion of various forms of internal governance because institutional administration influences how foundations go about the business of supporting a college or university. Foundations raise money in various ways, including through annual giving programs, planned giving, and major fund-raising campaigns. Institutional administration can play a very influential role in major fund-raising initiatives by providing direction for how a campaign should proceed and what areas of campus it is intended to benefit. This position was clearly articulated by the University of Iowa Foundation:

> Because the UI Foundation was established to facilitate the University's mission, the Foundation's major initiatives, such as large capital campaigns, are set the by University's President, Provost, and central administration with concurrence of the Foundation's management group and board of directors.
>
> (University of Iowa Foundation, n.d.)

In this way, presidents and other upper-level administrators provide guidance to the foundation as it seeks to support the institution's mission, and an external entity becomes critical to internal operations. Figure 3.5 highlights key features of foundations.

College and University Foundations are:

- Separate legal entities
- Integral to operation via fundraising
- Sometimes subject to open records requests
- Supportive through small gift programs, annual giving initiatives, and major fundraising programs

---

Figure 3.5 Foundations

CAMPUS-WIDE FORUMS

The campus-wide forum is a hallmark of higher education and can be a useful tool for promoting shared governance on campus and providing the campus community with information and opportunity for input. Campus-wide forums are called to address numerous issues—from social to political to financial—at the forefront of discussion at a college or university.

During periods of financial exigency, it can be useful and effective to hold a campus-wide forum to discuss budget procedures or explain methodologies for making budget reductions, thus providing transparency to the campus community. For example, the president of Western Carolina University called a campus-wide forum in January 2011 to address the impact of North Carolina's nearly $4 billion state revenue shortfall on university operations (Holcombe, 2011).

Forums are also useful to provide a framework for public discussion of campus-specific issues that may have caused acute controversy, such as the campus-wide smoking ban instituted at Texas State University. At two forums held in 2010, one for students and one for faculty and staff, the director of University Health Services discussed his review of the institution's smoking policy and his recommendations (Venable, 2010). Such forums also give members of the campus community an opportunity to express their feelings about decisions that can be used to guide good practice.

CONCLUSION

Shared governance on the not-for-profit college or university campus is an integral tenet of internal institutional operation. Postsecondary institutions are unusual in that, as corporate bodies, they seek input directly from so many constituents to effect operations, but this is a defining factor of higher education that has long been advocated, especially by the faculty. Faculty senates variously yield great power over institutional decisions or no power at all, depending on the context of the institution. They remain, however, a powerful voice through which faculty members can exert influence or, at a minimum, state a position on an issue of import to a particular campus.

Curriculum committees also provide a window for faculty input, as well as student and staff perspectives. Curriculum committees will continue to face challenges as they navigate an ever-changing set of demands from students, parents, and the public to respond to contemporary professional educational concerns, while seeking to remain true to traditional educational philosophies relative to the liberal arts curriculum and its role in the general curriculum. Likewise, facilities and space committees will remain challenged as enrollments increase without a corollary increase in physical space or campus facilities. The work performed by such committees requires a careful balance of the needs of several constituency groups, including faculty, staff, students, and members of the external community. These committees must be sensitive to the needs of all of these groups while working within the context of a finite physical environment.

Planning and budget committees are similarly challenged to balance the needs of a variety of constituencies, but must further consider those needs projected into the future in relation to forecasts of available resources. These committees work in concert with other campus committees to achieve campus academic and cultural missions within the framework of changing financial and physical resources.

Athletics committees are composed of a broad campus cross-section, and are responsible for overseeing athletics programs, protecting the academic and physical interests of student athletes, and ensuring compliance with NCAA regulations specific to a particular campus. Such committees have been challenged in the past by questions of academic integrity, scandals, and costly sanctions, but are charged with the important duty of marshaling the student-athlete's experience and providing alumni and other members of the campus community a valuable outlet to express institutional loyalty.

Service to institutions on committees, advisory groups, or task forces compels members of the campus community to balance individual needs with the collective needs of departments or the institution. This delicate balance requires a judicious inquiry into what is best for the professional health of all parties involved, and must be reached in order to maximize benefit to a particular campus's internal governance.

Foundations, although separate legal entities, are integral to the internal operations of publicly funded colleges and universities. They are charged with developing private funding to support a college's or university's mission while maintaining separation from direct internal administration. However, because foundations exist specifically to support an affiliated institution, their development activities are strongly influenced by members of central administration, thus yielding an external entity central to internal campus operations.

Finally, campus-wide forums provide a window of opportunity for members of the campus community to express opinions and receive information. Such forums can provide transparency into institutional administrative decisions across a range of issues, such as budgetary concerns or acute campus controversies. They are also used to address broader social issues and invite a robust discussion of concepts and events that help shape the contours of the marketplace of ideas that is the American college or university.

REFERENCES

American Association of University Professors. *1966 Statement of Government of Colleges and Universities.* Washington, DC: American Association of University Professors.

Aronowitz, S. (2006). Should academic unions get involved in governance? *Liberal Education, 92*(4), 22–27.

Bess, J. L., & Dee, J. R. (2008). *Understanding college and university organization: Theories for effective policy and practice.* Sterling, VA: Stylus.

Birnbaum, R. (1989). The latent organizational functions of the academic senate: Why senates do not work but will not go away. *Journal of Higher Education, 60*(4), 423–443.

Bornheimer, D. G., Burns, G. P., & Dumke, G. S. (1973). *The faculty in higher education.* Danville, IL: The Interstate Printers and Publishers.

Bright, D. F., & Richards, M. P. (2001). *The academic deanship: Individual careers and institutional roles.* San Francisco, CA: Jossey-Bass.

Brubacher, J. S., & Rudy, W. (1976). *Higher education in transition: A history of American colleges and universities, 1636–1976.* New York: Harper & Row.

Buller, J. L. (2006). *The essential department chair: A practical guide to college administration.* Bolton, MA: Anker Publishers.

Burgan, M. (2009). Faculty governance and special-interest centers. *Academe, 95*(6), 15–19.

Collins, A. B. (2006). Adding a course to the curriculum? Dilemmas and problems. *Journal of Travel and Tourism, 6*(4), 51–71.

Dooris, M. J., Kelley, J. M., & Trainer, J. F. (2004). Strategic planning in higher education. *New Directions for Higher Education, 2004*(123), 5–11.

Fink, I. (2004). Research space: Who needs it, who gets it, who pays for it? *Planning for Higher Education, 33*(1), 5–17.

Gayle, D. J., Tewarie, B., & White, Q. (2003). *Governance in the twenty-first century university: Approaches to effective leadership and strategic management* (ASHE-ERIC Higher Education Report *30*(1)). San Francisco: Jossey-Bass.

Gose, B. (2006). At a growing number of community colleges, fund raising is no longer optional. *Chronicle of Higher Education.* Retrieved from http://chronicle.com/article/At-a-Growing-Number-of/26509/

Guckert, D. J., & King, J. R. (2003–2004). The high cost of building a better university. *Planning for Higher Education, 32*(3), 24–29.

Helms, R. M. (2005). Who needs a faculty senate? *Academe, 91*(6), 34–36.

Holcombe, R. (2011, January 29). WCU chancellor to host campus-wide budget forum Monday. *Tuckasegree Reader.* Retrieved from http://www.tuckreader.com/wcu-chancellor-to-host-campus-wide-budget-forum-monday/

Kelderman, E. (2011). State spending on higher education edges down, as deficits loom. *Chronicle of Higher Education.* Retrieved from http://chronicle.com/article/State-Spending-on-Colleges/126020/

Kezar, A., & Eckel, P. (2004). Meeting today's governance challenges: A synthesis of the literature and examination of a future research agenda for scholarship. *Journal of Higher Education, 75*(4), 371–399.

Knight Commission on Intercollegiate Athletics. (2010). *Restoring the balance: Dollars, value, and the future of college sports.* Retrieved from http://www.knightcommission.org/images/restoringbalance/KCIA_Report_F.pdf

Lee, B. A. (1979). Governance at unionized four-year colleges: Effect on decision-making structures. *Journal of Higher Education, 50*(5), 565–585.

Lidsky, A. J. (2002). A perspective on campus planning. *New Directions for Higher Education, 119,* 69–76.

Lizzio, A., & Wilson, K. (2009). Student participation in university governance: The role conceptions and sense of efficacy of student representatives on departmental committees. *Studies in Higher Education, 34*(1), 69–84.

Miller, M. T. (2003). The status of faculty senates in community colleges. *Community College Journal of Research and Practice, 27,* 419–428. doi:10.1080/10668920390129022

Miller, M. T., & Miles, J. M. (2008). Internal governance in the community college: Models and quilts. *New Directions for Community Colleges, 41,* 35–44. doi:10.1002/cc313

Miller, M. T., & Pope, M. L. (2003). Faculty senate leadership as a presidential pathway: Clear passage or caught in a maze? *Community College Journal of Research and Practice, 27,* 119–129. doi:10.1080/10668920390128762

Minor, J. T. (2004a). Four challenges facing faculty senates. *Thought and Action: The NEA Higher Education Journal, 19,* 125–140.

Minor, J. T. (2004b). Understanding faculty senates: Moving from mystery to models. *The Review of Higher Education, 27*(3), 343–363. doi:10.1353/rhe.2004.0004

Mississippi Legislature, Joint Legislative Committee on Performance Evaluation and Expenditure. (2007). *An analysis of the legal status of university foundations, their oversight, and the authority of the PEER committee to review university foundations.* Retrieved from http://www.peer.state.ms.us/reports/rpt500.pdf

Muffo, J. A. (2001). Involving the faculty in assessing the core curriculum. *Assessment Update, 13*(2), 4–5.

National Collegiate Athletic Association. (2010). 2004–2009 NCAA Division I Intercollegiate Athletics Programs Report. Retrieved from http://www.ncaapublications.com/productdownloads/REV_EXP_2010.pdf

Olson, G. A. (2011). When to dissolve a faculty senate. *Chronicle of Higher Education.* Retrieved from http://www.chronicle.com/article/When-to-Dissolve-a-Faculty/126827/

Pope, M. L., & Miller, M. T. (2005). Leading from the inside out: Learned respect for academic culture through shared governance. *Community College Journal of Research and Practice, 29,* 745–757. doi:10.1080/10668920591006610

Rickes, P. C. (2009). Make way for the Millennials! How today's students are shaping higher education space. *Planning for Higher Education, 37*(2), 7–17.

Romano, C. R., & Hanish, J. (2003). Balancing multiple needs through innovative facility design. *New Directions for Student Services, 101,* 3–15.

Rudolph, F. (1977). *Curriculum: A history of the American undergraduate course of study since 1636.* San Francisco: Jossey-Bass.

Sacramento State University. (2011). *Space planning guidelines and criteria for the assignment of university space.* Retrieved from http://www.csus.edu/umanual/Campus.Space.Planning.htm

Salter, B., & Tapper, T. (2002). The external pressures on the internal governance of universities. *Higher Education Quarterly, 56*(3), 245–256.

Sander, L. (2007). Report: Faculty feel "disconnected" from college sports, think some coaches' salaries are excessive. *Chronicle of Higher Education*. Retrieved from http://chronicle.com/article/Faculty-Feel-Disconnected-From/68/

Sufka, K. J. (2009). How to make faculty senates more effective. *Academe, 95*(6), 20–21.

University of California. (2005). *UCOP space management principles*. Retrieved from http://www.ucop.edu/ucophome/coordrev/oppolicies/SpaceManagementPrinciples.pdf

University of Dayton. (2008). *Space management guidelines*. Retrieved from http://campus.udayton.edu/~UDCampusPlanning/index.htm

University of Iowa Foundation. (n.d.). *Frequently asked questions*. Retrieved March 30, 2011, from http://www.uifoundation.org/about/faq/

Venable, A. (2010). Smoking ban: Public forum tonight. *The University Star*. Retrieved from http://star.txstate.edu/node/2087

Wheeler, D. W., Seagren, A. T., Becker, L. W., Kinley, E. R., Mlinek, D. D., & Robson, K. J. (2008). *The academic chair's handbook* (2nd ed.). San Francisco: Jossey-Bass.

4

STUDENT GOVERNANCE AND INVOLVEMENT IN INSTITUTIONAL LEADERSHIP

Shouping Hu, Carrie E. Henderson, and Jennifer Iacino

INTRODUCTION

The year 2011 ushered in some very different yet somewhat familiar scenes to the world of higher education in the United States. After the "Occupy Wall Street" movement, there came the "Occupy Colleges" movement. A heightened, broad-based activism swept college campuses across the country, with students voicing their concerns about the stark inequality in American society as well as about issues directly related to their own lives, such as student indebtedness. Student activism of such breadth and intensity hasn't been seen since the 1960s and 1970s. Given what has been happening in colleges and universities, some questions may arise in the minds of those on the outside: Are there any governance structures on campus that represent students? If so, what role do they play in institutional leadership and in the policy-making process so that students' concerns can be heard?

This chapter briefly documents the historical evolution of student governance in U.S. higher education, discusses the various functions of student governance in institutional leadership, describes the diverse venues in which students can play a role in institutional leadership and related issues, and finally presents examples of notable practices in higher education.

American higher education has undergone drastic transformations since the establishment of Harvard College in 1636, successfully evolving from an elite to a mass system, and then to universal access. Student populations have also changed drastically, from primarily traditional-age college students to a much more diverse enrollment. The attention on students and the expectation of their roles have evolved along with the environments within and beyond higher education.

In the early stage, the "in loco parentis" doctrine permeated American colleges and universities, where students were treated as somewhat passive participants in higher education under the care and supervision of college administrators. As Horowitz (1987) documents in her historical analysis, campus life was defined with battles between the administration and students. Initially, student clubs and organizations were a way for students to enjoy campus life and deal with college administrators when frustrations surfaced. Eventually, college administrators introduced formal student governance structures as a way to work with students and better manage campus life (Laosebikan-Buggs, 2006).

As higher education has transformed, so has the relationship between students and the institutions they attend. In particular, the rising sentiment of consumerism reflects the increasing demand of students to participate in the decision-making process that impacts their education. Nowadays, student governance is a widely implemented customary practice for most institutions of higher education in the United States. It is even governmentally mandated for public colleges and universities in many states, including Wisconsin, Florida, and California.

Jones (1974) acknowledges that "governance" is a nebulous term that requires further explanation. The definition of student governance varies by scholar. Schenkel (1971) says governance is the process of direct control by different individuals within an institution. Love and Miller (2003) describe how student governance has evolved to mean student involvement in traditional areas of academic oversight, such as student activities and student organization funding. Miller and Nadler (2006) describe student governance as the involvement of students in institutional management, either through formal or informal organizations. Friedson and Shuchman (1955) characterize student governance through student governments: "By student government we mean a type of organization which by virtue of its composition and constitution is entitled to represent the student community as a whole" (p. 6). Finally, May (2009) links student governance to American democratic ideals:

> Student self-governance is emblematic of the democratic ideals of this country. The earliest student bodies desired to establish representative governments mirroring those of the emerging young nation. The evolution of student self-governance continues its healthy course on today's colleges and universities campuses, and it is truly a mark of this nation's democratic principles and standards. As higher education in the United States has matured and expanded, so has student self-governance, sustaining the argument that student governance is a key component to this growth. Student self-governance will continue to evolve and expand, particularly as a means to reach students where administration and faculty cannot—by engaging students in the campus community and by giving students a voice.
>
> (p. 486)

Birnbaum (1988) notes that there is no one common definition of campus governance; "a governance system is an institution's answer—at least temporarily—to the enduring question that became a plaintive cry during the campus crisis of the late 1960s and early 1970s: 'Who's in charge here?'" (p. 4). Accordingly, institutions often have wide discretionary range to shape and cultivate student governance opportunities in terms of scope, level of involvement, and impact. Institutional leaders must weigh pressures from students and other constituents for greater student involvement against personal leadership styles and institutional values to create student governance opportunities that have significance and meaning, opportunities for growth for both the student and the institution. Under such circumstances, student involvement will enhance the overall decision-making process of the institution.

IMPORTANCE OF STUDENT GOVERNANCE
AND ENGAGEMENT

The importance of student governance and involvement in institutional leadership lies in their unique ability to meet two major institutional purposes simultaneously: the development of students and the improvement of institutional effectiveness. Student learning and personal development are among the most important goals of higher education institutions. The higher education literature has unequivocally confirmed that the more students are engaged in college activities, the more they will gain and learn from their college experience (Astin, 1993b; Hu & Kuh, 2003; National Survey of Student Engagement, 2004, 2005; Pascarella & Terenzin, 1991, 2005). Research specifically on student governance experiences also shows their desirable effects on student development (Komivies, Wagner, & Associates, 2009; Kuh & Lund, 1994), especially in the areas of leadership development. The development of college student leadership has particular relevance to today's society. As American society is undergoing dramatic demographic changes and social transformation, many pressing issues such as inequality in educational and economic attainment for citizens of diverse backgrounds present challenges to the society as a whole (Smith, Altbach, & Lomotey, 2002; St. John, 2003). When reflecting on these challenges, Astin and Astin (2000) comment that "the problems that plague American society are, in many respects, problems of leadership" (p. 2), and they argue that American colleges and university have a responsibility to develop college students to become effective future leaders to make social changes. Encouraging student participation in governance and institutional leadership can be an effective means of fulfilling that responsibility.

Meanwhile, higher education institutions have been constantly criticized for not meeting the needs of students and the broader society. The general public perceives colleges and universities as organizations lacking in effectiveness and efficiency. With large sums of public funds being invested in higher education, the discontent about student learning outcomes has never been higher (Arum & Roksa, 2011; National Commission on the Future of Higher Education, 2006). Colleges and universities not only have some explaining to do but also need to find ways to improve the quality of undergraduate education.

Within the higher education community, student dissatisfaction is high as well, particularly in today's job market, where a college degree does not necessarily lead to advanced employment after graduation. As students and their families are footing the bills for college education, they are demanding a greater voice in institutional decision-making that could influence their education and future.

Student involvement in institutional leadership has the potential to improve the quality of institutional decisions and enhance student satisfaction on campus. The multiple potential benefits to the institution include improved implementation of decisions, evaluation of curricula and teaching practices, and the promotion of an atmosphere of openness, community, solidarity, and trust (Menon, 2003). While some scholars argue that students have relatively little impact on campus policy, the involvement of students has been shown to be an important aspect of campus decision-making (Jones, 1974; Miller & Nadler, 2006). Such participation varies by institution, but often is reflected in student government associations. Student governance can placate the need to speak out, it can improve the level of acceptance of a decision on campus, and it can allow students the opportunity to openly challenge administrators and faculty. In a broad sense, student involvement in institutional governance provides a system of checks and balances with administrators and faculty.

(Love & Miller, 2003, p. 522)

STRUCTURE AND PROCESS OF STUDENT GOVERNANCE

Institutional culture and organization play an important role in the structure and process of student governance opportunities. Kuh and Whitt (1988) define culture as

> persistent patterns of norms, values, practices, beliefs, and assumptions that share the behavior of individuals and groups in a college or university and provide a frame of reference within which to interpret the meaning of events and actions on and off campus.

(p. iv)

Cultural norms for individual campuses work to invisibly establish boundaries for student governance that fit the overall customs of the institution; these boundaries are not fixed, but instead are malleable and stretch or contract as specific players transition into and out of the institution.

Within formal structures, an officially chartered student government association, student senate, or student assembly is a common means of student governance, though the purpose of these bodies can vary widely. Students are often elected by their peers, have the authority to represent wider groups of students on the campus (by academic year or program of study, for example), and may cast official votes in the governance process. Laosebikan-Buggs (2006) describes the primary functions of formal student government associations:

- serves as the official voice of students to the administration (representation);
- allows students to participate in the decision-making processes of university governance (voice);
- ethical and responsible collection and dissemination of student fees; and
- recognition of student organizations as well as the coordination of the activities clubs and organizations on campus (advocacy) (p. 3).

This description is clearly reflected in the constitution of Florida State University's student body, which states that

> the mission of the Student Government Association (SGA), is to provide FSU students with representation, services and advocacy within the university structure. The Student Government Association provides quality leadership for, and accountability to its constituency by recognizing that strength arises from diversity, engagement, and dialogue.

(2009)

This statement not only highlights the role of student governance in "representation," "services, and "advocacy" for students in the university community, but also indicates that it provides opportunity for and accountability to its constituents.

Students are also often included in more informal processes of governance through invitation by faculty and administrators to join various committees and special project work groups. Students are typically a small minority on these committees but frequently have a powerful voice in the discussion; faculty and staff have varying and possibly somewhat limited exposure to student opinions on governance topics, and often are quite interested to know students' perspectives on critical issues. Informal opportunities rarely afford voting rights, but students gain power through access to institutional leaders and the forum to voice student opinions. At institutions that do not have formal student government associations, students may be invited to participate in some of the functions described above in a more informal, decentralized manner.

ROLES AND FUNCTION OF STUDENT GOVERNANCE

Significant differences exist by institution with regards to the role and function of student governance. For example, what issues are available or "on the table" for students to address through formal and informal governance structures? Some institutions, both public and private, may have a relatively consistent history of meaningful student participation in institutional governance, including a vibrant elected SGA and student involvement in fee allocation processes and a wide variety of campus committees and judicial boards. Others may have periods marked by student activism for greater levels of involvement, such as meetings with the university president on controversial issues or even a student vote on the institution's board of trustees. Still others (typically young and/or private institutions) may have limited experience with student governance and may be hesitant to open decision-making processes to include students. Community colleges and regional commuter campuses may provide student governance opportunities, such as student programming councils responsible for planning campus events, but face apathy and limited engagement from the student body. Braskamp, Trautvetter, and Ward (2006) discuss the centrality of shared governance on collaborative campuses, based on their study of 10 faith-based liberal arts colleges:

> Creating community—a community where faculty involvement in student development is supported—calls for collective responsibility. Faculty and staff mentioned that being part of a community means stepping outside oneself. As we have already suggested, faculty play a key role in this. We also learned that students play central roles in maintaining the campus community. Students are empowered and often provide input on the direction of the campus. This merits comment on two fronts: The students interviewed were highly involved in the campus community, and this involvement connects them with faculty. Faculty, students, and administrators work side by side as part of shared governance.

(p. 164)

Institutional leaders have the opportunity to involve students at many governance levels and in a wide variety of issues. Search committees often offer an opportunity for students to have a say in selecting new administrators or faculty, or even in selecting large campus vendors through a competitive bid process (such as the food service contract, which has a major impact on the quality of student experiences). For example, two students were among the search committee for the president at Florida State University in 2009, and they are also among the leadership team of the SGA. Funding committees can be a significant and highly valued responsibility assigned to student leaders; public institutions often collect "activity" fees through tuition payments, and SGAs or other committees may have discretion to allocate those funds within established parameters and guidelines (the senior student affairs officer typically has veto power over these student decisions). This is very important, as institutions are facing budgeting challenges as well as mounting criticism for increasing tuition.

Student participation in strategic planning and accreditation committees is less common, but can be a meaningful way to enrich student engagement experiences and also to provide decision-makers with critical feedback about student perspectives (participation on these types of committees might be seen at institutions with a long-standing tradition of high student integration at all levels of governance). Additionally, institutional administration and special topic committees such as the homecoming week planning committee or program review for the history department are often open to student participation. In these committees, decisions are often made by the chair or deferred to the consensus of the group, and it can be valuable to have the enthusiasm and creativity of students to energize what may be routine tasks.

Table 4.1 provides further information about these broad categories of student involvement in institutional leadership processes, including some desirable characteristics of students serving these groups, expectations for participation, and special challenges to consider. Each institution should expand these categories in consideration of its unique circumstances, purpose, values, and culture.

Many institutions have both undergraduate and graduate enrollment, so there is a need to consider the most suitable structure for involving different student populations in institutional leadership. Love and Miller (2003) find that the needs of undergraduates involved in student government differ from those of graduate students.

> It is increasingly important that similarities and differences between undergraduates and graduate students be identified and clarified in an effort to build a more cohesive and potentially powerful force that advocates for students on campus, particularly in light of the encroaching corporate model of institutional management.
>
> (Love & Miller, 2003, p. 534)

Although most institutions still combine graduate student representation into broader student government, some research universities have graduate student government associations that better serve the graduate student population.

Graduate students employed by the university have also sought representation through collective bargaining agreements and unions. For public institutions, collective bargaining

Table 4.1 Examples of Student Governance and Involvement in Institutional Leadership

Categories of Student Governance	Common Examples	Student Characteristics to Serve	Participation Expectations	Special Challenges
Search Committees	Food service vendor; dean of students; university president	Process-oriented; typically represent particular campus constituencies	Gather information and communicate to other students; provide critical feedback to those responsible for selection	Creating "meaningful" experiences for students when the ultimate decision does not rest with the committee
Funding Committees	SGA activity fees; building projects; student scholarships	Fiscally oriented; often engaged in campus politics or formal governance structures; often appointed or elected to committee	Follow established policies; make critical decisions; exercise responsible discretion	Holding students accountable to established policies and guidelines without overturning funding decisions
Strategic Planning and Accreditation Committees	Mission revision; Quality Enhancement Plans; re-branding initiatives	Values-oriented; interested in aligning policy and practice; interested in setting high standards	Focus on broad issues; bring student voice to the discussion	Communicating broader vision and context to students to allow for their meaningful participation in the discussion
Institutional Administration and Special Topic Committees	Academic program review; honor code/civility board; homecoming week	Task-oriented; able to take on projects as part of the group; able to communicate ideas and plans to other students	Contribute ideas; volunteer time to advance new initiatives; consistently participate for duration of committee	Setting reasonable limits on student ideas without discouraging creativity or enthusiasm

and unionization falls under state law. Some states encourage collective bargaining, while others restrict it. For private institutions, collective bargaining and unionization fall under federal law, specifically the Taft–Hartley Act. Overall, graduate student employees at public and private institutions have exercised their rights and attempted to influence institutional governance through unions (Berquist & Pawlak, 2007).

FACILITATING STUDENT GOVERNANCE IN INSTITUTIONAL LEADERSHIP

Even though student governance emphasizes the role and voice of students, campus administrators can effectively facilitate student governance in institutional leadership by following the steps described below.

Orienting Student Leaders to Governance Processes

Communicating expectations to students and orienting them to specific roles and customs are vitally important to their successful engagement in meaningful governance opportunities. Students should be guided to develop the knowledge and skills that will allow their participation to be useful to and well received by administrators, faculty, and other constituents. Students often perceive participation on governance committees to be a privilege and seek to exercise professionalism. Their mentors and advisors have a valuable opportunity to help them gain further appreciation for the importance of professional conduct and customs. Additionally, it is important that students understand the charge of the committee, as well as any relevant history of related work or the background of individuals on the committee or related to the project. Taking extra time to properly orient students to the governance process and cultivate their ability to positively contribute can ensure that both the students and the committee benefit from their participation in institutional governance processes.

Responding to Students

Where there are no state mandates for student governance, institutional leaders often have the authority to facilitate and authorize student participation in governance processes. What happens when students request (or demand) more responsibility than leaders want to allow? For example, students may become dissatisfied with a particular employee working in an area funded by student fees and demand authority to terminate his or her employment; should students be permitted to hire and fire employees? Another common example may be found in sponsorship agreements; if students become opposed to a particular corporate sponsor of university athletics or other prominent program, should they have the discretion to terminate a partnership that is lucrative for the institution? There are no "one size fits all" solutions to these complex and tumultuous situations, but there are some important considerations for institutional leaders to weigh:

- Am I facilitating adequate opportunities for student voices to be heard, recognized, and considered around this issue?
- Are we challenging students to engage in the deeper issues and to help generate solutions and/or options to consider?
- Are there important legal limitations or other legitimate reasons students should not be included in the decision-making process on this issue, and are these being communicated effectively and clearly?
- What precedents are being established by inclusion or exclusion of student voices on this issue?
- Am I truly open to hear the concerns students have on this issue?

Birnbuam (1988) notes that the culture of an institution may place high value on symbolic action, that is, the appearance of meaningful response to student concerns without the intention or desire for true interaction and inclusion. Institutional leaders must ensure that efforts to include students in important decisions or to respond to their concerns are not shallow symbolic gestures but, to the extent practical, meaningful opportunities for mutual learning and building community.

INSTITUTIONAL DIFFERENCES REGARDING STUDENT GOVERNANCE IN INSTITUTIONAL LEADERSHIP

The enterprise of higher education in the United States is diverse and complex, with more than 4,000 institutions nationwide. Different types of colleges and universities have different missions, student populations, campus cultures, and institutional contexts. There is no "one size fits all" for how to engage student governance in institutional leadership.

Even though over half of current college students attend community colleges, involving student governance in institutional leadership in those colleges can be a challenging task because their enrollment consists of non-traditional, part-time commuter students. Additionally, many students work full-time and support families. It is not surprising that community college student governments are "up and down" in their level of effectiveness. They might have a few strong leaders for a while, but then slip badly after those officers graduate. Many of these bodies have to start over from scratch just about every year (ASGA, 2011).

Despite the challenges, some community colleges manage to have student governance in institutional leadership. Grand Rapids Community College, located in the state of Michigan, has a student congress whose purpose

> shall be to represent the students at Grand Rapids Community College and promote their interests and welfare in the college decision-making process. The Student Congress is thereby the voice of the Student Body. The Student Congress will also be responsible for the allocation of funds for recognized student organizations and campus life.
>
> (GRCC Student Congress Constitution, 2011)

One specific way Grand Rapids students are involved in institutional governance is through Student Congress, the body that governs and manages campus activities fees. Additionally, members serve alongside college officials on the budget, campus elections, communication and technology, recognition and involvement, and rules committees.

Private institutions can also face challenges in engaging student governance in institutional leadership, mainly because of how they are funded, run, and structured. First, private schools are not required to provide public records. Second, their governing boards are appointed by the schools themselves, and not by the state or governor. Finally, private institutions have other challenges that are worthy of discussion.

Despite these challenges, a number of private institutions have sought to include students in their decision-making processes. Columbia College Chicago (CCC) is a private liberal arts college located in Chicago, Illinois. The American Student Government Association recognized CCC for making great strides in student governance:

> SGA now sits on several campus-wide committees that had been closed to students in the past. It has a representative on CCC's board of trustees—a position that even many long-established SGs do not possess. Members work together with administrators on issues facing students, such as coming up with alternatives to expensive textbooks.
>
> (Campitelli, 2007)

A number of activities demonstrate how students at CCC are engaged in institutional leadership. The SGA at CCC holds student forums, puts out a student-driven agenda, conducts student polls, reaches out to involved students, sends representatives to every college-wide event, finds common ground between faculty and administrators, provides tangible benefits to students, and takes on long-term projects.

Middlebury College is a private liberal arts college in Vermont. The Student Government Association provides the main vehicle for student involvement in institutional governance (Middlebury Student Government Association, 2012):

> The Student Government Association is the vehicle through which students can participate in the formulation of institutional policy affecting academic and student affairs and collectively express their views on matters of general interest to the student body. The SGA makes student appointments to student, joint student/faculty, and trustee councils and committees. The SGA also allocates student activities fees and authorizes student activities for their eligibility to receive funds. The SGA provides services to the student body as deemed necessary.

Public universities, particularly big research universities, have actively engaged student governance in institutional leadership. The University of California, San Diego, which has very high research activity, has a policy for student participation in institutional governance in its student conduct regulations. Purdue University, which also has very high research activity, boasts a graduate student government that operates separately from the undergraduate student government. Purdue Graduate Student Government has worked on a number of university governance initiatives, including smoking ban policy, travel grants, and negotiated health care costs. Additionally, Florida State University, a research university known as the "Berkeley of the South," has a long tradition of involving students in many avenues of student governance and institutional leadership (Marshall, 2006); most notably, the president of the Student Government Association is a voting member of the Board of Trustees.

Private research universities can also successfully engage student governance in institutional leadership. Students at Duke University in Durham, North Carolina, developed a general statement of rights and freedoms (Duke Student Government, 2011). This statement caused change in the Duke community as it was designed to guide future university actions to ensure that students were not only represented, but also had a voice in the decision-making process.

ENABLING FACTORS AND BARRIERS FOR STUDENT GOVERNANCE IN INSTITUTIONAL LEADERSHIP

A number of factors determine the extent to which students participate in institutional governance, specifically student government. However, there are ways in which institutions can encourage fruitful student participation in institutional leadership and decision-making. First, statutory requirements, when available, seem to promote the practice of including college and university students in institutional decision-making. These requirements do not exist in every state, but formal policies can serve the same purpose. Student congress, student government associations, and student conduct policies all describe good practices of shared governance among students and across a variety of institutions. The primary means for student involvement, however, appears to be student government associations, which vary in research universities based on undergraduate and graduate student participation. Additionally, graduate students employed by public and private institutions can seek representation through collective bargaining and unionization, when legal.

The literature highlights a number of factors that are conducive to effective student involvement in institutional governance. Campuses where involvement in student government is effective generally share many of the following characteristics: (1) Institutional culture that supports collaboration; (2) student-focused mission; (3) clear definitions of the rights of student government; (4) active advising; and (5) involvement from senior administrators. Love and Miller (2003) and Laosebikan-Buggs (2006) describe the importance of a campus culture that supports collaboration among students, faculty, staff, and administrators. In order for student involvement in governance to work, the campus must inherently support the students. Miller and Nadler (2006) suggest that a student-focused mission is paramount to effective student governance. A student-focused mission means that the institutions is dedicated to the students and will be more receptive to student involvement. Brunfield (2006) argues that campuses should clearly define students' role in campus governance. Finally, Miller and Nadler (2006) argue that active campus advising and involvement from senior administrators will support student involvement in institutional governance.

Student governance in institutional leadership can be very effective when supported by college or university that values the student government and student input. Many institutions that focus on students in their mission tend to support student governance. Additionally, institutions should have clearly defined goals and expectations for student governance to work appropriately. Active advising and involvement from senior-level administrators reflects on the institutional culture and values. Any and all of these characteristics could help foster effective student involvement. A good example is Florida State University. The university administration also intentionally stimulates student leadership interests and cultivates student leadership skills by emphasizing leadership education in undergraduate curriculum. In addition, the university administration and Student Government Association worked together to create a freshman leadership council and freshman leadership institute, along with the well-established Center for Leadership and Civic Engagement.

In addition to highlighting conditions conducive to student involvement in institutional governance, the literature indicates various barriers to such participation: (1) Lack of trust between students, faculty, and administrators; (2) internal and political strife among student body organization; (3) student leaders' beliefs that student government power is limited, which translates to apathy; and 4) student government that is not representative of the campus population.

Miller and Nadler (2006) explain that if students, faculty, and administrators do not trust each other, then creating a working relationship becomes difficult. Both Miller and Nadler (2006) and Laosebikan-Buggs (2006) see dangers in internal strife among student government associations or similar bodies. If these organizations do not function internally, then working collectively to advance the university is nearly impossible.

Miller and Nadler (2006) also describe how the mentality of students must be positive in order to impact institutional policies. Specifically, students must believe they can influence campus governance in order to do so. Finally, Miller and Nadler (2006) and Laosebikan-Buggs (2006) argue that student government associations, or any student body, must be representative of the general student body in terms of demographics and opinions of campus policy. If the representative body is not actually representative, then effective student governance may be threatened.

CONCLUSION

Student governance is a very important feature of American higher education. With skyrocketing college tuition and public discontent with the quality of undergraduate education, the pressure is on institutional administrations to hear students' voices and attend to their concerns. The "Occupy Colleges" movement should serve as a reminder of this urgent need to university administrations across the country. Administrators can effectively utilize student governance structures, formally or informally, to actively engage students in institutional leadership and other decision-making processes so that student voices can be heard and student needs can be met. In addition, administrators should realize that student participation in governance can have strong impacts on student learning and personal development, as well as lasting effects on individual students, the institution, and the society as a whole.

Even though there are big differences in institutional types and contexts, student governance can be a valuable channel for communication and dialogue, and a venue for effective partnership between institutional administrators and students to explore, design, adopt, and evaluate campus policies, programs, and practices. The opportunities for student governance to be a part of institutional leadership are abundant, as described in this chapter. All those who are concerned about student outcomes from college and institutional effectiveness can help eliminate the barriers and create favorable environments to facilitate and engage student governance in institutional leadership and decision-making processes. In particular, higher education leaders and administrators can intentionally design the structures needed for successful student participation; foster campus cultures that value collaboration between administrators, faculty, and students; and promote student involvement in institutional leadership. Ultimately, both the students and the institutions can benefit a great deal from effective and successful student governance in institutional leadership.

REFERENCES

American Student Government Association. (2011). *For every college.* Retrieved January 31, 2011 from http://www. asgaonline.com/ME2/Default.asp

Arum, R., & Roksa, J. (2011). *Academically adrift: Limited learning on college campuses.* Chicago, IL: University of Chicago Press.

Astin, A. W. (1993a). *Assessment for excellence: The philosophy and practice of assessment and evaluation in higher education.* Phoenix, AZ: American Council for Education and Oryx Press.

Astin, A. W. (1993b). *What matters in college: Four critical years revisited.* San Francisco: Jossey-Bass.

Astin, A. W., & Astin, H. S. (Eds.). (2000). *Leadership reconsidered: Engaging higher education in social change*. Battle Creek, MI: W. K. Kellogg Foundation.

Berquist, W. H., & P. K. (2007). *Engaging the six cultures of the academy*. San Francisco: Jossey-Bass.

Birnbaum, R. (1988). *How colleges work: The cybernetics of academic organization and leadership*. San Francisco: Jossey-Bass.

Braskamp, L. A.; Trautvetter, L. C. & Ward, K. (2006). *Putting students first: How colleges develop students purposefully*. San Francisco: Jossey-Bass.

Brunfield, R. (2006). A case of student governance. In M. Miller, & D. Nadler (Eds.), *Student governance and institutional policy: Formation and implementation* (pp. 43–59). Charlotte, NC: Information Age Publishing.

Campitelli, A. (2007). A solid foundation: Building blocks for SGA growth. Retrieved on July 2, 2012 from http://www.asgaonline.com/Media/PublicationsArticle/SLSpring2007_A-Solid-Foundation.pdf

Duke Student Government. (2011). Your rights. Retrieved March 25, 2011 from http://dsg.dukegroups.duke.edu/your-rights/

Florida State University Student Body (2009). Constitution of the Student Body. Retrieved on December 12, 2011 from http://sga.fsu.edu/PDF/CONSTITUTION_OF_THE_STUDENT_BODY.pdf

Freidson, E., & Shuchman, H. L. (1955). Student government in American Colleges. In E. Freidson (Ed.), *Student government, student leaders, and the American college* (pp. 3–28). Philadelphia: United States National Student Association.

GRCC Student Congress Constitution (2011). Retrieved on July 2, 2012 from http://web.grcc.edu/Pr/studentlife/2007/sc_constitution_1.22.07.pdf

Horowitz, H. L. (1987). *Campus life: Undergraduate cultures from the end of the eighteenth century to the present*. New York: Knopf.

Hu, S., & Kuh, G. D. (2003). Maximizing what students get out of college: Testing a learning productivity model. *Journal of College Student Development, 44*, 185–203.

Jones, D. H. (1974). *An analysis of students' perception of their role in governance at Gaston College*. Fort Lauderdale, FL: Nova University.

Komives, S. R., Wagner, W., & Associates. (2009). *Leadership for a better world: Understanding the social change model of leadership development*. San Francisco: Jossey-Bass.

Kuh, G. D., & Lund, J. P. (1994). What students gain from participating in student government? In M. C. Terell, & M. J. Cuyjet (Eds.), *New directions for student services: Developing student government leadership* (pp. 5–17). San Francisco: Jossey-Bass.

Kuh, G. D., & Whitt, E. J. (1988). *The invisible tapestry: Culture in American colleges and universities*. ASHE-ERIC Higher Education Report No. 1. Washington, DC: Association for the Study of Higher Education.

Laosebikan-Buggs, M. O. (2006). The role of student government. In M. Miller, & D. Nadler (Eds.), *Student governance and institutional policy: Formation and implementation* (pp. 1–8). Charlotte, NC: Information Age Publishing.

Love, R., & Miller, M. (2003). Increasing student participation in self governance: A comparison of graduate and undergraduate student perceptions. *College Student Journal, 37*, 533.

Marshall, S. J. (2006). *The tumultuous sixties: Campus unrest and student life at a southern university*. Tallahassee, FL: Sentry Press.

May, W. P. (2009). Student governance: A qualitative study of leadership in student government association. Educational Policy Studies Dissertation. http://digitalarchive.gsu.edu/eps_diss/36

Menon, M. E. (2003). Student involvement in university governance: A need for negotiated education aims? *Tertiary Education and Management, 9*, 233–246.

Middlebury Student Government Association. (2012). College governance. Retrieved on July 2, 2012 from http://www.middlebury.edu/about/handbook/governance/SGA

Miller, M. T., & Nadler, D. P. (2006). Student involvement in governance: Rationale, problems, and opportunities. In M. Miller, & D. Nadler (Eds.), *Student governance and institutional policy: Formation and implementation* (pp. 9–18). Charlotte, NC: Information Age Publishing.

National Commission on the Future of Higher Education (2006). *A test of leadership: Charting the future of U.S. higher education*. Washington, DC: U.S. Department of Education.

National Survey of Student Engagement (2004). *Student engagement: Pathways to collegiate success*. Bloomington: Indiana University Center for Postsecondary Research.

National Survey of Student Engagement (2005). *Student engagement: Exploring different dimensions of student engagement*. Bloomington: Indiana University Center for Postsecondary Research.

Pascarella, E. T., & Terenzini, P. T. (1991). *How college affects students: Findings and insights from twenty years of research.* San Francisco: Jossey-Bass.

Pascarella, E. T., & Terenzini, P. T. (2005). *How college affects students: A third decade of research.* San Francisco: Jossey-Bass.

Schenkel, W. (1971). Who has been in power? In Hodgkinson, H. L., & Meeth, L. R. (Eds.), *Power and Authority.* San Francisco: Jossey-Bass.

Smith, W. A. , Altbach, P. G., & Lomotey, K. (eds.) (2002). *The racial crisis in American higher education: Continuing challenges for the twenty-first century.* Albany, NY: State University of New York Press.

St. John, E. P. (2003). *Refinancing the college dream: Access, equal opportunity, and justice for taxpayers.* Baltimore, MD: Johns Hopkins University Press.

5

ADMINISTRATIVE ASPECTS OF ACCREDITATION AND ASSESSMENT

Kristina M. Cragg, Angela E. Henderson,
Barrie D. Fitzgerald, and Ross A. Griffith

INTRODUCTION

Moving is both exciting and stressful. A simple move in the same town and a cross-country relocation alike require a well-organized and clearly defined plan with specific deadlines for a successful outcome. When one's personal items finally arrive (hopefully all in one piece) at one's new home, the daunting task of opening boxes, unpacking, and getting organized in an unfamiliar space can feel like it will never end. Finally, after hours of work, those items begin to fit into place and context within the new location.

Accreditation is much like the process of moving, requiring a highly organized effort and a review of all items in house. The assessment process resembles unpacking in that one needs to review existing information in the context of a changed environment to determine not only how items at hand fit into the new place but also what new items are needed to create the best conditions possible given the available means.

This chapter focuses on accreditation and its integral connection to assessment. It begins with a general overview of accreditation and quality and moves on to a comparison of the regional institutional accrediting bodies. Institutional effectiveness, as it pertains to regional accreditation, is described, and a model assessment process is presented, complete with examples.

ACCREDITATION AND QUALITY

Accrediting agencies have ensured the quality of higher education institutions and programs for more than 100 years (Eaton, 2011). While the benefits of regional accreditation have a significant financial impact on institutional budgets, "receiving accreditation does not send a strong signal of high quality so much as the lack of accreditation by a well-known accreditor sends a signal of poor quality" (Weisbrod, Ballou, & Asch, 2008, p. 186). Establishing standards of quality have pervaded higher education through all accreditation agencies, of which there are four types:

1. Regional accreditors—accredit public and private, mainly non-profit and degree-granting, two- and four-year institutions.
2. Faith-based accreditors—accredit religiously affiliated and doctrinally based institutions, mainly non-profit and degree-granting.
3. Private career accreditors—accredit for-profit, career-based, single purpose institutions, both degree and non-degree.
4. Programmatic accreditors—accredit specific programs, professions and free-standing schools, e.g., law, medicine, engineering and health professions (Eaton, 2011, p. 2).

This chapter focuses on regional accrediting agencies before discussing assessment from the regional accreditation perspective.

REGIONAL ACCREDITING AGENCIES

Six regional accrediting agencies are recognized. Regional accreditation affords significant benefits to an institution by authenticating quality, providing access to federal and state funds, creating employer confidence, and enabling an easier transfer process for students (Eaton, 2011).

Regional accreditors require higher education institutions to demonstrate accountability and evidence of effectiveness on a regular basis, such as every 5 to 10 years. As demands on colleges and universities intensify from all stakeholders (i.e., federal, state, and local), so too has the emphasis on accreditation and the role of the administrator in ensuring that the institution is reaffirmed (Burke & Associates, 2005; Kramer & Swing, 2010).

Table 5.1 profiles the six regional agencies that accredit institutions throughout the United States. As shown, the North Central Association of Colleges and Schools, Higher Learning Commission (NCA-HLC) accredits more institutions than any other agency, while the Southern Association of Colleges and Schools (SACS) is responsible for the greatest number of students.

OVERVIEW OF THE INSTITUTIONAL ACCREDITATION PROCESS

All six regional accrediting agencies have the same overarching goals and responsibilities for ensuring institutional quality. They also all follow a similar four-step process:

1) Self-study: … a written summary of performance, based on accrediting organizations' standards; 2) Peer review: by faculty and administrative peers in the profession; 3) Site visit: by faculty and administrative peers in the profession; and 4) Judgment by accrediting organizations: commissions decide on accreditation status.

(Eaton, 2011, p. 5)

Table 5.1 Description of the Six Regional Accrediting Organizations

Accrediting Body	Est.	Duration of Accreditation	Number of States/Areas Included	States/Areas Included	Number of Standards	Number of Specific Requirements	Number of Institutions	Number of Students	Web
Middle States Commission on Higher Education (MSCHE)	1919	10 years	8	Delaware, the District of Columbia, Maryland, New Jersey, New York, Pennsylvania, Puerto Rico, and the U.S. Virgin Islands	14	165	483	2,894,963	www.msche.org
New England Association of Schools and Colleges, Commission on Institutions of Higher Education (NEASC-CIHE)	1885	10 years	6	Connecticut, Maine, Massachusetts, New Hampshire, Rhode Island, and Vermont	11	172	243	945,035	http://www.neasc.org/
North Central Association of Colleges and Schools, Higher Learning Commission (NCA-HLC)	1895	10 years	19	Arizona, Arkansas, Colorado, Illinois, Indiana, Iowa, Kansas, Michigan, Minnesota, Missouri, Nebraska, New Mexico, North Dakota, Ohio, Oklahoma, South Dakota, West Virginia, Wisconsin, and Wyoming	5	21	997	5,601,380	www.ncahigher learning commission.org

Organization	Established	Review cycle		Region			Institutions	Enrollment	Website
Northwest Commission on Colleges and Universities (NWCCU)	1917	10 years	7	Alaska, Idaho, Montana, Nevada, Oregon, Utah, and Washington	9	69	154	1,071,176	www.nwccu.org
Southern Association of Colleges and Schools, Commission on Colleges (SACS)	1895	10 years	12	Alabama, Florida, Georgia, Kentucky, Louisiana, Mississippi, North Carolina, South Carolina, Tennessee, Texas, Virginia, and Latin America	4	89	790	5,284,111	www.sacscoc.org
Western Association of Schools and Colleges (WASC)	1962	10 years (Colleges and Universities); 6 years (Community and Junior Colleges)	8	California, Hawaii, the United States territories of Guam and American Samoa, the Republic of Palau, the Federated States of Micronesia, the Commonwealth of the Northern Mariana Islands, and the Republic of the Marshall Islands	4	44 (Colleges and Universities), 118 (Community and Junior Colleges)	163 Colleges and Universities, 142 Community and Junior Colleges	2,662,681	www.wascweb.org

Sources: Regional Accrediting Organization websites, 2011.

Despite these commonalities, specifics of the reaffirmation process vary with each regional accrediting agency. Table 5.2 details the process of each agency.

One of the most obvious differences among the reaffirmation processes of the six regional accrediting agencies is SACS's requirement of a Quality Enhancement Plan (QEP). Required of all institutions seeking reaffirmation since 2004, the QEP is intended to engage the entire campus in continuous improvement that enhances student learning. Whether it is a new plan or an enhancement of an existing plan, the QEP needs to provide: (1) Depth of intended activities demonstrating substantial goals and learning outcomes as a result of the plan; (2) sufficient funding to support the plan; (3) a detailed five-year timeline for accomplishing all facets of the plan; and (4) a thorough assessment and evaluation process to determine if the goals and desired learning outcomes have been accomplished.

Table 5.2 Accrediting Process by Regional Accrediting

Accrediting Body	Evaluation Process
Middle States Commission on Higher Education (MSCHE)	1. Preparation of a Design for Self-Study, that outlines the approach to the self-study and peer review. 2. Completion of self-study process by Steering Committee and dissemination of the report to the Commission. 3. A Commission staff member assigned as liaison to the institution reviews the self-study and conducts a staff visit to the institution. 4. Prior to the full team visit, the Chair of the team makes a preliminary visit to the institution. 5. During the evaluation visit, the team conducts interviews with constituents that may be relevant to the self-study. The team discusses findings and arrives at a consensus. The Chair writes and submits the report to the Commission and institution and presents a brief to the Commission which includes the recommendation for Commission action. 6. The Institution may respond to the team report to clarify any issues of fact in the report. 7. The Commission delegates to the Committee on Evaluation Reports the in-depth discussion of the institution's self-study, the team report, the institution's response to the team report, the Chair's brief, and any comments by staff. The Committee makes a preliminary determination, which the full Commission then considers, approves, amends, or rejects. 8. The institution disseminates the Commission's action, which may include issuing an affirmation of accreditation, a requirement for follow-up activities, an order to show cause why accreditation should not be removed, or the removal of accreditation.
New England Association of Schools and Colleges, Commission on Institutions of Higher Education (NEAS C-CIHE)	NEASC accreditation is structured in a ten-year cycle of: (1) Self-study which engages the entire educational community in structured analysis, self-reflection, and planning in response to the standards. (2) Peer review which brings discipline and perspective to the process through the observations and judgments of a visiting committee of peers from other schools and colleges, informed by the self-study and based on the standards. (3) Follow-up which is monitored by a commission of elected peers and overseen by a professional staff to ensure that planned and prescribed institutional change is accomplished and which provides for intervention, as necessary, to respond to information gathered in regular reports from the institution or through complaints from the public concerning a failure to comply with the standards.
North Central Association of Colleges and	1. The organization engages in a self-study process for approximately two years and prepares a report of its findings in accordance with Commission expectations. 2. The Commission sends an evaluation team of consultant-evaluators to conduct

Table 5.2 (Continued)

Accrediting Body	Evaluation Process
Schools, Higher Learning Commission (NCA-HLC)	a comprehensive visit for continued accreditation and to write a report containing the team's recommendation. 3. The documents relating to the comprehensive visit are reviewed by a Readers Panel or, in some situations, a Review Committee. 4. The IAC takes action on the Readers Panel's recommendation. (If a Review Committee reviewed the visit, the Review Committee takes action.) 5. The Board of Trustees validates the IAC or Review Committee, finalizing the action.
Northwest Commission on Colleges and Universities (NWCCU)	1. Commission representative conducts a preliminary campus visit. 2. The institution analyzes itself through a self-study. 3. Review committee reviews the institutional self-study report, visits the campus, and prepares a "written report of its findings. 4. A draft report of the evaluation committee's findings is sent to the institution's chief executive officer for review of errors of fact. 5. The committee's final report is submitted to the Commission Office. The Commission Office provides the institution's chief executive officer with a copy of the final version of the report. 6. If it so chooses, the institution may provide the Commission with a written response to the evaluation committee report. 7. The Commission reviews all materials, verbal statements of the evaluation committee chair and the institution's chief executive officer, and the committee's accreditation recommendation.
Southern Association of Colleges and Schools, Commission on Colleges (SACS)	As part of the reaffirmation process, the institution will provide two separate documents. 1. Compliance Certification – completed by the institution to demonstrate its judgment of the extent of its compliance with each of the Core Requirements, Comprehensive Standards, and Federal Requirements. 2. Quality Enhancement Plan – The Quality Enhancement Plan (QEP), developed by the institution (1) includes a process identifying key issues emerging from institutional assessment, (2) focuses on learning outcomes and/or the environment supporting student learning and accomplishing the mission of the institution, (3) demonstrates institutional capability for the initiation, implementation, and completion of the QEP, (4) includes broad-based involvement of institutional constituencies in the development and proposed implementation of the QEP, and (5) identifies goals and a plan to assess their achievement. Review by the Commission on Colleges: 1. The Off-Site Review – The Off-Site Reaffirmation Committee, composed of a chair and normally eight to ten evaluators, meets and reviews Compliance Certifications to determine whether an institution is in compliance with all Core Requirements (except Core Requirement 2.12), Comprehensive Standards (except Comprehensive Standard 3.3.2), and Federal Requirements. 2. The On-Site Review – The On-Site Reaffirmation Committee will conduct a focused evaluation at the campus to finalize issues of compliance; provide consultation regarding the QEP; and evaluate the acceptability of the QEP. At the conclusion of its visit, the On-Site Committee will finalize the Reaffirmation Report. The Report of the Reaffirmation Committee, along with the institution's response to areas of non-compliance, will be forwarded to the Commission's Board of Trustees for review and action on reaffirmation. 3. Review by the Commission's Board of Trustees – The Committees on Compliance and Reports (C & R) review reports prepared by evaluation committees and the institutional responses to those reports. The C & R Committee's recommendation regarding reaffirmation is forwarded to the Executive Council for review. The Executive Council recommends action to the full Board of Trustees which makes the final decision on reaffirmation and any monitoring activities that it requires of an institution.

(Continued)

Table 5.2 (Continued)

Accrediting Body	Evaluation Process
Western Association of Schools and Colleges (WASC)	*Senior Colleges and Universities:* 1. The Institutional Proposal is the first stage in the accreditation review cycle and guides the entire accreditation review process. It establishes a framework for connecting each institution's context and priorities with the Standards of Accreditation for the accreditation review. Once accepted, the proposal serves as the primary basis for both institutional self-review and team evaluation, and is given to each evaluation team and the Commission, along with the Accreditation Standards, as the basis upon which the evaluation of the institution should occur. 2. The Capacity and Preparatory Review is designed to enable the Commission to determine whether an institution fulfills the Core Commitment to Institutional Capacity: "The institution functions with clear purposes, high levels of institutional integrity, fiscal stability, and organizational structures and processes to fulfill its purposes." In keeping with the goals of the accreditation process, the Capacity and Preparatory Review is intended to be a focused review which includes a site visit with clearly defined purposes and procedures. 3. The Educational Effectiveness Review is intended to be aligned with the Capacity and Preparatory Review. Its primary purpose is to invite sustained engagement by the institution on the extent to which it fulfills its educational objectives. Through a process of inquiry and engagement, the Educational Effectiveness Review also is designed to enable the Commission to make a judgment about the extent to which the institution fulfills its Core Commitment to Educational Effectiveness. *Community and Junior Colleges:* The full accreditation process has three stages: the self-study, the visit, and the follow-up. A school's philosophy and the WASC criteria serve as the underlying bases for these stages.

Sources: Regional Accrediting Agency websites, 2011.

ADMINISTERING AND FUNDING FOR A SUCCESSFUL REAFFIRMATION

With the limited financial and personnel resources available at many institutions, preparing for accreditation can be a substantial task. As accreditation is a constantly evolving process, many administrators have yet to experience reaffirmation under the most recent principles of their regional accreditor. In addition, many institutions experience significant institutional changes during the 6- to 10-year span between on-site visits, which can contribute to the challenges of a successful reaffirmation.

An analysis of the requirements of the six regional accrediting agencies, particularly those that require substantial attention from administrators in terms of time and careful resource allocation, provides a broader understanding of accreditation across regions. Table 5.3 identifies seven common categories of accreditation standards: administration, financial resources, institutional effectiveness, qualified faculty, planning, institutional conduct, and federal criteria. For each category, accreditation standards are identified by the specific regional accrediting standard number.

This analysis of accreditation standards demonstrates that there is a set of common standards essential to all institutions and administrators. Based on these commonalities, institutions can look to others outside of their regional accrediting agency for strategies.

Table 5.3 Common Topics and Standards by Regional Accrediting Agency

Topic Crosswalk Among Six Regional Accreditors

Category	Accreditation Standards	MSCHE	NEASC-CIHE	NCA-HLC	NWCCU	SACS	WASC[a]
Administration	Administration, Governance, and Leadership	4, 5, 6	3.1–3.12, 11.1	1d, 4a	2.A.1, 6.A.1–4, 6.B.1–9, 6.C.1–9, 6.2, 7.D.1–3, 9.A.4	2.1–3, 2.6, 3.2.1–8, 3.2.10, 3.2.11, 3.2.12, 3.10.4	1.3, 3.8–3.11, 4.6
	Student Admissions/ Retention/ Graduation	6, 8, 11, 13	4.3, 4.11, 4.23, 4.35, 4.41, 5.15, 5.17, 6.1–6.6		2.A.16, 2.F.1–6, 2.G.7, 2.G.10, 2.3, 2.5, 2.6, 3.C.1–4, 3.D.1–5, 3.E.3	2.6, 2.7.4, 3.4.3, 3.4.4, 3.4.6–9, 3.5.2, 3.5.3, 3.6.3, 3.6.4, 3.9.2, 4.1, 4.3	2.2, 2.14
	Student Support Services	6, 8, 9, 11, 13	6.4, 6.7–6.18	3d, 4d	2.C.5, 2.D, 3.A.1–4, 3.B.2, 3.B.4–6, 3.D.9–19, 6.E	2.10, 3.4.9, 3.4.12, 3.8.2, 3.9.1, 3.9.3, 3.11.2, 4.1, 4.5	2.11–2.13
	Curriculum	6, 11, 12, 13, 14	2.5, 4.1–4.43, 5.11	4a–d	2.A.1–12, 2.C.1–8, 2.D.1–3, 2.F, 2.G.1–12, 2.H.1–3, 2.1, 2.4	2.7.1, 2.7.2, 2.7.3, 2.7.4, 3.4.1, 3.4.2, 3.4.10, 3.4.11, 3.4.12, 3.5.1, 3.6.1, 3.6.2, 3.8.2, 4.2, 4.3, 4.4	2.1–2.9, 4.7
Resources	Resource Allocation/ Institutional Resources	2, 3, 4, 7, 11, 13	3.7, 4.3, 4.9, 4.21, 5.3, 5.6, 6.14, 7.1–7.12, 8.1–8.6, 9.1–9.14	2a, 2b, 3d, 4a	1.B.4, 2.A.1, 2.A.30, 2.E.1–6, 2.G.2, 2.G.3, 2.G.6, 3.A.4, 3.D.7, 3.D.8, 3.E.4, 4.A.4, 4.B.4, 5.A, 5.B.1–5, 5.C, 5.D.1–6, 5.E.1–3, 7.A.1–4, 7.B.1–8, 7.D.1–3, 8.A.1–7, 8.B.1–3, 8.C.1–4	2.9, 2.11.1, 2.11.2, 3.2.11–14, 3.8.1, 3.8.3, 3.9.3, 3.10.1, 3.10.2, 3.10.3, 3.10.4, 3.10.5, 3.11.1, 3.11.2, 3.11.3, 4.7	3.1, 3.5–3.7
Institutional Effectiveness	Institutional Assessment	2, 3, 6, 7, 10	1.5, 2.4–2.7, 5.7, 5.22, 6.18, 7.12, 8.6, 9.14, 10.14	2c, 3c, 5a–d	1.B.9, 2.B.1–3, 3.B.1, 3.E.1	2.5, 2.12, 3.2.10, 3.3.1, 3.7.2	2.7, 2.11, 4.4, 4.8
	Effectiveness and Student Learning	8, 11, 12, 13, 14	4.7, 4.15, 4.18, 4.24, 4.31–4.33, 4.37, 4.44–4.51, 5.11, 5.15, 5.16	3a–d, 4a–d, 5a–d	2.B.1–3, 2.2, 3.C.1, 4.A	2.5, 2.12, 3.3.1, 4.1	1.2, 2.3–2.7, 2.10, 4.3

(Continued)

Table 5.3 (Continued)

Topic Crosswalk Among Six Regional Accreditors

Category	Accreditation Standards	MSCHE	NEASC-CIHE	NCA-HLC	NWCCU	SACS	WASC[a]
Faculty	Faculty Credentials/ Search and Screening/ Evaluation	10	4.22, 5.1–5.10, 5.22		2.C.7, 2.E.3–6, 4.A.1, 4.A.5, 4.A.6, 4.A.8–10, 4.1	2.8, 3.2.9, 3.5.4, 3.7.1, 3.7.2, 3.8.3	3.1–3.4
	Academic Freedom	6, 10	5.13, 11.3		4.A.7, 4.B.7, 9.A.5	3.7.4	1.4
	Professional Development/ Methods of Instruction/ Function	7, 10	5.8, 5.11–5.22	3a, 3b, 4a	2.A.8, 4.A.2, 4.A.3, 4.B.1–7, 6.D	2.9, 3.7.3, 3.7.5	3.11, 4.6, 4.7
Planning	Mission and Goals	1, 6	1.1–1.4	1a–e	1.A.1–7	2.4, 3.1.1, 3.4.2	1.1
	Institutional Planning	2, 3, 7, 14	2.1–2.3, 4.9	2a–d, 5a	1.B.1–9, 3.A, 8.C.1–4	2.5	4.1–8
Institutional Conduct	Integrity	6, 10, 12	3.2, 4.36, 5.4, 5.14, 5.18, 6.1, 6.16, 11.1–11.11	1b, 1e, 4a–4d, 5a–d	3.C.5, 3.E.5, 3.1, 6.1, 9.A.1–5, 9.1	3.2.14, 3.4.5, 3.9.2, 3.10.4, 3.13, 4.5, 4.7	1.5–1.8
	Public Disclosure/ Availability of Information to Constituents	6, 9, 11	6.15, 10.1–10.14		1.B.9, 3.B.3, 3.B.4, 3.E.2, 3.E.6, 3.1, 4.A.4, 9.A.3	3.1.1, 3.2.9, 3.2.14, 3.4.4, 3.4.5, 3.6.4, 3.9.1, 3.9.2, 3.14, 4.3, 4.6	1.2
	Timely and accurate reporting to agency	6, 14		6.1	1.A.7, Policy A-2	3.10.2, 3.12, 3.13	1.9
Federal Criteria[b]	Federal					4.1, 4.2, 4.3, 4.4, 4.5, 4.6, 4.7	

Source: Analysis conducted by K. Cragg and A. Henderson, 2011.

[a] Refers to the WASC Handbook of Accreditation 2008, Accrediting Commission for Senior Colleges and Universities only. Does not include Accrediting Commission Standards for Community and Junior Colleges, which are in a separate handbook. (Source: Analysis of regional accrediting body standards, 2011.)

[b] SACS is the only accrediting agency that separates federal standards.

Table 5.3 provides a crosswalk to allow administrators to gain an understanding of standards that align across accrediting agencies. This enables administrators to use responses of peer institutions as benchmarks in formulating their own responses, and also to determine whether it is appropriate to include specific detailed data, such as number of students per major, or broad programmatic summaries.

This approach can save valuable time and prevent embarrassment, as the institution is able to provide a response modeled on those of peer institutions rather than one so generic that the accrediting agency might issue a judgment of non-compliance on the standard.

FINANCIAL IMPLICATIONS

Regional accreditation is optional for institutions; each institution must choose whether to undergo the rigorous application process. While participation is not mandatory, the financial gains associated with recognition by a regional accreditor far outweigh any cost. One of the most significant benefits of accreditation is that the federal government offers federal financial aid only to students attending an institution that is regionally accredited by one of the six agencies. For the more than 66% of students receiving some form of federal financial aid (National Center for Education Statistics, 2009), whether or not an institution has regional accreditation may mean the difference between attending college or not.

Simply applying for regional accreditation does not automatically guarantee that an institution will be accredited. Regional accrediting agencies are required by CHEA to publicly disclose the names of all institutions seeking accreditation and currently accredited. In the event that an accreditor finds an institution in non-compliance in one or more areas, the institution is given the opportunity to resolve the issues internally before receiving negative media attention that might harm its reputation. Regardless of the severity, every item judged to be non-compliant has a financial cost associated with correcting the issue. These costs can be avoided by maintaining compliance on all items in between reaffirmation periods, which also reduces the amount of work required prior to reaffirmation.

FOCUS ON INSTITUTIONAL EFFECTIVENESS

Institutional effectiveness, which has received much attention due to an increased focus on accountability at the federal and state levels, most recently notable in the Higher Education Opportunity Act of 2009. Regional accrediting agencies have thus been held responsible for ensuring positive outcomes of student learning and continuous institutional improvement.

Traditionally, public colleges and universities have had considerably more experience than private institutions with formal academic assessment. Because state legislatures and agencies have, in general, required public institutions to provide extensive assessment activities and outcomes, these institutions have larger professional staffs to conduct assessment activities than do their private counterparts. Additionally, private colleges and universities are often decentralized, with academic departments conducting their assessment according to their own standards. As a consequence, consistent and thorough assessment can be more challenging for private institutions.

Institutions undergoing the reaffirmation of accreditation process are finding that simply having an assessment process in place is no longer sufficient; it is expect that data are interpreted and there will be appropriate action to improve student success (Dunn, McCarthy, Baker, & Halonen, 2011). Institutions must not only systematically collect assessment data, but also show that those data have directly influenced programmatic or curricular changes aimed at fostering continuous improvement.

DESCRIPTION OF ASSESSMENT

Assessment, while large in process, is relatively simple in concept. In order for academic and administrative programs to function efficiently, they must be able to effectively evaluate their accomplishments and make corresponding improvements. While institutions may be more familiar with academic assessment, the term "assessment" has widened to include administrative units as well. The purpose of administrative unit assessment is to examine and review the performance and accomplishments of a department to ensure continuous improvement of the programs and services it offers. This process of evaluation is often interchangeably referred to as institutional effectiveness or assessment. Terenzini ([1989] 2010) acknowledges, "one of the most significant and imposing obstacles to the advancement of the assessment agenda at the national level is the absence of any consensus on precisely what assessment means" (p. 31). Another definition is "the gathering of information concerning the functioning of students, staff, and institutions of higher education" (Astin, 1991, p. 2). Most simply, assessment is the process of declaring goals, defining criteria for success, providing evidence to illustrate success of goals, and indicating changes to be implemented as a result. Within this section, assessment refers to the continuous process used to illustrate programmatic planning and attainment of related goals to ensure the ongoing quality of academic or administrative programs.

PURPOSE OF ASSESSMENT

Based on the results of a 2009 survey of campus provosts at over 1,500 institutions, Kuh and Ikenberry (2009) found that "the three most influential forces driving assessment were the expectations of regional accreditors, those of specialized accreditors, and an institutional commitment to improvement" (p. 10). In contrast, the results of the 2011 follow-up survey of program heads found at the "department/program level, the primary driver in assessment activity is faculty's interest in improving their programs—followed by accreditation" (Ewell, Paulson, and Kinzie, 2011, p. 8). Despite the varying motivations for programmatic assessment, the process required to demonstrate effectiveness is often the same. A systematic cycle of assessment allows academic and administrative units to set goals, determine measures of success, and make programmatic changes based on evidence-based feedback.

Once integrated with campus culture, it enables these units to align their goals and accomplishments with the larger mission and goals of the institution as a whole, and to select their own measures for gauging success. This flexibility allows the assessment process to function across distinct disciplines with minimal limitations.

One benefit of measuring academic program success, as Volkwein (2010a) points out, is that

> academic departments and programs that are able to provide presidents and provosts with evidence about the impacts they are having on their students will be more successful in the competition for campus resources than academic units not able to provide such evidence.
>
> (pp. 4–5)

In order to be successful, academic programs must show evidence of continuous improvement. Improvement represents the accomplishments of an academic program in relation to predetermined goals. To demonstrate continuous improvement, programs must provide evidence not only of improvement, but of improvement that builds upon and furthers prior improvements. Improvements must illustrate actions taken beyond the scope of everyday routine; accomplishment of daily tasks is not within the range of continuous improvement.

COMPONENTS

Components of a successful assessment process include definition of goals linked to clearly defined, quantifiable metrics; evidence of completion of goals; and discussion of changes made based on evidence (Bryan & Clegg, 2006; Middaugh, 2010; Nichols & Nichols, 2005; Palomba & Banta, 1999). Goals can be student learning outcomes or specific objectives related to other aspects of program quality. In general, departments are encouraged to express learning outcomes in measureable behavioral terms. Examples might include demonstrated proficiencies in a specific subject area or standard achievement comparable to that of the national student populace. The preferable methodology is to establish a combination of direct and indirect methods of assessing the success of stated learning outcomes achieved by students.

EVALUATION COMPONENTS

Regardless of whether a unit is academic or administrative, goals/outcomes must change annually to show continuous improvement; the same set cannot be used over and over again. Similarly, metrics used to measure success must change annually to reflect progress. Using the same goals and metric criteria each year does not provide evidence of continuous improvement.

Continuous improvement must use previous programmatic success as a foundation and seek to move beyond it; therefore, establishing valid metrics is critical to effective assessment. Careful attention should also be paid to the manner in which the assessment process is presented to, and perceived by, the campus. Presenting the process in simple terms with examples of goals, metrics, evidence, and results is essential to campus buy-in; simplicity of method makes the assessment process less daunting. Terenzini ([1989] 2010) suggests that assessment

> should be seen by all as a developmental, not punitive, undertaking. It should be a vehicle for individual and institutional improvement, not a search for documentation on which to evaluate individual faculty members, or to cut budgets, or retrench programs.
>
> (p. 34)

A well-developed institutional assessment process allows for a consistent internal review of units across the college or university and makes it possible to provide external reviewers with assessment documents that are thorough and uniform, regardless of program type. This approach eliminates ambiguity, helps with planning and training, and assists in standardizing the documentation.

ASSESSMENT WEBSITES

A number of institutions have developed websites totally devoted to assessment. At Wake Forest University, the Dean of the College of Arts and Sciences developed a site that provides a step-by-step guide for assessment, an FAQ page, and resources including relevant papers and other institutions' assessment websites. The Wake Forest website emphasizes learning outcomes for academic departments within the college. It includes an opening statement from the Dean attesting to the commitment of teaching and the necessity of assessing learning outcomes for providing a quality education to the students (Wake Forest College, 2011). She has referred all of the chairs and academic program directors to this website to guide them in their assessment and evaluation processes. One of the resources listed is the assessment website of Vanderbilt University, a peer institution of Wake Forest. As stated on that site:

> Vanderbilt University's commitment to institutional improvement through research-based planning and evaluation follows from its mission as a research university. The university continually reviews its objectives and operations, with the aim of improving the quality and the effectiveness of the institution. Outcomes of these activities are evident at all levels of the university—from the institution as a whole, through colleges and schools, to individual departments and administrative units—and demonstrate that Vanderbilt excels in its mission as a research university.
>
> (Vanderbilt University Assessment Website, 2010, para. 1)

AN EXAMPLE ASSESSMENT CYCLE

The Assessment Cycle: The Assessment Plan

The assessment plan is the first part of the assessment cycle and is often completed prior to the start of the assessment cycle year. The plan, in which programs identify the goals they will be targeting in the coming year, generally contains three main sections: definition of goals, statement of specific criteria for success, and indication of the methods that will be used to prove whether the goals have been attained.

In general, the plan should identify a minimum of three goals to be accomplished within the time frame identified with the assessment cycle. Goals may be specific student learning outcomes or items the program wishes to accomplish; however, goals should be achievable within the time frame. In general, goals that cannot be completed and documented within the assessment time frame are not suitable for inclusion on a formal assessment plan, unless a program intends to address a particular goal across several years.

In such a case, the larger goal should be broken into smaller goals that can be accomplished within a single assessment cycle to provide demonstrable evidence of progress. Similarly, programs should seek to define their goals as narrowly as possible to avoid potential problems resulting from vague language. By clearly and concisely defining goals, programs are able to create goals that are easy to measure.

The next element in the assessment plan is the definition of criteria for success. These criteria should include detailed and quantifiable targets for success. As programs must submit the criteria for success prior to the start of the assessment cycle, the possibility of selecting goals already known to be successful is limited. Criteria for success should align with appropriate goals and retain the same structure. If a program goal is to increase enrollment, the accompanying criteria for success should contain the specific enrollment increase target needed to declare the goal a success (e.g., 5%). A clear definition of success in relation to the goal makes it easy to determine whether the criteria have been met.

The final element of the assessment plan addresses the methods that programs will use to prove that they have met their goals. Methods can be any items used to gather data that will illustrate progress toward the goal, from student test scores to program enrollment reports.

Once completed by the department designee, the assessment plan should be forwarded to department heads and deans to verify that they support its goals. This will also ensure that program goals are aligned with larger scale goals. Table 5.4 provides an example of an assessment plan.

The Assessment Cycle: The Assessment Report

The assessment report concludes the assessment cycle, documenting the outcome of the evaluation process blueprinted in the assessment plan. In order to complete the report, programs have only to supplement the original plan with two additional elements: the results of the evidence collected using the method indicated in the plan and the changes made based on the outcome of the goal.

The results section asks programs to detail the supporting evidence or data they gathered regarding the accomplishment of their goals. In this portion, programs may

Table 5.4 Example Assessment Plan

Goal:	Improve student scores on program exit exam
Criteria for success:	Increase percentage of students scoring 85 or better on program exit exam by 2% over last year
Method of evidence:	Comparison of program exit exams for this year and last year

Table 5.5 Example Assessment Report

Goal 1:	Improve student scores on program exit exam
Criteria for success:	Increase percentage of students scoring 85 or better on program exit exam by 2% over last year
Method of evidence:	Comparison of program exit exams for this year and last year
Evidence:	75% of students taking the program exit exam scored 85 or better; an increase of 3% from last year's 72% of students who scored 85 or better
Changes made as a result:	The program is adequately preparing students for the exit exam; the exam will be revised next year to ensure that content remains current

elaborate upon the methods used and the resulting outcomes. If relevant, the discussion may also include contextual data such as previous years' results for comparison.

The final section of the report closes the assessment loop by asking programs to indicate the changes implemented in response to the completion of the goals. If the data collected proved that the goal was a success, programs should indicate the changes they are making to ensure continued success. In cases where the evidence collected during the year suggests that the unit did not meet the criteria for success, programs should indicate the changes they are making to improve the situation. Table 5.5 provides an example assessment report.

COMMON METHODS OF ACADEMIC AND ADMINISTRATIVE ASSESSMENT

According to the 2009 report by Kuh and Ikenberry for the National Institute for Learning Outcomes Assessment (NILOA),

> at the program level the most popular approaches to assessing learning outcomes were student portfolios, measures of specialized knowledge and other performance assessments, and rubrics, as more than 80% of institutions indicated at least one of their academic programs was using one of these approaches.
>
> (p. 3)

On the follow-up survey, the most commonly reported assessment methods at the program level included capstone courses, rubrics, performance assessments, final projects, tests, surveys (local and national), and portfolios (Ewell, Paulson, & Kinzie, 2011, p. 9). Wagenaar (2011) encourages the use of rubrics as they "help students see the organization and goals of a course more clearly, and help others assess the course and student learning more accurately" (p. 35).

Direct Methods of Assessment

Direct methods of academic assessment can include the following:

- Scores on "field tests" as compared to the "Norm" of all institutions
- Achievement in capstone courses "graded" by outside faculty

- Presentations by students at professional conferences evaluated by peer professionals
- Success after graduation, e.g., "placement" into graduate/professional schools and jobs

Indirect Methods of Assessment

Indirect methods of assessment can include the following:

- Surveys of graduating seniors
- Surveys of alumni
- Focus groups with students
- Exit interviews with students

Third-party nationally normed surveys such as the College Senior Survey (CSS) offered through the Higher Education Research Institute (HERI) and the National Survey of Student Engagement (NSSE) are excellent ways to gain information from seniors on their satisfaction in different areas, such as how they spend their time and how they have changed since their first year. Academic departments may choose to isolate results of their majors from these surveys to determine students' perceptions of the effectiveness of their academic experience in the respective major. Results of the surveys can also be compared to those of peer institutions to determine the relative "success" of the students.

Examples of Assessment Methods Used in Plans and Reports

Tables 5.6 and 5.7 list potential items that may be used in the assessment planning and/ or reporting processes. The purpose of these lists is to initiate ideas for items that can be used to demonstrate that assessment is occurring within academic and administrative units. Those new to assessment may find the lists useful in creating their first assessment plan and/or report.

Table 5.6 Potential Items for Academic Assessment Plans and Reports

1	Alumni survey data
2	Applied art/music jury examinations
3	Comparison of mid-term test and final exam grade
4	Comparison of program/department to other schools in system
5	Completion of teacher self-assessment/observation instrument
6	Course management software usage
7	Department committee meetings minutes
8	Distribution of test scores using program rating scales
9	Embedded test questions
10	Employer survey data
11	Evaluation of capstone projects
12	Evaluation of concert performances

(Continued)

Table 5.6 (Continued)

13	Evaluation of lesson plans
14	Evaluation of oral presentations
15	Evaluation of program application trends
16	Evaluation of student portfolios
17	Evaluation of teaching/ counseling method/style
18	Faculty course evaluation data
19	Faculty opinion survey data
20	Feedback from program focus groups
21	Internship survey data
22	Major field test data
23	Number of faculty attending training opportunities
24	Number of student/faculty conference attendees
25	Number of student/faculty conference presentations
26	Number of students successfully completing program
27	Pass rates of certification/licensure exam
28	Pass rates of specialized discipline exams
29	Pre- and post-first-year survey data
30	Pre- and post-test data
31	Program evaluation rubrics
32	Program exit exam data
33	Program exit survey data
34	Program feedback from students
35	Program satisfaction survey data
36	Student self-assessment data

Table 5.7 Potential Items for Administrative Assessment Plans and Reports

1	Alumni survey data
2	Client survey data
3	Course management usage data
4	Evaluation of annual events
5	Evaluation of areas for improvement
6	Exit exam data
7	Feedback from students, faculty, staff, and administrators
8	Grant recipient survey data
9	Impact of services offered data
10	Income received from sales
11	Number of applications processed

Table 5.7 (Continued)

12	Number of clients using services
13	Number of conference attendees
14	Number of conference presentations
15	Number of employees attending trainings
16	Number of new trainings provided
17	Number of publications
18	Number of requests for additional services
19	Number of services offered
20	Number of services offered
21	Number of training services offered
22	Orientation programs data
23	Placement test data
24	Productivity report data
25	Reports illustrating increased efficiency of services
26	Review of existing protocol
27	Services satisfaction survey data
28	Student activity data from card swipes
29	Total income from performances and coinciding attendance
30	Total money raised/donated
31	Training evaluations assessment
32	Training sessions attendance
33	Training workshop survey data
34	Tutoring survey results assessment
35	Usage reports
36	Website usability survey data

RESPONSIBILITY

An institutional effectiveness planning process should be integrated—that is, departmentally based but also connected to the planning efforts of the academic and administrative divisions and of the institution as a whole. In this model, student assessment data collected by the department feeds into evaluation and decision-making procedures that allow for the incorporation of assessment data into the planning cycles of departments and the overall institution. The planning mechanism described throughout this chapter is decentralized, employing the administrative philosophy that those most knowledgeable of, and closest to, the ongoing processes of the department should also be responsible for reviewing them and implementing changes (Peterson, Hurtado, & Dey, 2001).

Volkwein (2010b) notes that "program reviews under ideal conditions are integrated into the fabric of academic affairs and constitute a constructive process of self-examination and continuous improvement" (p. 21). Within this structure, assessment of academic and administrative programs is the responsibility first and foremost of

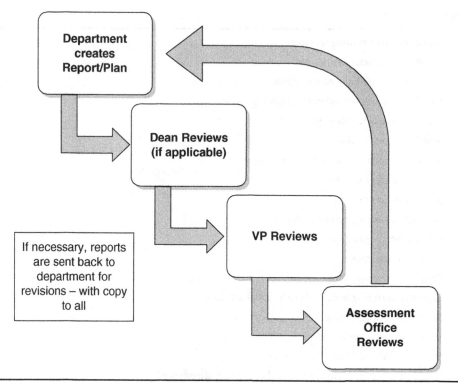

Figure 5.1 Assessment Report Creation and Review Process

the department itself. In most instances, the department head or program director completes the departmental assessment report. These are the individuals responsible for establishing the goals and directions of the program/unit. As such, they are the most informed regarding the program's accomplishments. Also, these individuals tend to be administrators who have an understanding of the program's role in the college or university. Awareness of the institution's direction and goals is necessary to the creation of a solid assessment report. Figure 5.1 presents a graphical display of the key stakeholders involved in creating and reviewing the assessment report/plan.

Having initial responsibility for the report allows the program/unit director to address programmatic goals and accomplishments in conjunction with larger institutional goals. The college's or university's direction/mission provides a framework and context for accomplishments of the program/unit. A subsequent review by the dean or vice president further ensures that the program's goals are in alignment with those of the institution. At this stage, the dean or vice president reviews the accomplishments of the program/unit for the prior year, as well as the goals for the coming year. The reviewer's responsibility is to verify that program/unit accomplishments accurately reflect departmental activity and that stated goals are appropriate for the program/unit.

Upon completing his or her review, the dean or vice president approves the assessment report created by the program/unit director. For academic programs, the report is then forwarded to the provost for final review. This system of multiple reviews illustrates that the responsibility for assessment is shared across levels.

Successful assessment requires shared responsibility to show that the process is not limited to a stand-alone report created by a program director. Shared responsibility allows the assessment process to be viewed as a collaborative endeavor rather than a routine report. Involving the provost, generally the highest-ranking academic officer on campus, emphasizes the importance of assessment, encouraging program directors to be accountable for the material submitted in plans and reports. Knowing that program goals and accomplishments will be reviewed by the deans, vice presidents, and provost helps program directors to focus on realistic and useful goals.

CONCLUSION

Former Secretary of U.S. Department of Education Margaret Spellings was most compelling when she stated in 2006,

> We have noted a remarkable shortage of clear, accessible information about crucial aspects of American colleges and universities. … Our complex, decentralized postsecondary education system has no comprehensive strategy, particularly for undergraduate programs, to provide either adequate internal accountability systems or effective public information.
>
> (U.S. Department of Education, 2006a, pp. 4, 13)

Since the release of the Spellings Commission report in 2006, there has been more emphasis nationally on accountability in higher education and thus greater pressure on institutions to demonstrate actual learning outcomes.

In conclusion, academic assessment in all programs is not only important to the quality of institutions of higher education but also an inherent requirement of accrediting associations and governmental agencies.

REFERENCES

Astin, A. W. (1991). *Assessment for excellence: The philosophy and practice of assessment and evaluation in higher education.* Westport, CT: The Oryx Press.

Bryan, C., & Clegg, K. (Eds.). (2006). *Innovative assessment in higher education.* New York: Routledge.

Burke, J. C., & Associates. (Ed.). (2005). *Achieving accountability in higher education: Balancing public, academic, and market demands.* San Francisco: Jossey-Bass.

Dunn, D. S., McCarthy, M. A., Baker, S. C., & Halonen, J. S. (2011). *Using quality benchmarks for assessing and developing undergraduate programs.* San Francisco: Jossey-Bass.

Eaton, J. (2011). *An overview of U.S. accreditation (revised).* Washington, DC: Council for Higher Education Accreditation.

Ewell, P., Paulson, K., & Kinzie, J. (2011). Down and in: Assessment practices at the program level. Urbana: University of Illinois and Indiana University, National Institute for Learning Outcomes Assessment (NILOA), 8–9.

Kramer, G. L., & Swing, R. L. (Eds.). (2010). *Higher education assessments: Leadership matters.* Lanham, MD: Rowman & Littlefield Publishers.

Kuh, G., & Ikenberry, S. (2009). *More than you think, less than we need: Learning outcomes assessment in American higher education.* Urbana: University of Illinois and Indiana University, National Institute for Learning Outcomes Assessment (NILOA), 3, 10.

Middaugh, M. F. (2010). *Planning and assessment in higher education: Demonstrating institutional effectiveness.* San Francisco: Jossey-Bass.

National Center for Education Statistics. (2009). *2007–08 National Postsecondary Student Aid Study (NPSAS:08): Student financial aid estimates for 2007–08.* Retrieved from http://nces.ed.gov/pubs2009/2009166.pdf

Nichols, J. O., & Nichols, K. W. (2005). *A road map for improvement of student learning and support services through assessment.* Flemington, NJ: Agathon.

Palomba, C. A., & Banta, T. W. (1999). *Assessment essentials: Planning, implementing, and improving assessment in higher education.* San Francisco: Jossey-Bass.

Peterson, M., Hurtado, S., & Dey, E. (2001). *Wake Forest University—A case study on the institutional dynamics and climate for student assessment and academic innovation.* Report of the National Center for Postsecondary Improvement (NCPI), June. Available: http://www.wfu.edu/ir/docs/michigan.pdf

Terenzini, P. (2010). Assessment with open eyes: Pitfalls in studying student outcomes. *New Directions for Institutional Research,* 2010, 29–46. (Reprinted from *Journal of Higher Education, 60*(6), 644–664, 1989.)

U.S. Department of Education. (2006a). *A test of leadership: Charting the future of U.S. higher education* (ED-06-C0-0013). Washington, DC: Education Publication Center, 4.

U.S. Department of Education. (2006b). *Action plan for higher education: Improving accessibility, affordability and accountability.* Retrieved from http://www.wiche.edu/info/agendaBook/nov06/presentations/Schray-factsheet.pdf

Vanderbilt University Assessment Website. (2010). *Assessment home.* Retrieved from http://virg.vanderbilt.edu/AssessmentPlans/

Volkwein, J. (2010a). The assessment context: Accreditation, accountability, and performance. *New Directions for Institutional Research,* 2010, 3–12.

Volkwein, J. (2010b). A model for assessing institutional effectiveness. *New Directions for Institutional Research,* 2010, 13–28.

Wagenaar, T. (2011). Why do I like assessment? Let me count the ways. *Chronicle of Higher Education, 57*(26), 35.

Wake Forest College. (2011) *Assessment of student learning website.* Retrieved from http://college.wfu.edu/assessment/

Weisbrod, B. A., Ballou, J. P., & Asch, E. D. (2008). *Mission and money: Understanding the university.* New York: Cambridge University Press, 186.

6

THE NATURE AND ROLE OF BUDGET PROCESSES

Patrick J. Schloss and Kristina M. Cragg

INTRODUCTION

When it comes to catastrophic events (e.g., Pearl Harbor, September 11, tsunamis, earthquakes, hurricanes), a media outlet's goals are to be the first on the scene and to show progress in the form of action. This captivates audiences, as they want to see what will happen next. Additionally, people volunteer in the wake of such disasters because they want to be part of something transformational. The common theme among these events is that action is needed in order for advancement to take place.

The same is true for declining economic times, especially for colleges and universities. It is important to act when problems arise. It is not enough to plan or even plan to plan; taking action is only thing that will enable an institution to move from its current place to a new place. Since change almost always involves finances, the focus is often on determining which action is appropriate in the face of limited resources. This chapter addresses this concept of action-oriented administration and responsibility when financial resources are scarce or dwindling.

IMPORTANCE OF PLANNING AND BUDGETING

Possibly no aspect of the management of postsecondary institutions is as important as planning and budgeting (Barr, 2002; Chabotar, 2006; Kezar & Lester, 2009). Nearly all initiatives depend on resources that are seldom sufficient to allow for every worthy activity. Consequently, effective organizations are able to prioritize activities, allocating resources to the most important.

The unique characteristics of postsecondary schools present distinct challenges for budget managers. Primary budget sources can be wide ranging and include student tuition, state appropriation, auxiliary income (e.g., residence halls, bookstores, food services), foundation income, incidental or targeted income (e.g., athletic receipts, performing arts receipts, parking fines), extramural funds that are the result of grants and contracts, and income that is the result of intellectual property (e.g., licenses, patents, royalties).

Restrictions on the use of this income can vary within an institution. For example, at a given school, tuition and state appropriations may not be spent on hospitality items and surpluses may not be carried forward from one year to the next. On the other hand, foundation income and endowments can grow indefinitely and be spent on dinners, social travel, and entertainment. Public institutions in one state may be able to accumulate a reserve of tuition money, while those in another may require that all funds be expended by the end of the fiscal year.

Further adding to budget challenges at postsecondary institutions, the relationship between mission and expenditure or cost is not often well defined (Weisbrod, Ballou, & Asch, 2008). In fact, in some cases it is illogical. A technical school may be charged with preparing the workforce for critical shortages in applied vocations such as nursing and welding. A careful analysis may reveal that these are among the two most costly programs offered. General education, as a transfer curriculum to colleges or universities, may be a peripheral focus offered solely for the convenience of young people in the region. One would expect budget support to follow the mission, with more dollars being allocated to nursing and welding and less to general education. In reality, the very costly welding and nursing curricula that require substantial equipment and staffing levels generate the same income per student as the less costly general education curriculum.

Finally, though managing extensive and complex budgets, many postsecondary school administrators have little or no formal preparation in finance. The typical university president first developed expertise as a musician, social scientist, or teacher educator. He or she advanced from faculty member to department chair to dean and eventually to president. Based on this career path, his or her sensitivity to curriculum delivery may be exceptional. Sensitivity to the financing of the curriculum may be lacking.

MONEY FOLLOWS MISSION

No single budget principle is more important than the philosophy characterized by the phrase "Money follows mission." The aforementioned example of nursing and welding is a case of the mission following the money, which most would agree is highly destructive. Carried to the extreme, this approach would cause technical schools to experience "mission creep" until their offerings were weighted heavily toward high-income and low-cost general education. The effect would be the loss of their central mission or workforce development.

"Money following mission" means that the institution must have a clear and well-vetted mission statement, for example, "to provide training in applied disciplines that are essential to meeting the workforce needs of the local region." Figure 6.1 presents additional examples.

Expenditures should be judged against this mission statement. All things being equal, welding instruction would maintain priority over college transfer sociology courses. Similarly, a liberal arts university's mission to provide education in the arts, sciences, and humanities leading to a broadly educated student would emphasize support for library holdings, lab equipment, and terminally qualified/student-centered faculty. A premium

Binghamton University, State University of New York

Our mission is to provide an affordable, world-class education to high-caliber students from culturally and economically diverse backgrounds. Our focus is always on the student. Our internationally renowned faculty members produce amazing scholarship and art, and bring their spirit of inquiry and discovery into the classroom.

Bowling Green State University

Bowling Green State University (BGSU) provides educational experiences inside and outside the classroom that enhance the lives of students, faculty and staff. Students are prepared for lifelong career growth, lives of engaged citizenship and leadership in a global society. Within our learning community, we build a welcoming, safe and diverse environment where the creative ideas and achievements of all can benefit others throughout Ohio, the nation and the world.

California Institute of Technology

The mission of the California Institute of Technology is to expand human knowledge and benefit society through research integrated with education. We investigate the most challenging, fundamental problems in science and technology in a singularly collegial, interdisciplinary atmosphere, while educating outstanding students to become creative members of society.

Cornell University

Cornell is a private, Ivy League university and the land-grant University for New York State. Cornell's mission is to discover, preserve, and disseminate knowledge; produce creative work; and promote a culture of broad inquiry throughout and beyond the Cornell community. Cornell also aims, through public service, to enhance the lives and livelihoods of our students, the people of New York, and others around the world. Our faculty, students, alumni, and staff strive toward these objectives in a context of freedom with responsibility. We foster initiative, integrity, and excellence, in an environment of collegiality, civility, and responsible stewardship. As the land-grant University for the State of New York, we apply the results of our endeavors in service to our alumni, the community, the state, the nation, and the world.

Massachusetts Institute of Technology

The mission of MIT is to advance knowledge and educate students in science, technology, and other areas of scholarship that will best serve the nation and the world in the 21st century. The Institute is committed to generating, disseminating, and preserving knowledge, and to working with others to bring this knowledge to bear on the world's great challenges. MIT is dedicated to providing its students with an education that combines rigorous academic study and the excitement of discovery with the support and intellectual stimulation of a diverse campus community. We seek to develop in each member of the MIT community the ability and passion to work wisely, creatively, and effectively for the betterment of humankind.

Notre Dame

The University seeks to cultivate in its students not only an appreciation for the great achievements of human beings, but also a disciplined sensibility to the poverty, injustice, and oppression that burden the lives of so many. The aim is to create a sense of human solidarity and concern for the common good that will bear fruit as learning becomes service to justice.

(Continued)

(Continued)

University of California, Los Angeles

UCLA's primary purpose as a public research university is the creation, dissemination, preservation, and application of knowledge for the betterment of our global society. To fulfill this mission, UCLA is committed to academic freedom in its fullest terms: we value open access to information, free and lively debate conducted with mutual respect for individuals, and freedom from intolerance. In all of our pursuits, we strive at once for excellence and diversity, recognizing that openness and inclusion produce true quality.

University of Illinois

The University of Illinois will transform lives and serve society by educating, creating knowledge and putting knowledge to work on a large scale and with excellence.

University of Michigan

The mission of the University of Michigan is to serve the people of Michigan and the world through preeminence in creating, communicating, preserving and applying knowledge, art, and academic values, and in developing leaders and citizens who will challenge the present and enrich the future.

Vanderbilt University

Vanderbilt University is a center for scholarly research, informed and creative teaching, and service to the community and society at large. Vanderbilt will uphold the highest standards and be a leader in the quest for new knowledge through scholarship, dissemination of knowledge through teaching and outreach, creative experimentation of ideas and concepts. In pursuit of these goals, Vanderbilt values most highly intellectual freedom that supports open inquiry, equality, compassion, and excellence in all endeavors.

Figure 6.1 Sample Mission Statements

might also be placed on small class sizes. All things being equal, less support would be given to business programs, engineering programs, and athletics.

Institutions of all types and levels build sufficient flexibility in their mission statement to allow for serious competition among diverse activities. For example, Ezra Cornell founded Cornell University with a commitment to providing for human development in all disciplines and skills that would advance society. The school assigns exceptional resources to many of the country's best programs, including engineering, agriculture, hotel management, and the liberal arts. It is not surprising that assigning resources is far more challenging at Cornell than at a more homogenous institution.

One caveat to the money/mission axiom—introduced here to avoid the appearance of idealism—involves supporting a program or activity that is distinct from yet "enables" the mission.

Big Ten schools, for example, are famous for their football programs, which have had a major impact on the quality and effectiveness of their mission, itself clearly embedded in teaching, research, and scholarship. For example, applications to Penn State skyrocketed following their National Championships. Revenue generated by ticket sales, sports apparel, and television contracts drives a wide range of programs at the schools. Finally, Big Ten football programs are a magnet for private gifts, which are often used to provide scholarships to outstanding students.

A related exception may be that of the "cash cow." Many institutions offer programs on the fringe of their curriculum to generate revenue for their core mission. For example, many proud "liberal arts" institutions offer professional programs clearly not grounded in the liberal arts tradition. It can easily be demonstrated that business or education majors can be produced at a substantially lower cost than music majors. Removing the professional programs that run with 30 students to the professor would eliminate a revenue stream that offsets the 6:1 student-professor ratios in the performing arts.

Administrators are often tempted to ignore their institution's mission when assigning resources. Sometimes an administrator would like to keep his or her favorite program, even if it's costly. Other times an administrator wants to eliminate a costly or otherwise burdensome program, even if it is central to the institution's mission.

Organizing and managing to focus on the school's mission, not that of any one individual, is critical to strengthening the core of the institution (d'Ambrosio & Ehrenberg, 2007; Mactaggart, 2007, Martin & Samels, 2009; Miller, 2007). What follows is a description of a number of practices that ensure, to the extent practical, that money finds its way to the mission. These should be read with only a modest level of confidence. As has been said, "There are a number of ways to skin a cat." The practices shared below are included as they are simple, yet effective methods for managing an institution.

IDENTIFY FUNDS AND EXPENDITURES

At the simplest level, the budget process advocated in this chapter involves laying all funds on one side of a budget and all potential expenditures on another. This enables leaders to compare the value of their institution to another in an effort to reduce costs and put into perspective which item is more "valuable" than another. When dealing with required budget reductions, it is critical to reduce costs in lieu of layoffs (Brown & Gamber, 2002). Since there are invariably more needs than funds, needs must be prioritized. Those most important to the mission should be funded, those least should not be funded.

For the process to have integrity, all available funds and all potential expenditures should be known to budget managers. Projected expenditures are seldom "hidden" from budget managers; a portion of available funds frequently is. As the experienced reader will know, the "hidden" funds are typically used by the less-than-forthcoming manager to support "pet projects" that may not be central to the mission.

As an example, a small southeastern university suffered severe budget reductions. Following the major principle of "transparency," all funds were placed on a ledger with fund requests. Because of the reductions, low-priority and unfunded projects included library acquisitions, scientific equipment, and professional travel. Though replacements for four-year-old vehicles were not on the funding request list, new vans appeared on campus. When questions were raised, it was found that a director had not disclosed income from parking fines, room service fees, and other miscellaneous sources. He had independently directed this income to the vehicle purchase without considering the overall budget process.

The problem is that the value of library holdings, equipment, and travel, when judged against the mission, may have been greater than that of new vehicles. Because the income was hidden from the budget authority, this judgment could not be made.

To reemphasize, all available funds and all fund requests should be known to decision makers. Hidden funds will likely be directed to special projects that are not as important as the least important project known by budget managers. Essentially, "a budget doubles as an accountability and control device, against which expenditures can be monitored for compliance" (Lasher & Greene, 2001, p. 475).

Being aware of all funds available is not an easy task for most postsecondary institutions. Below is a description of typical sources.

Tuition Payments

Depending on the governing board, tuition can be collected and retained entirely by the school or remitted to a central agency (e.g., state system office) with a portion being returned to the school. Further, the board may determine that only a portion of the tuition should be returned for institutional expenditures and another be directed to grow the school's endowment or financial reserves. Tuition rates at public institutions are generally established directly or indirectly (with consultation) by a statewide or local governing board. These may include boards of regents, trustees, or school boards. Private-school tuitions are generally set by trustees, who, in keeping with general business practices, attempt to strike a balance between student willingness and ability to pay and the funds required to offer a quality education.

The governing board also balances local tuition rates with those of competitors. The goal is to achieve full enrollment while accruing sufficient tuition from each student to provide high-quality instruction in a well-managed physical plant. If tuition is excessive, the school will not achieve full enrollment. The loss of students will result in a loss of revenue, and the quality of instruction and attractiveness of the physical plant will suffer. This may further inhibit the ability to fill seats, leading to a downward spiral. Conversely, if tuition is too low, a school may achieve full enrollment but have insufficient revenue to maintain quality programs.

Tax Appropriations

State governments or local governing bodies may provide tax receipts to postsecondary institutions based on a funding formula or an annual decision. The formula may be as simple as a dollar amount for each credit generated or as complex as assigning a portion of an overall tax pool based on variables such as credits generated, student head counts, physical plant size, or participation in special programs. Appropriations can be earned immediately, with formula results being directed into the current year budget, or can lag, with formula funds generated in a given year being paid out years later.

Public institutions almost always balance appropriated funds with tuition rates. During the post-World War era, when higher education access proliferated, appropriations accounted for the largest portion of institutional budgets. A ratio of 70% appropriations to 30% tuition was common. In recent years, state budget problems, the cost of the "war on drugs," and possibly a loss of cachet for higher education, has reversed this ratio, so that many students now pay 70% of the cost of their education. Some state institutions have cynically described themselves as "state-related" or private, as government support has fallen below 20%.

In a manner similar to tax appropriations, private schools must strike a balance between tuition payments and funds drawn from their endowment. While the institution may announce a cost of $30,000 in tuition and fees, it budgets for a "discounted" cost of $20,000 dollars per student because, on average, students receive a $10,000 "scholarship" package against the full cost of tuition.

If there is a quick check of the fiscal health of a private or public institution, it is that the endowment in the former case and reserves in the latter are increasing year to year. Of course, this increase must be in the context of full enrollment of high-quality students, full staffing, and a well-maintained physical plant.

Auxiliary Income

A majority of colleges and universities generate income outside of the tuition-based cash stream. Typical sources include food service contracts, parking fees, residence hall rents, and health fees. These fees may be segregated from the overall budget but applied to the purpose for which they were collected. Parking fees may be used exclusively to maintain lots and structures. Residence hall rents may be applied to debt services and maintenance on dormitories. Health fees may be applied to professional salaries, equipment, and pharmaceuticals.

As emphasized earlier, these funds, though segregated, should be known to the overall budget authority. A case in point: At one school that collected one of the highest health service fees in its state, the funds were not disclosed to the general budget manager and so duplicate expenditures were made from auxiliary funds and appropriated funds, with both the auxiliary director and student life director funding and managing very similar health education programs.

Extramural Funds

Postsecondary institutions generally derive income from grants and contracts. At the high end, this income can exceed hundreds of millions of dollars. At the low end, it can be measured in the tens of thousands. In any case, direct costs budgeted in each grant or contract are generally assigned for the purpose of the project and not transferable to other purposes.

A project to train migrant workers may have a substantial budget, but the granting agency expects funds to be directed toward project objectives—travel to migrant worker housing, tuition expenses for migrant workers, staff salaries, telecommunications, and so on. Funds cannot be shifted to non-project expenses such as technology used in the university library, salaries of general departmental secretaries, graduate student stipends for teaching assistants in introductory classes, or student scholarships.

Many federal grants reimburse the institution for "indirect costs" that are incidental but critical to project objectives. These expenses include utilities for project offices, administrative time, and custodial care of program space. Indirect costs are generally figured as a percentage of the direct costs and can provide flexibility in the institution's budget. Because custodial support, administrative salaries, and utilities are already budgeted, grant money frees general operating funds for other institutional practices. Since grants and contracts are often a key part of an institution's mission, it is a common practice to direct money generated by indirect costs to objectives related to grant and contract procurement.

Foundation Funds

Foundations have been established at almost all public institutions. Though they operate independently, their explicit purpose is to support the mission of the institution. Foundation income is generally from private gifts, special projects, and investments. Expenditures are free of state and federal restrictions that constrain the general operating budget.

The effectiveness of a foundation is measured in several ways. The first method is by determining the amount of funds raised through annual campaigns. This may include routine annual solicitations of alumni and friends via phone, mailings, or personal contacts. Another method is to determine funds gathered through capital campaigns or periodic fundraising efforts. These activities generally focus on special projects important to the development of the school. A campaign may occur over several years, procuring major gifts and pledges for an athletic complex, library, or scholarships. Funds may be raised through special projects such as sales of intellectual property generated through foundation assets, admissions receipts from foundation events, and sponsorships from university performing arts and athletic activities.

The success of a foundation is also measured by the growth of assets from year to year as well as the overall size of the endowment. The endowment is the total liquid and illiquid assets managed at any one time. Finally, the foundation can be judged by the total funds distributed in support of the college or university each year. This may be to all institutional interests, such as endowed chairs, equipment, and facilities, or specifically to scholarship support.

All funds of private institutions are generally free of restrictions imposed by state government. Consequently, foundations are not needed to avoid governmental restrictions. Further, a private school's development office can generate funds equivalent to those accrued through a public school's foundation. The growth may include tuition and fee revenue and overall value of the private school's endowment not expended in a given year. Finally, while foundations of public institutions operate independently, the equivalent body of a private institution is most often an integral part of the administration.

MATCH FUND SOURCE RESTRICTIONS WITH FUNDING NEEDS

Unfortunately, the use of funds generated by public postsecondary schools may be restricted based on the fund source. For example, in the state of Georgia, tuition cannot be discounted or used to provide scholarships, and it can be spent by the institution the day it is received. State appropriations carry similar restrictions but may be spent two years after the year in which they are earned. Neither can be used for student scholarships, athletic support, alcohol, or purchases of over $5,000 that have not been bid in the manner prescribed by the State Purchasing Manual. Also, on frequent occasions, the legislature restricts the use of tuition and appropriations for such purchases as vehicles and major equipment.

In Georgia, fee money can be used only for the explicit purpose for which the fee was generated, with athletic fees being used in part to provide athletic scholarships. Fees and appropriations cannot be carried forward from one year to another. Auxiliary funds (generated by dorm rents, food service deposits, parking fees, etc.) can be carried forward indefinitely. Foundation money can be used for nearly any legal purpose, including hospitality (including alcoholic beverages), student scholarships, athletic support, and major purchases from a single source. Foundation funds can also be carried forward and invested indefinitely in common financial vehicles including stocks, bonds, and bank instruments.

There may be a temptation by university administrators to align the budget authority to the fund source without regard to the funding need. For example, the director of auxiliary services may claim authority over all auxiliary income, including revenue from the bookstore, the residence hall, food services, the print shop, and parking. Allowing this to happen would cost the institution a major source of flexible funds and would deviate from the principle that money follows mission.

An example, based on funding restrictions at a major state system, makes the case. Auxiliary income, while relatively plentiful, is not needed to support mission-related critical needs. Although the bookstore generates substantial income, the expenses are fairly low—a few employees, utilities, modest advertising, and maintenance. It is not uncommon for the operation to accrue tens of thousands of dollars annually. At the same time, appropriation and tuition policy have resulted in the biology faculty not having an adequate vehicle for student work at a field station, and the state has imposed a freeze on the use of tuition and appropriations for vehicle purchases.

Given that there are no unmet needs in the bookstore that rival the need for a vehicle, the institution-wide budget committee should be able to recommend that bookstore revenue be used for the vehicle purchase (even against the objections of the director of auxiliary services). There are a lot of ways to justify this encroachment on the director's "turf"; the most simple is that money follows mission.

PROMOTE TRANSPARENCY OF INCOME AND EXPENDITURES

It has been said that no single factor is more likely to be associated with the failure of an organization than for key decision makers not to understand the budget. No single budget process or principle is as important as the recognition that money follows mission. Knowledge of this principle must be embraced by those concerned about the overall financing of the school as well as those operating at the lowest level. For money to follow mission, personnel at all levels must know the mission and income sources. They must know how to connect the two for the optimum advantage of the mission.

It is noteworthy that "money follows mission" examples exist outside of higher education. For example, top accountants at major public firms do not have offices. Their mission is fiscal support for firms that are distant from the home office. Securing office space in a single building would not be conducive to that mission and would be a drag on the budget.

Conversely, because they support firms across the country, much of their time is spent on the road. Obviously, their travel budgets are very large—money follows mission.

To the casual observer, MIT and Cal Tech have very "industrial" physical plants. There are few signature rooms with "picture postcard" architecture. Loading docks and ventilators are often the prominent architectural features. It is clear that institutional resources are directed to a physical plant that is optimal for engineering research and production.

Promoting knowledge of the institution's mission and budget processes should be a core part of institutional culture. One best practice is to view the budget units in the form of a pyramid, as illustrated in Figure 6.2. At the top of the pyramid would be the university budget council; at the bottom, each individual staff or faculty member with discretion over a set pool of funds. The top committee would advise the president and account for the oversight and, with the president, distribution of all fiscal resources. In the case of a moderate-sized state or private university, this could be over $200 million. A small technical school or community college budget might be under $5 million dollars. The very bottom of the pyramid might be occupied by the advisor of the school newspaper, who operates on a budget of several hundred dollars.

All funds at the lower echelons of the pyramid would be included in the upper echelons of the pyramid. Oversight and distribution of funds at the top echelon would be to the second echelon, oversight and distribution of second-echelon funds to the third, and so on.

As an example, the university budget council might assign funds to the academic affairs division or provost and council of deans. It might also distribute funds to the division of finance and administration through the vice president for administrative affairs and directors council. A portion would also go to the division of student life through the dean of students and council of student affairs directors.

The university budget council, through open sessions and public reporting, would determine the relative needs for each of the second echelon units. It would also establish

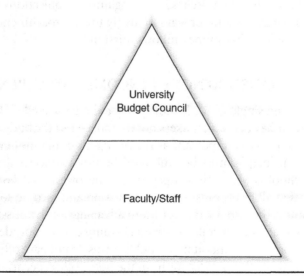

Figure 6.2 University Budget Council Structure

regulations on how funds would be expended. These regulations would include whether funds could be shifted from line item to line item (e.g., using operating money to hire personnel). The budget council might also establish budget policy for all levels based on input from those affected.

The university budget council would not direct expenditures for the second echelon or lower. For example, it might provide a line item of $40 million for academic faculty but would not determine how much would be allocated to each department or whom to hire in each department. This authority would rest with the provost and council of deans at the second level.

Similarly, the provost and deans would assign funds to each college and might establish additional regulations beyond those indicated by the university budget council. They might indicate the overall amount authorized for personnel in each college. The dean and council of chairs would determine the amount to be assigned to each department and the specific individuals to be employed. Finally, each academic department would receive an allocation for personnel, determine the specialty for each faculty line, and make the actual selection of faculty.

While respect for the authority of each level is important, one cannot understate the value of communication and consultation between levels. To maximize interaction, there should be substantial overlap between professionals at each level. The university budget council must have representatives from each level. Meetings must be open so that budget managers can understand directly how and why distributions are made at the upper echelons. There must be periodic opportunities to revisit the mission statement and conceptualize strategic plans in order to keep campus leaders focused on activities that support mission and plans alike.

The typical university budget council might include each of the vice presidents, a faculty member from each college, a couple of deans, the director of the physical plant, the human resources officer, the director of auxiliary services, and several members of the plant staff. Though non-voting members, deans and key directors should attend all meetings.

It is advisable that the council membership be over represented with faculty to emphasize that the mission is education and training, and that faculty are closest to the mission. Also, because the vice president for finance and administration has the closest functional knowledge of the budget, he or she may be the most important consultant to the council. The provost and vice president for academic affairs should chair the council—money follows mission.

Of course, the president should attend all meetings. He or she should set the tone for the council through strategic planning, periodic state-of-the-institution addresses, and reports to and from the governing board. He or she should also select and evaluate administrative personnel at the top echelon. Finally, as the council is advisory to the president, he or she should have ultimate budget authority.

INSTITUTION-WIDE FOCUS

The university budget council and each subsequent budget manager in the pyramid must possess all information relevant to the council or individual manager's authority. It is equally important that the information be presented in an easily understood manner. Owing to the complexity of most institutions, the actual budget document may be a 6-inch-thick sheaf of 15-inch-wide green bar sheets. While this level of detail may be needed for an individual budget manager or auditor, it is of little use to the university budget council. In fact, there is no possible way that a chief academic officer, dean, or plant manager will have the inclination, time, or ability to extract or aggregate critical information from all other entries.

It is important to provide budget summaries containing only the level of information needed by the budget manager or advisory group. As shown in Figure 6.3, this can be done in a page or two. The university budget council would generally focus on the overall balance of funds distributed to units, the relationship between income and expenditures (hopefully they balance), and the impact of major expenditures or revenues. It might also be concerned about year-to-day expenditures against revenue but would have little need for details regarding departmental personnel, equipment, or operating expenditures.

Though the council would work from a one- or two-page sheet containing this information, the institutional budget officer would have the green bar reports as back-up. He or she would also have the abstracted reports provided to managers and committees lower in the pyramid. These documents could be used to answer any questions requiring more granular responses.

ADOPT MODIFIED ZERO-BASED BUDGETING

Zero-based budgeting requires that all funds in the annual budget be zeroed out at year's end. Either the fund manager fully depletes the budget line item (i.e., spends all available funds) or the remaining funds are "swept up" at a given date and returned to the central budget, at which point a zero fund balance is indicated in the line item.

Each line item is replenished in the next fiscal year based on an indication of need as it pertains to the mission. In the extreme, all line items go to zero and returning funds in the next fiscal year must be fully defended. One year's budget may bear no relationship to funds assigned in the previous year.

The extreme version of zero-based budgeting is seldom used because few organizations are so dynamic as to require a full overhaul of all line-item distributions. At a technical school, the number of students in welding classes is set by the capacity of the facility. Since enrollment does not change from year to year, the number of instructors does not change. Consequently, there is little need to defend relatively stable personnel costs. The same would apply to materials, utilities, and supervisory expenses. In this case, all that would be addressed would be incremental inflation adjustments and possibly new expenditures required by changing missions or equipment made necessary by technological advancements.

Conversely, an electrical technology program may have a steady decline in enrollment. Without appropriate consideration and defense, the program may be substantially overstaffed. Annual review would result in funds being reduced in the personnel line item proportionate to the loss of students. Similar reductions could occur in supplies. Of course, the funds could be reassigned to programs with growth potential.

FY12 BUDGET – April 19, 2011 Assumptions: – 4 % enrollment decrease.	BASELINE	Based upon 9% reduction in state appropriations	4-19-11 – Update from the System Office	4-19-11 – less additional 2%	NOTES
1 REVENUES					
2 State Appropriation Revenue	48,849,407.00				
3 Less: ERS cost increases			601.00	601.00	
4 Less: Unemployment Insurance			23,766.00	23,766.00	
5 Add: Formula Funding increase	—				
6 Total State Appropriation Revenues	48,849,407.00	45,918,443.00	45,942,810.00	45,942,810.00	42% E&G Funds
7 Reductions from FY11 – 6% total	(2,930,964.00)				
8 REDUCTION TARGETS for FY12		(4,132,659.87)	(1,439,980.00)	(2,297,140.50)	
9 Tuition/Student Revenues					
10 Annual tuition projection (Includes: WebMBA, Erate, 12–15 CH, new stu)	47,853,337.92	47,853,337.92	47,853,337.92	47,853,337.92	
11 GOML	2,577,000.00	2,577,000.00	2,577,000.00	2,577,000.00	
12 Institutional Fee per student per semester (annualized)	8,022,246.97	8,022,246.97	8,022,246.97	8,022,246.97	$295 per student per semester
13 Total Tuition Revenues	58,452,584.89	58,452,584.89	58,452,584.89	58,452,584.89	56% E&G Funds
14 Other Revenues	2,568,734.00	2,568,734.00	2,568,734.00	2,568,734.00	
15 Other Estimated Lapse	3,000,000.00	3,000,000.00	5,000,000.00	5,000,000.00	
16 Academic Lapse funding	500,000.00	500,000.00	500,000.00	500,000.00	
17 Tuition Carryover from FY11 (One time funds)	1,543,729.00	1,543,729.00	1,543,729.00	1,543,729.00	
18 Interest and Dividends	175,000.00	175,000.00	175,000.00	175,000.00	
19 MRR Funds	1,400,000.00	1,400,000.00	1,400,000.00	1,400,000.00	
20 TOTAL REVENUES	112,158,490.89	109,425,831.02	114,142,877.89	113,285,717.39	
21 EXPENDITURES					
22 Off The Top					

(Continued)

Figure 6.3 (Continued)

	FY12 BUDGET – April 19, 2011 Assumptions: – 4% enrollment decrease.	BASELINE	Based upon 9% reduction in state appropriations	4-19-11 – Update from the System Office	4-19-11 – less additional 2%	NOTES
23	FY12 Estimated Expenditures from FY11 original and earlier scenarios	88,217,550.00	88,217,550.00	88,454,952.00	88,454,952.00	
24	ERS cost increases (employer matching)			601.00	601.00	
25	Unemployement Insurance, DOAS			23,766.00	23,766.00	
26	Electricity and Natural Gas Increase			285,651.75	285,651.75	
27	Employee Health Insurance Increase			732,848.54	732,848.54	
28	New Retiree Employer portion of Health Insurance			130,943.52	130,943.52	
29	GOML Expenditures	2,577,000.00	2,577,000.00	2,577,000.00	2,577,000.00	
30	Faculty FY11 from increased enrollment	1,446,229.00	1,446,229.00	1,446,229.00	1,446,229.00	
31	FY11 Academic Personnel Pool Additions	185,298.00	185,298.00	185,298.00	185,298.00	
32	FY11 Staff Personnel Additions – Finance and Admin	243,749.00	243,749.00	243,749.00	243,749.00	*131,187 Available*
33	FY11 Staff Personnel Additions – Student Affairs	68,373.00	68,373.00	68,373.00	68,373.00	*21,420 Available*
34	FY11 Staff Personnel Additions – Unaligned	65,284.00	65,284.00	65,284.00	65,284.00	*55,284 Available*
35	QEP	100,000.00	100,000.00	100,000.00	100,000.00	
36	Strategic Focus Pool	2,000,000.00	2,000,000.00	2,000,000.00	2,000,000.00	
37	Capital Fund (Bailey Addition)	2,700,000.00	1,605,491.00	1,605,491.00	1,605,491.00	
38	Capital Fund (Ashley Hall)		750,000.00	1,687,397.00	1,687,397.00	
39	Capital Fund (Ashley Hall) – MRR Funds		649,416.00	900,000.00	900,000.00	
40	Capital Fund – Remaining MRR Funds		250,584.00	—	—	

#						Notes
41	Restoring Operating Budgets by 10%			500,000.00	500,000.00	
42	**Subtotal**	97,603,483.00	98,158,974.00	101,007,583.81	101,007,583.81	
43	**Flexibility pools**					
44	University Pool for Deferred Maintenance, Enrollment, Utilities	3,233,995.24	842,956.98	2,373,655.66	2,547,929.95	
45	Capital Projects, unallocated	2,808,182.23	988,608.00	1,978,808.00	947,373.21	*Spring Release*
46	Tuition Carryover to FY13 (See Col E for Estimated Maximum Carryover) **One Time Funds**	1,512,910.14	1,512,910.14	1,512,910.14	1,512,910.14	*Maximum Tuition Carryover* 1,512,910.14
47	Flexibility Pool – **(One time funds)**	—	—	—	—	
48	**New Personnel**					
49	Academic Affairs for FY12 enrollment	—	—	—	—	*$0 allocated due to no anticipated enrollment growth.*
50	Academic Affairs Pool remaining for FY12 enrollment, including conversions	—	—	—	—	*$0 allocated due to no anticipated enrollment growth.*
51	Academic Promotions and Tenure	114,400.00	114,400.00	114,400.00	114,400.00	
52	FY12 Other Divisions Personnel additions	—	—	—	—	*$0 allocated due to no anticipated enrollment growth.* *Fall Release*
53	**Pools for Divisions:**					*Spring Release* *Pool Manager*
54	*Academic Affairs*					
55	Graduate Assistant Stipend Pool	500,000.00	700,000.00	500,000.00	500,000.00	

(Continued)

Figure 6.3 (Continued)

FY12 BUDGET – April 19, 2011 Assumptions: – 4 % enrollment decrease.		BASELINE	Based upon 9% reduction in state appropriations	4-19-11 – Update from the System Office	4-19-11 – less additional 2%	NOTES
56	Academic Equipment/Materials and Maintenance Pool	600,000.00	400,000.00	600,000.00	600,000.00	300,000.00
57	Library Reference/Special Collections	100,000.00	25,000.00	100,000.00	100,000.00	50,000.00
58	Faculty Scholarly Travel	200,000.00	175,000.00	200,000.00	200,000.00	100,000.00
59	Release Time for Research, Reassigned Time	200,000.00	140,000.00	200,000.00	200,000.00	100,000.00
60	Major Scientific Equipment for Research	250,000.00	200,000.00	250,000.00	250,000.00	125,000.00
61	Summer Faculty Pool	3,000,000.00	2,500,000.00	3,000,000.00	3,000,000.00	3,000,000.00
62	Erate Pool	150,000.00	100,000.00	150,000.00	150,000.00	75,000.00
63	Art Pool	50,000.00	50,000.00	50,000.00	50,000.00	50,000.00
64	*Finance and Administration*					
65	Instructional Setting Renovation Pool – MRR Funds	500,000.00	300,000.00	—	500,000.00	250,000.00
66	General Maintenance Pool	428,500.00	200,000.00	428,500.00	428,500.00	228,500.00
67	Vehicle Maintenance and Replacement Pool			170,000.00	170,000.00	85,000.00
68	Equipment Maintenance and Replacement Pool			100,000.00	100,000.00	50,000.00
69	*Student Affairs*			—	—	—
70	Student Affairs Equipment Pool	50,000.00	50,000.00	50,000.00	50,000.00	50,000.00
71	*Advancement*			—	—	—
72	Showcase University Events	50,000.00	10,000.00	50,000.00	50,000.00	50,000.00
73	*Unaligned*			—	—	—
74	Computer Replacement Pool	300,000.00	300,000.00	300,000.00	300,000.00	150,000.00
75	IT Infrastructure	400,000.00	400,000.00	400,000.00	400,000.00	200,000.00
76	**TOTAL EXPENDITURES**	112,051,470.61	107,167,849.12	114,035,857.61	113,178,697.11	2,335,000.00
77	**Estimate of Funds Available / (Further Reduction Needed)**	107,020.28	2,257,981.90	107,020.28	107,020.28	107,020.28

Figure 6.3 Sample Two-Page University Budget

Some form of zero-based budgeting is critical to all educational programs. However, as emphasized above, it is seldom rational to expect a full defense of every line item in a budget. In most educational institutions, tenure and employee loyalty create very stable employment patterns. Programs with declining enrollment may be staffed by fully tenured faculty members, making proportionate staff reductions either awkward or impossible. The opportunity to shift personnel funds to other programs occurs only upon the resignation of a faculty member.

The university budget council should identify line items that must be defended annually and others that are static (allowing for inflation adjustments). Alternatively, the council could assign a percentage of a unit's budget that must be defended annually. These practices allow funds to be redistributed based on the shifting needs of the institution. They avoid, however, defending funds that cannot or should not be shifted under any circumstance. This hybrid approach also conserves resources, as individual managers and budget committees can rest easy with stable base funding while focusing on strategic plans and marginal budget changes.

Rising enrollment and revenues present a unique opportunity. The budget committee can distribute funds following the same budget used in the past year. New funds resulting from enrollment/income increases can be assigned based on proposals that enhance the mission.

Declining enrollments and revenue present obvious problems. To bring order and avoid destructive concern, it is advisable to assign a budget reduction target proportionate to twice the loss expected in the overall budget. While strains on fiscal resources in the 1980s and 1990s were difficult (Mumper, 2001), the current state of the economy calls for new ways of dealing with reductions, which are unprecedented.

Individual units defending an increase should be referred back to the institutional budget reduction target or the proposed higher budget reduction. Doing so is politically charged and highly challenging. No budget manager wants to deal with budget reductions. It is not the loss of money that is distressing, it is the loss of valued personnel, promotion opportunities, merit salary increases, and other amenities that enhance morale in challenging times. The recommendation to deduct twice the amount needed to balance the budget and require a defense to earn funds back to the unit would seem to exaggerate the potential trauma.

The justification for following the recommendation lies in the next budget principle, which involves redistributing and investing one's way out of a budget challenge. Put in the form of a simple parable, no matter how bad conditions were for depression-era farmers, they would always buy seed, even if it meant depriving their families of gifts, clothing, even food. The next year's crop, resulting from this redistribution and investment, was the best chance the family had to break free of the bad economic circumstances.

Similarly, the best chance a school has to overcome challenging economic circumstances is to shift resources and energy from less productive activities that are peripheral to the mission to activities that may be more productive and mission centered. No matter how great the challenge, the budget process must provide an opportunity to shift funds to unfunded or underfunded activities that have a better chance of advancing the mission and returning revenue.

CREATE A STRATEGIC INITIATIVE POOL

Strategic planning and initiatives are the hallmarks of reengineering an institution. Research (Bolman & Deal, 2003; Middaugh, 2010; Morrill, 2007) points to strategic planning as a key first step. Once a plan is devised, action is needed; otherwise the plan simply sits on the shelf. Individual departments and colleges may engage in strategic planning and shift funds from existing activities to new programs as indicated by the plan.

In a similar manner, there should be a process that encourages strategic planning between units and facilitates the shifting of funds as appropriate. Since no single unit would have the funds, technical expertise, or interest to support interdepartmental initiatives like living-learning communities that integrate the academic curriculum with residence life, international programs that engage faculty from a number of departments and students from a number of nations, new athletic teams that require additional facilities, scholarships from university relations, and coaches who may be members of the faculty, a university-wide budget council facilitates the discussion and funding of such interdepartmental activities.

It is strongly recommended that the university budget council set aside a pool of money annually for broad-based strategic initiatives that cannot be accomplished with typical departmental allocations. Ideally, the money would come from increased institutional funding resulting from revenue sources discussed previously, such as enrollment growth, tuition increases, gifts to the school, increases in research indirect costs, and so on.

If such funds are not available, there may be an assessment to each budget area that is either "across the board" or based on centrality to the mission and productivity. The latter is the better of the two options, as it is consistent with the overarching principle that money follows mission. Across-the-board reductions are indiscriminate and will adversely affect mission-critical and marginal operations equally. They will also disproportionately affect offices with little discretionary budget. A 3% reduction may not be remarkable for a continuing education program that uses temporary part-time staff in rented class space. A 3% reduction to residence life, where 90% of the budget is spent for bond debt on new buildings and utilities, can be catastrophic.

Once the fund pool is established, the university budget council may request proposals for new funding from all campus constituents. Figure 6.4 shows a sample strategic initiative process. To ensure attention to interdisciplinary and cross-unit proposals, various vice presidents, deans, and directors may cultivate relationships that result in joint submissions. A proposal for a new athletic team may be fostered by the athletic director but also involve the facilities manager, provost, and vice president for university relations. A proposal for living-learning communities may be prompted by the dean of students but include the provost, dean of arts and sciences, and director of auxiliary services.

This request and the subsequent review of proposals should be consistent with the aforementioned principle of transparency. Specifically, the committee should establish the criteria for proposals and the method of evaluation in open session. All members of the academic community should have the opportunity to provide feedback on the standards. In some form, the standards should ensure that the successful proposals will be those that most directly advance the mission and have the greatest chance of being economically self-sustaining. To ensure that proposals deliver against their promise, it

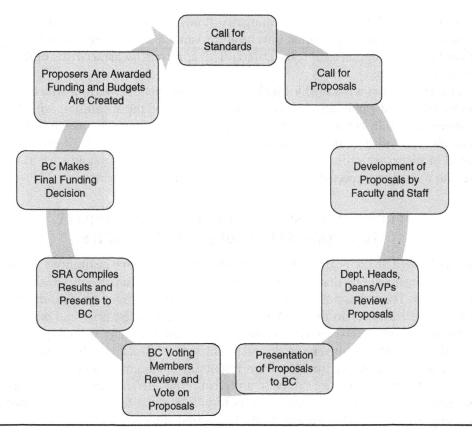

Figure 6.4 Sample Strategic Initiative Process

may be desirable to require that each new initiative be reviewed annually for three years. If the program delivers as proposed during that period, the funding becomes permanent and an annual defense is no longer required.

In keeping with the hierarchical budget authority discussed previously, it is desirable for all proposals to be reviewed and approved by higher-level budget managers within the institution. For example, a nursing educator responsible for basic skills instruction may have an idea for increasing lab size that requires funding for simulation units. The cost of the units would easily be covered by an increase in student/faculty ratio from 6:1 to 10:1. The faculty member would draft the proposal for review and approval by the coordinator of the basic skills center, then the proposal would be reviewed and approved by the dean of health sciences and chief academic officer. Finally, it would be reviewed and approved by the university budget council.

This example further illustrates the importance both of the hierarchical budget authority and of transparency. Acting in isolation, the university budget council would not be likely to assess the impact of the new lab arrangement on nursing accreditation, nor would it be fully sensitive to staffing issues in the nursing program. Because all meetings are open and reviews occur from the department up to the university budget council, issues of pedagogy, staffing, and accreditation would be addressed.

As described, the process for obtaining new funds should be clear and unambiguous. A faculty or staff member should thus be able to anticipate funding simply by judging his or her own proposal against the criteria. This approach is characteristic of the overall budget process.

This chapter has advocated a highly structured budget approach in which all processes are vetted publically, known by all members of the institution with budget authority, and fully consistent with the view that fiscal resources are assigned based on their ability to advance the institutional mission. Sadly, it would only be in the fantasy world of higher education that one could lay out a spending plan and stick to it. The need to manage unexpected events forms the basis of the next principle.

PROVIDE FOR SUFFICIENT BUDGET FLEXIBILITY TO ADDRESS PROBABLE CONTINGENCIES

As emphasized at the beginning of the chapter, postsecondary institutions are highly complex organizations that include a vast array of fund sources, each with its own restrictions. Their missions are not captured by a single activity like "promoting the most absorbent towel on the market" or "providing the lowest price and outstanding customer service." Postsecondary school missions generally refer to multiple areas of attention, such as "teaching, research, and public service." Teaching is frequently divided among wide-ranging departments, from restaurant management and performing arts to math and physics. Service can be to a myriad of private and public individuals and organizations. Research can range from multimillion-dollar federally funded institutes to a single faculty member evaluating stock selection strategies.

In short, the typical sources of income and diversity of mission in business and industry would be comparable to those of a jewelry store at the mall. The usual income sources are retail purchases and repairs; the mission is to sell high-quality jewelry in a trustworthy and friendly atmosphere. This is comparable in complexity to a single academic department at a postsecondary school. To extend the simile, a postsecondary institution is more like the entire mall, with each college or department resembling a store and a corner hotel, food court, and paid parking included.

The budget process must be sufficiently flexible to accommodate the diverse character of the institution. The wide range of income sources and mission-related activities exposes the school to a wide range of risks and opportunities. Any variable can change without warning, and a school must be able to react to an unexpected threat or unanticipated opportunity.

The "hurricane cone" often used in television weather is a good analogy for the planning and budget cycle. Budgets are generally planned three to six months from the start of the year, just as hurricane tracking often begins days or weeks ahead of landfall. Early on, little is known about the final path of the hurricane. The predicted path therefore begins across the breadth of a tropical depression and produces a very wide possible track. As the days pass and the hurricane forms and approaches land, more is known about atmospheric conditions, and the expected path becomes increasingly narrow. A week from landfall, the region predicted to be affected by the storm may cover two or three states; a day from landfall, the range may be a few miles.

Similarly, it is often impossible when budgeting to predict key variables with a high level of certainty. The further out from the first day of class, the less focused and more potentially inaccurate the prediction. As time passes and more accurate data are acquired from budget-related events (e.g., enrollment, fee payment, financial aid applications, residence hall receipts), the budget predictions become increasingly accurate.

Events that occur during the year may also be highly dynamic. Local boards and state legislatures have been known to remove portions of appropriated money mid-year. Utility companies may introduce a rate hike early in the year. Contract settlements may unexpectedly increase staff and faculty costs. The budget must be sufficiently flexible to adapt to these contingencies through "reserve" holdings or optional expenditures that can be made late in the year.

Early in the formation of a hurricane, forecasters inform the public of "remote" possibilities but encourage very basic planning. Regardless of how far out the eye of the storm is, residents should have an evacuation plan, and a plan to secure their structure. In other words, buy a few sheets of plywood and a map—just in case.

Administrators of postsecondary schools may need more than a few sheets of plywood and a map to adjust to the myriad of contingencies that may come their way. Strategies for ensuring flexibility differ from the time budget planning begins to the moment the budget is in force. Many institutions develop the first budget draft six months prior to the start of the fiscal year. Consistent with the earlier discussion of zero-based budgets and the high level of fixed expenses, the first draft appears remarkably similar to the previous year's budget.

Notwithstanding this tendency, there will be changes in circumstances that introduce small modifications. Most likely, there will have been salary increases, utility increases, enrollment changes, initiation of new programs, personnel changes, and so on. Obviously, the first budget scenario will reflect all of these changes. It will also reflect changing events that are anticipated throughout the year.

Like the hurricane prediction, however, that original scenario will only be a rough approximation of what will actually occur. Every couple of weeks until the start of the fiscal year, the institutional finance officer and institutional budget committee will evaluate the current scenario against any new information relevant to its appropriateness. Increased applications/expected enrollment, increased appropriations, a major gift, and so on may lead the committee to increase income and expenditures. Approval of a new program may lead to the redistribution of funds during the start-up year.

If the budget officer and committee judge that the changes require a better budget forecast, they may agree on a second budget scenario. Of course, this scenario would replace the original scenario. The process of evaluation and revision continues until the start of the fiscal year, at which time the last of the budget scenarios becomes the operating budget.

Incidentally, as scenarios are approved, the institutional budget director and/or committee may allow the eventual fund recipient to begin operating with the line item (or a portion of the line item) or may require that funds not be encumbered until the budget year begins. Obviously, personnel costs involving contractual staff would be released, while one-time non-essential purchases would be held.

Restrictions on funds and enrollment will determine the best course for maintaining flexibility. Below are several key approaches to engineering flexibility into the budget. Of course, others are possible.

DEFERRED ENROLLMENT AND INCOME

Some schools admit only a portion of available applicants. This practice offers the immediate advantage of ensuring that a budget problem is not the result of declining student numbers. The admissions office can always dig deep enough to fill the student ranks and the tuition-driven portion of the budget. If application rates are high, admissions can be increased to offset shortfalls in other budget sectors, such as declining appropriations or declining private gifts.

The process normally involves placing the most qualified students who are not admitted on a waiting list. As budget needs and the admissions yield (number of students admitted who enroll) materializes, the admissions office may accept wait-listed students. Of course, to meet a budget shortfall, students admitted from the wait list must be served at little additional cost over the value of tuition and appropriations (if available). The challenge of this approach is that as the school digs deeper into the wait list and overall applicant pool, the reported selectivity of the institution is diminished. The loss of status associated with reducing selectivity may further erode the institution's reputation and limit future applicant pools. In addition, serving additional students at little additional cost generally means increasing class size and instructional resources available on a per-student basis, which has a similarly negative impact on the reputation of the institution.

HOLDING FINANCIAL RESERVES

The institutional budget committee may establish a "contingency reserve" line item. If all goes well during the year, the fund will not be depleted and will be available for year-end capital projects (e.g., repairing cracked sidewalks, reroofing a building, creating a parkway). Of course, it can be drawn down to address a contingency such as lower than expected enrollment, unexpected damage to the physical plant, or higher salaries. It is important to maintain discipline in the use of this reserve. If the school needs to repair roofs, roof repair should be an explicit line item in the budget. Keeping it as a "contingency item" puts the physical plant at risk of deteriorating year after year while less important items are supported.

LOANS FROM OTHER FUND SOURCES

Many institutions have flexible fund sources that exist outside of the annual operating budget. A private school, for example, may have a substantial endowment that can be used for virtually all purposes. Public schools in many states can maintain a reserve that allows for flexible spending when challenging financial circumstances occur. Universities are rightly cautious about reducing their endowments or reserves; once those funds are eliminated, there are few options for handling a financial challenge other than reducing staff or cutting into critical programs. For this reason, a reduction in reserves or endowments is best treated as a short-term loan.

When an institution finds it necessary to draw funds against its reserves or endowment, the university budget council should draw up an explicit payback schedule as well as a budget scenario for the payback period that ensures that the fund is replenished. Obviously, this means that whatever circumstances caused the shortfall must be corrected and additional income and/or efficiencies identified. It is generally best to use a loan only when an explicit change in circumstances is expected. This may include the start of a new endowed fund, a change in state funding formula, or an amendment of tuition policy. If these guidelines aren't followed, the problems that required the loan may be magnified by the requirement to replenish the funds.

CONCLUSION

It is typical for faculty and staff to emphasize that higher education is not a business and should not be bound to strictures associated with commercial enterprise. To the contrary, postsecondary schools have income in the form of tuition and fees, and have expenses in the form of salaries and operating expenditures. The most successful institutions balance these elements, leaving substantial reserves to assure stability (Prowle & Morgan, 2005). Harvard, for example, carries an endowment that has exceeded $35 billion. This endowment can fluctuate by as much as $8 billion annually. Without a doubt, administrators at Harvard University are fully aware of dynamics involving income and expenses. In fact, more has been written about the management of a school's endowment relative to enrollment and educational expenditures than just about any topic in higher education.

This chapter repeatedly emphasized that planning and budgeting center on one dominant principle: money follows mission. Even the best financial managers can do a disservice to a university if they are unfamiliar with its priorities and thus do not support those priorities in the budget. One of the most interesting controversies in higher education is the extraordinary growth of the Harvard University endowment. Harvard's mission includes world-class teaching, research, and service. Many have argued that an insufficient amount of endowed funds are being directed to the mission. They would argue that the mission of Harvard University appears to be to grow its endowment.

The typical technical school, college, or university should have a well-developed mission statement, and there should be a strong connection between the allocation of resources and this statement. A majority of income for technical schools should be directed to facilities, supplies, and faculty that enable high-quality technical education. The budget of a research university should include major expenditures for scientific equipment, graduate assistantships, and research scholars. Community colleges should spend a majority of money on classroom instruction and facilities.

Of course, to make a connection between money and mission, all sources of funds and all expenditures should be known. A cynical observer might suggest that institutions that "hide" money from key decision makers do so to obscure inconsistencies between money and mission. There is no reason to hide that 80% of the institutional budget goes to high-quality faculty and staff or that references were acquired for the library. Conversely, there are far too many examples of schools that unknowingly pay for executive hotel suites, elegant homes, or luxury vehicles. These purchases are often hidden from those most directly concerned with achieving the mission of the institution.

REFERENCES

Barr, M. J. (2002). *Academic administrators guide to budgets and financial management*. Hoboken, NJ: Jossey-Bass.

Bolman, L. G., & Deal, T. E. (2003). *Reframing organizations: Artistry, choice and leadership* (3rd ed.). San Francisco: Jossey-Bass.

Brown, W. A., & Gamber, C. (2002). *Cost containment in higher education: Issues and recommendations* (Vol. 28). New York: John Wiley & Sons.

Chabotar, K. J. (2006). *Strategic finance: Planning and budgeting for boards, chief executives, and finance officers*. Washington DC: Association of Governing Boards of Universities and Colleges.

d'Ambrosio, M. B., & Ehrenberg, R. G. (Eds.). (2007). *Transformational change in higher education: Positioning colleges and universities for future success*. Northhampton, MA: Edward Elgar Publishing.

Kezar, A. J., & Lester, J. (2009). *Organizing for higher education: A guide for campus leaders*. San Francisco: Jossey-Bass.

Lasher, W. F., & Greene, D. L. (2001). College and university budgeting: What do we know? What do we need to know? In J. L. Yeager, G. M. Nelson, E. A. Potter, J. C. Weidman, & T. G. Zullo (Eds.), *ASHE Reader on Finance in Higher Education* (2nd ed.). Boston: Pearson Custom Publishing.

Mactaggart, T. (Ed.). (2007). *Academic turnarounds: Restoring vitality to challenged American colleges and universities*. Lanham, MD: Rowman & Littlefield.

Martin, J., & Samels, J. E. (2009). *Turnaround: Leading stressed colleges and universities to excellence*. Baltimore: The John Hopkins University Press.

Middaugh, M. F. (2010). *Planning and assessment in higher education: Demonstrating institutional effectiveness*. San Francisco: Jossey-Bass.

Miller, B. A. (2007). *Assessing organizational performance in higher education*. San Francisco: Jossey-Bass.

Morrill, R. L. (2007). *Strategic leadership: Integrating strategy and leadership in colleges and universities*. Lanham, MD: Rowman & Littlefield.

Mumper, M. (2001). State efforts to keep public colleges affordable in the face of fiscal stress. In Paulsen, M. B., & Smart, J. C. (Eds.), *The finance of higher education: Theory, research, policy and practice*. New York: Agathon Press.

Prowle, M., & Morgan, E. (2005). *Financial management and control in higher education*. New York: Routledge.

Weisbrod, B. A., Ballou, J. P., & Asch, E. D. (2008). *Mission and money: Understanding the university*. New York: Cambridge University Press.

Part II

Functional Activities of Institutions

7

A GUIDE TO THE DEVELOPMENT OF
AN INSTITUTIONAL STRATEGIC PLAN

John L. Yeager, Hana Addam El-Ghali, and Shruti Kumar

INTRODUCTION

This chapter discusses the purpose, development, and implementation of an institutional strategic plan. Globally, higher education is experiencing rapid changes, requiring postsecondary institutions and their students to adapt accordingly. These rapid changes are associated with increasing and competing stakeholder demands. Colleges and universities need a clear focus to achieve their missions—deliberate decisions are needed to steer an institution in a particular direction (Cowburn, 2005).

The literature points to several major drivers of change:

- Diminishing and changing availability of resources.
- Changing workforce requirements.
- Escalating postsecondary expenditures.
- Changing student diversity and enrollment patterns.
- Increased competition among the various postsecondary sectors.
- Changing institutional missions in response to external changes.
- Rapid growth and development of the community college sector.
- Increasing reliance on various modes of distance education.
- Rapid growth of the for-profit private education sector.

These drivers, coupled with a myriad of other domestic and global factors, make it increasingly difficult for higher education institutions to prosper and survive. No longer is it possible for an institution to simply react to whatever happens; rather, it must understand how new circumstances will affect its operations, and respond proactively.

The higher education scene began a critical evolution in the late 1960s and early 1970s and started to experience notable uncertainties in the latter decade as a result of the aforementioned demographic, economic, and technological fluctuations (Dooris,

Kelley, & Trainer, 2004). Many academic institutions began seeking new processes and procedures to respond to these emerging challenges.

At the same time, there was an increasing interest on the part of institutional boards of trustees, many with members from organizations outside of higher education such as business and industry, to investigate the applicability of business practices and procedures to the operation of higher education institutions—an approach encouraged by public and state agencies. Such practices included process reengineering, the application of multiple attribute decision models, facilities fast-tracking, zero-base budgeting, project management, benchmarking, and cafeteria benefit systems. The primary goals were to contain and reduce costs for both private and public institutions and to assist them in more effectively and efficiently achieving their stated vision and mission.

The public media repeatedly reported these changes and demanded that appropriate actions be taken, since the general public strongly believed that institutions of higher learning, through their practices and pricing policies, were denying many potential students access to a college education. Further, there was a growing concern on the part of the public that these institutions were not providing quality educational programs that enabled students to obtain jobs upon graduation.

Of particular interest both to the public and to higher education administrators, was the application of institutional planning and budgeting processes adopted from business and industry. It was believed that the combination of quality strategic planning processes and proven budgeting practices could significantly improve institutional effectiveness and efficiency. Strategic planning, which was increasingly being used by business and industry to address issues of organizational effectiveness, was of particular interest.

Organizational strategic planning stresses effectiveness. It is essential to do the important and right things, as opposed to doing the wrong things correctly with a high level of efficiency. Only effectiveness can foster mission success. The strategic plan is important because it provides a baseline for specifying the institution's future direction, priority setting, program development, resource allocation, and evaluation. Strategic planning is increasingly seen to be about learning and creativity, with the recognition that college and university leaders need to challenge assumptions and consider radically changing existing structures and processes (Dooris et al., 2004).

Strategic planning provides the tools and processes for developing a map that clearly charts organizational goals and pathways for achieving them. Creating an institutional planning process is an important, although often neglected, first step. Staff often want to begin "planning" immediately, without carefully considering the ramifications of their actions. This can lead to wasted resources or, worse, a failed planning effort—something from which an institution may have great difficulty recovering.

This chapter will provide university administrators with an effective approach for developing and implementing an institutional strategic plan. There are many types of organizational plans, such as operating plans, financial and budget plans, technology plans, project plans, academic plans, human resource plans, and enrollment plans; however, the strategic plan is *the* foundational institutional plan upon which all other plans rest. It's important to remember that a strategic plan is an institutional leadership document built on consensus and trust. The president is recognized as the leader of the

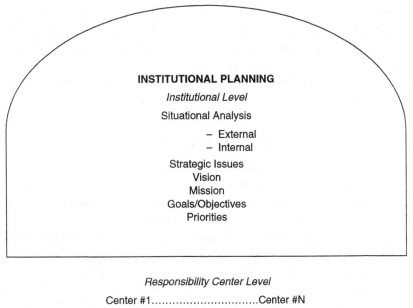

Figure 7.1 Conceptual Framework of a Strategic Plan

institution, although the board of trustees, supported by management, faculty, and staff, has ultimate responsibility and authority for institutional development.

Many conceptual frameworks are used in the organization and development of an institutional strategic plan. Figure 7.1 shows one example. This particular framework indicates that all parts are linked and reflects a top-down approach to strategic planning. At the institutional level, merging issues are identified, and institutional direction is determined by the vision, mission, goals, and planning priorities. These components in turn provide guidance to each of the subordinate academic and administrative planning units—the schools and departments where the actual work is conducted. Each of these entities then creates its own strategic plan within the given framework.

When developing an institutional strategic plan, it is vital to articulate to all relevant parties the steps to be followed. Colleges and universities are complex organizations, and if an institution-wide strategic plan is to be successfully elaborated, all participants and stakeholders must understand the process involved and commit themselves to completing tasks well and on time.

Therefore, the first step should be to develop the Plan to Plan, a formal document prepared and propagated by the institution's leadership to inform stakeholders of the specific priorities, and procedures to be integrated into the strategic planning process. This crucial roadmap explains both the need for the plan and the issues that must be considered (Steiner, 1979). The following sections provide an overview of each component of the Plan to Plan.

THE PLAN TO PLAN

Rationale and Purpose

The first component of the Plan to Plan justifies the development of the strategic plan. It is important to identify the particular needs of the given institution, as this will determine the steps to be followed and the various individuals and committees that should participate. The planning and execution of an institution-wide strategic plan is a significant and heavily resource-laden undertaking, and this needs to be clearly communicated. The president, in conjunction with the board of trustees, should therefore announce to the university community the rationale for establishing the new or revised plan. Such rationales cover a wide range of needs, as shown by the examples in Table 7.1.

The appointment of a new chief executive often triggers the development of a new strategic plan. Most new executives want to implement their own plan, not their predecessor's. The reason for developing the plan should be clearly and concisely articulated in a statement that identifies major current issues confronting the campus and acknowledges the success or limitations of past planning efforts.

Plan Specifications

The Plan Specification component informs stakeholders about what will be included in the plan and relevant planning parameters. It addresses such factors as the timeframe to be covered, the organizational units to be included (academic, research, student affairs, administrative), and the organizational levels to be considered (institutional, school, or department). Undergraduate students usually complete their degree within four to six years; this often becomes a major consideration in determining the length of the planning period. Most colleges' and universities' strategic plans cover 4 to 10 years. If a longer timeframe is required, the process should include a planning updating system.

The Specification section indicates not only the number of years to be covered by the plan but also the amount of time that will be devoted to the preparing the plan. For example, it could take a committee with modest previous planning experience between

Table 7.1 Examples of Reasons for Creating an Institutional Strategic Plan

1. Appointment of a new president
2. Changing student populations, such as the inclusion of coeducational programs
3. Emerging new competitors
4. Changes in the marketplace for graduates
5. Changes in availability of resources
6. State mandate that all public institutions develop a new or revised strategic plan

9 and 24 months to develop a strategic plan for an institution of medium size (4,000–8,000 students) and medium program complexity. Regardless of the exact amount of time and effort that will be needed, it should be recognized that developing and implementing the plan will demand significant resources. A truncated preparation period may lead to the omission of key elements required for a successful plan or prevent adequate involvement of the institutional community.

Finally, this component should specify any enterprise system plans that may be developed during the same timeframe. These plans might focus on a given organizational structure, process, or function of the enterprise, for example, institutional facilities, human resources, admissions, development, technology, or financial plans. If the institution is to be effectively managed, the strategic plan must be more than a simple summation of individual unit sub-plans and processes, which tend to fragment institutional planning. As useful as sub-plans may be, it is important to have a comprehensive map for major areas and functions that cut across the institution.

Organization of Planning Process

A major step in the development of any strategic plan is to determine the organizational units that will serve as the primary focus for planning. While it is possible to use functional areas such as research, public service, and instruction, this can make it difficult to analyze how resources are utilized. It is more pragmatic to use extant academic and operational budget units that parallel the resource allocation process. This facilitates the use of historical information and data interpretation and assists in directly aligning planning activities with resource allocation activities and institutional governance.

All participants should understand how the planning process will be organized. While there are many ways of structuring this process, there should always be a close alignment of the planning task structure and the institutions' organizational decision structure. Figure 7.2 illustrates a simplified organizational planning structure.

STRATEGIC PLANNING ORGANIZATION

Figure 7.2 Simplified Organizational Planning Structure

As indicated in Figure 7.2, the core of the organizational structure is a strategic planning committee (SPC) that reports to the president. Responsible for supervising and coordinating the entire planning process, the SPC oversees subcommittees devoted to specific areas such as external scanning, internal assessment, and vision and mission. The SPC typically receives staff support from the institution's planning office or office of institutional research.

The SPC performs essential planning functions, such as:

- Representing all key institutional constituencies.
- Providing leadership and oversight to the planning process.
- Designing and approving the planning process.
- Setting planning agenda and schedule.
- Receiving planning reviews and approving planning documents.
- Recommending planning documents to the president.
- Approving participants to serve on the various planning subcommittees.

Planning Roles and Responsibilities

Determining the roles and responsibilities of the people involved in the planning activities is another essential step in developing a strategic plan. It is critical to establish committees to assist in the planning process. If the plan is to include the best possible ideas, the best available minds must contribute to its development. Moreover, active encouragement of participant engagement can facilitate higher levels of "buy-in"; if faculty, administrators, staff, and students recognize that their ideas and suggestions are included they will more likely support and accept the planning process and the resulting plan.

There are a number of strategies for achieving effective participation. Planning subcommittees can be assembled from faculty and staff organizations or other elected governing bodies that have broad representation that cut across the institution, with care being taken to include as many categories of participants as reasonably possible. In addition, priority should be given to encouraging the best available minds to participate. This could be accomplished both by having some individuals with expertise that crosses multiple areas serve on several committees and by using nominations and/or appointments to help ensure that the best and the brightest will be *actively* engaged in the planning process. An invitation to participate from the provost or president can be very persuasive in recruiting outstanding committee members.

The committee selection process must reflect both the principles of representation and the need for creative and dedicated participants. While this process will presumably be challenged by numerous political agendas, individual interests and the academic and cultural traditions of the institution will likely provide the university community with sufficient direction and openness to engage in meaningful planning discussions. Most faculty and staff want to make valuable contributions to the planning process and have a voice in the organization's future direction.

Another way to facilitate participant engagement is to accompany institutional-level planning with the development of school and department plans, since most faculty are interested in plans that directly affect their programs. The vertical planning activities that will result will cut across multiple levels of the organization, helping to ensure active alignment and integration. Examining both horizontal and vertical impacts will make it easier to assess the overall effect of activities.

Key Committees

Key committees are essential for the development of the plan, as they provide structure for decision making. One approach to forming key committees is to determine the decision-making hierarchy that has been imposed on the organization as a result of its operations. A university's board of trustees is its highest decision-making entity and is thus key to the strategic planning process. Depending on a number of factors, such as size of the institution, the board may play a direct role in the process or may appoint a subcommittee to monitor and receive planning documents from the president and present them to the full board for information or approval. This subcommittee would work in close cooperation with the SPC. The board usually has the chief institutional planning officer (e.g., the director or coordinator of institutional planning), serving as its staff.

One of the most important committees to be selected by the president with board concurrence is the SPC, responsible for oversight of the planning process. The SPC appoints members to the various other planning committees and approves those committees' roles, responsibilities, charges, assigned tasks, and deadlines. It also reviews draft committee reports and can reject the material received or ask for modification as necessary. The SPC is the final institutional planning authority, subordinate only to the president and board. Its members should be recognized as both the de jure and de facto institutional leaders representing both faculty and staff in the planning process.

Although the board has final approval, it is the president's plan. In fact, in many cases one of the first tasks the board will assign to a new president is the development of an institutional strategic plan. Although the president may not publicly appear to play a major role in its preparation, the plan is recognized by all participants as a leadership document.

The SPC, with presidential consultation, usually appoints various ad hoc committees, such as an external scanning committee, an internal assessment committee, and a committee to examine institutional competitors. A number of other committees may also be established depending on the particular situation confronting an institution; these might focus on enrollment, technology, facilities, undergraduate education, graduate education, continuing education, or distance education. This approach allows individuals across the institution to contribute to the overall institutional strategic direction (Birnbaum, 2001).

While appointing a large number of committees has the advantage of increasing stakeholder involvement in the process, monitoring and coordinating the resulting work can be a difficult task. Also, it must be recognized that the participants are volunteers, most of whom have other, full- time assignments. The more participants that are involved in institution-wide projects, the greater the amount of time that will be necessary for meetings and the creation, review, and discussion of position papers to reach consensus, significantly slowing the process.

Three traditional planning subcommittees—external scanning, internal assessment, and competitor assessment—are of key importance. Their joint activities summarize the environment in which the plan will be developed.

Work Plan

The development and coordination of an institutional strategic plan is a major undertaking that requires not only a careful delineation of all work tasks but also an understanding of how the different tasks and decision processes are linked. Once the structural components of the Plan to Plan have been identified, a work plan should be designed to map the different tasks to be executed.

Among the various models that might be employed, the Program Evaluation and Review Technique (PERT) has proven to be effective. This technique makes it possible to specify and sequence tasks, allot time and resources, estimate work schedules, and assign responsibility for task completion. (Several desktop PC programs are available to assist in data and schedule preparation.) Further, the various reports, networks, and diagrams that PERT produces are excellent communication tools in that they can provide accurate status reports on different aspects of the project.

The Communication Plan

Good communication is indispensible throughout the planning process and key to its success. An important function of the SPC is to design and implement an effective communication system. It is imperative that the university community be kept informed of the development of the institutional plan; in too many cases, planning efforts that extend over several years lose their visibility, and therefore support, especially when the tasks involved are distributed across many participants.

It must be remembered that the development of an institutional strategic plan is not high on the individual agenda of many members of the university community. Further, with few exceptions, typically no one is hired for the explicit purpose of developing an institutional strategic plan. Faculty and staff fully understand that the institutional reward system awards little individual recognition for plan development activities; for example, the tenure system places little value on a faculty member's role in the development of administrative projects. Therefore, it is not surprising that strategic planning activities can quickly drop from an individual's radar screen, making it essential that the SPC develop a well-orchestrated communication strategy to continuously update the university community on the status of the plan and reiterate the importance of the plan to current and future institutional operations.

The objectives of the communication strategy are to inform and educate all constituencies engaged in the planning process of the status of the various activities, to distribute key planning documents to relevant parties, to continuously emphasize the importance of the process, and to facilitate the development and support of an institution-wide planning culture by actively soliciting broad-based participation. The following are examples of activities that might be included in a communication strategy:

- Sending letters and memos from the president or the chair of the SPC to university constituents concerning the status of planning activities and the completion of major milestones. The leadership must appear knowledgeable, interested, and supportive of the planning activities being conducted.
- Publishing in-house and alumni planning newsletters.

- Maintaining a strategic planning website that features information about the plan and provides an open-ended mechanism for receiving input from the university community.
- Conducting periodic open hearings that not only encourage the dissemination of information but also facilitate the questioning of plan specifics.
- Publishing products resulting from the planning process, such as the external scan, internal assessment, and school and department plans and policies.
- Holding school and department forums to discuss specific subunit planning activities.

Supporting Offices

Owing to the many support activities required to initiate and conduct a comprehensive planning process, it is often desirable or even necessary to have support for the SPC's activities through a senior level administrator's office (e.g., president, vice president). This can be accomplished by creating a new office, designating a planning associate, or expanding an existing unit, such as the office of institutional research. If possible, the last is probably the best solution, since the creation of a new office is likely to raise funding questions (i.e., where will the funds come from to support this effort?). Moreover, as the staff of the existing office will already have experience in developing and working with institutional data, only a modest temporary expansion may be necessary. If staff resources are sufficient, this office could be assigned responsibility for assisting the academic and administrative areas in developing their plans, coordinating planning activities across the institution, and conducting specialized studies related to the planning process. Regardless of the specific solution that is selected, it is imperative that sufficient staff be assigned since a large number of supporting tasks need to be completed; these range from preparing reports, collecting institutional data, and scheduling committee meetings to editing and publishing planning materials.

It is critical to estimate and provide sufficient resources, both fiscal and human, to support the planning processes. Many colleges and universities attempt to develop plans by reassigning staff from existing offices before verifying that there is sufficient organizational slack to accommodate a major increase in workload with no additional personnel or resources. This proves less than satisfactory if critical work goes neglected, deadlines are missed, and staff resentment builds due to workload pressures and the amount of overtime required.

Finally, if the institution has little planning experience it may decide to employ an external consultant to assist in designing the planning process and the plan. Care must be taken, however, that the resulting plan reflects the needs of the institution and not the consultants. In addition, key institutional representatives could attend strategic planning workshops conducted by entities such as the Society for College and University Planning or the Association for Institutional Research prior to working on the various planning committees.

DEVELOPING THE PLAN

The development of the strategic plan follows many of the steps specified in the Plan to Plan. Having specified its goals and objectives, the institution focuses on how to attain them in its current situation. It explores the principal external macro-trends and

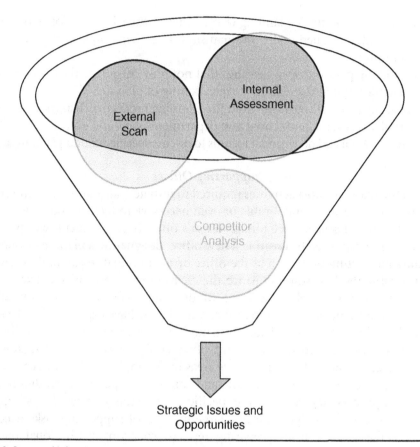

Figure 7.3 Sources of Information

internal micro-trends likely to influence the institution and its programs. The external scan looks at opportunities and threats; the internal assessment, at strengths and weaknesses. A third component is an analysis of existing or future competition in the higher education sector. Figure 7.3 presents a graphic of these concepts. Examples of competing institutions include those offering programs in the same geographical region or distance education programs; businesses and industries offering pre-seminar and in-service programs.

The situational analysis results in preliminary information that guides the selection of priority issues for which specific plans will be developed. This process not only identifies major external opportunities and threats, but also provides a basis for analysis of future program investments (Servier, 2000).

It is imperative that the situational analysis explore both micro and macro environments in examining the institution's individual circumstances and the local milieu. One of the first steps in this analysis is to identify who will be responsible for the process. Although all staff and committees play a role, leadership is necessary to ensure an inclusive approach. Once a leader has been chosen the scanning techniques may be selected.

In order to manage the large amount of information that could be generated by the situational analysis, it is useful to categorize internal factors as strengths and weaknesses and external environmental factors as opportunities and threats.

Conducting the External Scan

The external scan must be an organized process for determining the impact of external forces, which may involve actual events or potential trends relating to political environments, economic situations, social dynamics, technological advancements, demographics, competitors, or legislation. This scan highlights the importance of context and awareness of the external environment when considering the formulation and implementation of strategies (Cowburn, 2005). It is thus important to define potential threats and opportunities, as well as the institutional changes implied by those factors.

Responding to opportunities can propel the institution forward (Servier, 2000). For example, a new employer with educational needs could move into the area, or a national report could list the institution among the most tech-savvy in the country. On the other hand, threats such as a decline in the number of area high-school graduates, the collapse of a major employer of the institution's graduates, or an erosion of the tax base used to fund education in the state represent unfavorable trends or specific events that could lead to stagnation, decline, or demise of the institution or one of its programs (Servier, 2000).

Philip Kotler (1981) outlines three questions necessary to guide the analysis of the external environment:

- What are the major trends in the environment?
- What are the implications of these trends for the institution?
- What are the most significant threats and opportunities?

An external scanning committee needs to be established for the purpose of segmenting the environments into at least four primary areas: political, economic, social, and technological (PEST) (King & Cleland, 1987; Alfred, 2006). In many cases additional areas such as education or health are added to provide a more comprehensive map. A scanning process is then initiated to identify events and trends for each of these areas; these are in turn classified as opportunities or threats, which are often further classified by importance and potential impact.

Events and trends are identified through a variety of techniques, such as the establishment of a committee that systematically reviews journals or papers for potential topics, which it then researches, forwarding the results to the external scanning committee to determine their relevancy for inclusion in what is known as the Delphi process. This technique requires the use of an expert to guide the process and to provide feedback to participants. The Delphi panel typically consists of experts who are requested to respond to a series of questions concerning a preselected number of topics or issues. The panel is not permitted to know the individual responses of the various experts. A coordinator summarizes the responses, and this information is distributed to the panel, which again responds to the topic questions and may also be asked to justify their answers. Typically, after three or four rounds of questions a consensus begins to emerge. While this example is relatively simple, the exercises can be highly complex.

Finally, many planning offices gain substantial information by simply reviewing the strategic plans of other institutions, particularly those in similar sectors, such as community colleges, or within a defined geographical region.

Conducting the Internal Assessment

The internal assessment examines the situation within the institution itself. It looks at components such as—but not limited to—the institutional culture, key staff, financial resources, and operational capacity. By assembling and truthfully critiquing existing information about these subjects, the analysis provides insight into the institution's strengths and weaknesses. The internal environment can also be reviewed by creating an inventory of resources available within the institution and determining in which capacity these resources can function and be used.

Developing the Vision and Mission Statements

The vision and mission statements are the core of any higher education institution's strategic plan (Cowburn, 2005). These are companion pieces. Although many believe that they should be represented by two distinct documents, institutions often combine the statements, along with a brief history, into a single document, thereby orientating the organization in a comprehensive context. Many institutions of higher education share similar missions and compete to attain similar goals and objectives. Therefore, it is essential for the strategic planning process to shape the institution in ways that ensure mission attainment by capturing and maintaining a market niche in the quest for resources, faculty, and students (Dooris et al., 2004).

It has only been in the last half-century that institutions of higher education have seriously begun to engage in strategic planning, and many have only recently begun to develop institutional vision statements. Simply defined, a vision statement is an expression of how an organization would like to be perceived in the future. It is intended to identify the organization's core values and to reflect the level of quality and excellence being pursued. A vision statement should (1) focus on a better future, (2) motivate and inspire by encouraging individuals to pursue ambitions that will allow them to realize their hopes and dreams, (3) communicate enthusiasm and excitement, and (4) state positive outcomes.

The mission statement is the keystone of the organization and should define the organization's purpose, qualities, and contributions in clear, concise terms. Simply put, it states what the organization does and does not do. As stated by Ansoff (King & Cleland, p. 49), "It is the common thread that binds together the programs and activities of an organization." A mission statement should articulate the organization's fundamental purposes and goals, unique qualities and characteristics, key constituencies, geographic area of service, major areas of emphasis and commitment, and civic obligations.

An important function of the mission statement is to provide the criteria for judging what new programs should be initiated and what existing programs should be considered for termination. This is essential, since all programs and activities must support the organization's mission. Mission statements are almost clinical in style and have a past-to-present-oriented time frame.

Both the vision and mission statements should be regularly reviewed and widely disseminated throughout the organization. This is particularly important for colleges and universities since their purposes do not center on budgetary "bottom lines." As all subunits in the institution must support its overall goals, they all must clearly understand its mission. Indeed, one of the primary criteria for the existence of a subunit is the degree to which it supports the institution's mission. The mission statements of each subunit should thus reflect some aspect of the institutional mission.

At the institutional level, the mission statement is reflected through a series of goals and objectives. Each part of the mission statement should be supported by one or more goals. There are several types of goals: those that satisfy specific stakeholder groups, those that are designed to improve the institution's operating efficiency, those that are related to the institution's assets, and those that refer to organizational development. As goals are typically rather long term and broad in nature, making them difficult to measure, each goal statement should specify a series of measurable objectives. The assumption is that if objectives associated with a specific goal are successfully achieved, the goal will be achieved.

The institutional vision, mission, goals, and objectives flow down to the school and department levels that provide a structure and interconnect to frame and link institutional activities. Once the higher order goals and objectives have been selected, programs are prepared for the various subunits. It should be recognized that this is an iterative process, with program activities continually being adjusted. As program activities are developed, funding decisions are made, responsibilities are assigned, and evaluation processes are established in accordance with the objectives.

Program Development

Program development activities can be organized, planned, and evaluated based on the information generated from the internal and external analyses in association with the institutional mission statement, goals, and objectives. At the institutional level, consideration is given to the establishment or termination of major programs that span several organizational areas, for example a new program in computer-assisted instruction or international law. Since these programs are not exclusively part of a single department and could have institution-wide implications, they could become a joint school or central administration initiative.

It is anticipated that each school and its respective departments will be responsible, within the context of the institution's planning parameters, for developing a program agenda for the coming planning period. The academic plans will include a brief rationale and program description, as well as intended outcomes and resource requirements (estimated number of students, faculty, funding, facilities, and instructional and library resources).

Linking Strategic Planning to Resource Allocation

It is important to recognize the link between the planning and budgeting systems, and to understand the degree to which that link may be exploited. The relationship can be difficult to describe. Many times universities separate decision-making about academic planning, physical development, and finance from one another (Cowburn,

2005). The strategic plan describes the various activities that must be conducted, their relative importance, and their relationship to the overall mission and goals of the institution. Since these activities represent the core mission of the institution, they have a major claim on the institution's assets. In almost all cases, there is cost overlap because individual activities are interrelated, making it very difficult to determine the full cost of a given activity or any enhancement of performance that can result from an increment of additional resources. The plan provides the activities and direction and specifies associated budget requirements. One of the major purposes of the plan is to identify the critical requirements of the institution and to link these needs with institutional resources.

Almost all postsecondary institutions engage in an annual budget process that provides an opportunity to examine the current implementation status of the strategic plan, reexamine priorities, modify budgets based on performance, and assess the need for program modifications or termination. In addition, this is an ideal time to review new planning proposals. (It is assumed that throughout the previous fiscal year academic and administrative units were submitting new planning activities for funding consideration.) The strategic plan is exactly that: a plan; it is not cast in concrete and is based upon anticipated performance outcomes and changing external and internal conditions. Therefore, when conditions warrant, it can and should be modified to align with reality. The annual budget review process provides an ideal time not only to assess plan achievements over the last year, but also to review and modify goals and objectives for the coming year. It is also closely linked with the program evaluation process.

Plan Implementation

Strategic planning is of little value unless the plan is effectively implemented. It is therefore necessary to give due importance to the plan implementation process. Since there are often significant discrepancies between the ideal and reality and between aims and available capability and resources (Cowburn, 2005), an overall implementation plan must be developed.

Today, more and more administrators are asserting that the purpose of planning is not to make a plan but to make a change that can only be achieved through plan implementation (Dooris et al., 2004). The implementation plan basically provides a series of summaries and overviews of programs, budgets, and unit action plans, as well as specifying who is responsible for overseeing the implementation. It could be presented in the form of a project plan showing the sequencing of steps and the tasks and associated time schedule.

Developing action plans is the first step of the "doing" stage. Specific action plans need to be created for each objective and for each priority area. The task of developing the implementation plan is often assigned to a committee, although responsibility for the implementation itself typically falls to a single individual, usually the person in charge of the relevant unit or subunit. When this responsibility is distributed among several individuals, accountability becomes difficult.

Table 7.2 presents a simple format for an implementation plan. As shown, only a limited amount of information is required, primarily focusing on specific control. Naturally, larger, more complex initiatives involving several units would necessitate greater detail.

Table 7.2 Implementation Plan

FORMAT FOR ACTION PLAN			
Priority area:			
Goals/objectives:			
Associated strategy:			
Resource requirements:			
Action Plan	Person Responsible	Start Date	Evaluation Date
Stage-1 (Program details)			
Stage-2 (Implementation steps)			
Final stage (Completion)			

A frequent criticism of the strategic planning process is that it produces a document that ends up collecting dust on a shelf. In order to ensure that institutions approach the implementation of the plan seriously, the planning committee needs to adhere to the following guidelines (McNamara, 2007):

- Develop the implementation plan with the people who will be responsible for carrying it out.
- Ensure the plan is realistic and achievable in terms of time, personnel, and budget.
- Document and distribute the implementation plan, and invite review input from all affected parties.
- Organize the overall strategic plan into smaller action plans.
- Specify and clarify the roles and responsibilities of those who will be implementing the plan.
- Translate the strategic plan's actions into job descriptions and personnel performance reviews.
- Consider the use of project management techniques to manage the implementation process.
- Communicate the role of follow-ups to the plan.
- Appoint one staff person to chart the progress of implementation activities. This person should report to the president or provost.

Many people who contribute to the planning process expect their plans to be implemented exactly as described in the plan, which seldom happens. It is normal to deviate from the original plan. In fact, it is desirable to modify the plan in response to significant external or internal changes. A strategic plan should be seen as an evolving, living document (Cowburn, 2005). It is only a guideline, not a strict roadmap that must be followed under all circumstances.

Usually the institution ends up altering its direction during the period covered by the plan. Modifications to the plan usually result from changes in the institution's external environment and/or stakeholders' needs, which affect institutional goals, or changes in the availability of resources to carry out the original plan.

If the strategic planning committee is to be responsible for overseeing the revision and implementation process, that role must be carefully defined in terms of plan review and modification. Members of the implementation committee can be drawn from the original strategic planning committee, the benefit being that they will be very knowledgeable about the plan. However, a major drawback must be considered: Having already devoted a considerable amount of time to developing the initial plan, many may be reluctant to now assume responsibility for plan implementation.

An important aspect of deviating from the plan is knowing the reasons for doing so, that is, having a clear understanding of what's going on and why. McNamara (2007) has proposed some guidelines for changing the plan:

- Be sure some mechanism is identified for changing the plan. For example, what is causing changes to be made; why the changes should be made (the "why" is often different than "what" is causing the changes); the changes to be made, including to goals, objectives, responsibilities, and timelines. Always discuss and record what can be learned from previous planning activity to make the next strategic planning activity more efficient.
- During planning, clarify how the plan can be changed. A good approach is to require that any changes be approved by the board, if the changes might be to the overall mission, vision, values, and top-level goals, but not to the action plans. Any changes in action plans should require the approval of the unit where the actions will take place and the strategic planning committee that has oversight of the implementation process.
- If frequent changes are made, produce a new version of the plan. On plan revisions, note the change and reference previous versions. If changes are made several times a year, then a new plan document should be prepared. With faculty and staff turnover it is essential to have a written track of plan changes over time.

A final decision that must be made is when the plan revisions will be reviewed for implementation. Whenever a new revision is submitted, should it be reviewed and if approved implemented, or should a selective review be conducted on a regular basis, such as quarterly? Or should all reviews take place once a year at a specific time, such as during the annual budget review? While each process has its relative merits, it is important that a review process be selected and disseminated. Since many planning changes require the allocation of new funds, it makes sense to consider such reviews when annual budgets are being developed.

Monitoring and Evaluation

Monitoring and evaluation are increasingly emerging as indispensible activities for any institution looking to enhance itself. At the overall institution level, the responsibility for monitoring and evaluating the plan is also given to a committee, one of whose important roles is to recommend mid-course corrections triggered by unexpected environmental changes. Some changes may be major, such as dropping or adding a program or inclusion of a new program. These would go through the prescribed approval procedure of the institution. For example, the new program information requirements would include the following:

- The name of the originator.
- Identification of program to be developed or expanded.
- The objectives and reasons for the proposed change.
- A detailed description of the change.
- Effects, both short-term and long-term, of the change on various parts of the institution, such as libraries or computer centers.
- A description of an evaluation procedure to assess the attainment of the objectives.
- A detailed resource allocation plan including personnel and revenue sources and anticipated expenditures. (The plan should be multi-year, preferably covering a three- to five-year time frame.)
- Enrollment projections and special requirements.

The operating-level monitoring and evaluation of the programs and projects included in the strategic plan are also vital activities. This work is best carried out by the specific constituencies responsible for implementing the programs concerned. The institution must be extraordinarily vigilant and transparent in monitoring implementation efforts set forth in the plan, reporting results and taking corrective actions to ensure success. An important part is the development of relevant, meaningful indicators/metrics of progress towards strategic plan execution.

Responsibilities for Monitoring and Evaluation

In addition to designing a mechanism for monitoring and evaluating the plan, it is essential to identify the responsibilities expected throughout the process. The strategic plan should be monitored throughout its implementation, and decisions made based on the results. For example, the board might expect the chief executive to regularly report to the full board the status of implementation, including progress toward each of the overall strategic goals. In turn, the chief executive might expect regular status reports from middle managers regarding their assigned goals and objectives assigned (McNamara, 2007).

Senior management teams are generally responsible for monitoring the implementation of the strategic plan. They also need to establish a reporting mechanism to keep the university community informed of the progress being made (HEFCE, 2000). Senior management can obtain its monitoring information in various ways, for example (HEFCE, 2000) in an operating statement directly from the person responsible for implementing a task, through verbal or written reports from the senior manager overseeing implementation of a task, or by conducting a systematic evaluation. These can be regular or exception reports. It will help if the reporting formats and the frequency of reporting are decided in advance.

Key Questions While Monitoring and Evaluating the Implementation of the Plan
The key questions to be examined while monitoring and evaluating the status of the implementation of the plan include the following (McNamara, 2007):

- Are goals and objectives being achieved or not? If they are, then acknowledge, reward, and communicate the progress.
- Will the goals be achieved according to the timelines specified in the plan? If not, then why?
- Should the deadlines for completion be changed (be careful about making these changes—know why efforts are behind schedule before times are changed)?
- Do personnel have adequate resources (money, equipment, facilities, training, etc.) to achieve the goals?
- Are the goals and objectives still realistic?
- Should priorities be changed to put more focus on achieving the goals?
- Should the goals be changed?
- What can be learned from monitoring and evaluation to improve future planning activities and future monitoring and evaluation efforts?

Frequency of Monitoring and Evaluation
The frequency of reviews depends on the culture of the institution and the environment in which it is operating. Institutions experiencing rapid internal and/or external changes may want to monitor implementation of the plan at least monthly. Boards of directors should see the status of implementation at least quarterly; chief executives, at least monthly.

Monitoring can take place at several levels and at various frequencies depending upon the type of institutional structure (HEFCE, 2000). Table 7.3 gives examples of different types of monitoring at various levels and frequencies.

Reporting Results of Monitoring and Evaluation
It is essential to report the results of the monitoring and evaluation exercises conducted. Status reports should always be prepared and include specific updates on progress to goals as well as outlining any necessary next steps that are not already outlined in the plan. When highlighting an issue for attention, the monitoring report ought to propose a course of action (or offer alternatives) to deal with it, particularly in the case of financial reports (McNamara, 2007).

Developing and implementing a successful plan has several benefits. It provides a public statement as to direction, value, programs, and priorities; a mechanism to monitor external changes and develop responses; a baseline to ensure that progress is being achieved; and a baseline for quality improvement.

Annual Progress Report and Evaluation
The annual progress report and evaluation indicates the degree to which the plan is or is not being successfully implemented and those situations where expected outcomes have not met previously determined standards. A detailed analysis could be conducted to uncover the reasons for these unmet expectations, such as insufficient resources, increased competition or other changes in the external environment, a change in

Table 7.3 Monitoring at Various Levels

Level of Monitoring	Nature of Monitoring	Frequency
Overview	To maintain an ongoing awareness of progress on issues of timing, general significance, or financial impact To receive assurance that objectives and tasks are being implemented	At least annually
Management	To ensure that tasks are being implemented in accordance with the plan	Monthly
Financial	To provide a detailed review of a plan or project budget at the center	Monthly
Budget holder	To provide a detailed or general review of a plan or project budget at line management level	Monthly
Resources	To review resource use To review recruitment efforts and resources	Quarterly
Academic Quality	To provide a detailed or general review of quality assurance arrangements	Annually

organizational priorities or organizational economic status, new leadership, absence of appropriate technology, changes in consumer demand, or poor management or inadequate execution of plan implementation. Determining why an initiative failed can provide valuable lessons as to how future implementation processes can be modified to increase the likelihood of success.

Once this evaluation has been completed, the information can be used to adjust individual unit plans through changes in resource allocations, modification of activities, or even termination of activities. It is only through a careful formative assessment of performance over periods of time, coupled with a partial summative evaluation every few years, that an institution can obtain an accurate picture of its plan's effectiveness.

CONCLUSION

Institutional strategic planning involves a considerable investment of institutional time and resources, and if done correctly can provide a number of major benefits:

- A public articulation and declaration of the purpose and direction of the institution.
- A common understanding of the important external factors that might affect the institution.
- The identification of major internal weaknesses.
- A series of important initiatives to enable the institution to achieve major goals.
- The development of a participatory process to achieve a high level of community buy-in.
- A linkage between the budget and the plan.
- The creation of a baseline to judge institutional progress.

To achieve these benefits, it is necessary to develop a pre-plan (or a Plan to Plan) that carefully outlines and describes the process to be followed in the development of the strategic plan. As the president's leadership document, the plan must have widespread institutional support and provide a framework for institutional decision-making in terms of both academic and administrative functions. Key elements of the plan are the institution's mission and vision, which represent the foundation for all institutional development. Since a strategic plan, by definition, must represent how an institution will impact and be impacted by environmental changes, an external scanning process must be implemented in conjunction with an assessment of the institution's internal strengths and challenges.

Developing an open process and encouraging institution-wide participation can foster a culture of trust. The plan provides a framework for forming decisions to enhance the growth and success of the institution. It is not a precise set of specifications but rather a general set of propositions as to how the institution will respond to change, a strong force that can either help the institution move forward or hold it back in a competitive market. Since the plan is not set in concrete, it can be modified as necessary. Indeed, it is all about change and how the institution can adapt in pursuit of its vision and mission.

In conclusion, it is significant to acknowledge that the plan put forth by a postsecondary institution must combine the aspirations of academic departments with the global purposes of the entire institution (Duke, 1992). In today's competitive higher education marketplace, it is important to allow for differentiation, recognizing that significant effort and resources must be invested to ensure that an institution "stands out from the crowd" and attracts the students, staff, and resources it needs to fulfill its strategic objectives (Cowburn, 2005).

REFERENCES

Alfred, R. L. (2006). *Managing the big picture in colleges and universities: From tactics to strategy.* Westpost, CT: Praeger Publishers.

Al-Omari, A. A., & Salameh, K. M. (2009). Strategic planning effectiveness in Jordanian universities: Faculty members' and academic administrators' perspectives. *Research in Post-Compulsory Education, 14*(4), 415–428.

Birnbaum, R. (2001). *Management fads in higher education.* San Francisco: Jossey-Bass.

Bottom, T. L., Gutierrez, R. E., & Ferrari, J. R. (2010). Passing the torch: Maintaining faith-based university traditions during transition of leadership. *Education, 131*(1), 64–72.

Choban, M. C., Choban, G. M., & Choban, D. (2008). Strategic planning and decision making in higher education: What gets attention and what doesn't. *Assessment Update, 20*(2), 1–14.

Cowburn, S. (2005). Strategic planning in higher education: Fact or fiction? *Perspectives, 9*(4), 103–109.

Dooris, M. J., Kelley, J. M., & Trainer, J. F. (2004). Strategic planning in higher education. *New Directions for Higher Education, 2004*(123), 5–11.

Duke, C. (1992). *The learning university.* Buckingham, UK: SRHE/Open University.

Higher Education Funding Council for England. (2000). *Strategic planning in higher education: A guide for heads of institutions, senior managers and members of governing bodies.* No. 00/24). England: Higher Education Funding Council for England. Retrieved from http://www.hefce.ac.uk/pubs/hefce/2000/00_24.pdf

Kettunen, J., & Kantola, M. (2007). Strategic planning and quality assurance in the bologna process. *Perspectives: Policy & Practice in Higher Education, 11*(3), 67–73.

King, W. R., & Cleland, D. I. (1987). *Strategic planning and management handbook.* New York: Van Nostrand Reinhold Company.

Kotler, P., & Murphy, P. E. (1981). Strategic planning for higher education. *The Journal of Higher Education, 52*(5), 470–489.

McNamara, C. (2007). *Field guide to non-profit strategic planning and facilitation.* Minneapolis, MN: Authenticity Consulting.

Servier, R. A. (2000). *Strategic planning in higher education.* Washington, DC: CASE.

Sirat, M. B. (2010). Strategic planning directions of Malaysia's higher education: University autonomy in the midst of political uncertainties. *Higher Education, 59*(4), 461–473.

Steiner, G. A. (1979). *Strategic planning: What every manager must know.* New York: The Free Press.

Tolmie, F. (2005). The HEFCE guide to strategic planning: The need for a new approach. *Perspectives: Policy & Practice in Higher Education, 9*(4), 110–114.

Welsh, J. F., & Nunez, W. J. (2005). Faculty and administrative support for strategic planning: A comparison of two- and four-year institutions. *Community College Review, 32*(4), 20–39.

Welsh, J. F., Nunez, W. J., & Petrosko, J. (2006). Assessing and cultivating support for strategic planning: Searching for best practices in a reform environment. *Assessment & Evaluation in Higher Education, 31*(6), 693–708.

West, A. (2008). Being strategic in higher education management. *Perspectives: Policy & Practice in Higher Education, 12*(3), 73–77.

8

STRATEGIC PLANNING WHEN ALIGNING CURRICULUM AND RESOURCES

Steven T. Breslawski

INTRODUCTION

For millennia, man has attributed great importance to celestial alignments, believing them to be harbingers of great events. The location of the planets and stars determined the date on which the Roman emperor Julius Caesar was assassinated. In AD 96, 140 years later, the emperor Titus Flavius Domitianus was also killed by assassins. They chose the date and hour of his death based upon the alignment of the planet Mars, whose position in the sky suggested that the emperor's protection would be at its weakest.

IMPORTANCE OF ALIGNING CURRICULUM AND RESOURCES

This chapter and the next consider some organizational alignments that, while a bit more down to earth, are the key to unlocking the great mystery of organizational performance. Specifically addressed are the issues and challenges associated with three different alignments: (1) curriculum, (2) strategic, and (3) resource alignment. These three constructs have meaning as individual concepts as well as in gestalt, with the cumulative alignment of strategy, curriculum, and resources commonly referred to as *resource alignment*. The overarching goal of resource alignment, in concert with strategic and curriculum planning, is the effective allocation of available resources to the delivery of curricula.

This chapter discusses the importance of the strategic and curriculum planning environments in which resource alignment occurs, focusing on the significant challenges that tertiary education institutions face in this regard. In contrast, the next chapter focuses on some of the economic and tactical issues associated with resource alignment, including increasing curriculum capacity within the constraints imposed by the contemporary public policy and funding environment.

Given the decreasing support for higher education discussed in Chapter 1, the careful allocation of resources to curricula has never been more important. Done well, resource alignment will ensure a number of positive outcomes. First, resources devoted to delivering curricula will support the strategic goals of the institution. Second, resources expended will reflect the learning goals and outcomes defined by the institution's curricular units on behalf of its stakeholders. Third, resource alignment will help institutions to be more responsive to calls for improved outcomes in terms of the knowledge and skills possessed by the students that they graduate. Finally, alignment provides a necessary foundation as institutions seek to reduce per-student costs through increased efficiency and enhanced curriculum capacity. This will help educational institutions as they try to do more with less in response to the current funding environment.

This discussion of resource alignment, within the broader curricular and strategic context of higher education, is presented in five sections, the first of which has been this section on alignment of curriculum and resources. The next section introduces and defines the concepts of curriculum alignment and strategic alignment, and lays the foundation for understanding how both are important to successful resource alignment. The third section considers the issue of strategic curriculum planning, and discusses the challenges faced by many educational institutions. It makes the case that, despite the challenges, resource alignment efforts will be most effective in environments where strategic plans include a curriculum component. The strategic roles of curricula are also discussed. In the fourth section, the focus turns to actually achieving curriculum alignment, whose relationship to resource alignment is developed more fully. Matters of personnel, including aptitudes, buy-in, and training, are also considered. The chapter closes with concluding remarks and recommendations.

DEFINING ALIGNMENT

Resource alignment, in the context of higher education, requires the melding of two bodies of thought. The first, referred to as *curriculum alignment*, is a topic frequently encountered in the education literature. The second, referred to as *strategic alignment*, has been advanced by strategic management practitioners and theorists.

Curriculum Alignment

In the lingo of the discipline, curriculum alignment ensures that that which is written (i.e., educational standards/goals), that which is taught, and that which is tested are consistent. As perspectives on assessment have evolved beyond traditional testing, *learning outcomes assessment* now extends the curriculum alignment process to include assurance of learning. The concept of *curriculum alignment* has been discussed for some time, primarily in the K-12 education literature. English's work (1992) is seminal. Curriculum alignment has received increased attention in the K-12 literature in part due to some of the mandates associated with the No Child Left Behind legislation and the emergence of strong accountability frameworks adopted in many states (Dingman, 2010; Glatthorn, 1999).

More recently, authors have extended the alignment paradigm to include instructional resources such as media, technology, and library resources (Lowe, 2001). Others have contemplated extension of the basic concept to include better alignment of formal curriculum with informal learning that takes place in classrooms (Glatthorn, 1999). While the adoption of formal curriculum alignment processes has found increasing support among practitioners and in the literature, it also has its detractors. The most common derogatory characterization is "teaching to the test." See Wraga (1999) for a discussion of competing perspectives.

As learning outcomes assessment and assurance of learning have found more prominence in the regional and programmatic accreditation standards set forth for higher education organizations, the topic of curriculum alignment has been discussed with increasing frequency in the higher education literature. For the purposes of this chapter, curriculum alignment is defined as the process of ensuring that the subject matter taught in a course, the pedagogy employed for a course, and the assessment protocols assigned to the course are consistent with the learning goals established for that course. Resource alignment extends the curriculum alignment paradigm to include the allocation of resources sufficient to support the aligned curriculum, including resources to support assessment. Resource alignment and curriculum alignment are thus closely linked.

Strategic Alignment

The concept of strategic alignment comes from the management planning literature. Strategic alignment proponents espouse the critical importance of aligning functional area or subunit goals and activities with the strategic plan of the organization. Thus, an organization's human resources (HR) strategy, manufacturing strategy, logistics strategy, financial strategy, risk strategy, and information technology (IT) strategy must be consistent with its strategic plan and any changes in its strategic direction.

Consider, for example, a company that has decided, strategically, that it must internationalize its operations. The HR strategy has to evolve so that qualified candidates with aptitudes and interests related to international business can be hired or developed. The financial strategy has to evolve to include foreign currency transactions and hedges against exchange-rate fluctuations. The logistics strategy has to now consider potential problems associated with inventory crossing international borders, the navigation of customs processes, and the need to rely on international carriers for transport. The risk management strategy must protect the organization and its agents when an employee inadvertently violates international laws. In short, the plans and activities of an organization's subunits may need to change dramatically, to the point of undertaking activities that are completely novel, in order to perform consistently with the strategic direction of the organization.

Strategic alignment has been a challenge for many organizations. Consequently, various authors have proposed frameworks for achieving strategic alignment; see, for example, the Balanced Scorecard (Kaplan & Norton, 1996) and One Strategy (Sinofsky & Iansiti, 2009).

Failure to achieve strategic alignment can have profound negative consequences. The quintessential case study is Dell Computer®, a company that began with the (then) revolutionary idea of eliminating the middleman through the direct sale of computers to customers. However, after achieving monumental success with this model, Dell decided to augment its direct-to-consumer channel by partnering with major retailers, including Best Buy and Wal-Mart.

Traditionally, 85% of Dell's sales had been to businesses and government. Therefore, it did not have the systems in place to support individual consumer sales at retail locations. Many of Dell's operating divisions failed to plan for and implement the changes necessary to support retail operations. As a consequence, the company encountered significant problems in its retail endeavors. For example, numerous customers seeking warrantee service or software upgrades were told that they had passed their warrantee date and were no longer eligible for support, even though their receipt clearly indicated otherwise. The problem was that Dell's information systems indicated that the purchase date was not the retail purchase date, but rather the date that the big-box store purchased the computer from Dell.

Other problems included reliability issues due in part to additional product handling at retail and a product development process that failed to differentiate between the demands of the typical retail customer and those of Dell's traditional customers. The poor performance of the retail division, combined with a faltering economy, hardware glitches, and recent trends in consumer demand resulted in deteriorating financial and stock performance. This was followed by lawsuits and accounting scandals that culminated with stiff fines from the Securities and Exchange Commission. In short, failure to align company activities to changes in company strategy and the business environment led to a downward spiraling of performance. See Kopytoff (2010) and Vance and Helft (2010) for more details.

Strategic alignment is no less important for higher education institutions. Chapter 2 of this text discusses the strategic planning process in some detail. Planning must be followed by implementation and alignment. Alignment must be comprehensive and consider all aspects of the strategic plan i.e., alignment, like the strategic plan, pertains to all aspects of the organization. For higher education, this means alignment must include curriculum; this chapter thus focuses primarily on strategic alignment as it pertains to the curricular aspects of strategic planning.

The Relationship Between Strategic, Curriculum, and Resource Alignment

English (1992) supports his discussion of curriculum alignment with a triangular model that places the curriculum at the top, the teacher at the lower left, and the test at the lower right. Curriculum alignment is necessary to ensure that these three elements are consistent with one another, or aligned. Figure 8.1 presents a parallel model to convey the relationship between strategic, curriculum, and resource alignment.

Effective resource alignment depends on both competent curriculum alignment and consideration of curricular priorities within the strategic plan. Specifically, resource alignment and curriculum alignment efforts must be preceded by thoughtful and purposeful strategic curriculum planning (discussed in the next section). Thus, several key processes, required to ensure both a high-quality education and efficiency, are inexorably linked, as shown in Figure 8.2.

This chapter will attempt to make the case that an optimal allocation of resources cannot occur in the absence of competent strategic curriculum planning and without thoughtful curriculum alignment. An example will help support that assertion.

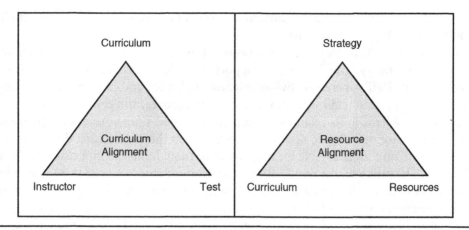

Figure 8.1 Curricula and Resources Applied Must Be Consistent with the Strategic Plan

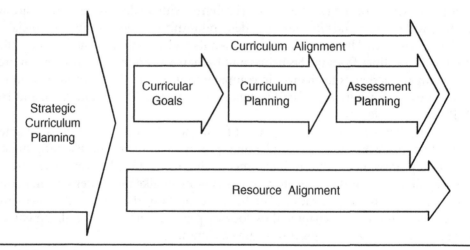

Figure 8.2 Resource Alignment Must Be Preceded by Strategic Curriculum Planning

Consider a hypothetical course, philosophy 101, taught at hypothetical institution XYZ University. How should resources be allocated to this course? Should the course be taught in a large lecture format or as a seminar? Should it be writing-intensive and/or require students to do substantial library research? Should it be staffed by full-time faculty or adjunct staffed? Do the faculty assigned to this course require Ph.D. credentials? How many sections should be offered? How extensive and intensive should the outcomes assessment process be? How many resources should be devoted to the assessment process?

These questions cannot be answered without understanding the role of this course in the broader curriculum and within the strategic context of the institution. Institutions offer courses for many reasons, some programmatic, others learning-related. These reasons include:

(a) Developing desired skills (e.g., communication, critical thinking);
(b) Remediating weak skills (e.g., math skills, reading skills, writing skills);
(c) Satisfying the requirements of licensure or mandate;
(d) Providing a foundation of knowledge necessary to succeed in a sequel course;
(e) Supporting a general education component of an undergraduate degree program;
(f) Supporting a program major, minor, or certification;
(g) Providing breadth or depth in subject offerings;
(h) Providing an integrative, capstone experience;
(i) Supporting the contemporary interest of some stakeholder group (including faculty); and
(j) Inertia: The course has been taught for many years and continues to be taught.

The reasons listed above are not intended to be either mutually exclusive or collectively exhaustive, but rather to make the point that it is necessary to understand the role and purpose of a course, and the strategic role of the program(s) it supports, in order to properly assign resources to the course.

STRATEGIC CURRICULUM PLANNING

This section addresses the importance of strategic curricular planning, the planning and alignment challenges faced by institutions of higher education, and the strategic role that curricula play as the institution assembles its competitive portfolio of programs.

As discussed in Chapter 2, the strategic planning process helps determine how an organization will define and fulfill its mission, compete with other organizations, and distinguish itself from competitors. For educational institutions, curricular planning decisions (including curricula offered, scope, focus, and delivery methods) represent a critical aspect of competitive differentiation and are a primary determinant of revenues and costs. For this reason, the importance of strategic curriculum planning as a prerequisite to resource alignment cannot be overstated. A strategic curriculum plan must be included in the outcome of any strategic planning process (see Figure 8.3).

Challenges to Planning and Alignment

Educational institutions are not the only organizations that find strategic planning and alignment difficult. Even if a stellar plan is produced, implementation presents its own challenges. To draw an analogy, wedding vows are fairly simple to utter; following through on them is the real challenge. The challenges faced by educational institutions can be organized into four groups: (1) challenges faced by any organization (business and non-business alike), (2) challenges stemming from the unique nature of postsecondary schools and curricula, (3) challenges due to organizational structure, and (4) the expertise and interests of college personnel.

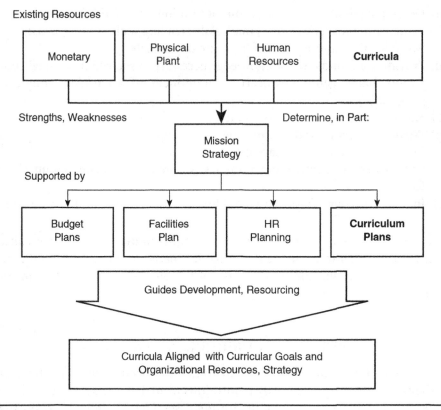

Figure 8.3 Curriculum Is an Important Component of Strategic Planning

Challenges Faced by All Organizations

Studies of organizations with alignment problems (e.g., Miller, 1997) reveal four common underpinnings of misalignment:

1. *The strategic planning process is flawed:* It's impossible to align a bad strategic plan. Therefore, a robust planning process is crucial to avoid strategy misalignment. The vision may be brilliant, but vision and goals must be driven down into the organization through detailed planning and execution. A poor strategic planning process will fail to adequately define goals that are concise and measurable. Plans often lack detailed operational planning and change management components. Most of all, plans often fail to assign specific responsibility for activities and deliverables. A fundamental tenet of organizational management is that if no one is responsible for a task, the task is unlikely to be completed. The devil is in the details (although a concise executive summary is also nice).

2. *Faulty strategic plan governance:* Plan governance is essentially a form of project management and ensures that the plan is managed through to execution. Plan governance requires that the plan goals are consistently measured and brought back in line quickly if the organization heads off course. Without governance, strategy misalignment will almost certainly occur.

3. *Poor communication of the strategic plan:* Alignment requires the development of a communications strategy that includes helping individuals who will be responsible for the plan's success to know what it is they are expected to do, when they are expected to do it, and what the deliverables are to be. Failure to communicate the plan nearly guarantees strategic misalignment down the road. The plan should define who needs to know what, when they need to know it, how they'll be expected to execute a given portion of the plan, and how communication will be maintained moving forward. An important part of communication is periodically reporting progress and success while also acknowledging challenges and shortcomings.

4. *Poor buy-in and motivation:* Unfortunately, especially when an organization has a history of poor strategic planning and plan execution, cynicism can creep into the ranks and the plan can become an administrative charade. If the rewards structure of the organization is not aligned with the plan, it is difficult to generate and maintain buy-in and ownership. It is important for individuals at all ranks to develop the sense that the plan's success will help them succeed and prosper in their professional life.

The Nature of Colleges and Curricula

While the four pitfalls delineated above are germane to all organizations, they seem to be particularly salient in the domain of higher education, especially with regard to strategic curriculum planning. It is striking to discover the frequency with which a strategic curriculum plan or a curriculum planning process is omitted from a college's or university's strategic plan. References to curriculum are often limited to platitudes such as "strengthen existing programs" or broadly stated goals such as "increase graduate enrollments by 20%." However, there is rarely a serious assessment and articulation of how existing or proposed programs fit into the strategic goals of the institution.

There are a number of reasons that postsecondary institutions fail to consider curricula explicitly in their strategic plans. To begin with, educational institutions are relatively new entrants to the realm of strategic planning and are therefore notoriously bad at developing strategic plans. Strategic planning begins with defining a mission (i.e., a purpose for existence). Many educational institutions were established by mandate and thus, to some, their reason for existence is a matter of franchise rather than contemplation. Similarly, their programs (curricula) exist because they always have; the notion that programs should serve a (sometimes competitive) purpose is a foreign concept. The "not-for-profit" designation assigned to many colleges and universities may play a factor in diminishing the competitive focus of their strategic plan. However, an old adage reminds us that "just because an organization is not-for-profit does not mean it has to be for loss." A strategic evaluation of existing and planned programs is always important.

Another reason curriculum is frequently absent from the strategic plans of educational institutions may be that these plans are often developed in a spirit of collaborative, shared governance. While this may assist in developing buy-in to the plan, the resulting mission statement often lacks focus and instead describes an institution that is everything to everyone. The mission statement may describe (or justify) the school as it is rather than as it should be. In the absence of a more dictatorial structure, it may be difficult to identify programs and courses that lack strategic value and should thus be subject to

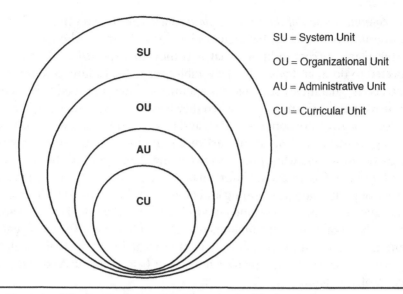

SU = System Unit

OU = Organizational Unit

AU = Administrative Unit

CU = Curricular Unit

Figure 8.4 Alignment and Planning May Be Inconsistent Across Levels of the Organization

termination or diminished with regard to resources. Tenure and seniority rights come into play as well. Educational institutions do not like to retrench programs; it is an ugly business. Strategic curriculum planning may be viewed as a "Pandora's Box" that no one wants to open.

As always, honesty is the best policy. It is important that faculty and staff in each academic program understand how their curriculum fits into the strategic plan of the institution. This will help them to better understand budget and resource decisions made in support of the strategic plan. If there is a discord between the personal aspirations of some individuals and the strategic role that they (and the program they support) play in the institution, those individuals can make more informed choices about their continuing professional development, career path, and future with the school.

Impediments Due to Administrative Structures

A final but key reason that strategic curriculum planning is difficult for educational institutions has to do with their often concentric organizational structure, as depicted in Figure 8.4. It is clear from the discussion in Chapter 1 that educational institutions vary greatly in their administrative structure; however, in whole or in part, Figure 8.4 is representative of the organizational context in which a great number of educational institutions operate. This unique context, in which strategies evolve and curricula are typically designed and delivered, presents some very real challenges. In explaining this assertion, it is helpful to begin by defining a few terms.

- *Curricular Unit (CU):* Refers here to the organizational unit within an educational institution that is directly responsible for the design and delivery of a particular curriculum. Typical names include area, program, or department. An individual commonly referred to as a head, director, coordinator, or chair has administrative authority to assign resources to ensure that a curriculum is implemented and curricular goals are achieved. This individual typically has direct supervisory control over the faculty delivering said curriculum.

- *Administrative Unit (AU):* Refers to a high-level span of (primarily administrative and resource) control that includes one or more CUs. Common names include school, college, or division. The AU may span a set of closely related curricular units (e.g., college of applied sciences, school of medicine) or, alternatively, the AU may span a set of CUs that have a common purpose (e.g., division of continuing education). An individual such as a dean, director, or assistant provost is charged with administrative and budget oversight for the AU.

- *Organizational Unit (OU):* The aggregate organization in which educational services are delivered (i.e., the educational institution itself). As delineated in Chapter 2, the OU may be a community college, major research institution, liberal arts college, or trade school. An individual with a title such as president, working with a board of directors, is commonly responsible for developing a vision, mission, and brand for the OU and for developing corresponding strategies for achieving the mission.

- *System Unit (SU):* The OU may be part of a broader SU (e.g., state university system) and subject to the policy requirements, political concerns, and resource constraints set forth by that system. While organizational theory would suggest that policy directives at the highest (SU) level of the organization would be highly strategic in nature and, as such, far removed from the curriculum and operational decisions of the CU, the opposite may be true. Liberal course transfer policies or lax transfer student admission policies set forth by the SU may make it difficult for the CU to ensure that certain learning outcomes are achieved and measured. General education mandates set forth by the SU may limit or complicate curriculum design decisions and reduce the OU's control over the assignment of resources. SU policies may limit the degree to which the OU, AU, or CU is able to develop the resources necessary to obtain curricular goals, forcing curriculum and resource decisions (e.g., class size, staffing levels) that conflict with strategic and curricular goals of the lower levels.

Depending on mandates, statutes, tradition, or leadership preferences and skills, strategic curriculum planning may occur, in whole or part, at any level of the organization. A poor plan (or constraints imposed by a plan) at any level will impact the ability of inner levels to align resources and curriculum.

A second impediment to strategic alignment is that in higher education, strategic planning has traditionally been viewed as something done by administrators at the OU level, while curriculum design and implementation has been viewed as the franchise of the faculty at the CU level. In such environments, a curriculum planning component is likely to be absent from strategic plans. Often, curriculum design and implementation has more to do with the interests and expertise of the faculty than the broader strategic goals of the institution.

However, curriculum decisions can be made at any level of the organization. For example, in secondary education, curricula are often specified (mandated) by an authorized board or committee at the SU level. Curricular decisions can be made at the SU level in tertiary education as well. For example, at the system (SU) level, the organization may adopt a cost-reduction strategy that limits duplication of programs. Consider a hypothetical state university system consisting of 20 campuses. The SU's plan may dictate that any particular program (e.g., a bachelor of arts in psychology degree) will be offered by at most five campuses. This limitation will obviously place constraints on the strategic plans of the 20 campus units in terms of programs offered.

Another example might be a CU accredited by an organization that requires it to develop detailed strategic plans that define its mission and differentiate its programs from other business programs. During accreditation review, the CU is judged on the degree to which its curricula, and the resources that support them, are consistent with its stated mission. However, it is very difficult to do meaningful strategic curriculum planning at the CU level if plans are nebulous or absent at the AU and OU levels. The CU cannot develop strategic plans without guidance, authorization, and buy-in at the AU and OU levels. Further, strategic planning at the CU level cannot run counter to plans at the AU and OU level.

Thus, curriculum planning can occur at any level of the organization, but the curriculum planning process may or may not be strategic in nature or related to the institution's strategic plan. However, resource alignment will be most effective if strategic plans at each level contain a curricular component, even if that component is nothing more than a coordinated and purposeful delegation of curriculum decisions to the next lower level of the hierarchy. For example, the SU of a state university system may delegate any and all curriculum decisions to the OU level.

The Expertise and Interests of College Personnel

One strategic planning and alignment problem that is unique to institutions of higher education has to do with the expertise, skills, and abilities of the individuals involved in the planning process. Administrators at universities are often culled from the faculty ranks. Many administrative assignments are temporary in nature. The consequence is that those charged with developing and implementing strategic plans at each level are likely to differ greatly in their understanding of strategic planning, the skill level they bring to the task, and the importance they place on the task. The degree of coordination in planning, between levels, can vary greatly. Very much like outcomes assessment, strategic curriculum planning does not work very well if people are doing it only because they have been told that they should do it or that they have to do it. Benefits are likely to accrue only if the individuals involved embrace the purpose and importance of strategic planning. In another similarity to outcomes assessment, buy-in from the faculty is particularly important if strategic curriculum planning is to be meaningful and if alignment is to occur. As discussed later in this chapter, organizations may need to invest heavily in training and education in order to convey the importance of, and methods for, competent strategic curriculum planning.

Because of these challenges, strategic plans and implementation efforts have the potential to be ineffective. As illustrated in Figure 8.5, multiple agents will be "pulling" in different ways (i.e., the organization will lack unity of purpose). Under these circumstances, alignment of curriculum and resources will be very difficult and will likely produce sub-optimal results.

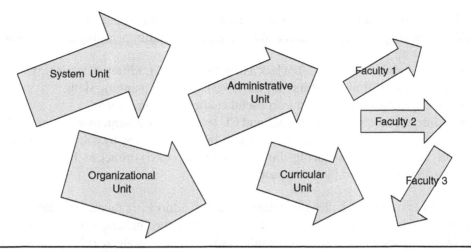

Figure 8.5 Plans, Efforts, and Resources Lack Unity of Purpose—Faculty Act as Free Agents

In contrast to Figure 8.5, an ideal strategic planning process will be competently executed at each level of the organization and coordinated with organizational levels above and below. Strategic plans at all levels will be explicit and purposeful in their consideration of curricula as tools for achieving the mission of the institution. The individuals involved will be knowledgeable about developing missions and strategies and have the leadership skills necessary to develop buy-in from those impacted by their plans. When this level of coordination and curricular planning occurs, the organization is more likely to be unified in its purpose and more successful at moving in the desired direction; see Figure 8.6.

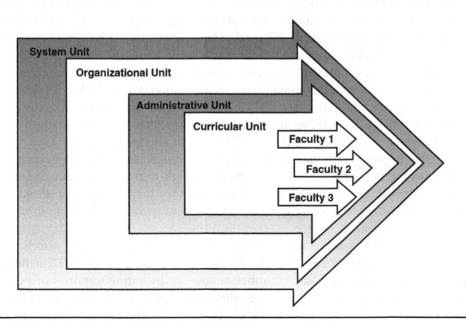

Figure 8.6 Coordinated Planning at Each Level Leads to Unity in Purpose and Direction

To summarize, educational organizations face the following challenges when undertaking strategic planning in general and strategic curriculum planning in particular:

- Educational institutions often lack a long history and tradition of strategic planning.
- Educational administrators may have weak strategic planning skills.
- Strategic plans often lack a purposeful curriculum component.
- Strategic plans at the SU, OU, AU, and CU levels may be absent, weak, or inconsistent.
- At any level of the organization, buy-in by those affected by a strategic plan may be lacking. Without faculty buy-in, faculty are likely to act as free agents with regard to what and how they teach.

An awareness of these challenges is the first step to addressing them. Training and professional guidance from experts are important. Once the challenges are addressed, the institution will be in a position to consider and specify the strategic role(s) of each of its programs and curricula.

Strategic Roles of Curricula

With regard to strategic curriculum planning, one of the most important decisions that any educational institution must make is to determine what academic programs it will offer and what strategic role each will play. As summarized in Table 8.1, the reasons for offering various programs, and the courses that support them, are myriad.

The first programs referenced in Table 8.1 are those designated strategically as *medallion programs* (i.e., programs of priority and strong repute for which the institution is to be known). Typically, the prominent reputation of a medallion program will attract students, faculty, resources, and employers from outside the normal calling population of the institution. There are profound resource implications for assigning this designation to a program. Specialized facilities and equipment will need to be updated and maintained on a regular basis. Courses will need to be staffed by individuals that have a strong reputation in their field. Course offerings may need to be extensive and include a high degree of specialization. It may be crucial to obtain and maintain program accreditation and to devote the resources required to meet accreditation standards. Accreditation standards are likely to limit class sizes and adjunct staffing as well as require a substantive assessment initiative. Even if they do not, it may be difficult to maintain program reputation if class sizes are too large or the use of adjunct faculty too pervasive.

To maintain program reputation, entrance requirements are likely to be competitive, resulting in a high-parameter student body. While high-parameter students are unlikely to need remedial courses (which saves resources), they may require specialized placement support or other types of support (e.g., visa and specialized housing support for international students).

Another reason that an institution might choose to offer a program is perceived *high demand* (i.e., the program is popular among the calling population). Demand for a program can be inferred from a number of sources, including inquiries of potential students and their parents, search terms entered by visitors to the institution's website, or the student career interest survey published annually by the National Research Center for College and University Admissions, a not-for-profit organization.

High-demand programs are strategically important as they can bolster institutional enrollments and generate strong, steady cash flows (thereby supporting smaller, esoteric programs). According to the College Board, between 50% and 70% of college students will change their major at least once. It is likely, therefore, that a strategy of attracting students to high-demand programs will serve a secondary purpose of providing enrollments for less popular or less visible programs, as some of the students in the popular program will probably change their course of study.

Running large (popular) programs has obvious resource consequences. The program and curriculum must be structured to efficiently manage large numbers of students. This might include running large course sections or, alternatively, many smaller sections. If many sections of a course are offered, reliance on adjunct faculty resources may increase, as will the need to coordinate course content and assessment protocols. Support services, such as academic advisement, must also be conducted in an efficient manner (e.g., in a web-based or mass advisement format). More time and thought may need to be devoted to course, room, and facilities scheduling. Depending on institution and program entrance requirements, large programs are likely to contain a broad

Table 8.1 Strategic Aspects of Various Program Types

Program Type	Strategic Role of Program	Resource Implications
Medallion	Program of high repute, used to attract local and non-local students to the institution (OU)	Program is heavily resourced in terms of Ph.D. faculty, specialized (depth) course offerings, support staff, program marketing, etc. Program accreditation likely to be maintained. Enrollments may be carefully managed
High-Demand	Responds to popular demand and bolsters institutional enrollments. Strong cash flows help pay for smaller, esoteric programs	Program structured to efficiently manage large numbers of students (e.g., larger sections, mass advisement, increased use of adjunct faculty to ensure sufficient staffing)
Niche	Responds to niche presented by local environment, e.g., a Southern California school offers specialized degrees in seaport management and container logistics	Program may receive support from local business partners. Program may be practice-focused and include strong experiential learning component
Complementary	Program is a logical complement to existing programs and used to convey a sense of "completeness" of program offerings	Program likely to share foundation and core courses with existing programs, with incremental resources required to staff specialization courses
Mission-Obligated	Program is almost necessitated by mission of institution, e.g., a liberal arts school will have a general education program	Resources required will vary with the scope and purpose of program and how it is intended to support the mission of the institution
Inertial	No strategic role. Program exists because it has always existed	Institution should decide whether this program can be incorporated into its strategic goals or whether resources might be better applied elsewhere

spectrum of students, with a substantial number needing tutorial or remedial support. The institution will need to work purposely to develop a sense of community so that students do not feel "lost in the crowd."

Resources applied to large programs can vary drastically. Consider that an institution may choose to designate one of its large programs as a medallion program; this will demand a serious commitment of resources. At the opposite end of the spectrum is a large program that acts as a cash cow for the university. A cash cow is the term applied to one of the four categories (quadrants) in the Boston Consulting Group (BCG) market growth/market share matrix (Stern & Stalk, 1998). Cash cows generate substantial revenue while consuming minimal resources.

Another strategic role is the *niche program*. A niche program, as the name suggests, is an institutional response to a specialized educational need, often pertaining to localized circumstances or stakeholder(s) that have unique needs. For example, a school near Las Vegas may provide specialized education opportunities for casino workers or managers. A school near Los Angeles (and its seaport) might offer programs focused on international trade and maritime logistics or specialized programs associated with some aspect of the music or film industry. A niche program may emphasize practice over theory and may include significant experiential learning opportunities for students.

Niche programs offer a (strategic) opportunity for the educational institution to set itself apart and may provide development opportunities if the institution is effective at developing strong relationships with key stakeholders. Stakeholders may be willing to provide external funding support for the program, donate specialized equipment, arrange for guest speakers for classes, support experiential learning opportunities for students, and offer placement opportunities for program graduates.

While niche programs provide certain strategic opportunities, they can be unique in their resource requirements. The liaison function, for the purpose of maintaining strong relationships between the niche program and key stakeholders, is critical. Experiential learning opportunities need to be identified on an ongoing basis and practicum experiences need to be supervised. Specialized equipment or facilities may be required. The applied nature of many niche programs suggests the need to staff courses with (or provide other exposure to) practitioners and not just theorists.

Complementary programs provide an opportunity for the institution to convey an air of completeness, focus, or "one-stop shopping." By sharing a common foundation and core component with other programs, a complementary program will allow the institution to offer a broader curriculum with minimal incremental resources. For example, it may be relatively easy for a university with several traditional engineering programs (electrical, mechanical, and civil) to add programs in materials engineering, nano-engineering, and environmental engineering with very few incremental resources (assuming the programs share the same foundation courses). As a result, the school will appear to have more of an engineering focus. The breadth of offerings at this institution may attract students who want to go into engineering but are unsure of what type.

The resource implications, however, are important to understand. A complementary program will generate enrollments in both shared and specialized courses. If, for example, the shared courses are slightly under-enrolled in their current state, the addition of a few students in a complementary program may increase enrollments in core courses to an optimal size. However, the institution will also need to be willing to allocate resources to staff a few specialty seminars with potentially low enrollments. Worse yet, if core courses are already full, the few extra students generated by the complementary program may require more sections of core courses *and* tolerance of small enrollments for specialty seminars. Enrollment and section planning become very important in this context.

Mission-obligated programs are those that are arguably required given the mission of the institution. A liberal arts college must have a general education program that ensures that each student gets a broad exposure to the liberal arts. A denominational school is almost obliged to have a program called "religious studies" (or its equivalent).

However, an institution has many degrees of freedom in determining the scope and nature of a mission-obligated program and the resources to be expended. In the case of general education, schools vary greatly with regard to use of large vs. small lecture, adjunct vs. full-time faculty, required course structure, and breadth of course offerings. An institution that has many liberal arts programs may be able to compose its general education program entirely from the foundation courses required by the various liberal arts degrees. In contrast, an institution with a technical focus may have to develop general education courses for no purpose other than to provide a general education core for its students.

In contrast to the program types described above, an *inertial program* exists for no other reason than that it has always existed. Unfortunately inertial programs are often more the rule than the exception. An inertial program may be a strong program by some metric or it may be a weak program, but its status and existence is happenstance rather than purposeful and planned.

A number of factors can contribute to the existence of inertial programs. For example, tenure and union contracts may make it difficult for institutions to shut down certain programs and shift resources to emerging needs. However, the reasons that inertial programs exist can always be summarized as lack of strategic curriculum planning. In an environment that embraces such planning, inertial programs do not exist; all programs contribute (in a planned way) to the mission and/or the competitive strategy of the institution. An optimal allocation of resources to the delivery of curriculum cannot occur without thoughtful inclusion of curriculum in the strategic planning process.

ACHIEVING CURRICULUM ALIGNMENT

Once the strategic role of a curriculum has been specified and a preliminary budget range for the curriculum is available, it is time to pursue curriculum alignment. This section considers activities associated with curriculum alignment in the higher education context, including the establishment of specific educational goals. It examines challenges and how to address them, focusing primarily on the training that is likely to be required. Also discussed is the possibility of broadening the curriculum alignment concept from the alignment of a single course to the alignment of a complex and integrated curriculum through comprehensive curriculum planning. The section concludes with thoughts on how the aforementioned issues relate to the alignment of resources and curriculum.

Establishment of Learning Goals

At its most basic and focused level, curriculum alignment is the process of making sure that students are taught that which they are expected to learn. This requires that (1) learning goals are identified, (2) corresponding curricula are developed and specified with some detail, and (3) competent instruction (consistent with the curriculum design) takes place. Assessment is the process that determines the degree to which learning goals have been achieved (see Figure 8.7). Assessment may be embedded within instructional delivery as a part of normal classroom activities or it may occur "downstream" in the form of a criterion- or norm-referenced exam, e.g., a state or national exam (see McGehee & Griffith, 2001 for a discussion of these terms). As Figure 8.7 illustrates, curriculum alignment, similarly to assessment, is never "done," rather it is an iterative process informed by assessment outcomes.

The traditional alignment paradigm begins with the establishment of educational goals relating to both knowledge and skills. These goals should reflect the requirements of various stakeholders and may reflect national and state curriculum standards, educational traditions, and/or mandates by state legislatures, boards of regents or their equivalents, and accrediting bodies. Goals may also result from benchmark comparisons with other institutions or recognized educational best practices.

Once goals are established, a curricular response can be devised and an assessment protocol developed. Table 8.2 depicts two curricular responses to a national standard; the first response demonstrates weak alignment, the second demonstrates improved alignment (Council, 2001).

Alignment is easiest to achieve when educational goals are clear and well-articulated. Unfortunately, any educational goal—even one of recognized importance—can be expressed with varied levels of specificity and scope. For example, consider the following goals associated with students understanding the concept of the 75th percentile:

- Students will define and explain the concept of the 75th percentile of a data set.
- Students will identify the score that represents the 75th percentile in a data set.
- Students will identify the definition of the 75th percentile from a multiple-choice list.
- Students will use the PERCENTRANK spreadsheet function to identify the 75th percentile of a data set.

Each definition requires a different assessment and may require different pedagogy and/or different resources (e.g., access to computer software).

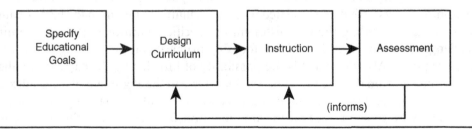

Figure 8.7 Alignment Requires Goals, Design, Instruction, and Assessment to Be Consistent

Table 8.2 Varying Degrees of Alignment Between Curriculum, Instruction, and Assessment

Goal	Alignment	Local Curriculum	Instruction	Assessment
Topic/Course: World War I (U.S. History or World History class) National Standards: The student will be able to analyze cause–effect relationships pertaining to WWI	Poorly Aligned	A curricular unit is designed to focus on causes, consequences, and major developments of WWI	The instructor teaches about the weapons used during WWI	The unit test assesses student knowledge of the effect of WWI on the home population of the United States
The student will understand the global scope, outcome, and human costs of WWI	Alignment Improved	A curricular unit is designed to focus on causes, consequences, and major development of WWI. The unit is also designed to help students determine cause–effect relationships	The instructor has students read primary and secondary sources of information focused on WWI and create flow charts showing cause–effect relationships pertaining to the war	Students present and explain their flow charts to their peers and are evaluated by their instructor and peers using a rubric designed by the class under the instructor's guidance

The example above suggests that goal specification may be difficult even when the construct to be learned (the 75th percentile) is fairly well defined. Many educational outcomes are more difficult to define. For example, we can all agree that it is important that students write well. However, we may be less certain how to specify the associated outcome goal(s). Consider three possibilities:

- Students will be able to compose a paragraph whose meaning and sentence structure is easy to comprehend; the student's writing will incorporate basic rules of grammar.
- Students will be able to write narrative texts for varied purposes.
- Students will be able to propose and support ideas using facts, opinions, examples, and details appropriate to audience and purpose.

Each of these goal statements is relevant to the broad goal of writing well. Each, however, has a different focus, implying different pedagogies and resources required.

The "write well" example above is a specific instance of a broader class of learning outcomes sometimes referred to collectively as "soft skills." Examples of outcomes related to soft-skill development include:

- Students are able to independently conduct online research.
- Students are able to make an effective presentation.
- Students are able to compare and contrast competing solutions to a problem.
- Students are able to work effectively in teams.
- Students are able to determine cause-and-effect relationships.
- Students are able to think critically.

While it may be clear that these are important outcome goals, it is unclear whether these outcomes belong to any particular subject matter or course. It is also unclear whether they should be "taught" in a single course, taught in a single course and reinforced in others, or taught sequentially across several courses. Faculty and programs will need to work collaboratively to determine appropriate curricular solutions and assessment protocols, consistent with available resources. Administrators will need to recognize that, done well, this is not a trivial task. Workloads and rewards systems will need to be adjusted to encourage success.

Curriculum alignment, like strategic curriculum planning, is a required condition if resources are to be effectively assigned to curricula. Consider a course that is designed, in part, to focus on development of writing skills and presentation skills. Suppose also that the instructional design requires students to give three impromptu presentations and complete a series of significant written assignments, intended as platforms to provide detailed constructive feedback to students on their writing. Suppose further that this feedback is iterative and accompanied by several opportunities for students to revise and resubmit work. Unless significant additional instructional resources were assigned to this course, it is unlikely that this curriculum design could be well executed in a 500-student large-lecture format. Any instructor assigned to the course would need to be skilled at coaching both oral presentations and writing.

Thus, the outcome of the curriculum alignment process will place constraints on how resources are applied to a curriculum and to the individual courses within that curriculum; curriculum alignment is a necessary companion to resource alignment. Given that a particular curricular solution will exceed the resources made available to a program via the strategic planning process, it is likely that alignment of curriculum and resources will need to occur concurrently as suggested in Figure 8.2 and iteratively as suggested in Figure 8.7. It is a waste of time to specify a curricular design only to find out that the necessary resources are not available.

While a well-aligned curriculum design is a necessary condition for effective resource alignment, it is not a sufficient condition. Faculty buy-in and ownership of the curriculum design (including assessment) must occur for the design to be successful. Sufficient resources must be made available to support the assessment process, and assessment measures and results must be actionable if the curriculum design and instruction are to evolve to address gaps suggested by assessment results.

Obstacles to Curriculum Alignment

The success of curriculum alignment (and, therefore, resource alignment) is subject to the competence with which the four processes identified in Figure 8.7 are executed. These processes have been discussed in the primary and secondary education literature for some time; trained career specialists are now available to support the alignment process, either as full-time school district staff or as consultants.

In contrast, curriculum alignment (including assessment) is very much in its nascent stages for many postsecondary schools. As discussed below and summarized in Table 8.3, higher education institutions face a number of challenges related to curriculum alignment.

Table 8.3 Hurdles to Achieving Curriculum Alignment

Issues and Challenges for Curriculum Alignment in Higher Education	
Issue to Be Addressed	**Challenges**
Novel nature of the task	Many tertiary CUs have never undergone a comprehensive curriculum review and alignment process
Nature of faculty expertise	Likely to be narrowly focused in a particular academic domain related to program of instruction. Not likely to be focused on curriculum design and assessment
Faculty roles and rewards	Unlikely to recognize stewardship of curriculum. Unlikely to hold faculty accountable for broader curriculum outcomes (e.g., development of soft skills)
Ownership of curriculum	Likely to be course-/faculty-centric. Faculty may be hesitant to give deference to, or participate in, a broader curriculum design
Reactive nature of traditional curriculum oversight	Curriculum design and oversight needs to be comprehensive, integrative, planned, and process driven. However, it is more likely to be reactive to specific course-/faculty-centric proposal
Academic freedom	Need to allay fears that academic freedom is curtailed by curriculum planning, alignment, and assessment

Faculty Expertise

In higher education, curricula are often devised by faculty whose training and background are unlikely to encompass the intricacies of education theory. In most university disciplines, faculty training and expertise are generally associated with researching a very narrow subject matter. Ph.D. faculty are unlikely to have significant training in issues of curriculum design and it is doubtful that they would be hired for their expertise in these areas.

Consequently, there is often a discord between faculty expertise and the expertise required for broad curriculum planning. This discord is likely to be exacerbated as higher education relies increasingly on part-time staffing to meet budget constraints. Adjunct staffing relationships are apt to be ephemeral, and adjuncts are likely to be hired for their expertise in a subject area, not for their stewardship of curricula and expertise in curriculum design.

Faculty Roles and Rewards

A second challenge is that traditional faculty roles and rewards systems may undervalue curriculum development and stewardship efforts. Recognition and incentive systems are much more likely to reward stellar teaching evaluations, strong publication records, and successful procurement of grants than they are to reward stewardship of the broader curriculum design. Senior faculty, through happenstance, may develop an interest in curriculum design and integration as they mature in their career and teach a broader set of courses. However, curriculum alignment is too important a process to leave to the chance that someone's stewardship interests will evolve in a helpful way.

Ownership of Curriculum

In primary and secondary education, curricula are often devised or dictated by a board of regents or other body of authority. A parallel structure may be seen in higher education when licensure is involved (e.g., nursing programs or registered accounting (CPA) programs). Organizations that grant professional accreditation may also dictate certain curriculum content, but the requirements are generally broad, leaving the details to the curricular unit (CU).

In the absence of discipline-specific standards, curriculum is generally developed at the CU level. In environments where faculty expertise is narrowly focused, individual courses, their content, and the pedagogy applied are often proposed and "owned" by specific faculty. Courses may be developed as stand-alone silos, with little consideration given to integration between courses and with limited thought expended on broader curricular goals. Goals such as "develop the students' ability to test ideas and evidence" and "develop the capacity of students to plan and manage their own learning" are likely to be included in the curriculum only if they happen to serve a particular course.

A Tradition of Reactive Oversight

In many academic settings, curriculum oversight is assigned to a committee. However, traditional curriculum committees are often reactive bodies (i.e., they respond to a proposal, perhaps for a new course or perhaps for a program change). The committee considers the proposal, then approves it, rejects it, or makes a recommendation to a higher authority.

In contrast, the role and outcome of curriculum alignment is prescriptive rather than reactive. Integration requires faculty to cooperate and coordinate amongst themselves and to relinquish ownership of courses and their content. For many institutions and faculty, this represents a major shift in how they view curriculum development, ownership, and oversight. Without proper training, education, and buy-in, resistance to change is probable. Concerns over academic freedom are likely to develop.

Academic Freedom

Academic freedom has long been a controversial but cherished privilege granted to the stewards of higher education. Curriculum alignment and assessment planning have emerged as lightning rods for charges that academic freedom is being curtailed.

Edward Deming, referred to as the "father" of total quality management (TQM), delineated the 14 fundamental principles of his approach. One of these is "Drive out fear." With regard to academic freedom, it is important to anticipate faculty concerns and, as discussed in the next section, help faculty to overcome these fears.

Overcoming Obstacles Through Education

Where curriculum alignment is novel or where existing processes are weak, an institution is unlikely to achieve alignment without first educating participants (faculty, staff, and administrators) and then formalizing a process. Curriculum alignment is also subject to the ability of the faculty to eventually deliver the (sometimes broader) educational goals defined in the alignment process. As summarized in Table 8.4 and discussed below, education and training will need to occur at three levels.

Education Leading to Buy-In

As in outcomes assessment, curriculum alignment must be embraced and supported by the faculty, not just mandated by administration. Those involved in curriculum development and delivery will embrace curriculum alignment only when understand the nature and necessity of the process. Therefore, it is important to educate faculty, staff, and administrators about the process and potential benefits of curriculum alignment and to contrast the alignment paradigm with the status quo. This is also a good opportunity to establish and reinforce linkages between strategic curriculum plans and the alignment process.

Depending on the nature of the institution and the current state of curriculum alignment, the scope of attempts to educate participants and develop buy-in might be institution-wide (all programs) or sequential, based on some metric of program priority. Priorities may reflect the strategic importance of the curriculum in question (most important programs first), the value of the resources at risk (larger programs first), or the perceived size of the gap between what currently exists and the desired state (most egregious offenders first).

While many types of training are possible, given the importance of the exercise, it is not unreasonable to envision a retreat-style format where faculty, staff, and administrators can meet to learn about and discuss curriculum alignment. A retreat format lends an air of seriousness and importance to the exercise, allows individuals to focus without competing distractions, and provides an opportunity for all involved to express their thoughts and concerns.

Efforts to educate participants about the nature and necessity of curriculum alignment will benefit from external validation. It may be useful to bring in consultative talent, that is, individuals who are adept at defining the task and advocating its necessity, and who can provide evidence (literature- or experience-based) of benefits that can accrue, best practices, and competitive trends. Where possible, accreditation or professional standards can be used as evidence of the need to align and integrate the curriculum and to expand educational goals beyond delivery of basic knowledge.

If the CU or AU works with an advisory board, the board can also participate in the alignment process. Advisory boards are often impressed to discover the amount of effort and thought required for curriculum alignment and will also benefit from understanding how the program that they support fits into the OU's strategic plan. Boards are often a good source of ideas for developing curricular goals that transcend a specific subject

Table 8.4 Proper Training in Support of Curriculum Alignment Is Essential

Education and Training Required to Support Curriculum Alignment

Type of Training	Purpose of Training
Education leading to buy-in	Training that helps faculty, staff, and administrators understand why curriculum alignment is necessary and important
Process training	Teach individuals how curriculum alignment is done
Goals training	Teach faculty how to support broader educational goals

matter and will provide external validation for the importance of incorporating such goals into the broader curriculum.

The outcome of said training should be that faculty, staff, and administrators understand what curriculum alignment is and why it is necessary and important. Moreover, with reference to buy-in, it is important that all individuals understand what they are buying into, as it represents a major shift from traditional practice. Specifically, faculty and staff need to understand the following:

1. Curriculum alignment goes hand in hand with resource alignment and strategic alignment. Each program will be resourced (in terms of faculty lines, class sizes, instructional support, equipment support, and facilities support) according to its role in the strategic plan. The "winners" in this regard should understand that with greater strategic importance and resources come higher expectations with regard to curriculum planning, assessment, attainment of educational outcomes and program quality. There may also be greater expectations with regard to research quality, research productivity, and external support.
2. Curriculum planning will become more formal, more process-driven, more integrated, and probably more extensive in terms of the scope of learning outcomes considered in the process.
3. The development of course content is likely to require more collaboration, formal specification, and a commitment to pursue the learning outcomes eventually defined for a particular course. A commitment to outcomes assessment is implied.
4. Administrators will need to ensure that the rewards system provides incentives for those that embrace and support curriculum alignment.

Process Training

Once general buy-in is achieved, it is time to identify and train specific individuals to lead the curriculum alignment process. Curriculum alignment is a non-trivial exercise. For many faculty, the process is outside the scope of their experience and training; process training is implied. Even without the curriculum alignment component, systematic, process-driven curriculum review will be something that many CUs are unfamiliar with, having relied traditionally on reactive and/or ad hoc curriculum review procedures. It may be appropriate to invest in consultative training and support at this time. Ideally, the trainer should be able to provide prescriptive guidance, including articles and/or cases from the literature and a description of best practices.

It is important to select a team of individuals who profess buy-in to the curriculum alignment process. If possible, the inaugural team should be devised of experienced and trusted leaders from the faculty. In lieu of training, the inaugural team can begin its charge by reviewing the literature for relevant articles. It may also be appropriate for the team to review the practices of peer and aspiration schools and perhaps report back to the broader faculty with a summary of what they have learned and how they would like to proceed.

Once consensus has been reached on a curriculum review process (in which curriculum alignment is embedded), the process should be codified and become part of the governance structure of the CU. The process definition should include, among other things, scope, frequency, inputs, outputs, required activities, timelines, and roles. This codified process will serve as a "contract" between those directly involved in the process, the broader faculty, and those that administer the CU. It will also serve to convey standard operating procedures to future teams of faculty that periodically undertake the review and alignment process. See Figure 8.8 for an example.

Continuous (future) curriculum alignment is unlikely to occur unless the process becomes part of the broader curriculum strategy and makes its way into operational plans with appropriate resources provided and proper recognition given through the faculty roles and rewards structure of the institution.

Process training also needs to include methods for specifying and communicating the learning goals and outcomes for each course. For example, the faculty may jointly develop a set of "course guides" (master syllabi) for each course in the curriculum. Teams of faculty who teach a particular course could develop these guides, which would thus clearly reflect the faculty's view of appropriate knowledge content and associated skills. Each course guide would specify course objectives, learning outcomes, relative

---

Codification of Periodic Curriculum Review and Alignment Process: An Example

Review and Alignment of Curriculum

Every five years the Curriculum Committee shall undertake a comprehensive review of the foundation and core curriculum of the *XYZ program*. The review shall include, but is not necessarily limited to, consideration of accreditation standards for content and integration, a competitive review of the curriculum of several peer (public and private) institutions, the curriculum of several programs generally recognized as outstanding, outcomes assessment results, and input from faculty at large, faculty supporting curricular specialty areas, students, alumni, advisory boards, and employers.

The review shall begin with confirmation that the course guide for each course is up to date and reflects the activity that occurs in said course; in this regard, the committee shall meet with the course coordinator of each course. The committee shall consider whether the integrative relationships between each course need to be modified and whether the development of broader "soft skills" (writing, teamwork, etc.) identified in the course guides are still consistent with the contemporary expectations of program stakeholders in terms of scope and intensity.

The committee shall also consider changes in the faculty complement since the last curriculum review (as well as any anticipated changes) and explicitly indicate how said changes have impacted the Department's ability to staff the curriculum.

The outcome of this review is to be a written report to the faculty describing the review process, identifying areas of concern, and offering proposals for addressing issues that have been identified during the review. Explicit reference shall be made to the consistency of the curriculum design with regard to (1) accreditation standards, (2) the Department and College strategic plans, and (3) the Department's Assessment Plan. An appendix to the report will document and detail interaction with, and input received from, various stakeholder groups.

The comprehensive review and alignment of *specialty area curricula* is the responsibility of specialty area faculty. However, the Curriculum Committee shall review all proposals made concerning changes to these programs and make a written recommendation to the faculty that indicates whether the Curriculum Committee supports said proposal. The Department faculty shall vote on the Curriculum Committee's recommendations.

Figure 8.8 Curriculum Review/Alignment Process Should Be Part of the Unit Governance

emphasis for various topics, and discipline-related skills outcomes. It might also identify integration relationships with other courses, and whether the course is targeted for the development of broader outcomes, such as development of (written or verbal) communication skills, persuasive argument skills, and research skills.

This type of framework is useful in overcoming faculty concerns about academic freedom. Because the course guides are developed collaboratively, faculty have an opportunity to include coverage of topics that they deem important and to influence curriculum design. Faculty retain flexibility with respect to delivery of curricula. They have authority to select supporting material (texts, articles, etc.) as well as to determine, among other things, their own pedagogy, testing protocols, grading schemes, and course policies. As long as the learning outcomes defined in the course guide are achieved and assessment protocols supported, faculty have broad latitude in how they teach their courses. Process training should directly address, and seek solutions to, concerns about academic freedom.

Training Related to Expanded Learning Outcomes

Various stakeholder groups are asking that education evolve beyond the transfer of knowledge and skills. Table 8.5 delineates a number of educational goals that (1) transcend subject matter, and (2) have been argued to be important in the literature (e.g., Baxter Magolda, King, & Drobney, 2010).

A well-aligned curriculum will explicitly consider the attainment of many of these goals based on their importance to a particular discipline. The alignment process will determine the priority to be assigned to each goal according to stakeholder needs and the strategic role of each program. The alignment process will also determine the platforms (e.g., courses) where related knowledge and skill development is to occur. Some goals may be assigned to the general education curriculum, while others will be pursued (or reinforced) within a specific curriculum.

Regardless of where these goals fall in the curriculum design, it will be the responsibility of the faculty to ensure that they are attained. Unfortunately, even if faculty members accept that a particular goal is important, they may lack skill in helping

Table 8.5 Skills and Traits that Transcend Curricular Subject Matter

Skills and Traits We Want Our Students to Develop

Important Skills that Transcend Subject Area	Important Traits that Transcend Subject Area
• Moral reasoning skills	• Socially responsible leadership
• Ability to think critically	• Personal health and psychological well-being
• Oral and written communication skills	• Willingness to give back to society
• Ability to argue persuasively	• Diversity awareness and openness to diversity
• Ability to effectively work in teams	• Political and social involvement
• Ability to identify and use sources of data	• Love of learning
• Ability to resolve conflicts	• Ethical behavior and interactions with others
• Ability to determine cause-and-effect relationships	• Self-direction as a learner
• Ability to compare and contrast competing solutions to a problem	

students achieve it. Making students give presentations is not teaching them to do so. Making students work in teams is not teaching them how to work in teams. Making students write is not teaching them to write. Curriculum alignment is unlikely to have the desired outcomes if faculty are not appropriately trained.

While the importance of training is self-evident, the literature offers very little prescriptive guidance in this regard, and a successful track record by tertiary institutions has yet to be documented therein. To the contrary, Munter and Reckers (2010) report, for example, that of 500 accounting educators surveyed, the vast majority (91%) said that it was either important or very important that accounting graduates have a strong grounding in ethics. Yet of those respondents ($n = 387$) who said they would be directly responsible for teaching ethics, 64% said that they had received no financial or release-time support for training in ethics. The same study reports that 98% of accounting educators believed that accounting majors should have strong critical thinking skills. However, most reported no training in the development of said skills. These results suggest that getting faculty to embrace broader curricular goals is not the problem; the mean response on the critical thinking question was 4.8/5.0, where 5.0 is "very important." The challenge, rather, is to ensure that faculty are equipped to help students achieve the desired outcomes.

Broadening the Scope of Curriculum Alignment

Many curriculum alignment initiatives in secondary education are based on a process call "backloading" (English, 1992). In the backloading approach, those responsible align curricula by examining the assessment (e.g., a statewide mathematics exam) and then devising a consistent curriculum. Detractors of this type of alignment have deemed it "teaching to the test," which is probably a fair characterization. In addition to promoting a fairly narrow curriculum (only topics that appear on the test are emphasized), it has the more insidious effect of limiting the curriculum to learning outcomes that the test designer was able to devise a test for. As broader educational outcomes, such as those listed in Table 8.5 are notoriously hard to assess via exam, they are unlikely to be part of any curriculum design resulting from backloading.

In contrast to backloading, "frontloading" involves specifying the curriculum first and then identifying or devising an assessment capable of measuring the degree to which students have learned the subjects. Administrative oversight should include ensuring that a frontloading approach, and not a backloading approach, is used. This allows for outcomes such as those found in Table 8.5 to figure in the curriculum and in the assessment protocols. However, oversight must also be used to ensure that frontloading is not applied to a weak curriculum. A curriculum that lacks rigor, depth, and breadth can just as easily be assessed via frontloading as can a more robust curriculum.

Ideally, curriculum alignment will represent a fundamental shift in how the role of each course, within the broader curriculum, is determined. In particular, if curricular goals are to be expanded beyond the traditional impartment of knowledge, it will be important to understand the role and contribution of each course. Certain courses may be designated, for example, as "writing courses" or "team-oriented courses." While faculty will still bear primary responsibility for determining the knowledge outcomes associated with each course, they will now be obliged to provide opportunities for students to achieve mastery of all the outcomes associated with that course. This may require additional training on the faculty's part, and the institution should view the strategic planning process as an opportunity to make a commitment to this type of training and begin to plan accordingly.

Curriculum alignment, within comprehensive curriculum design, also requires the development and implementation of assessment protocols; faculty will be obliged to support (perhaps broader) assessment protocols than just those pertaining to the subject matter of a particular course. For example, course assignments may now be used to assess students' writing skills.

An extension of the curriculum alignment concept is vertical alignment, where the curriculum design considers knowledge and skills required at the next level of education. For example, an eighth-grade curriculum that prepares students for success in the ninth grade would be considered vertically aligned. A number of authors have considered vertical alignment between high-school and college curriculums. For example, Fitzgerald (2004) provides a review of three different research studies that seek to determine what students must know, and be able to do, in order to succeed in entry-level university courses. Curriculum alignment may also represent an opportunity for the CU to fundamentally change how it approaches curriculum oversight and planning.

Resource Alignment

One of the primary motivations of curriculum alignment is to facilitate the efficient assignment of resources to curriculum. It is important for faculty to understand that the outcome of curriculum alignment will determine, in part, class-size and staffing decisions. For example, courses that do not contribute meaningfully to broader curricular goals such as the development of writing skills, presentation skills, and teamwork skills, may be candidates for large section delivery formats and various forms of automation. Conversely, faculty and courses that embrace and support broader curricular goals may need to have limits placed on class sizes or have faculty resources augmented with additional resources such as teaching assistants, grading support, and laboratory support.

A review of Figure 8.2 will remind us that resource alignment depends on an understanding of the strategic role of a particular program, and coincides with the development of curricular goals and designs. As not all programs will have the same resource base (consistent with strategic plans), broader curricular goals will necessarily be more modest in some programs than others. Similarly, resources devoted to assessment may be substantially different in various programs depending on each program's strategic role.

CONCLUSION

This chapter examined some alignments that are important to unlocking the power of organizational performance. More specifically, it examined the interplay between various aspects of strategic planning, curriculum planning, and the alignment of strategy, resources, and curriculum. The basic premises of the chapter are that (1) resources cannot be optimally allocated to curricula until the strategic role of each component of the curriculum is defined (strategic alignment), and (2) allocation of resources to curriculum that are not aligned in terms of learning goals, course content/pedagogy, and assessment (curriculum alignment) is inefficient. It is unlikely that learning goals will be achieved (as measured by assessments) unless the curriculum is aligned. Hence, neither the institution nor its students will derive maximum benefit from the resources applied.

The importance of strategic curriculum planning and the nature and outcome of curriculum alignment were emphasized. The curriculum alignment process must occur after the strategic role of a program has been defined. The scope and intensity of the alignment process must reflect the program's strategic role and the resources made available to support the program. Curriculum planning in general and curriculum alignment in particular are necessary for the proper allocation of resources. Resources cannot be thoughtfully allocated to curriculum unless there is a clear understanding of how various educational goals will be achieved in the curriculum design. Broader curricular goals that transcend specific courses, such as the development of learning skills and communication skills, can be a challenging aspect of curriculum design.

A number of challenges to achieving alignment between strategy, resources, and curriculum were discussed. These included the nature of faculty expertise, traditional faculty roles and rewards systems, traditional concepts of curriculum ownership, and the reactive nature of traditional curriculum oversight. The importance of education and training as a tool for overcoming these challenges was developed in some detail. Education is required both to achieve broad buy-in of the alignment process and to provide the training necessary for individuals to review and align the curriculum successfully.

Finally, we discussed the need to codify curriculum review and alignment processes and to integrate the process into operational plans. Roles and rewards systems must be adjusted to recognize the important contribution made by stewards of the curriculum.

REFERENCES

Baxter Magolda, M. B., King, P. M., & Drobney, K. L. (2010). Practices that provide effective academic challenge for first-year students. *Journal on Excellence in College Teaching, 21*(2), 45–65.

Council of Chief State School Officers. (2001). *The Comprehensive Social Studies Assessment Project (CSSAP) professional development manual.* Washington DC. Retrieved from ERIC database (ED474133).

Dingman, S. W. (2010). Curriculum alignment in an era of standards and high-stakes testing. *Yearbook of the National Council of Teachers of Mathematics, 72*, 103–114.

English, F. W. (1992) *Deciding what to teach and test: Developing, aligning, and auditing the curriculum.* Newbury Park, CA: Corwin Press.

Fitzgerald, M. A. (2004). Making the leap from high school to college: Three new studies about information literacy skills of first-year college students. *Knowledge Quest, 32*(4), 19–24.

Glatthorn, A. A. (1999). Curriculum alignment revisited. *Journal of Curriculum and Supervision, 15*(1), 26–34.

Kaplan, R., & Norton, D. (1996). Using the balanced scorecard as a strategic management system. *Harvard Business Review,* January–February, 75–85.

Kopytoff, V. G. (2010). Dell settles a client's claim that it hid computer defects. *New York Times,* September 24.

Lowe, K. R. (2001). Resource alignment: Providing curriculum support in the school library media center. *Knowledge Quest, 30*(2), 27–32.

McGehee, J. J., & Griffith, L. K. (2001). Large-scale assessments combined with curriculum alignment: Agents of change. *Theory Into Practice, 40*(2), 137–144.

Miller, S. (1997). Implementing strategic decisions: Four key success factors. *Organization Studies, 18*(4), 577–602.

Munter, P., & Reckers, P. M. (2010). uncertainties and budget shortfalls hamper curriculum progress on IFRS. *Issues in Accounting Education, 25*(2), 189–198.

Sinofsky, S., & Iansiti, M. (2009). *One strategy: Organization, planning, and decision making.* New York: John Wiley & Sons.

Stern, C. W., & Stalk, G. (1998). *Perspectives on Strategy from the Boston Consulting Group.* New York: John Wiley & Sons.

Vance, A., & Helft, M. (2010). Investors chide Michael Dell. *New York Times,* August 17.

Wraga, W. G. (1999). The educational and political implications of curriculum alignment and standards-based reform. *Journal of Curriculum and Supervision, 13,* Fall, 4–25.

9

ECONOMIC AND TACTICAL CONSIDERATIONS FOR ALIGNING CURRICULUM AND RESOURCES

Steven T. Breslawski

INTRODUCTION

There are any number of cost-analysis and cost-cutting strategies that can be borrowed from the private sector and applied to the management of educational costs. These strategies include automation, substitution of part-time labor for full-time labor, and outsourcing. Virtually any activity can be reduced, eliminated, or consolidated. Campuses, like factories, can be closed. However, it is important to realize that for-profit organizations have been developing these strategies for many years, making many mistakes and learning many lessons along the way. If misapplied, these tools will deliver poor results, just as they sometimes do in the private sector.

In the case of automation, for example, there have already been profound developments in how educational content is packaged and delivered. Emerging technologies make it possible to deliver educational content in ways that contrast starkly with the traditional lecture-centric approach, which is bound by time and location. Lectures can now be broadcast and/or recorded and delivered to remote locations either synchronously or asynchronously. Notes and instructional resources can be compiled and made available via instructional portals. Assessments can be automatically graded and grade books updated in real-time.

As complex as the college or university budget setting can be, it is possible to simplify the task at hand. Figure 9.1 depicts resource alignment as a machine with four levers that must be adjusted in order to achieve balance between revenues and costs. The first lever alters the funds available to support all campus programs and activities. On a good day, the lever can be adjusted to bring in more funds, perhaps as a result of a tuition increase or the generosity of a donor. On a bad day, however, the state budget process might adjust the lever in the opposite direction, leaving fewer funds available.

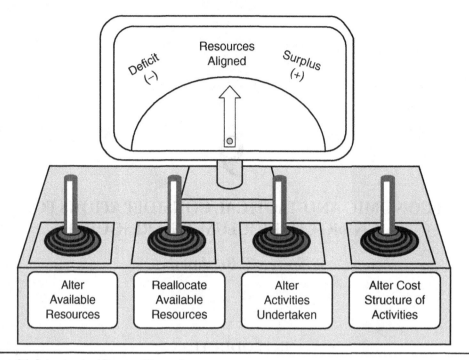

Figure 9.1 Determinants of Resource Alignment

The second lever (moving left to right) reallocates funds between activities; an adjustment could mean less spending on campus grounds maintenance and more spending on computer laboratories.

The third lever can be adjusted to change the activities that the institution undertakes. The school might phase out two undergraduate programs, which may allow it to decrease costs (but perhaps decrease revenue as well), or perhaps replace those programs with a new graduate program.

The fourth lever changes the cost of some activity. The institution might, for example, choose to staff a course with part-time faculty rather than full-time faculty.

Without loss of generality, it is possible to limit the use of this machine to issues of curriculum. The institution can increase or decrease the funds available to support curricula (lever 1), reallocate resources between curricula (lever 2), choose to add or delete curricula (lever 3), or change the cost structure of its curriculum (lever 4). All of the issues addressed in this chapter can be associated with one of the levers depicted in Figure 9.1.

In a general sense, higher education institutions face the same cost–volume–profit relationships as a typical business enterprise. The more that any business sells, the more revenue it generates. However, there is typically a variable cost that accompanies each unit of sales, i.e., the more items sell, the more costs accumulate. In a successful business, the profit on each unit (unit revenue minus unit cost) will be large enough so that the sum of the profits on all sales will exceed the total fixed costs of doing business and the business will make money.

Similarly, the number of credit hours "sold" by a college or university will increase with the number of students and the number of courses each student takes. More students mean more revenues; however, more students also mean more costs. Thus, for higher education institutions, the number of students and the number of credit hours taught are primary drivers of both revenues and costs.

Unfortunately, beyond these basics, the numbers get muddled by some of the unique characteristics of university economics. These include the following:

- Some students pay less (or pay zero) because of scholarships.
- Adding one student to the class does not necessarily increase costs. Sometimes more students require more sections of classes. Other times they fit nicely into the classes already being offered.
- At many schools, students are not charged for additional courses once a certain threshold is achieved, e.g., the tuition charged for five courses may be the same as that charged for four.

Whatever the revenue is, costs must be managed to align revenues and costs. In its simplest form, unit curricular cost can be envisioned as:

$$\text{Cost Per Student} = \frac{\text{Cost of Curriculum}}{\text{Number of Students}}$$

This equation suggests that cost management can be approached from two related perspectives. The first is to determine whether the same curriculum can be offered for a reduced cost, i.e., driving down the numerator will decrease the cost per student. The second approach would be to find a way to offer the same curriculum to a larger number of students, i.e., driving up the numerator will decrease the cost per student. Both of these perspectives are examined throughout this chapter.

The remainder of the chapter is presented in five parts. It begins by exploring the funding and resource environment in which alignment of budgets and curricular cost takes place. This will reveal which of the levers portrayed in Figure 9.1 are likely to be the most helpful in balancing revenues and costs. The chapter then examines the economics of curriculum capacity in more detail. Specification of a cost function indicates the issues that drive costs and invites analysis of which policies might be applied most effectively. Next comes a discussion of business process reengineering (BPR), a framework for determining whether activities are worthy of the resources applied to them. Other tools and issues associated with the alignment of curriculum capacity and available resources, including enrollment modeling and collaborative relationships with other institutions, are then examined. After a summary of findings, the chapter closes with a detailed example of how BPR-type analysis can be a powerful ally in driving cost efficiencies.

TRENDS IN HIGHER EDUCATION FUNDING

This section considers sources of higher education funding, which include public support, tuition and fees, contracts for services such as dormitory and meal plans, gifts and endowments, research grants, and (for a small number of schools) revenues associated with sports programs. In keeping with this chapter's focus on aligning curriculum resources, the discussion will be limited to those funding components most directly related to curriculum, tuition, and public tuition subsidies.

Traditionally, higher education institutions have relied on activity-based metrics, such as credit hours generated, as the primary determinant of revenues received and as the primary basis for allocating resources. Whether tuition income represents the majority of an institution's instructional budget (as in private universities) or whether that income is augmented by state and federal sponsors, the revenue generated has traditionally been based on student credit hours or some related metric such as full-time equivalent (FTE) students. Even ancillary funding sources, such as dorm room and food service contracts, as well as alumni giving, occur in direct proportion to FTE students.

Public Subsidies

The State University of New York (SUNY) provides an interesting microcosm of FTE funding models and trends in higher education funding. For example, in the late 1970s, SUNY used the "40-Cell Matrix," an FTE -based funding model with 4 rows representing instructional levels (undergraduate/graduate, introductory/advanced) and 10 columns representing discipline groups (humanities, sciences, etc.). The model identified state support levels for each student in a particular cell, making it fairly easy to conduct cost/benefit analysis of new program proposals and to review the economics of existing programs, since both cost and revenue functions could be derived based on enrollment assumptions.

Unfortunately, by AY94-95, the 40-Cell Matrix was suggesting that state support was inadequate, as total funding made available to SUNY through the state budget process was only 75% of that specified by the funding model. However, given significant shortfalls in the state budget that year, an alternative interpretation was accepted—the funding was right, the funding model wrong. The funding model was revised and simplified to a 12-cell matrix in 1998 and augmented to include other funding considerations (e.g., mission, location, quality, and performance). However, by AY03-04, it became clear that the new model shared the previous model's flaw; it too suggested that state support was too low— 20% below the funding level required to operate the university system.

And thus SUNY, like many other institutions, abandoned traditional credit-hour funding models or, with the economic crisis of 2008, even turned them on their heads. In contrast to operating under a funding model, institutions now operate under a *cut-allocation model* that allocates shortfalls and cuts in state funding to the various state-operated campuses. More generally, many states are significantly reducing tertiary education funding. It is widely believed that federal funding is likely to erode as well since the growing federal budget deficit has placed all discretionary federal programs "on the table" for budget reductions.

Even before the economic crisis that began in 2008, educational institutions had been facing a long period of budget difficulties arising from declining state support. For example, at SUNY Brockport, state support has decreased from 90% of the operating budget to about 18% over a period of about 20 years. The school has evolved into more of a "state-supported university" than a "state university," consistent with the privatization of public universities theme discussed in Chapter 1.

Administrators at the tertiary level should not expect the funding pendulum to swing back any time soon. Even if state budgets recover, other demands for budget resources are likely to overshadow the needs of higher education. While the causes of declining support are myriad, Ehrnburg and Rizzo (2004) cite studies that suggest that (1) the significant expansion of state spending on Medicaid, and (2) court-mandated K-12 finance reforms (to equalize spending across school districts in 22 states) explain much of the decrease in state support for higher education. If these assertions are correct, it can be inferred that the problem will not correct itself any time soon. Similarly, the rapid growth of entitlement spending at the federal level is likely to confiscate dollars that might otherwise go to colleges and universities.

To summarize, administrators in higher education should operate under the assumption that state and federal support will be stagnant at best. More likely, funding will fall, in real terms if not in absolute terms.

Increasing Tuition

Assuming that authorities with oversight of the institution will allow it, both public and private colleges and universities have the option of raising tuition in order to respond to budget shortfalls. However, it will be increasingly difficult for institutions of higher education to pursue this option. Between 1960 and 2005, the price of a public higher education rose from about 5% of median family income to more than 17%, with estimates that it will reach 30% by 2020 (Burd, Brush, & Selingo, 2005). Undergraduate tuition and fees in the United States have increased by an average of 2.5 to 3.5 percentage points above the inflation rate since about 1980 (Ehrenberg & Rizzo, 2004). According to the Bureau of Labor Statistics, the cost of tuition and fees grew by 439% between 1982 and 2005, after adjusting for financial aid. Education costs have outpaced other fast-growing sectors of consumer spending during the same period, such as energy (108%) and medical costs (251%) (Wang, 2009). According to the College Board, the average price for public, four-year university tuition and fees was $7,020 in 2010, up 6.5% from 2009. The corresponding private school average was $26,273, up 4.4%.

The middle class is in danger of being priced out of public education, especially as financial aid programs are cut and eligibility requirements stiffened. The blogosphere is full of discussions questioning whether college is even worth the expense, and rising costs are clearly part of the frustration (Khadaroo, 2010). With the possible exception of the most prestigious schools, which always seem to have a waiting queue of individuals who will pay dearly for their pedigree, it is doubtful that most institutions will be able to use significant tuition increases as the answer to their budget shortfalls. Furthermore, any income from tuition increases is likely to be consumed by decreases in public support or rapidly increasing costs such as employee benefits, especially healthcare, and the cost of energy. For example, since 1997, the University of Minnesota's spending on fringe benefits, a large portion of which are healthcare costs, have risen by nearly 13% a year, from about $152 million to more than $400 million (Post, 2011).

Options

If revenues cannot be enhanced, then administrators have a very stark choice before them: (1) shrink programs and institutions, consistent with available funds, (2) offer lower-quality programs at a lower cost, or (3) become more efficient in the use of available resources. With respect to the first option, there may be room for institutions to "prune" selective programs, but a wholesale retreat is unlikely. There is a general sense that education has never been more important for individual success and economic well-being. Based on earning and employment differentials between those with and without college degrees, there are calls to greatly increase the proportion of the population that is college educated. In a February 2009 speech to a joint session of Congress, President Obama asserted his desire for the United States to reclaim, by 2020, its status of having the highest proportion of college graduates in the world (White House Press Office, 2009).

Further, we live in a consumer society where choice and selection have almost become dogma. Consumers of education increasingly want more choices, more flexibility, and more convenience. Contraction is, at best, a short-term strategy for dealing with budget imbalances and will probably hurt the competitive profile of an institution in the long run.

Reducing costs by reducing quality is also problematic. Colleges and universities have come under increasing scrutiny as stakeholders have begun to express concern over the emerging caricature of undergraduate education typified by lax standards and large lectures taught by teaching assistants. There is a general sense that higher education needs to improve and to deliver more in terms of both what students know and what graduates can do.

The 2003 National Assessment of Adult Literacy indicates that average literacy levels among adults with bachelor's degrees are disturbingly low and continue to decline over time (Fitzgerald, 2004). The National Survey of America's College Students reveals that

> 20 percent of U.S. college students completing four-year degrees—and 30 percent of students earning two-year degrees—have only basic quantitative literacy skills, meaning they are unable to estimate if their car has enough gasoline to get to the next gas station or calculate the total cost of ordering office supplies.
>
> (Connor & Ching, 2010)

Constituency groups such as the Business-Higher Education Forum and the Partnership for 21st Century Skills argue that a profound gap exists between the knowledge and skills most students possess and those they will need in the 21st century. Employers also suggest that transcripts, the primary way that schools convey the competence of their graduates, are not seen as a meaningful measure of students' skills, abilities, and potential (Bassis, 2009).

THE BASIC ECONOMICS OF CURRICULUM

The introduction to this chapter suggested that curriculum costs per student, in their most simple form, could be modeled as follows:

$$\text{Cost per student} = \frac{\text{Cost of curriculum}}{\text{Number of students}}$$

For purposes of illustration, consider a single section of a single course. Let NS_j be the number of students enrolled in course j. Let CF_j be the cost of the faculty resource assigned to the course (faculty and assistants) and CO_j be the sum of other course-related costs (e.g., copying, visual aids, laboratory materials, guest speakers). The cost per student (CPS) enrolled in course j is defined as:

$$CPS_j = \frac{CF_j + CO_j}{NS_j}$$

The economics are fairly straightforward. To reduce CPS, the institution may:

1. Decrease the faculty costs (CF) associated with course j.
2. Decrease other course-related costs (CO).
3. Increase the number of students (NS) enrolled in course j.
4. Eliminate the course and channel students into less expensive venues.

Each option is discussed below.

Decrease Faculty Cost

Having faced budget pressures for some time now, educational institutions have already pursued many of the "easy" policies, especially those pertaining to the cost of faculty. Today's caricature of teaching at large state universities often involves an inexperienced graduate student, possibly with poor English language skills, staffing undergraduate courses. In fact, the practice of staffing undergraduate courses with graduate students was already pervasive at four-year public institutions by 1995, with 32% of course sections staffed by graduate students (Benjamin, 2002). While certainly less expensive, this approach to staffing is generally perceived as offering an inferior educational experience.

Time has witnessed a decrease in the proportion of classes staffed by full-time, tenure-track faculty, while the number of classes staffed by "adjunct" or "contingent" faculty (other than graduate students) continues to grow. As reported in Umbach (2007), between 1970 and 2003, the number of part-time faculty increased by 422%, while full-time faculty increased by only 71%. This shift can be traced directly to the growing financial pressures faced by public and private higher education institutions (Ehrenberg & Zhang, 2005).

While many contingent faculty are gifted instructors, there are some indications that over-reliance on them has hurt the quality of education (Jaeger & Eagan, 2009; Jaeger & Hinz, 2008). Full-time faculty spend substantially and (and proportionately) more out-of-class time on activities that support student learning than do part-time faculty. Over 50% of part-time faculty at two-year colleges and 31% of part-time faculty at four-year colleges report holding no office hours, while only 2% and 7% of their full-time counterparts (respectively) made the same assertion (Benjamin, 1998). A study by Ehrenberg and Zhang (2005) found that an increase in the proportion of contingent faculty had an adverse effect on graduation rates. Umbach (2007) found that part-time

$$CPS_{FT} = \frac{22500 + 1200}{35} \qquad CPS_{PT} = \frac{4000 + 1200}{35}$$

$$CPS_{FT} = \$677 \qquad CPS_{PT} = \$149$$

Figure 9.2 Full-Time (FT) Staffing Is About 450% More Expensive Than Part-Time (PT)

faculty tend to be less effective in their instruction and are less committed to teaching than their full-time peers.

Despite the problems with contingent staffing, the economics are fairly compelling. Consider a section of 35 students staffed by a full-time faculty member paid $90,000 per year. Taking fringe benefits and salary devoted to professional obligations such as scholarship and research out of the equation, if said professor teaches four courses per year (as is common at many research-oriented schools), one-fourth of his or her salary may be attributed to this course. Compare this structure with that of a class of 35 students taught by a part-time instructor who receives $4,000 per section taught.

For the moment, assume that other course-related costs (CO), such as copying, are $20 per student plus $500 of fixed expenses for both courses. The two cost structures are compared in Figure 9.2.

The 450% differential does not take into account the other expenses associated with full-time staffing, such as travel, research support, and sabbatical. If, in the example above, the part-time faculty member were to be replaced with a full-time lecturer paid $60,000 per year to teach eight courses, the CPS would be $249; tenure-track staffing under the stated assumptions is still about 270% more expensive.

Because the economics are so compelling, institutions will continue to rely on adjunct staffing. Proper direction, supervision, training, and incentives can address many of the problems associated with contingent staffing. Adjunct faculty assignments should be consistent with strategic and curricular goals (as discussed in the previous chapter). Table 9.1 lists factors to consider when making adjunct staffing arrangements.

Another strategy to reduce faculty costs is to increase the revenue-generating activity base across which faculty salaries are distributed. For example, suppose that the institution has traditionally hired non-tenure track full-time faculty (henceforth lecturers) for $55,000 per year with an obligation to teach four courses in the fall semester and four courses in the spring. Salary per course would be $6,875. In the future, an alternative contractual arrangement for newly hired lecturers might be $60,000 per calendar year with an obligation to teach 10 courses per year: 4 in the fall, 4 in the spring, and (assuming the institution runs sessions in winter and/or summer) 2 courses in the special sessions. Salary per course would be $6,000, a modest savings of about 13%. However, revenue generated in the special session would also be retained by the institution.

Given that the proportion of available tenure-track positions is shrinking, these positions are becoming (comparatively) harder to obtain and, therefore, comparatively more attractive to faculty seeking employment. This may offer colleges and universities an opportunity to negotiate a more favorable activity level compared to historical practices. For example, instead of negotiating a three-year contract requiring 6 courses (3/3 load) per year (18 courses total), the contract might specify a total of 19 or even 20

Table 9.1 Factors to Consider When Assigning Contingent Faculty

Factor	Outcome Favoring Adjunct Staffing	Comments
Class size	Small	• Isolate problems to a small number of students • CPS is high when full-time tenured faculty staff small courses
Supervision	Supervision available	• Need to ensure convergence of specified learning outcomes, participation in assessment protocols, and rigor in course content and grading consistent with traditional faculty
Program size	Large	• Multiple sections require flexibility in staffing • Students have option of choosing to take course from traditional faculty • Supervision and guidance should be available from full-time faculty teaching same course • Large programs are likely to have some strategic importance and therefore well-defined and documented learning outcomes and assessment protocols, providing maximum guidance
Strategic role	Niche program	• Specialized, practitioner knowledge often required
Strategic role	Inertial, low-priority, or terminated program	• Minimize cost by using adjunct faculty while program being phased out or until future direction determined
Strategic role	Medallion program	• Use adjunct faculty within accreditation guidelines • Learning outcomes and assessment protocols are more likely to be well defined and documented, providing maximum guidance • Enhanced administrative support associated with medallion status fosters direction and supervision • Specialized expertise may be required
Learning outcomes	See below	• Left side of continuum most appropriate for most contingent faculty

Nature of Learning Outcomes

Dissemination of Knowledge	Discipline-Based Skills, Methods	Skills that Transcend Discipline	Development of the Person

$$\longleftarrow \qquad\qquad\qquad\qquad\qquad\qquad \longrightarrow$$

Note: See previous chapter for definition of strategic niches referenced in table.

courses, with the faculty member having significant control over when the additional courses would be taught. This would allow the faculty member to arrange and manage his or her other obligations (service and research) as required. The same contract might allow the faculty member to trade teaching a large section for one or both of the additional courses. This would of course be subject to union and other workload rules and competitive forces. The institution might have to maintain traditional contract terms for medallion programs (consistent with market practices), programs of high strategic importance, and in disciplines where Ph.D. faculty are in short supply.

Decrease Other Course-Related Costs

Two recent developments are worth noting in this regard. One represents an opportunity and the other, for many institutions, a strategic threat.

Large lecture formats often require teaching and grading support. Online homework grading systems have evolved rapidly over the past decade and offer a substantial opportunity to lower the cost of grading support. In a somewhat more recent development, online tutoring systems are now a reality for many subjects. As described in Carey (2009), a company called Smarthinking provides 24/7, on-demand, one-on-one tutoring in a range of introductory college courses. The tutors have bachelor's and master's degrees in their fields and communicate with students via computer, using an onscreen, interactive "whiteboard." Writing tutors give feedback on essays within 24 hours.

While it would likely be cost prohibitive for a single college to provide on-demand 24/7 tutoring for an esoteric course like organic chemistry, Smarthinking pools demand from hundreds of postsecondary institutions and tens of thousands of students. In addition to economies of scale, they take advantage of lower wages paid to tutors in places such as India and the Philippines. Institutions can buy multi-hour blocks of 24/7 tutoring in various subjects for much less than it would cost them to provide that service on their own.

Online tutoring offers institutions a substantial opportunity to lower tutoring costs. However, recent developments in the pricing of online courses may represent an existential threat to some traditional schools. Unfettered by costs associated with classrooms, research, building maintenance, student unions, groundskeeping, and so on, organizations that offer courses in a strictly online format are poised to be a disruptive and strategic threat.

To date, most of the online providers have used convenience, rather than price, to compete with traditional forms of higher education. In fact, some providers charge a premium for online courses in the form of a technology fee. However, as described in Carey (2009), one organization has begun to offer students as many courses as they want for a flat rate of $99 per term. Students can choose from a large array of standard introductory classes. The organization is currently trying to navigate some recent problems with regional accrediting bodies, but the future is clear. Unless traditional colleges and universities can overcome the cost disadvantage and differentiate their educational products from some of the emerging formats, all but the most desirable pedigrees will be at risk. Sound assessment protocols and responsiveness to assessment results will be important in providing this differentiation.

Larger Classes

As stated earlier, educational institutions have faced budget pressures for some time now and have already pursued many of the "easy" policies. To a degree, large lectures have become a hallmark of big state universities and, unfortunately, are generally perceived to offer an impersonal and inferior educational experience (especially when staffed by graduate students). The economics, however, are compelling.

$$CPS_{400} = \frac{27300 + 9000}{400} \qquad CPS_{35} = \frac{22500 + 1700}{35}$$

$$CPS_{400} = \$90.75 \qquad CPS_{PT} = \$691.43$$

Figure 9.3 Cost per Student Comparison 400 Students vs. 35 Students

Consider a large section of 400 students staffed by a full-time professor paid $90,000 per year. Taking fringe benefits and salary devoted to other professional obligations such as scholarship and research out of the equation, if said faculty member teaches four courses per year, one-fourth of his or her salary may be attributed to this course. Assume also that the professor of the large section is assigned two teaching assistants at a per-course cost of $4,800. Compare this structure with that of a class taught in a (rather large) seminar format of 35 students, with no grading support. For the moment, assume that other course-related costs (CO), such as copying, are $20 per student and $1,000 fixed for both courses. Figure 9.3 compares the two cost structures.

The economics are hard to ignore. While large-section classes have, over time, become associated with lower-quality education, a number of technology developments that have occurred over the last 10 years may change public perception. These technology-based enhancements include the following.

Interactivity

Wireless audience response systems (WARS), more commonly known as "clickers," have made it possible for large classes to become more interactive while at the same time providing immediate feedback on learning. Although the clicker is essentially equivalent to a "show of hands," its anonymous nature promotes participation, and there is no need to waste time counting outstretched arms. Instructors can pose a question to the class, ask students to "vote" with their answer, and then immediately discuss the correct response(s). Authors have found positive benefits to WARS across a wide range of courses, in terms of either student attitudes and/or improved learning. Relevant studies include Guthrie and Carlin (2004), Barnett (2006), Graham, Tripp, Seawright, and Joeckel (2007), Hunsinger, Poirier, and Feldman (2008), and Milner-Bolotin, Antimirova, and Petrov (2010).

WARS technology transforms large lectures from passive experiences to active expreriences, suggesting that the benefits of active learning may accrue. It can help instructors achieve some of the practices associated with high-quality undergraduate education (Chickering & Gamson, 1987). These include:

- Keeping students engaged during the entire class period.
- Gauging the degree to which students understand material presented.
- Providing students with prompt feedback on their understanding.

Access to Materials

Both within and outside of the lecture environment, technology has improved access to materials. Large flatscreen monitors now help those in the rear and sides of the lecture hall see what the instructor is doing on the whiteboard. Campus portal systems allow instructors to post notes, examples and exemplars, and taped versions of the lecture for students that miss class. The same portal systems allow students to ask each other questions and participate in discussion groups.

Automated Homework Grading Systems

Textbook publishers have begun to provide sophisticated automated evaluation and grading systems for homework. Historically, in the absence of substantial (and talented) grading support, the assignment of significant graded homework as a learning aid has been impractical in a large lecture format. Yet certain disciplines, such as mathematics, statistics, and micro-economics, rely on providing opportunities for students to actively learn through solving a large number of similar but not identical problems. Traditionally, this has meant assigning a substantial number of "back of chapter" homework problems.

The new online systems are very sophisticated in that they have evolved beyond simple "right/wrong" grading responses, i.e., they can diagnose where the student went wrong. Further, students' responses to practice problems are used to generate directives as to what material they should review to improve their performance on the final assessment. Students receive immediate feedback, including a grade, and instructors receive formative feedback concerning topics where students are struggling.

In short, these are not necessarily your parents' large lectures any more. A recent experiment described in Mervis (2010) and Deslauriers, Schelew, and Wieman (2011) compared two large (250-student) physics classes. For the first 11 weeks, both courses were taught by an experienced (and apparently well-regarded) professor using traditional lecture techniques. In the 12th week, the professor taught one section, and two graduate students taught the other using an interactive approach that used clickers. Through week 11, the test scores in the two sections were similar. However, on exam questions pertaining to the material covered in week 12, students in the interactive section answered 74% of exam items correctly, while students in the traditional lecture answered only 41% correctly. The best exam scores in the lecture-based section were below the average of the interactive section. While a number of alternative hypotheses could explain the observed difference in performance (attendance in the interactive class was higher, Hawthorn effect, etc.), the results of the study suggest that learning outcomes can be substantially improved for large lectures.

Beyond the compelling cost per student benefit, there are a host of factors that should be considered before pursuing large lecture formats, as shown in Table 9.2. Finally, large sections make sense only if justified by sufficient enrollment. However, it may be possible, in a cross-disciplinary sense, to generate said enrollment. Assume that a university has several degree programs with similar, but not identical, courses in some content area, say, introductory statistics. Introductory statistics courses are found in economics, business, psychology, criminal justice, math, and sociology curricula to name a few. The knowledge and skills outcomes for all of these courses (i.e., sampling methods, descriptive statistics, basic probability, and applications of sampling distribution theory) are likely to be very similar, although each discipline may place different emphasis on each outcome. Only the supporting computer software and domain of the applications used in examples and problems is apt to change.

Table 9.2 Factors Favoring the Use of Large Sections

Factor	Outcome Favoring Large Sections	Comments
Strategic brand	Large comprehensive university	• Not consistent with a brand image of small, intimate college
Strength of student body	More capable	• Not appropriate for students that need significant coaching and individual attention
Program size	Large	• Efficient delivery of curriculum to large numbers of students
Strategic role	Cash cow	• Generate maximum revenue at lowest cost and at an acceptable level of quality
Facilities	Large-lecture–oriented	• Lecture halls • Media support, including ARS • Recitation support if required
Faculty skills	Strong teaching skill, experienced	• It takes a special instructor to do this well
Assessment protocols	Well-established, highly efficient	• Assessment data should be easy to collect, code, and analyze
Learning outcomes	See below	• Left side of continuum most appropriate for large lectures

Nature of Learning Outcomes

Dissemination of Knowledge	Discipline-Based Skills, Methods	Skills that Transcend Discipline	Development of the Person

$$\longleftrightarrow$$

Note: See previous chapter for definition of strategic niches referenced in table.

The disciplines may be able to convene and identify a common core of knowledge and skills that all of their courses share. If that core is substantial, it may be possible to teach the core in a large lecture format, with students assigned, by discipline, to recitation sessions to focus on discipline-specific issues. Alternatively, the discipline-specific issues might be covered in another course staffed by the particular discipline. For example, a topic unique to the introductory psychological statistics course might be taught later in the research methods course. A variation would be to allow the most strategically important programs to maintain their own course and use a combined course for the other programs.

Eliminate the Course in Question and Channel Students into Less Expensive Venues
Depending on the work and compensation rules in place at the institution, it is not unusual for salary discrepancies to exist between disciplines. Hypothetically, there are

courses staffed by faculty in one discipline that might be staffed (with less expense) by faculty in another. Courses in statistics that support psychology, mathematics, economics, business, teacher education, and so on, come to mind. As another way to manipulate the CF factor, the common component of the various course curricula could be defined and staffed by the least expensive program in terms of average faculty cost. Similarly, certain general education courses (e.g., ethics courses) are potentially staffed by several disciplines. It may be worthwhile to have instructors from the low-cost discipline teach the course, assuming that they are willing and able to satisfy the learning outcomes required by the other programs.

The Problem of Small Classes

Much of the previous discussion has been about using large classes as tools to reduce costs and the conditions that would permit such an approach. It is equally important, though, to consider the justification for small classes. The discussion of strategic curriculum planning and curriculum alignment in the previous chapter should serve as a guide.

Class size is the most sensitive factor in determining the cost per student. Given the magnitude of full-time faculty salary, the per-student cost of running a small class will normally exceed the revenue that its enrollments generate unless it can be staffed with a less expensive resource. If such a resource does not exist, the course must be "subsidized." This provides a convenient definition of a small class, i.e., a class that has not generated sufficient revenues to cover its cost. Frankly, there are relatively few instances when subsidization can be justified; these include the following:

- The small class size is a temporary development based on unforeseen circumstances.
- The small class size is a temporary development resulting from planned circumstances such as a new program startup.
- The small class size is planned, the small size is deemed necessary, and the course supports a curriculum that is of primary strategic significance to the institution.
- The course supports a faculty research agenda or project that is monetarily or strategically important to the institution.
- There are critical learning outcomes for (an important) program that can only be achieved by running a small class.
- The enrollment cannot be deferred, for example by running the course every two semesters instead of every semester.

If the justification is strategic in nature, then the strategic curriculum plan should have identified the source of funds to support the cost. For example, the instructor of the small class might also teach a large lecture. Otherwise, if the shortfall in enrollment is perennial and unplanned, it is indicative of an enrollment model that needs to be revised or a program for which a critical level of demand is not being met by enrollment management processes. If the enrollment management process cannot resolve the issue, then a less expensive curricular solution should be sought. If none exists, the program that the course supports may not be viable.

BUSINESS PROCESS REENGINEERING

Business process reengineering (BPR) is the practice of understanding and deconstructing current organizational processes to improve quality and organizational efficiency and effectiveness. In essence, the organization identifies everything it does and begins by questioning the reason(s) for performing each activity in order to determine if the activity is really necessary. If the activity is deemed necessary, the next step is to question the way it is done currently in order to determine whether it could be done better. Figure 9.4 illustrates these steps.

BPR can be applied to either manufacturing or service processes and has the potential to significantly improve efficiency and reduce costs.

Consider, for example, a manufacturing firm that runs a foundry in order to produce a particular casting. As foundries are energy-intensive operations with environmental consequences, the manufacturer is motivated to look for alternatives. It would first explore whether the casting itself is necessary, i.e., can the product be redesigned (without excessive expense) to function without this part? If the part is necessary, the next question is whether the part has to be produced in a foundry. Perhaps a numerically controlled milling machine could craft the part from a block of solid material for reduced costs, better quality, and/or less environmental impact. Finally, the company should question whether it should be producing this part at all, or if that task would be better left to another company whose core competencies would allow it to manufacture the part with the best possible quality and at the lowest possible cost.

BPR gained much attention in the management literature during the 1970s and 1980s as business began to automate more and more processes to capitalize on the enhanced capabilities and decreased costs of computer and information technology. Many companies discovered that they were automating "bad processes" and that, prior to investing in automation, they should first scrutinize each process to make sure that it was actually required. For example, it would be pointless for the Ford Motor Company to spend millions of dollars to automate the production of the Model T. No matter how efficient production became or how optimally resources were aligned, the Model T would be irrelevant to the contemporary needs of the driving public.

Tertiary education formats, in some cases, have changed little over the last half-century. Lecture-based teaching comes to mind. Educational institutions are likely to

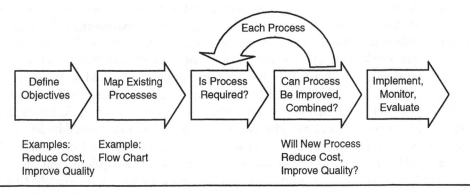

Figure 9.4 Business Process Reengineering

benefit from undergoing BPR-inspired review prior to pursuing resource alignment. Even very small changes can have profound results.

Consider the case of a major American technology giant that used BPR to examine its computer monitor assembly process. The original process began with opening boxes that contained glass cathode ray tubes (CRTs) purchased from a company in Korea. The CRT was the removed from the box, placed in a new monitor frame, and sent down the assembly line. The now empty CRT boxes were sent for crushing and recycling, and the foam inserts that had held the fragile CRTs safely in the box were sent out for shredding and disposal. The partially assembled monitors continued down the assembly line, with circuit boards and wiring being attached. The outer plastic housing was then added, and decals were pressed onto the housing. Following a quick bench test, a box printed with the manufacturer's logo and product information was taken from a stack of flattened boxes and "inflated," with glue applied to the box tabs to hold them in place. The monitor was packed in the box with customized foam blocks to protect it during shipping. This would appear to be a reasonable process, and all activities would appear to be necessary.

During the BPR exercise, however, someone noticed that the process required opening and destroying boxes at one end of the assembly line and inflating and using new boxes at the other end. Similarly, large foam blocks were being discarded (entering the waste stream) at the beginning of the assembly process and new blocks were being introduced at the end. Ultimately, the computer manufacturer was able to arrange for the CRT supplier to package the CRTs in boxes displaying the computer manufacturer's name and finished monitor information (rather than the CRT supplier's name and details about the CRTs). The foam packing blocks were redesigned so that flipped one way they would hold the CRT safely and flipped another way they would hold the finished monitor. The production line was changed from a straight line to a U shape. Now, each time a box was opened and a CRT placed into production, a finished monitor was placed into that same box and the foam inserts were reused instead of discarded. These were such simple changes, but the results were profound!

Applying BPR to the curriculum development and resource alignment processes can have equally profound results. Further, embracing BPR with regard to administrative processes could potentially liberate resources that could be shifted to the core mission of education.

Returning to the topic of large classes, consider the example of an institution with a very limited number of large lecture facilities. The compelling economics of large lectures notwithstanding, the school could offer very few classes in that format. The obvious solution, building new lecture halls, is expensive and not economically feasible in the current budget environment. Further, the payback period would be measured in decades.

A BPR-like process revealed an alternative solution. Lecture times would be shortened by 10 to 15 minutes per class period for a total of 30 minutes per week. For example, class periods for courses that met Monday, Wednesday, and Friday would be 50 minutes long, rather than 60, consistent with practices at other colleges and universities. The change would make one more time-slot per day available. This would permit each large lecture facility to be used one more time per day, allowing for approximately 10 additional sections per semester in the larger format.

An alternative solution to the problem might be to design a course that meets once a week in a large-capacity venue while also providing students with self-directed learning opportunities supported by on-demand video, interactive homework sites, and so on. This self-directed component of the course would be completed in lieu of a second (large-format) weekly meeting, freeing up the lecture hall for a second course of the same type. While some might object to the loss of contact hours, the growing body of data on online learning suggests that contact hours are not always the key to effective instruction.

Our discussion of BPR has been purposefully short; interested readers can see Vakola and Rezgui (2000) for a deeper treatment of the subject. BPR is one tool available to educational administrators; we discuss others in the next section.

OTHER TOOLS

This section considers other tools for increasing curriculum capacity or improving curricular efficiencies. The first, enrollment modeling, will help to ensure that curriculum capacity is neither too high nor too low. The second, enrollment management, is used to balance curriculum demand and curriculum capacity. The third is collaboration, in which partner institutions can expand curriculum capacity by working together.

Enrollment Modeling and Planning

Scheduling mistakes have huge consequences with regard to costs, on-time graduation rates, student satisfaction, and overall student success. There is no better way to lose future alumni support than by delaying a student's graduation because the student could not get into a course that was full. Graduation rates are a key metric on which educational institutions are compared and ranked.

The number of sections scheduled for a particular course should be based on anticipated demand; demand modeling is implied. The time-slots into which courses are scheduled should take into account availability of classroom or laboratory facilities. Most important, a course should not conflict with another course that students are likely to want to take at the same time, either within or outside the curricular unit. For example, international business students at a particular school may need to take upper-level language courses in their junior and senior years. Therefore, it would not make sense to schedule upper-level international business courses into the same time slots as upper-level French and Spanish courses.

Optimal scheduling cannot be expected without training those who are assigned the responsibility. Experience matters, and experienced schedulers should be engaged to train the inexperienced. Unless enrollments are steady-state, data on past, current, and projected enrollments are also required to model enrollments with any accuracy. A good enrollment model is absolutely necessary for competent section planning. Section planning, in turn, drives the staffing plan.

Enrollment Management

In a static resource environment, growing demand for a particular program can feel more like a curse than a blessing for those who staff the program. Unless budget resources flow freely in response to increases and decreases in activity level (they often do not), it will be difficult for any program to service increased demand.

Some programs will have too much curriculum capacity, while others will not have enough to meet demand. This may happen frequently if an institution focuses primarily on student quality metrics in admissions decisions. One alternative is to manage or "right size" program enrollments.

Enrollment management can occur in the admissions office or at the program level. In the former instance, applications requesting admission to a specific program need to be monitored and tallied. Using some criteria (first-come-first-served or student quality metrics), enrollments into a particular program are controlled. Students not admitted to a particular program can be encouraged to consider other programs (especially those that are under-enrolled). Admissions data can also be used to identify programs that are likely to be under-enrolled; proactive and targeted recruitment efforts can be useful for offsetting under-enrollment. Unfortunately, this approach suffers from the fact that students are exceptionally fluid in their choice of major at the time of college application.

In cases where a curricular unit has additional entrance requirements, enrollments can be managed by tweaking those preconditions. The same demand model used for enrollment modeling and planning can be adapted to model anticipated changes in demand resulting from changes in program entrance requirements. As described in S. Breslawski and K. Breslawski (2000) and S. Breslawski (2008), econometric models can be surprisingly accurate in predicting the success of students based on their performance vis-à-vis program entrance requirements, making it possible to refine admissions policies. Specifically, econometric models can help institutions to be confident that (1) students eliminated by more rigorous program standards are weaker students, and (2) students eliminated by program entrance standards are likely to select another major rather than leave the institution. Tailoring admissions policies accordingly can mitigate over-enrollment problems in the program in question, as well as under-enrollment in some of the other programs to which students migrate.

A final thought on enrollment management is that, for all intents and purposes, resources are wasted when an unqualified student is admitted to the institution. Students who are not able or not ready to pursue college-level work are likely to be problematic in terms of classroom performance and retention. Adding course sections to accommodate students who have a low probability of success takes resources away from other needs. Budgets are now so restrictive that most institutions simply can't afford to waste resources.

Two emerging trends are for schools to use "holistic" admissions standards and to inflate student SAT scores by combining the highest verbal score and the highest math score (attained over repeated tests). Administrators that adopt these policies must monitor results carefully to ensure that any gains from increased enrollments are not negated by falling rates of retention and wasted classroom seats.

Partnering with Other Institutions

Another way to increase curriculum capacity is through partnerships with other institutions. Transferred coursework is essentially a form of partnership with a transfer institution, where credit-hour-generating capacity is outsourced to another school. Unfortunately, the other institution generally gets all the revenue as well. In cases where courses are being subsidized (taught at a financial loss), however, accepting transferred courses can make sense.

Other opportunities exist beyond the traditional transferred course scenario. For example, consider five colleges in a state university system that offer (or are contemplating offering) an online business degree program. As business curricula are similar at many schools, it is not difficult to imagine a cooperative arrangement between programs. For the sake of simplicity, it may be assumed that the general education requirements of each program are satisfied outside of this example, either through online or traditional means.

Assume also that each school, if it were to offer its own online program, would enroll between 20 and 100 students each semester and that these individuals would begin by taking introductory-level courses. Some minor variation in enrollments will occur in courses at each level (sophomore, junior, senior) due to some students transferring credits, repeating courses, and/or taking more or less credits in a given semester. Assume that a minor level of attrition from the program (less than 100% retention) will also occur at each level, randomly varying between 0 and 5% per semester. Assume further that the target enrollment for each online course section is 28 students, with a minimum class size of 16 and a maximum of 32. Section sizes over 28 are used only to avoid having to introduce a new section with fewer than 16 students. Assume that each school requires the same or similar courses for its degree program.

A typical single-semester enrollment pattern, that satisfies the above assumptions, can be derived using Monte Carlo simulation, as shown in Table 9.3.

Note that the pattern shown in Table 9.3 is one of many that would satisfy these assumptions. However, any pattern would be equally useful in demonstrating the potential benefits of partnering with the other institutions.

Suppose that each school elects to staff its own program. Given the enrollment pattern shown above, each school will have to have the expertise and resources to staff 16 different online courses; this alone is a substantial assumption. Further, the faculty involved will have to *maintain* 16 different courses, some of which (e.g., information systems) require constant updating as their content changes rapidly. What's more, the individual schools will need the resources to staff a total of between 16 and 48 sections per semester, per the section totals at the bottom of Table 9.3. As the courses are myriad, it is likely that a substantial number of faculty will have to be involved, subjecting the program to substantial risk from faculty resignations, retirements, administrative assignments or leave, and so on.

It is also important to note that many high-quality online degree programs already exist. To launch an online degree program and compete with the better players in the arena, each of the five schools will need to invest significant resources in the production, maintenance, and delivery of 16 outstanding online courses.

Alternatively, suppose that the schools decide to collaborate and divide the course assignments among the five colleges, with each college staffing only three courses plus its own version of the strategic management (capstone) course, to maintain some uniqueness between programs. The first advantage to accrue is efficiency in terms of sections offered. In general, for a particular course, it will be more efficient for one program to offer enough sections to serve all students (from all schools) than for each program to offer enough sections to serve its own students. As shown in Table 9.4, the difference can be striking; 15 sections were saved in this example.

Table 9.3 Hypothetical Semester Demand Profile for Five Online Business Programs

Course Title	School 1		School 2		School 3		School 4		School 5	
	Students	Sections	Students	Sections	Students	Sections	Students	Sections	Students	Sections
Accounting 1	19	1	87	3	85	3	89	3	43	2
Accounting 2	16	1	91	3	89	3	96	3	40	2
Micro Economics	21	1	93	3	89	3	96	3	43	2
Macro Economics	21	1	92	3	87	3	92	3	41	2
Statisics 1	18	1	86	3	82	3	88	3	41	2
Statistics 2	18	1	86	3	81	3	84	3	40	2
Finance	17	1	84	3	81	3	82	3	39	2
Marketing	19	1	82	3	78	3	84	3	41	2
Business Law	19	1	83	3	78	3	83	3	40	2
Organizational Behavior	17	1	87	3	83	3	82	3	38	2
International Business	16	1	82	3	83	3	79	3	36	2
Business Ethics	16	1	78	3	81	3	78	3	36	2
Operations Management	13	1	79	3	80	3	79	3	38	2
Human Resources	15	1	75	3	78	3	77	3	36	2
Information Systems	19	1	75	3	84	3	75	3	34	2
Strategic Management	16	1	79	3	81	3	80	3	36	2
Total Students/Sections	280	16	1339	48	1320	48	1344	48	622	32

Table 9.4 In General, Fewer Sections Are Required if Enrollments Are Shared

Course Title	A Total Enrollment	B—Sections Required if Staffed by Five Schools	C—Sections Required if Staffed by One School
Accounting 1	323	12	12
Accounting 2	332	12	12
Micro Economics	342	12	12
Macro Economics	333	12	12
Statisics 1	315	12	11
Statistics 2	309	12	11
Finance	303	12	11
Marketing	304	12	11
Business Law	303	12	11
Organizational Behavior	307	12	11
International Business	296	12	11
Business Ethics	289	12	10
Operations Management	289	12	10
Human Resources	281	12	10
Information Systems	287	12	10
Strategic Management	292	12	NA–12 sections (offered as before)
Total Students/Sections	**4,905**	**192**	**177**

Columns A and B in Table 9.4 are summations of results from the five schools shown in Table 9.3. Column C is derived by applying the enrollment policy of 28 students per section, with a maximum of 32 students. Recall that section sizes over 28 are used only to avoid having to introduce a new section with fewer than 16 students and that each school will continue to staff its own strategic management (capstone) course to maintain an element of uniqueness between the programs.

Obviously, a different set of enrollment figures will generate different savings. However, a Monte Carlo simulation based on 1,000 scenarios (generated using the previously stated assumptions) yields an average of 15.1 sections saved, with a maximum of 35 sections saved. The minimum sections saving was –4, i.e., it is possible to construct a data set where it is actually more efficient (in terms of sections) for the individual schools to offer the required section.[1]

---

[1] This will occur when enrollments in each course are near to a multiple of 32 (maximum section size). In these circumstances, the number of students over the target enrollment of 28 (or its multiple) will be insufficient to spawn a new section and the sections will be overloaded instead, increasing productivity versus the combined model. Based on 1,000 trials, the probability of this occurrence is less than 2%.

The second efficiency enjoyed is that each school is now only preparing and supporting (grading, testing, office hours, tutoring) and maintaining four courses (capstone course plus three others). It may be assumed that courses are allocated to each school based on some system that takes consideration of the expertise or strengths of the particular faculty at each school, although a more arbitrary assignment is possible. If courses are allocated based on comparative strength, then it can be argued that the resulting program will be superior to those that would result if each school staffed all of its own courses.

With regard to the number of students served by each program, in the shared arrangement, each program would serve approximately the same number of students, with variation depending primarily on which courses they staffed and capstone course enrollments. Larger programs would serve fewer students than if they offered the entire program on their own; smaller programs, more.

Schools would need to find a mutually agreeable way to allocate revenue to reward the larger programs for attracting more students but also compensate smaller programs for serving more than they otherwise would. If the individual programs were approximately the same size, they would just split revenues in equal shares.

It is evident that the intricacies, difficulties, and start-up costs of partnering with other institutions can be significant. As the Chrysler and Daimler-Benz corporations discovered when they merged (and later divorced), integrating cultures, practices, business systems, information systems, and control structures can be daunting. However, with regard to allowing schools to gain efficiencies and to focus on core competencies, the results can be impressive.

Other Collaborative Opportunities

While this discussion has focused primarily on instructional costs, a number of non-instructional collaborative initiatives can be envisioned. The same technology that makes "distance learning" possible should allow for "distance administration." One can imagine several colleges within a university system or geographic area sharing bursar, registrar, and financial aid personnel. For example, students might be able to talk to a financial aid counselor or academic advisor via Skype®-like technology; required student records can be accessed remotely. The potential savings are large in terms of personnel and space. Savings generated could be used to support the institution's core mission of learning.

Facilities can also be shared. For example, the Boston Conservatory has arranged for its students to use Northeastern University's dining and athletic facilities. SUNY Brockport has shared a downtown Rochester, NY, classroom facility with a local community college and also partners with the Rochester Public Library to provide library resources to students who use the downtown satellite location.

THINKING OUTSIDE THE BOX: A FINAL BPR EXAMPLE

The BPR framework discussed earlier can be used to examine instructional programs, administrative processes, and facilities in order to determine whether partnerships can free up resources for the core mission of the institution. What follows is a final, rather grandiose example of enhancing curriculum capacity in the spirit of BPR.

The essence of BPR is to question everything that an organization assumes and everything it does and to understand the reasons and premises behind each activity. One of the most fundamental assumptions and basic building blocks of tertiary education is the student credit-hour system and the three-credit-hour college course. Credit hours (contact hours) are supposed to represent the amount of learning undertaken, and grades are supposed to reflect the degree of subject mastery. Many would argue that neither is true. The use of student hours has a long history and many critics; see Shedd (2003). However, until another system is devised, credit hours will remain important in terms of financial aid, student billing, course transfer, and financial analysis of educational institutions.

While it is possible to argue the need for a measuring system, it is not possible to argue that the current system is precise or comparable across institutions. At some institutions, a credit hour means 50 minutes of contact; at others, it means 60. Some colleges have 13-week semesters; others have 15-week semesters. Some colleges count two hours of lab time as one credit; others, as two. Students can receive credit for experience or credit by exam—with no hours of contact in a classroom. The online revolution brings the notion of contact hours as a measure of learning very much into question.

Consider also that stakeholders demanding that educators do more and that education be more. In response, textbooks have grown to include chapters on, among others, ethics, diversity, sustainability, and technology. Educators are being asked to cover more information, to do a better job of teaching so-called soft skills, and to incorporate service learning into their courses. If the knowledge content and rigor associated with a particular course remain constant, and these other learning outcomes are to be added, then how can a course still be awarded three credit hours?

Juxtaposing this discussion of credit hours with the earlier discussion of costs, revenues, and the budget environment raises an interesting question: What if there were a new generation of courses of four credit hours each (or more if needed)? In this new generation of courses, students would actually learn more (beyond basic knowledge transfer), and technology would enable professors to have contact with students outside of the classroom. To complete the fantasy, suppose that assessment results actually indicated that students were learning more and had more of the traits outlined in Figure 8.8 of the previous chapter (e.g., critical thinking skills, communication skills).

Simulation can be used to explore the economics of this switch from three to four credit hours. To simplify the example, consider two undergraduate-only institutions, each with 4,000 students, all of whom pay in-state tuition rates. At one school, all courses are three credit hours; at the other, they are four. The institutions fund no scholarships. Assume that the definition of full-time attendance (for financial aid purposes) is 12 credit hours at both schools. Assume also that students need to take one course above the full-time rate to graduate in four years. Said another way, instead of taking 40 three-credit courses (five per semester) and graduating in four years (with 120 credits), the student will take 32 four-credit courses (four per semester) and graduate in four years (with 128 credits).

Assume also that the commonly used "flat fee" rule applies, i.e., after paying for full-time tuition (12 hours), students do not incur additional tuition charges for taking additional courses. At both schools, 50% of the students take a sufficient number of courses to graduate in four years, and 10% take an additional course beyond this level. Another 20% are full-time for financial aid purposes (12 hours). Students who take just one course per semester constitute 5% of the population, as do students taking two courses. See Figure 9.5 for remaining assumptions.

Under these assumptions, in a single semester, the four-credit model generates approximately $1,398,000 more revenue in excess of costs versus the three-credit model. This reflects, in part, a lower proportion of students taking "free" courses above the 12-hour (full-time) threshold. Part-time students are also paying more per course; price sensitivity could be built into the model to reflect fewer part-time students, but the results would still favor the four-credit model.

Obviously, the parameters specified for this model are arbitrary, but these can be challenged. For example, based on a 1,000-trial Monte Carlo simulation, if the enrollment patterns associated with the number of courses taken per semester are randomly

Tuition Per credit	$210.00
Course-Related Fees Per Credit	$50.00
Revenue Per Credit	$260.00

	Salary	Teaches Courses/yr	Percent Of Classes Staffed
Average Salary FT Tenure-Track Faculty	$85,000	6	50%
Average Salary Full-time Lecturer	$60,000	8	20%
Average Part Time Salary	$3,500	4	30%

Average Course Size	25	students

Average Course Cost Per Student		
Salary Cost Per Student	$385.33	(weighted avg from above)
Incidentals per student	$50.00	
Total Per Student	$435.33	

Courses Per Semester	Enrollment Patterns	
	School 1 (3cr)	School 2 (4cr)
1	5%	5%
2	5%	5%
3	9%	20%
4	20%	50%
5	50%	10%
6	9%	9%
7	2%	1%
	100%	100%

Figure 9.5 Assumptions Underlying the Simulation

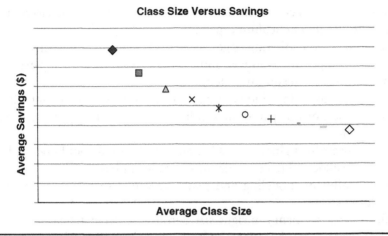

Figure 9.6 For Classes Size < 70, Four-Credit Savings Increase as Class Size Decreases

varied ±5% in all categories,[2] the four-credit model generates average savings of approximately $1,116,000 each semester, with a minimum savings of $703,000 and a maximum savings of $1,610,000. Savings are directly proportionate to the number of students assumed; double the students and double the savings. Altering the class-size assumption yields the pattern of savings shown in Figure 9.6.

From the faculty's point of view, there is little to dislike. Faculty teaching loads, in terms of number of courses per semester, remain unchanged. Faculty are being asked to do more in terms of active learning and soft-skill development, but these pressures will exist regardless of the credit-hour structure. The four-hour structure at least acknowledges the evolution away from the traditional lecture.

As for the students, those graduating in four years need to take only four courses per semester instead of five. Class scheduling becomes easier and there are fewer textbooks to purchase. Given that more students are now working more hours to pay for their education, this may be a more realistic definition of full-time.

Obviously, an institution would have to consider such a radical change with great care. For example, how would the school handle transfer of (primarily) three-credit courses? While these challenges are significant, it is worth noting that Binghamton University, which is part of the State University of New York System, has adopted this model and is consistently ranked as one of the best public universities in the nation.

CONCLUSION

This chapter, which considered resource alignment and curriculum capacity from an economic and tactical perspective, reached the following conclusions:

- Budget problems in higher education are unlikely to be solved through large tuition increases or increased levels of public support.

---

[2] The category representing a four year-graduation rate is adjusted to maintain a total of 100%.

- Addressing costs and efficiencies should be the primary approach to aligning available resources with curriculum capacity.
- The economics of (1) offering large classes, and (2) using less expensive contingent staffing are compelling. However, some schools may have already exploited these alternatives to their maximum potential.
- There are various factors and contingencies to consider when contemplating the use of large sections or part-time faculty. A number of these were delineated in Tables 9.1 and 9.2.
- Business Process Reengineering (BPR) and similar tools should be applied before resources are allocated to curricula on a permanent basis.
- Careful enrollment modeling and planning can prevent excess or insufficient curriculum capacity.
- Enrollment management can right-size enrollments to match available resources.
- Inter-institutional collaboration can be used to increase curriculum capacity and to lower costs.

REFERENCES

Barnett, J. (2006). Implementation of personal response units in very large lecture classes: Student perceptions. *Australasian Journal of Educational Technology, 22,* 474–494.

Bassis, M. (2009). Reining in college costs. *Business Week,* December 21, p 7.

Benjamin, E. (1998). Declining faculty availability to students is the problem—but tenure is not the explanation. *American Behavioral Scientist, 41*(5), 716–735.

Benjamin, E. (2002). How over-reliance on contingent appointments diminishes faculty involvement in student learning. *Peer Review, 5*(1), 4–10.

Breslawski, S. (2008). The impact of business program entrance requirements on enrollment outcomes. In *Proceedings of the Business Research Consortium of Western New York Conference,* Rochester, NY, April.

Breslawski, S., & Breslawski, K. (2000). Business program entrance requirements as predictors of program success. In *Proceedings, 2000 Annual Meeting of the Decision Sciences Institute,* Orlando, FL, November.

Burd, S., Brush, S., & Selingo, J. (2005). Rising tuition and Bush's budget top agenda at meeting of college leaders. *Chronicle of Higher Education, 51*(25).

Carey, K. (2009). College for $99 a month. *Washington Monthly.com,* September/October. Retrieved March 20, 2011 from http://www.washingtonmonthly.com/college_guide/feature/college_for_99_a_month.php?page=1

Chickering, A., & Gamson, Z. (1987). Seven principles for good practice in undergraduate education. *AAHE Bulletin,* (39), 3–7.

Connor, R. W., & Ching, C. (2010). Can learning be improved when budgets are in the red? *Chronicle of Higher Education, 56* (33), April 30.

Deslauriers, L., Schelew, E., & Wieman, C. (2011). Improved learning in a large-enrollment physics class. *Science, 332*(16031), 862–864.

Ehrenberg, R. G., & Rizzo, M. J. (2004). Financial forces and the future of American higher education. *Academe, 90*(4) 28–31.

Ehrenberg, R. G., & Zhang, L. (2005). Do tenured and tenure-track faculty matter? *Journal of Human Resources, 40*(3), 647–659.

Fitzgerald, M. A. (2004). Making the leap from high school to college three new studies about information literacy skills of first-year college students. *Knowledge Quest, 32*(4), 19–24.

Graham, C. R., Tripp, T. R., Seawright, L., & Joeckel, G. L. (2007). Empowering or compelling reluctant participators using audience response systems. *Active Learning in Higher Education, 8,* 233–258.

Guthrie, R. W., & Carlin, A. (2004). Waking the dead: Using interactive technology to engage passive listeners in the classroom. In *Proceedings of the Tenth Americas Conference on Information Systems,* New York, August.

Hunsinger, M., Poirier, C. R., & Feldman, R. S. (2008). The roles of personality and class size in student attitudes toward individual response technology. *Computers in Human Behavior, 24,* 2792–2798.

Jaeger, A. J., & Eagan, M. K. (2009). Effects of exposure to part-time faculty on associate's degree completion. *Community College Review, 36*(3), 167–194.

Jaeger, A. J., & Hinz, D. (2008). The effects of part-time faculty on first-year freshman retention: A predictive model using logistic regression. *Journal of College Student Retention: Research, Theory & Practice, 10*(3), 265–286.

Khadaroo, S. T. (2010). American frustration with college costs reaches all-time high. *Christian Science Monitor*, February 17.

Mervis, J. (2010). Nobelist "coach" takes on U.S. science education. *Science, 29*(10), *572.*

Milner-Bolotin, M., Antimirova, T., & Petrov, A. (2010). Clickers beyond the first-year science classroom. *Journal of College Science Teaching, 40*(2), 14–18.

Post, T. (2011). State funding cuts not the only reason for rising college tuition, Minnesota Public Radio, March 2. Retrieved March 18, 2011 from http://minnesota.publicradio.org/display/web/2011/03/02/minn-tuition/

Shedd, J. M. (2003). The history of the student credit hour. *New Directions for Higher Education, (122)*, 5–12.

Umbach, P. D. (2007). How effective are they? Exploring the impact of contingent faculty on undergraduate education. *Review of Higher Education, 30*(2), 91–123.

Vakola, M., & Rezgui, Y. (2000). Critique of existing business process re-engineering methodologies: The development and implementation of a new methodology. *Business Process Management Journal, 6*(3), 238–250.

Wang, P. (2009). Is college still worth the price? *CNNMoney*, April 13. Retrieved on April 28, 2011 from http://money.cnn.com/2008/08/20/pf/college/college_price.moneymag/

White House Press Office. (2009). Remarks of President Barack Obama—As prepared for delivery address to Joint Session of Congress, February 24. Retrieved March 20, 2011 from http://www.whitehouse.gov/the_press_office/Remarks-of-President-Barack-Obama-Address-to-Joint-Session-of-Congress

10

EFFECTIVELY MANAGING HUMAN RESOURCES IN 21ST-CENTURY COLLEGES AND UNIVERSITIES

Valerie Martin Conley and Kent J. Smith, Jr.

INTRODUCTION

At any given postsecondary institution there are several different categories of employees. Most institutions categorize full-time employees as faculty or staff. The latter may be administrative, professional, or support staff. Regardless of their category, all employees are expected to contribute in some way to student success as well as to the overall mission of the institution. As a result, effectively managing human resources in 21st-century colleges and universities is a challenging and complex endeavor.

Consider the following new employees at a given institution:

- Assistant Professor of English
- Director of Buildings and Grounds
- Instructional Technology (IT) Specialist
- Assistant Director of Student Activities.

It is their first day on the job and they are all required to attend the same new employee orientation given by the Office of Human Resources. While this is not a requirement at all universities and colleges, most institutions have some type of new employee orientation, which often places all categories of employees together.

While to some this may not seem like an important event in the life of a university or college employee, it is actually fascinating as it may be the only time during that person's career at the institution that he or she will be intentionally partnered with personnel from all other employee groups for the same training. Colleges and universities depend on people in order to fulfill their institutional missions. Students, staff, faculty, and administrators are all necessary participants in the operation of effective postsecondary schools. The complex interplay of roles, responsibilities, and authority on college and university campuses makes human resources management in higher education a challenging undertaking! For example, student employees have dual roles. They are simultaneously "students" and "employees" of the institution, making them both "customers" and "service providers."

The 1940 Statement on Academic Freedom and Tenure highlights the importance of freedom and economic security as "indispensable to the success of an institution in fulfilling its obligations to its students and to society" (AAUP, 1940). Tenure protects academic freedom. Yet, the percentage of tenured faculty members has decreased relative to other types of instructional employees in higher education, and recent legislative proposals have sought to eliminate or curtail it, raising questions about the best way to ensure academic freedom in the 21st century.

However, many argue that the tenure debate centers not on academic freedom, but instead on productivity and performance. Numerous articles, book chapters, and monographs describe ways to enhance the productivity and performance of tenured faculty members. Universities and colleges nationwide have implemented post-tenure review processes with varying levels of success.

As the tenure debate rages on, Leslie (2007) concludes that the American academic workforce is being dramatically reshaped by "tectonic" forces (p. 3). Tectonics is a branch of geology that focuses on the structure of the crust of planets or moons, and in particular on the fault lines that produce jagged effects that are not uniformly distributed. Are colleges and universities appropriately staffed to deliver high-quality, affordable (i.e., effective) postsecondary education, research, and outreach? Do jagged staffing patterns denote a strength of postsecondary education or a cause for concern?

A description of the types of personnel employed in colleges and universities provides context for this discussion. Next, the chapter outlines strategies for selecting and developing traditional and non-traditional faculty and staff, approaches for improving performance, and ways to combat short- and long-term budget reductions necessary to enhance productivity and efficiency in today's environment. It concludes with a discussion of the need to engage in purposeful, mission-driven, data-informed human resources planning and decision making that takes into consideration the complexity of employment relationships in 21st-century colleges and universities.

PERSONNEL

It is an understatement to say that the distribution of employees in higher education by primary functional area or occupational activity looks vastly different today than it did just 20 years ago. The number of academic support professionals, including those in technology and student affairs, has increased substantially in the past two to three decades. For example, the *Digest of Education Statistics* notes: "The proportion of other non-teaching professional staff rose from 10% in 1976 to 21% in 2009" (http://nces.ed.gov/programs/digest/d10/ch_3.asp, para 11). Researchers (Gumport and Pusser, 1995) dubbed the growth "A Case of Bureaucratic Accretion."

The U.S. Department of Education's National Center for Education Statistics (NCES) collects data from institutions on human resources through its Integrated Postsecondary Education Data System (IPEDS) Human Resources Surveys: Employees by Assigned

Position (EAP), Salaries, and Staff. All institutional employees are classified by full- or part-time status, faculty status, and occupational activity on the EAP. Occupational activities, or primary functions, are based on the Standard Occupational Classification (SOC) codes and categories as defined by the Bureau of Labor Statistics (BLS).

The IPEDS HR categories include individuals whose primary responsibility is instruction, research, and/or public service; graduate assistants; executive/administrative/managerial; other professionals; technical and paraprofessionals; clerical and secretarial; skilled crafts; and service/maintenance. The extent to which these categories adequately reflect staffing practices of postsecondary institutions varies. Categorizing employees by "primary" responsibility is an attempt to normalize the variability.

In fall 2009, colleges and universities employed approximately 3.7 million employees nationwide. The majority of employees were professional staff (75%). Figure 10.1 shows the change in the number of employees by primary responsibility for full-time professional faculty and staff for selected years from fall 1989 through fall 2009. While the number of full-time professional employees increased across the board, there was more rapid growth in non-faculty positions than in faculty positions between 1999 and 2009.

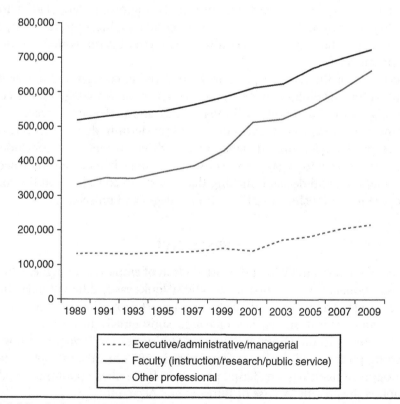

Figure 10.1 Full-Time Professional Employees in Degree-Granting Institutions, by Primary Occupation: Selected Years, Fall 1989 Through Fall 2009

Source: Table 253. *Digest of Education Statistics*, 2010.

The number of full-time executive/administrative/managerial employees rose by 45%; full-time other professional employees, by 53%; and full-time faculty, by 23%.

Figure 10.2 shows the change in the number of employees by primary responsibility for *part-time* professional faculty and staff for selected years from fall 1989 through fall 2009. Among part-time professional employees, there was a 35% increase in executives, a 16% increase in other professionals, and a 62% increase in faculty. Additionally, there was a 43% increase in graduate assistants during the period. The shift to a contingent faculty workforce is characterized by modest growth in full-time faculty positions coupled with rapid growth in part-time faculty and graduate assistants.

It is also interesting to note the relatively small percentage of part-time executive employees overall. Figures 10.3 and 10.4 show the distribution of all professional employees by primary occupation and employment status for 2009 and 1999, respectively. The most notable change is the decrease in the relative number of full-time faculty compared to other types of employees. Does this drop reflect a change in the

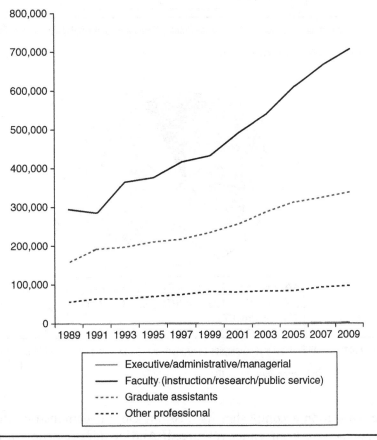

Figure 10.2 Part-Time Professional Employees in Degree-Granting Institutions, by Primary Occupation: Selected Years, Fall 1989 Through Fall 2009

Source: Table 253. *Digest of Education Statistics*, 2010.

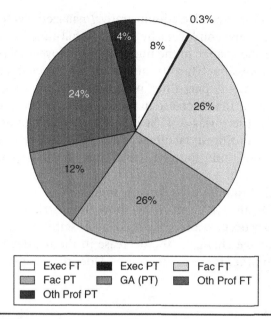

Figure 10.3 Distribution of All Professional Employees by Primary Occupation and Employment Status, Fall 2009

Source: Table 253. *Digest of Education Statistics*, 2010.

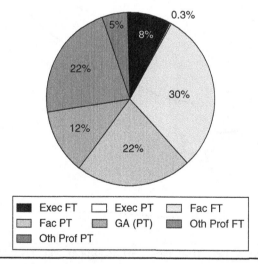

Figure 10.4 Distribution of All Professional Employees by Primary Occupation and Employment Status, Fall 1999

Source: Table 253. *Digest of Education Statistics*, 2010.

way higher education accomplishes its mission? Does it demonstrate that colleges and universities have been under-resourced? And/or does it denote a purposeful redirecting of resources away from the academic mission of institutions? An informed discussion requires an understanding of faculty and instructional staff, who they are, and what they do.

Faculty

IPEDS defines faculty as:

> Persons identified by the institution as such and typically those whose initial assignments are made for the purpose of conducting instruction, research or public service as a principal activity (or activities). They may hold academic rank titles of professor, associate professor, assistant professor, instructor, lecturer or the equivalent of any of those academic ranks. Faculty may also include the chancellor/president, provost, vice provosts, deans, directors or the equivalent, as well as associate deans, assistant deans and executive officers of academic departments (chairpersons, heads or the equivalent) if their principal activity is instruction combined with research and/or public service. The designation as "faculty" is separate from the activities to which they may be currently assigned. For example, a newly appointed president of an institution may also be appointed as a faculty member. Graduate, instruction, and research assistants are not included in this category.
>
> *(IPEDS Glossary)*

This definition highlights, but does not fully address, the complexities associated with determining accurate aggregate counts of faculty across institutions. Many researchers choose to restrict the definition of faculty to those individuals who hold tenure or are on the tenure track. Limiting the scope of analysis to tenured or tenure-track faculty poses little difficulty when conducting analyses on campuses where traditional lines are drawn between employees (i.e., faculty vs. non-faculty), but these lines are characterized by more and more shades of gray as all types of institutions hire more contingent faculty, including those hired less than full-time and full-time off the tenure track, with and without full benefits eligibility.

The National Study of Postsecondary Faculty (NSOPF), a sample survey of faculty and instructional staff last conducted by NCES in 2004, took these shades of gray into consideration. The target population included full-time and part-time employees who had faculty status, regardless of whether or not they had teaching responsibilities for credit, and anyone who had instructional responsibilities, regardless of whether or not they held faculty status. By casting a wide net, the NSOPF sample included a broad cross-section of professionals responsible for the instructional and research missions of colleges and universities of the day. The data, which offer a glimpse into the lives of some of these individuals, have been used in numerous studies.

In *Teaching Without Tenure,* for example, Baldwin and Chronister (2001) used NSOPF data to trace the growth of full-time non-tenure-track appointments and describe their characteristics. Their findings coalesced around five key themes:

1. The traditional full-time tenure-track faculty model is no longer adequately meeting the educational needs of a complex dynamic society.
2. A two-class faculty system has emerged in American higher education.
3. At present, many institutions with long-term needs are treating full-time non-tenure-track faculty as short-term solutions who are expendable and easily replaced.

4. No consensus has yet emerged within higher education on the terms and conditions of employment of full-time non-tenure-track faculty.
5. The quality of students' educational experience and the overall health of our higher education system depend on a vigorous academic profession—including faculty in non-tenure-track positions (Baldwin & Chronister, 2001, pp. 7–8).

These themes still resonate today. From their extensive research, including analyses of data from NSOPF; a survey of institutions about their use of full-time non-tenure-track faculty and policies in place to govern such appointments; a review of available institutional policies; and interviews with faculty, department chairs, faculty leaders, and administrators at 12 institutions, Baldwin and Chronister (2001) identified 11 components of a good practice model:

1. A defined probationary period (p. 147)
2. Explicit evaluation criteria (p. 149)
3. Multi-year contracts following a probationary period (p. 150)
4. Defined dates for contract renewal or termination (p. 151)
5. An equitable salary system (p. 153)
6. An equitable fringe benefit program (p. 154)
7. A system of sequential ranks (p. 155)
8. Support for professional development (p. 156)
9. Meaningful involvement in governance and curriculum development (p. 159)
10. Recognition of and reward for contributions (p. 160)
11. Procedures for protecting academic freedom (p. 161)

To aid institutions in meeting these goals, the authors developed a framework for self-assessment that guides users through a series of questions designed to determine the extent to which the institution is engaging in good practice regarding personnel policies and practices affecting full-time non-tenure-track faculty. The self-assessment covers four areas: the purpose and procedures for hiring, contractual arrangements, integration into the campus community, and oversight and monitoring (Baldwin & Chronister, 2001, pp. 206–210).

Examples of the types of questions in the first section include: "Does the institution have a comprehensive faculty staffing plan?" (p. 206) and "Has the institution clearly articulated the reasons for hiring non-track faculty?" (p. 207). In the section on contractual agreements, questions include: "Has a clearly defined position description been articulated for each non-track position?" (p. 207). One of the questions in the section on integration into the campus community asks: "Is there a formal orientation program for new full-time non-tenure-track faculty?" (p. 209). The final section poses questions such as: "What type of monitoring is conducted to ascertain that the policies and procedures governing the employment of full-time non-tenure-track faculty are consistently and equitably implemented?" (p. 210).

While the self-assessment guide was developed with full-time non-tenure-track faculty in mind, it could be modified to focus on each specific employee type to determine how well policies and practices in place are meeting the needs of the institution and the individuals. An important element is developing clear and reasonable expectations for each employee group.

Davis (2003) discusses managing people and encouraging development, as well as the important role of leaders in maintaining a positive work environment. Davis (2003) cites the dimensions of healthy work environments: (a) open communication, (b) employee involvement, (c) learning and renewal, (d) valued diversity, (e) institutional fairness, (f) equitable rewards and recognition, (g) economic security, (h) people-centered technology, (i) health-enhancing environments, (j) meaningful work, (k) family/work/life balance, (l) community responsibility, and (m) environmental protection (p. 178).

One employee group that has received a lot of attention is tenure-track faculty. Reported as "not surprising," findings from the 2008 *Tenure-Track Faculty Job Satisfaction Survey* conducted by the Collaborative on Academic Careers in Higher Education (COACHE) clearly demonstrate that what pre-tenured faculty members want are clear and transparent tenure processes and expectations (p. 2). Again, while these results are specific to one employee group, there is applicability to others.

As postsecondary work environments become more complex and the roles of employees more ambiguous, it will become even more critical to focus attention of the policies and procedures that delineate management of personnel functions. Effective human resource management practices in business and industry do have relevant application in postsecondary education settings. Davis (2003) emphasizes the importance of "a commitment to core values such as respect for all, lifelong learning, and celebrating diversity" in promoting healthy work environments (p. 178).

Other Professional Staff (A.K.A. Non-Faculty)

It is becoming more difficult to distinguish when, where, and how instruction takes place as programming related to first-year experience programs, retention, and learning communities become commonplace on college campuses. A philosophy that puts student learning at the center of the mission of the entire institution further blurs academic vs. non-academic lines. The Student Personnel Point of View (SPPV) emphasizes development of the whole student, inside and outside of the classroom. The emergence of student affairs as a field within higher education and commensurate growth in the number of professional staff employed in related positions is an indicator that institutions are embracing this philosophy. IPEDS does not collect separate data on individuals whose primary occupation is student affairs.

Winston and Creamer (1997) provide guidance to student affairs practitioners in *Improving Staffing Practices in Student Affairs*, which encompasses the contexts and values for staffing in student affairs to a model—dubbed synergistic supervision—to ensure quality in the profession. The components of the model include recruitment and selection of staff, orienting staff to new positions, supervising and managing staff, staff development, and performance appraisal. Conley (2001) adds "separation," noting that it is an integral aspect of the staffing process. While focused on student affairs, Winston and Creamer's model is applicable to other employee groups in higher education institutions. Given the complexity of employment relationships in colleges and universities today, effective staffing practices incorporating strategies for selecting and developing traditional and non-traditional faculty and staff are critical.

STAFFING PRACTICES

In any staffing practices model, recruitment and selection, orientation, supervision, performance evaluation, professional development, turnover, and retirement must be considered. Yet, colleges and universities occupy a unique position within our society, which requires postsecondary institutions to go beyond effective human resources practices and embrace the tenets of a learning organization that transcends business and industry practices. This is particularly challenging given the fiscal constraints facing many institutions, prompting some to question the priorities of those responsible for hiring decisions. Davis (2003) recommends a four-step process:

1. Describe the job
2. Identify skills, knowledge, and personal characteristics required to do the job
3. Establish selection criteria
4. Develop an assessment procedure to guide the selection.

The last step is critical to ensure consistency and fairness. Even so: "Vigilant efforts need to be maintained to see that the process is fair, that discrimination is absent, and that adequate records of the process are kept" (Davis, 2003, p. 182). Attention to process contributes to vigilance, a positive workplace environment, and compliance with state and federal workplace laws.

By way of example, Table 10.1 presents an excerpt from Ohio University's *Hiring Process Overview*.

Table 10.1 Example Hiring Process Overview: Excerpt from Ohio University's Hiring Process Overview

Step	Procedure
Job description	Complete a job description and submit to University Human Resources compensation for proper classification if it is a new position, the job description is more than 3 years old, or the primary duties and responsibilities have changed more than 50%
Essential position review	Complete and submit the essential position review form to the Office of the President for approval to post. The following employment categories are exempt from the essential position review process: positions fully (100%) supported through grant funding, student employee requests, internal postings of existing bargaining unit positions, and non-benefits-eligible term appointments
Posting	Concurrent with step 2, the hiring manager creates an electronic requisition to post via the University's employment website. University Human Resources will complete the posting process and contact the hiring manager to coordinate the posting and advertising dates
Recruitment and advertising	University Human Resources will post all benefits eligible vacancies to the University web-site as well as OhioMeansJobs.com and HigherEdJobs.com. Additionally, University Human Resources will place all advertisements for classified positions. The hiring department is responsible for all recruitment activities including ad placement for administrative, faculty and student employment opportunities

Table 10.1 (Continued)

Step	Procedure
Screening and interviewing process	University Human Resources will pre-screen to identify classified candidates that meet the minimum qualifications for classified positions. For all other employment types, departments are responsible for conducting screening processes to determine finalist candidates
Selection process	The hiring department is responsible for checking references for potential offerees. Once the department has identified the candidate(s) that are potential hires, the hiring manager must complete the online hiring forms and make their selections via the University's employment website to submit to either University Human Resources or the Office of Institutional Equity (depending on employment type) prior to any offer or negotiation with the candidate
Negotiation	University Human Resources will extend the official offer of employment as well as negotiate compensation and starting date for classified position. For all other employment types, the hiring department is responsible for these negotiations. As part of the negotiation process, being familiar with the University benefits, relocation policy, and compensation policy can be extremely beneficial
Complete the hire	University Human Resources will process all new hire information for classified employees and will prepare and submit the official offer letter. Unsuccessful classified candidates will receive regret email notification from University Human Resources. University Human Resources will schedule new hire orientation for classified employees
	The hiring department is responsible for completing the on-line appointment form; offer letter, letters of regret, and scheduling new employee orientation for faculty and administrative hires. Note: I-9 forms *must* be completed within 48 hours of employment start date. If the employee is not scheduled for orientation until a later date, please ensure the employee comes to University Human Resources within the first two days of employment to complete the I-9 in order to be in compliance with this important Federal Regulation
On-boarding	The first few weeks of the new employee's experience will shape their lasting impression of Ohio University. Please be sure to make the new employee feel welcome in their new environment. Checking in with them regularly, assigning a mentor, providing departmental handbooks, are all good ways to help ease their transition. You might also consider a "welcome" package that includes helpful information about the department and planning unit

Source: http://www.ohio.edu/hr/employment/upload/hiring_processes_overview.pdf

Vacancies

Individuals leave, or separate from, their positions for many reasons—some voluntary, others involuntary. Individuals may leave a position for professional reasons (e.g., to accept a promotion or for a higher salary) or personal reasons (e.g., to relocate closer to family). As the age of the population increases, more individuals are retiring from postsecondary institutions than ever before. Vacancies create losses but also opportunities. Winston and Creamer (1997) recommend conducting a thorough job analysis as a prerequisite to filling a vacancy. However, their case data reveal "that such practice is nowhere near universal or consistent" (p. 125). Davis (2003) also recommends conducting a careful job analysis: "Ask the person currently in the job, superiors, sub-ordinates, and colleagues to describe the job. Examine existing job descriptions. Consider what exemplary performers of this job or similar jobs do and set reasonable performance standards" (p. 181).

The resulting data can be used to prepare exemplary job descriptions; the basic elements required are described below.

Job Descriptions

Job descriptions help articulate the most important outcomes needed from an employee performing a particular job. The basic elements of a job description include the position title, the name of the unit in which the position is located, responsibilities, and qualifications. Job descriptions for faculty positions may include other elements as well. Winston and Creamer (1997) call the position description "a crucial outcome of position analysis" and note, "A position description normally is thought of as the formal statement of duties that defines a position" (p. 130). These descriptions may be posted in a number of ways; potential avenues include the institution's human resources website, external employment websites, email, and social media. Typically, multiple methods of posting are used.

Job Posting Best Practices

It is typical for the hiring department to be responsible for all recruitment activities including ad placement for administrative, faculty, and student employment opportunities (Ohio University *Hiring Process Overview*, November 2009, Step 4, p. 1). Davis (2003) summarizes:

> Developing a job description, statement of qualifications, and a job posting that is distributed widely, avoids the tendency to "build a job around a promising person' or to become attracted to people 'close at hand." Not only are such practices risky from a legal standpoint, they do not serve the institution well in the long run in locating the very best talent.
>
> (p. 182)

It is often a challenge to coordinate these activities in higher education because most vacancies are filled based on the recommendation of an ad hoc search committee convened for the intended purpose of completing the search.

Search Committees

Most searches in postsecondary institutions are filled with the assistance of a search committee. It is imperative that the roles and responsibilities of the search committee be clear from the outset. This can be accomplished through written invitations to serve on the committee and a charge from the supervisor or individual vested with hiring authority. Generally, research on what makes a search committee successful suggests that clarity throughout the process is a critical factor. Clarification upfront can ensure a smoother process later. For example, a key question to consider before the search begins is whether the committee should forward a ranked or unranked list of qualified candidates to the hiring authority. Knowing the expectations from the outset can reduce tensions at the conclusion of the search.

One of the most critical steps in the hiring process is conducting interviews. There are several types of interviews. Denham (2009) lists (a) informational interviews, (b) screening or telephone interviews, (c) individual interviews, (d) small group or committee interviews, (e) the second or on-site interview, (f) behavioral-based interviews, (g) task-oriented or testing interviews, and (h) stress interviews.

In higher education, most of these interview types are utilized. The typical flow begins with the telephone interview (some institutions are now conducting video phone interviews during this phase), followed by the individual (on-campus) interview, which can last one to two days and include group meetings and possibly a presentation on a given topic.

Reference checks are also interviews. A reference check is an interview of an applicant's former employer, former supervisor, current supervisor, or colleague. In higher education, a member of the search committee, the hiring supervisor, or a search firm hired by the institution usually conducts reference checks. The timing of the reference check varies by institution and by search committee; for instance, some choose to conduct reference checks prior to campus visits, while others wait until finalists are named for the vacant position.

Background checks go beyond reference checks to include criminal records and credit reports. Such checks are commonplace for administrative positions and are being utilized more and more in faculty searches.

Candidates should also be aware that search committees, search firms, and hiring authorities usually conduct Internet searches as a means of better understanding a candidate's background and breadth of experience. Yet, there is growing concern about the legalities associated with using information from cyberspace to make hiring and firing decisions.

Once the search process has concluded and a candidate has been identified for the position, a salary offer is made. Salary offers are handled differently in different institutions. The next section provides a general overview.

Salary Offer

The salary offer can come in a variety of ways, the most common being in person or by telephone call from the hiring supervisor. Another method institutions sometimes use is to send a formal offer letter to the candidate and schedule a follow-up call to discuss its contents.

In part, institutional culture determines where the hiring decision and responsibility for making salary offers reside. For faculty positions, department chairs may have authority to hire adjunct, temporary, or part-time faculty. Deans may reserve the right to negotiate offers with full-time tenure-track or non-tenure-track faculty. Hiring decisions for staff in administrative units are typically made at the director level or above.

Budget constraints provide justifiable pressures and may tempt those responsible for hiring decisions to bring individuals into the organization at the lowest possible salary. Women, on average, still earn less than men in similar positions. In academia, the wage gap has narrowed in recent years but is still between 4% and 6% even after controlling for factors that are generally accepted as impacting faculty salaries (e.g., publications, grants, etc.) (Toutkoushian & Conley, 2005). One reason for the persistent gap may be that women do not negotiate as well as men (Miller & Miller, 2002). Starting salary has implications for future earnings, and a lower starting salary is compounded over time. Salary information is widely available today, especially for public institutions. Making this information transparent during the hiring process is one strategy for safeguarding against salary equity issues.

Hiring is an expensive process. Given the amount of time and effort that goes into such decisions, it is no wonder that recruitment and retention are seen as critical human resource issues in higher education. As discussed below, an effective orientation process will help to ensure there is return on the investment.

Orientation

There is no shortage of resources on designing effective orientation programs for new higher education employees. For example, *The Missing Professor: An Academic Mystery* (Jones, 2005) takes a lighthearted approach by providing informal case studies and discussion stories that can be used as part of new faculty orientation, faculty development, and campus conversations. Winston and Creamer (1997) offer a comprehensive resource on staffing practices in student affairs, including new employee orientation.

These excellent resources notwithstanding, orientation is often defined by a planned event or series of events organized at the beginning of each academic year for a cohort of newly hired employees. These events are important because they introduce the new employee to the institution and its culture and provide an opportunity to process necessary paperwork for health insurance, retirement plans, and of course parking.

Effective orientation is associated with processes that integrate the employee (faculty or staff) into the institution on an ongoing basis. As individuals take on new responsibilities and institutions take on new initiatives, orientation and professional development have the potential to become seamless synergistic processes that incorporate new and existing staff. Issues important to consider for existing staff are highlighted below.

Existing Staff

The number of new employees hired at an institution in a given year is small compared to the number of continuing employees. It goes without saying that highly effective organizations depend upon the productivity of the latter group. Effective management of human resources in higher education requires institutions to focus more attention on existing staff. Bolman and Deal (1997) describe one useful tool for doing so—the human resources framework. The simple constructs of this theoretical framework are a reminder that organizations and people need each other. Organizations need the talent, skills, and abilities that individuals bring to positions. Individuals need the jobs and resources provided by the organization.

Highly effective human resource managers understand the importance of professional development in helping employees achieve continued personal and professional growth. College and university faculty and staff are experts on student development and the importance of the development of the whole student. The same constructs should be applied to understanding employee development.

However, separation is also a natural part of the staffing process. Individuals leave organizations for many reasons. Accepting a position at another institution and retirement are two of the most common. As the age of the population increases, retirements in higher education are becoming more commonplace. As the economy recovers, there will be opportunities for advancement. Understanding employees' strengths, opportunities for improvement, and aspirations will better position highly effective institutions to respond to demands for innovative strategies for delivering higher education to 21st-century learners. Approaches for improving performance are essential to success; these conducting honest and accurate evaluations appropriate for the type of employee, employing progressive discipline techniques, providing recognition and incentives, and identifying and empowering change agents.

Evaluations

Evaluations are key to understanding employees. Organizations perform evaluations in an effort to assess employee performance accurately. While evaluations serve a similar purpose for all types of employees, the process involved differs from group to group even within the same institution. For example, Winston and Creamer (1997) focus on supervision as the central mechanism for achieving effective staffing practices in student affairs. Evaluations are the primary tool supervisors use to provide feedback.

Evaluations are equally critical for faculty, but evaluation processes are typically different for faculty members than for administrative and other staff members at an institution. Faculty members value autonomy. Supervision, then, is not the primary mechanism for achieving effective staffing practices for faculty. Faculty performance evaluation is a continuous, multifaceted process including input from students, peers, department chairs, and deans.

Indeed, faculty members are evaluated in a variety of ways, one being based on the courses that they teach. Course evaluations provide instructors with feedback on students' perceptions of the course overall and the effectiveness of instructional methods used. Their primary purpose is to enable instructors to make informed decisions about improving the course. Institutions also use course evaluations to assess the instructor's teaching abilities.

Faculty members are also evaluated through peer review, which is typically conducted annually by a committee made up of colleagues at the same or higher rank within an academic department. The committee makes recommendations to the department chair and the dean regarding the performance of each faculty member within the department. The process for determining merit increases and the decision-making authority for allocating such increases varies from institution to institution. In their role as supervisor, department chairs are typically required to conduct their own evaluations of the faculty within their department.

When a faculty member goes up for tenure and/or promotion, that individual's accomplishments to date are reviewed more thoroughly. Evaluations of his or her portfolio are solicited from faculty in the discipline outside of the institution. Other forms of faculty peer review include proposal processes for conferences, publications, and grants. It is important to note that administrators are increasingly being evaluated through peer review as they engage in similar activities. The extent to which research and creative activity are expected or considered part of the normal duties of the position varies from institution to institution.

All individuals involved in evaluation processes at an institution should be provided with information regarding expectations for the position and their role in evaluating performance. According to the 2008 survey conducted by the Collaborative on Academic Careers in Higher Education (COACHE), pre-tenured faculty members who reported that expectations for tenure and promotion were clear and reasonable were more satisfied with their positions (p. 2). Indirectly, these data suggest that effective evaluation is critical to ensuring expectations are clear and reasonable. Yet, there are few tools specifically designed for higher education environments and little guidance for academic administrators, department chairs, and tenure review committees on handling evaluation for pre-tenured faculty members. One tool that has been implemented with employees generally is progressive discipline, described below.

Progressive Discipline

Progressive discipline is a process for dealing with job-related behavior that does not meet expected and communicated performance standards. Progressive discipline's primary purpose is to assist the employee in understanding that a performance problem or opportunity for improvement exists. Many institutions have a defined progressive discipline protocol. While progressive discipline processes may vary by institution, most include a verbal warning or reprimand. Should the performance problem continue, the discipline progresses to a written reprimand, suspension, and ultimately termination if the issue is not resolved.

Progressive discipline is typically applied differently with different employee groups. For example, a progressive discipline policy for addressing job-related behavior of student employees usually involves four basic steps: a documented verbal warning, a written warning, a suspension, and termination. Similar protocols are usually followed for non-faculty employees. Table 10.2 provides an example progressive discipline policy.

Table 10.2 Example Progressive Discipline Policy: Excerpt from The University of Alabama's Progressive Discipline Policy

Sections Included	Example Excerpted Wording
Purpose	The purpose of the procedure listed here is to encourage and help employees work together harmoniously according to the standards of The University of Alabama
Policy statement	Progressive steps will be followed in employee disciplinary matters except in matters the University, its representatives, or its management determine need to be addressed outside of the progressive system
Types of disciplinary action	*Verbal Counseling:* Verbal counseling sessions may take place between employees and supervisors in situations that are deemed less serious in nature. Every effort to determine and resolve the cause of the problem should be made. At the same time, however, it should be specifically stated that the employee is receiving a formal warning. Documentation of the verbal counseling should be made and maintained in departmental files for verbal counseling sessions.
	Written Counseling: Written counseling sessions take place between a supervisor and an employee when the behavior of the employee: is a repeated violation and verbal counseling has been administered; hinders the progress of the department in which the employee works; or hampers the progress of the University. Copies of all written warnings should be distributed as follows: one copy to the employee, one copy to the

Table 10.2 (Continued)

Sections Included	Example Excerpted Wording
	University's Department of Human Resources for inclusion in the employee's file, and one copy maintained in departmental files under lock and key.
	Suspension: Suspension, or release from duty, is a more severe action that may be used to continue investigations and/or for constructive improvement. Suspensions are issued when it is determined that a second warning would not suffice or that an initial incident is too severe for a warning yet not sufficiently severe for dismissal. Suspensions may vary in length, according to the severity of the offense or deficiency. Where a suspension has failed to produce the proper results, consideration should be given for a more lengthy suspension or the dismissal of the employee.
	Suspension notices should indicate the following: a. the reason(s) for the discipline, b. the inclusive dates of the suspension, and c. the employee's right of appeal.
	Dismissals: An employee's employment may be terminated after other disciplinary measures have failed or when a first time incident occurs that is extremely serious
Behaviors that may result in disciplinary action	Displaying a disrespectful and/or inappropriate behaviors toward a student, employee or supervisor;
	Refusing to do assigned work or failing to carry out the reasonable assignment of a manager, supervisor or department head;
	Falsifying a time card or other University record or giving false information to anyone whose duty is to make such record;
	Being repeatedly or continuously absent or late, being absent without notice or reason satisfactory to the University or leaving one's work assignment without appropriate authorization;
	Smoking within no-smoking areas or no-smoking operations or any area of the University that must be entered for the conduct of University business;
	Conducting oneself in any manner which is offensive, abusive or contrary to common decency or morality; carrying out any form of harassment including sexual harassment;
	Operating state-owned vehicles, equipment or private vehicles on state business without proper license or operating any vehicle on University property or on University business in an unsafe or improper manner;
	Having an unauthorized weapon, firearm or explosive on University property;
	Appropriating state or student equipment, time or resources for personal use or gain;
	Computer abuse, including but not limited to, plagiarism or programs, misuse of computer accounts, unauthorized destruction of files, creating illegal accounts, possession of unauthorized passwords, disruptive or annoying behavior on the computer and non-work related utilization of computer software or hardware;
	Conviction of a felony;
	Unlawfully distributing, selling, possessing, using or being under the influence of alcohol or drugs when on the job or subject to duty;
	Interfering in any way with the work of others;
	Stealing or possessing without authority any equipment, tools, materials or other property of the University or attempting to remove them from the premises without approval or permission from the appropriate authority;
	Willful violation of safety rules or University policies

Source: http://hr.ua.edu/empl_rel/policy-manual/counseling-discipline.htm

Different protocols are followed for faculty members—especially those with tenure, which is earned through an extensive review process after a probationary period. Afforded a high level of autonomy in their work, tenured faculty members have a responsibility to their subject—to seek and to state the truth as they see it—and devote their energies to developing and improving their scholarly competence. Tenured faculty members are guided by ethical principles of the profession and accept the obligation to exercise self-discipline and judgment in using, extending, and transmitting knowledge. Termination for cause of a tenured faculty member is a serious matter. The faculty handbook of an institution outlines the process. For example, the *Ohio University Faculty Handbook* states:

> Termination for cause of a continuous appointment, or the dismissal for cause of a teacher previous to the expiration of a term appointment should, if possible, be considered by both a faculty committee and the governing board of the institution. In all cases where the facts are in dispute, accused teachers should be informed before the hearing in writing of the charges against them and should have the opportunity to be heard in their own defense by all bodies that pass judgment upon their case. They should be permitted to have with them an advisor of their own choosing who may act as counsel. There should be a full stenographic record of the hearing available to the parties concerned. In the hearing of charges of incompetence, the testimony should include that of teachers and other scholars, either from their own or from other institutions. Teachers on continuous appointment who are dismissed for reasons not involving moral turpitude should receive their salaries for at least a year from the date of notification of dismissal whether or not they are continued in their duties at the institution.
>
> (Section I.4.A.d)

Care should be taken to distinguish between human resources management issues and breaches of ethics. If they are to enhance individual and institutional productivity, mechanisms for handling performance problems or opportunities for improvement among faculty must be based on clearly articulated expectations, and acceptable and trustworthy evidence (Braskamp & Ory, 1994).

An important provision for faculty is the ability to appeal a decision. "Faculty have the right to question a decision and be given an opportunity without threat of retaliation, to question the fairness of the assessment process" (Braskamp & Ory, 1994, p. 162). Disciplinary action cases for faculty should be handled with sensitivity given the nature of the tenured faculty member's position in the institution and within his or her academic field of expertise because these cases have the potential to affect an individual's status and the institution's reputation (Braskmap & Ory, 1994).

In addition to applying discipline fairly, effective human resources management also emphasizes recognition and incentives. The next section explores strategies that can be used to acknowledge the value of higher education employees, something particularly important in today's economy.

Recognition and Incentives

In a difficult economy, supervisors are always searching for ways to recognize dynamic employee efforts and simultaneously create a motivational environment where employees work at optimal levels to accomplish agreed-upon objectives. The term "incentives" most often calls to mind monetary rewards. It is important to keep in mind, particularly given the tough economic climate, that incentives take a variety of forms. Perhaps one of the most effective incentives an institution can provide is a positive work environment and campus climate.

Workplace motivators include both monetary and non-monetary incentives and should vary based on the career stage and generation of the employee. It should be noted that not all employees are solely motivated by monetary incentives. Although the use of positive reinforcements is good practice in the workplace, it must be done correctly. A balance between monetary and non-monetary incentives should be used to satisfy the diverse needs and interests of employees.

Evidence suggests that different incentives are important to employees from different generations. The generations covered in the AARP surveys include "Mature Workers" (those born between 1930 and 1945), "Baby Boomers" (those born between 1946 and 1963), "Generation X'ers" (those born between 1964 and 1981), and "Generation Y'ers" (those born after 1982) (Nelson, 1999). Nelson recommends flexible schedules as a non-monetary incentive for all employees. Other non-monetary incentives vary for the different generations, however. Mature and baby boomer workers are more similar than generation X'ers and generation Y'ers. Nelson suggests (a) flexible schedules and part-time hours for mature employees; (b) retirement planning and sabbaticals for baby boomers; (c) professional development, feedback, tangible rewards and an emphasis on the work environment for generation X'ers; and (d) increased attention on accomplishments for generation Y'ers.

Generational non-monetary incentive differences are affected by career stage and proximity to retirement. The older the individual, the greater the focus on retirement or supplementing retirement income with part-time or temporary jobs. The younger the individual, the greater the focus on job satisfaction and work environment. The bottom line is that organizations must tailor incentives to the needs of employees rather than using a "one-size-fits-all" approach, which is impersonal and sometimes ineffective.

Budget Reductions

In most colleges and universities today, budget reductions are a regular occurrence. Regardless of whether the budget reduction is short-term or long-term, it is not an easy task because it will affect something or someone adversely. In order to develop a strategy for combating reductions, one must understand why the cuts are being implemented, how much of a reduction is needed, how the reduction can be distributed across departments, and in what time frame the reduction will have to be absorbed.

It is important to know whether the reduction is happening because of occurrences, or trigger events, within the college or university (e.g., low enrollment, reduction in investment income, increased expenses, need for infrastructure improvements) or as a result of external factors (reduction in state subsidy or federal grants, down economy, or legislative changes). Once the reason for the reduction is known, the institution can plan accordingly to prevent future cuts, finding alternative methods of replacing the lost income and/or finding ways to absorb the reduction. Because higher education relies heavily on human resources, many budget reductions impact personnel.

Some strategies that can be employed to assist in combating short-term and long-term budget reductions include: (a) increasing revenue, (b) implementing hiring freezes and/or reductions in staff, (c) conducting environmental scans, (d) making tough decisions, and (e) involving faculty, staff, and students in the process.

CONCLUSION

This chapter began by examining trends in the distribution of higher education employees. The discussion continued with a review of recommended strategies for selecting and developing faculty and staff, and then explored approaches for improving performance and ideas for combating short- and long-term budget reductions necessary to enhance productivity and efficiency in today's postsecondary education environment.

The chapter now concludes with an overarching recommendation to engage in purposeful, mission-driven, data-informed human resources planning and decision-making that takes into consideration the complex employment relationships found in 21st-century colleges and universities. Specific advice focused at the institutional level and at individuals responsible for managing human resources is intended to provide guidance on how to create and maintain highly effective organizations composed of highly effective employees.

First, clarify, simplify, and streamline processes while respecting the autonomy of units engaged in searches. Even small institutions often have multiple job searches going on at the same time. Leverage mechanisms to make the most of the institutional resources available to support these searches. For example, provide a template for job descriptions; delineate the key steps in the process from approval of the search to making an offer; organize and make widely available tips on key questions to ask (and not to ask).

Attending to basic structural issues and clarifying policies and procedures will go a long way in ensuring organizational effectiveness. Of course, the culture of the institution influences the structure and the extent to which processes are centralized or decentralized. While structure matters, there should be a degree of flexibility inherent in human resources processes, particularly given the increasing complexity of employment relationships in colleges and universities today. Instead of thinking about processes as centralized or decentralized, highly effective organizations will strike an appropriate balance between the two.

Second, use a human resources framework and synergistic supervision to guide decision-making to improve performance. Review language in accrediting bodies' guidelines related to human resources. Mission-driven staffing practices that align with these guidelines will be most effective.

Third, budgets are value statements for colleges and universities, and unfortunately budget reductions are a harsh reality. Institutions must have a great understanding of what they are trying to accomplish and why. In combating short-term and long-term budget reductions, several options can be deployed. These include increasing revenue, implementing a hiring freeze or reduction in staff, conducting an environmental scan, doing less with less, and involving faculty and students in the entire conversation.

Finally, it should be clear from the complex employment relationships that exist on college and university campuses today that effective human resources management requires multiple processes and structures. Winston and Creamer (1997), among others, emphasize that at its core human resources involves people. It is possible to take this a step further by suggesting that everyone in higher education is involved in human resources. This approach requires constant, consistent communication; knowledge of institutional policies; and budget training.

REFERENCES

AAUP (1940). *1940 statement of principles on academic freedom and tenure.* Retrieved July 7, 2011 from the AAUP website: http://www.aaup.org/AAUP/pubsres/policydocs/contents/1940statement.htm

Baldwin, R. G., & Chronister, J. L. (2001). *Teaching without tenure: Policies and practices for a new era.* Baltimore: The Johns Hopkins University Press.

Bolman, L. G., & Deal, T. E. (1997). *Reframing organizations: Artistry, choice, and leadership* (2nd ed.). San Francisco: Jossey-Bass.

Braskamp, L. A., & Ory, J. C. (1994). *Assessing faculty work: Enhancing individual and institutional performance.* San Francisco: Jossey-Bass.

Collaborative on Academic Careers in Higher Education (COACHE). (2008). *Highlights report.* Retrieved July 7, 2011 from the Harvard Graduate School of Education website: http://isites.harvard.edu/icb/icb.do?keyword =coache&tabgroupid=icb.tabgroup103414

Conley, V. M. (2001). Separation: An integral aspect of the staffing process. *The College Student Affairs Journal, 21*(1), 57–63.

Davis, J. R. (2003). *Learning to lead: A handbook for postsecondary administrators.* ACE/Praeger Series on Higher Education. New York: Rowman & Littlefield.

Denham, T. J. (2009). *The 8 major types of interviews.* Retrieved July 7, 2011 from the Career Center Toolbox website: http://www.careercentertoolbox.com/interviews/the-8-major-types-of-interviews

Gilbreath, B., & Montesino, M. U. (2006). Expanding the HRD role: Improving employee well-being and organizational performance. *Human Resource Development International, 9*(4), 563–571.

Gumport, P. J., & Pusser, B. (1995). A case of bureaucratic accretion: Context and consequences. *The Journal of Higher Education, 66*(5), 493–520.

Hearn, J. C., Lewis, D. R., Kallsen, L., Holdsworth, J. M., & Jones, L. M. (2006). Incentives for managed growth: A case study of incentives-based planning and budgeting in a large public research university. *The Journal of Higher Education, 77*(2), 286–316.

Jones, T. (2005). *The missing professor: An academic mystery.* Sterling, VA: Stylus Publishing.

Kim, J. (2010). Strategic human resource practices: Introducing alternatives for organizational performance improvement in the public sector. *Public Administration Review, 70*(1), 38–49.

Leslie, D. W. (2007). The reshaping of America's academic workforce. TIAA-CREF institute. *Research Dialogue, 87*, 1–23.

Miller, L. E., & Miller, J. (2002). *A woman's guide to successful negotiating: How to convince, collaborate, and create your way to agreement.* New York: McGraw-Hill.

Nelson, B. (1999). *Incentives for all generations.* Retrieved July 7, 2011 from the Nelson Motivation Inc. website: http://www2.inc.com/search/16431.html

Ohio University Faculty Handbook (n.d.). Retrieved July 7, 2011 from the Ohio University Faculty Senate website: http://www.ohio.edu/facultysenate/handbook/index.cfm

Toutkoushian, R. K., & Conley, V. M. (2005). Progress for women in academe, yet inequities persist: Evidence from NSOPF:99. *Research in Higher Education, 46*(1), 1–28.

U.S. Department of Education. (2010). *Digest of Education Statistics.* Retrieved June 14, 2011, from the National Center for Education Statistics Website: http://nces.ed.gov/programs/digest

U.S. Department of Education. (n.d.). *IPEDS Glossary.* Retrieved June 14, 2011, from the National Center for Education Statistics Website: http://nces.ed.gov/ipeds/glossary/?charindex=F

Winston, Jr., R. B., & Creamer, D. G. (1997). *Improving staffing practices in student affairs.* San Francisco: Jossey-Bass.

11

SHAPING PHILANTHROPIC EFFORTS THAT SUPPORT INSTITUTIONAL PRIORITIES

John D. Crawford

INTRODUCTION

Over the past decade, philanthropic support for colleges and universities has become critical due to the economic recession, and increasingly so for public institutions as public resources have declined. Even in times of robust economic growth, the general feeling among higher education policy makers is that there will not be a significant return of public financial support for higher education institutions. While private colleges and universities have long relied on philanthropic support for survival, many public institutions have only recently realized the need to focus attention on attracting private support.

This chapter focuses on the main tenets of college and university fundraising. The process follows a building-block approach, beginning with step one, staffing a development office, and progressing through each step all the way to stewardship. Those steps are: establishing an accurate database of donor contact information, conducting prospect research, writing an institutional case for support, building support from within the organization, rating prospects, aligning prospect interest with institutional needs, determining the ask amount and who should make the ask, making the ask, and stewarding donors. Each of these steps is critical to the philanthropic success of a postsecondary school. In an era of declining state support for public higher education, advancement divisions have moved from the fringes of the institution to in many instances a central role in its administration (Kozobarich, 2000).

STAFFING A DEVELOPMENT OFFICE

University development or advancement in higher education institutions is becoming increasingly professionalized. However, university fundraising as a profession is considered a relatively new field (Caboni, 2010). No academic journal existed for the study of university advancement and fundraising until 2000 and the advent of the *International Journal of Educational Advancement* (Caboni, 2010). This relative lack of academic study in the field has yielded a generation of self-taught development professionals who adhere to similar theories on the subject of fundraising. As the field has become more professionalized, several academic programs have emerged to provide formal training for development professionals. Three popular programs are the Center on Philanthropy at Indiana University, the master's program in advancement at Vanderbilt University, and the certificate program in development at the University of San Francisco (Kozobarich, 2000).

The role of the development office is two-fold. First, the office must raise funds to support a variety of institutional needs, from operational expenses to the creation of endowments that will finance different university projects in perpetuity (Caboni, 2010). The development office is also responsible for ensuring that donor wishes regarding the expenditure of gifts are always honored as the donor intended.

In order for its development office to achieve these two functions, an institution must select development officers who are able to establish personal relationships with donors of significant character and integrity. Communication skills are essential, as is organizational ability.

While no two development offices will be organized exactly alike, a basic structure will typically be directed by a vice president. Depending on the size of the institution, development officers will be assigned to a specific college or academic department, to a geographic region, or to a combination of the two. Development officers will have responsibility for major-gift fundraising. A major gift is usually defined as a gift in an amount larger than an annual gift. Each development officer model will likely be supported by a central advancement services structure composed of the following:

- Database and research staff, who will maintain donor records, prepare reports, and identify potential donor prospects.
- Corporate and foundation staff, who will identify potential donors from these categories and establish the prescribed relationships for each, including preparing any reports required by grants received from these entities.
- Planned-giving staff with specialized knowledge in gift strategies such as wills, trusts, annuities, stocks and bonds, real estate, and other gifts that can be made as part of a donor's estate.
- Annual-giving staff, who organize and execute direct mail, telephone, and electronic solicitations.
- Gift-processing and accounting staff, who record gifts and ensure that all gifts are accounted for according to prescribed standards (Kozobarich, 2000).

THE DATABASE AND PROSPECT RESEARCH

Building and maintaining an accurate database has been described as the most frustrating challenge in most development offices. Keeping track of donor contact information, marital status, children, and professional information is a time-intensive but necessary function. The most widely used database software is

Blackbaud's Razer's Edge; however, all database software programs allow for the entering and updating of donor contact information, giving information, and so on. The records maintained in the database are the foundation to all future steps in the fundraising process. Both the collection of information and the manner in which it is stored should be given careful consideration. The basic building blocks of an accurate database are staff, time, data, tools, and partnerships.

Staff should possess the technical knowledge necessary to manage the database, but also appreciate that accuracy and confidentiality are critical. Building an accurate database takes time; it might be necessary to postpone other development activities until the task is completed. Data should include a prospect's name, all contact information possible, marital status, parental status, business information, degree information, events attended, volunteer roles, and virtually any other information that can be found. Tools include the database software already mentioned but also Internet search engines, data-mining companies, prospect-rating sessions (which will be discussed later), news accounts, and other verifiable information-gathering sources. Partnerships with institutional research offices, academic deans, athletic coaches, and other campus resources that might house information on prospective donors should be developed.

Once the database structure is in place, the database must be populated with the names of and information concerning prospective donors. For colleges and universities, alumni are prime donor prospects. Alumni have an intimate relationship with the institution, almost a built-in affinity for their alma mater. Information about alumni should be the most easily accessible for database managers and prospect researchers (Kozabarich, 2000).

Other than alumni, there are other constituents who might have an inclination to give to a university, such as corporations, foundations, and individual philanthropists who have been cultivated because of an interest in a particular segment of the institution. In order to determine if an alumnus, corporation, foundation, or philanthropist might be inclined to make a private gift, they must be researched. It is not possible to develop a personal relationship with each potential donor; the staff and resources are not available even at the largest and most endowed universities to accomplish this (Nicoson, 2010).

A system must be established to assess a prospect's ability to make a gift as well as his or her affinity for the institution. Indiana University's Center on Philanthropy teaches a method called "LAI" or Linkage, Ability, and Interest. The following methods can be used to determine the LAI of a prospect:

- *Electronic Screening.* Many vendors are available and for a wide range of fees will screen all or a segment of a donor database against a set of criteria to determine the giving ability of individual donors. Gifts to other organizations can also usually be discovered, which could help in identifying an area of donor interest. Depending on the information sought by the university, many different reports can be developed utilizing these findings.
- *An In-House Review of Data.* The past institutional giving history of donors and other non-donor constituents can be reviewed in a confidential round-table format. A donor's age, degree information, marital and parental status, as well as career information can be updated from these sessions. This type of review is most

useful for alumni, as much of the information is available from a variety of university resources.

- *Peer Evaluations.* Individuals with particularly close affiliations with institutions, such as trustees or foundation or alumni board members, are often in a position to know information about potential donors. While many times this information is not available due to professional courtesy or sometimes even legal obligations, this is an effective way to gather information about donor interests, ability to give, and circles of influence, as well as other information that might be useful in a future gift solicitation (Nicoson, 2010).

The above examples are the most commonly identified forms of prospect research. Adding a full-time professional researcher to the development staff will allow for these functions to be coordinated by one person, thus eliminating the need to draw valuable staff time away from other tasks in order to research prospects.

THE ANNUAL FUND AS A MARKER FOR FUTURE MAJOR GIFTS

The annual fund is traditionally the main feature of college and university fundraising programs. It is a barometer for an institution's ability to raise money from alumni. The annual fund also provides the most opportunities for contacts with alumni and other non-alumni donors. The benchmark for including donors in an annual fund appeal is no longer a simple appearance on the alumni roll. If the case can be made that a donor's interest will be served by an institution, then that donor should be included in the annual fund appeal (Sevier, 2004).

Response to the annual fund appeal can be used to determine donor satisfaction, areas of interest for specific donors, donor loyalty, and involvement. Most donors do not give out of a sense of duty to their alma mater; rather, they give to support programs that are perceived as valuable and successful. A high response rate to a particular program might indicate a high level of satisfaction with that program, while a low response rate could mean that the program is perceived as being ineffective or of little value. If this is the case, a targeted communications piece that highlights a program's achievements and explains the impact it is having could lead to more annual fund support (Sevier, 2004).

DEVELOPING THE CASE FOR SUPPORT

The first step in a case for support is the development and communication of a strategic set of priorities for the institution. It is this plan that will lead to donor confidence and create an atmosphere in which fundraising can occur (Hodson, 2010).

The case for support is as much an internal document as it is an external document for the institution. Developing the case for support allows administrators and faculty to collaborate on establishing fundraising priorities. It is the nature of presidents and deans to provide strategic direction for the institution as a whole and for individual academic departments that they lead. The expectation for campus leaders to increase philanthropic support for their institutions is growing (Hodson, 2010).

In many instances, the process of writing a case for support serves as a way to share information about various projects among internal campus constituencies. This is known as the case statement. The case statement should not be considered complete until it has the support of a broad section of the campus. Internal support for the projects outlined in the statement will benefit solicitations to external constituents.

From a donor's perspective, the case for support should be brief but also very specific about how private gifts will benefit the projects outlined in the documents. The case statement should align with the institutional mission and should be transparent (Nicoson, 2010). Many financial advisors have begun urging their clients to ask specific questions before making a major gift. The case statement should be the first place to which a development officer or administrator turns to answer donors' questions (Stannard-Stockton, 2010). The case for support should allow for conversations between university leaders and prospects that focus on the donor's aspirations for a gift. In short, the case for support will allow donors to envision their gifts manifested in an institutional fundraising priority (Hodson, 2010).

PROSPECT RATING AND ALIGNING DONOR AND UNIVERSITY INTERESTS

Prospect rating or qualifying gift prospects is simply the process or method of determining: (1) a prospect's interest in or affinity for a college or university; (2) the level of interest or affinity; (3) the ability of a prospect to make a gift; (4) the area or project in which the prospect is most interested. From these determinations, a formula develops; simply stated, the higher the degree of affinity and the higher the level of capability coupled with an ask for an area in which the donor has a high level of interest, the higher the chances for a major gift (McClintock & Shimp-Bowerman, 2006).

Affinity markers might include whether or not the prospect is a graduate, the number of previous gifts to the institution, the number of events attended, whether or not the spouse or children attended the institution, or whether or not the prospect's business benefits from internships or campus research projects. Ability markers might include the amount of previous gifts, profession, address, type of cars owned, real-estate holdings, stock holdings, amounts of gifts made to other organizations, political contributions, or board memberships. Markers that might denote areas of interest include the college from which the prospect graduated, profession, profession of spouse or children, previous areas of giving, board memberships, gifts to other organizations, attendance at events, or personal statements.

Prospect affinity will most likely be revealed by internal university records. Alumni and fundraising records will document attendance and giving histories and whether or not the prospect's spouse or children attended the institution. Campus information sources will in many cases also provide a glimpse into what interested the prospect as a student (if the prospect is an alumnus). Electronic screening services as well as peer reviews will probably provide the best information for ability markers. Electronic screens will be able to locate stock and real-estate holdings as well as political and charitable contributions. Peer reviews will reveal information such as marital status, legal judgments, bankruptcies, inheritances, board memberships, club memberships, and personal giving habits. Peer reviews should always be conducted with very small groups in confidential settings. Any questions related to the confidentiality of the information being provided should always dictate whether or not that information should be used in rating prospects (Nicoson, 2010).

THE ROLE OF PRESIDENTS, VICE PRESIDENTS, ACADEMIC DEANS, AND VOLUNTEERS IN FUNDRAISING

Fundraising is a shared responsibility among an institution's leadership and should include the president, vice presidents, academic deans, faculty members, and staff members. Volunteer leadership is also a critical component of fundraising. Developing an ask strategy for a specific donor can take several months or even years.

The president shoulders much of the responsibility for successful fundraising. It is the primary responsibility of the president to create the campus culture from which goals and objectives will flow. These goals and objectives will be the backbone for the strategic direction of the institution and therefore the foundation for all fundraising (Kaufman, 2004). It will also most likely be the president who directs a campus-wide process for identifying fundraising projects and to inspire internal and external support for fundraising (Kaufman, 2004).

Just as presidents will determine the strategic goals for the institution, deans and department chairs will determine the academic goals that will support those strategic goals. Deans many times will have spent the most time cultivating relationships with potential donors. Deans and vice presidents are typically closer to students than presidents. This proximity to students allows deans to have closer relationships that can continue after a student graduates. It is important for deans and vice presidents to recognize that sharing information with the development office about potential donors does not mean that they are giving away "their" donors. In many cases, the development staff will conclude that the dean or vice president is best positioned to make an ask or to attend an ask meeting (Hodson, 2010).

The role of cultivation and solicitation will vary among the president, vice president, deans, and faculty depending on the donor. The decision on the role each will play in interacting with, and eventually soliciting, donors should be made collectively and with a focus on which individual is likely to receive a positive response.

Another factor in determining the roles for cultivating and soliciting donors is the ability to "to tell the story." In other words, the ability to convey to the donor in clear terms what a project will do, why it is important, who will benefit from it, how much it will cost, and precisely how that donor's gift will be used should determine the role of anyone involved in donor cultivation and solicitation. Donors will expect the president to be knowledgeable about the institution as a whole, but a dean or faculty member might best explain the benefits of a complex academic project.

Many professional fundraisers suggest that presidents should spend a quarter to half of their time on university fundraising activities. Given the schedule demands of most chief executives, this type of commitment is impractical if not impossible. The time of the president is often his or her most valuable commodity. To maximize the time that he or she can devote to fundraising, the president should focus attention on those activities that have the greatest yield. Using the donor-screening techniques referenced earlier in this chapter, the development office should create a prioritized list of donors and prospects and should work with the president's office to schedule opportunities for interaction between these individuals and the president.

Universities can enhance their fundraising organizations by utilizing volunteers with influence in the community or personal affluence. Governing boards, foundation boards, and alumni boards are fertile fields from which to select fundraising volunteers. These boards are traditionally populated with individuals who have a demonstrated commitment to the institution through past giving and involvement in university events (Hodson, 2010).

For academic deans, college and departmental advisory boards are likely resources to discover both donors and volunteers. Individuals who have made significant gifts to the institution are naturally committed to its mission and goals. When possible, those major donors should be invited to participate in development activities, including making asks of colleagues and associates. Major gift donors have an unparalleled moral authority to solicit others because they have made a financial commitment of their own to the institution. They are well positioned to explain their reasons for making a gift and can often inspire or even challenge others in similar circumstances to follow their lead.

In almost every case, it will be the role of the fundraising professional to make asks. Presidents, deans, vice presidents, and faculty can tell the story and make the case, but the role of asking a prospect for a gift should fall to the professional fundraising expert. Fundraisers should be knowledgeable about the different gift vehicles, including cash pledges, stocks and other securities, real estate, as well as gift instruments such as bequests and trusts.

THE ASK STRATEGY

Everything discussed in this chapter up until this point informs some aspect of preparing for the gift ask or gift presentation. Every function of the development office—from staffing to data collection and analysis to prospect identification and rating to writing the case for support and then determining the roles of campus leaders in the cultivation and solicitation of donors—is done in advance of a gift ask.

The ask process begins many months and possibly years before the actual solicitation visit occurs. As prospects are identified and then qualified or rated, a series of activities designed to increase the connection between the institution and the donor will need to occur. A lunch or a dinner at the president's home, invitations to cultural events on campus, invitations to sporting events, specially arranged tours highlighting a particular project or program, and specially designed mailings about projects and programs taking place at the institution all contribute to the cultivation of potential donors prior to an ask. Each of these activities is intended to inform the donor, with pieces of the case for support sprinkled among social and entertainment activities. The ultimate goal of course is to strengthen the bond between the institution and the donor, which in many cases will illuminate an area of interest for the donor.

Each scheduled interaction is a contact. Development officers should record notes and make a report for each donor contact. Included in a contact report should be anything of substance learned, such as the names of family members, financial or business

---

State University
Donor/Prospect Contact Report

Date: _____

Prospect/Donor name: _____

Contact made by: _____

Contact conducted via (circle): *Personal Visit*   *Telephone*   *Correspondence*

Purpose of the contact (circle): *Preliminary Visit*   *Solicitation*   *Follow-up*   *Stewardship*

Summary of the contact (key information shared or gathered):

The next move with this prospect/donor should be:

_____ Preliminary meeting (gift proposal will not be presented)

_____ Solicitation meeting (gift proposal will be presented)

_____ Follow-up call:

Date the proposal was presented:_____

Ask amount and terms:_____

Purpose of the proposed gift:_____

Strategy for the next move:

Development Officer signature:_____

Complete this form immediately after a donor/prospect contact. Enter information into database weekly. Retain original and provide a photocopy to Vice President for University Advancement by Friday of each week.

Figure 11.1 Donor/Prospect Contact Report

information, level of interest expressed by the donor for a particular project, the prospect's general attitude toward the institution, and any next steps that need to occur. If a donor asks for information or indicates a desire for any type of follow-up, this should be noted, and the proper follow-up should occur within 72 hours. A good contact report (see example in Figure 11.1) will be a bridge between meetings, and a series of contact reports will serve as a guide through the solicitation process.

Determining the point at which to move from cultivation to ask is more art than science. Pushing a donor to the ask too soon can damage relationships or result in a smaller gift than might otherwise have been possible. Waiting too long to make the ask could also result in a smaller gift because the donor's interest in a particular project or program might wane or, worse, another charitable cause from a competing organization might garner his or her attention. In some cases, donors will subtly signal their desire to receive a gift ask.

A discovery, or a preliminary meeting with a donor, will often be helpful in gauging the individual's readiness to make a gift. Before the meeting, a development officer should research the donor by becoming familiar with all of his or her previous gifts (if any) and reviewing all contact reports. The development officer should be well informed about any projects that might be discussed and have a preliminary gift ask amount determined in his or her mind. During preliminary meetings, donors should be made aware that the institution considers them to be donor prospects and is in the process of raising money for a particular project. Accurately reading a donor's reaction to this information is critical in determining the next steps to be taken. It may take several preliminary meetings before a prospect is ready to be solicited.

Donor contacts and preliminary meetings will provide answers to the following questions:

- Who should make the solicitation? The person who has established the most trust with the donor should be included in the solicitation.
- What is the correct ask amount? This step is by no means scientific. The prospect rating process, contact reports, and preliminary visit information will inform this decision.
- What issues might prevent a prospect from considering a gift proposal? Any negative experiences that the donor has had with the institution will usually be revealed during a contact or a preliminary visit. While unpleasant, it is best to address these types of issues early on rather than during solicitation visits.

THE SOLICITATION MEETING

Once it has been determined who should be included in a solicitation meeting, what the ask amount will be, and what project or program will be the suggested beneficiary of the potential gift, it is time to conduct the solicitation. When requesting an appointment with a prospect to make a gift proposal, the purpose of the meeting should be shared with the prospect. By this time in the relationship, the individual will likely know that the institution is interested in making a solicitation request, but a prospect should never be solicited for a major gift without being expressly informed of the reason for the requested meeting.

As illustrated in Figure 11.2, there are four general steps to be followed during a solicitation meeting:

1. *Small talk.* This step breaks the ice and builds rapport with the donor. The solicitation team should mention topics of interest to the donor to put him or her at ease.
2. *Purpose of the meeting.* This step is usually the responsibility of the development officer and serves to call the meeting to order. While the donor will already be aware of the subject of the meeting, the development officer will restate the purpose and share the institution's plans or objectives regarding to the project to be discussed. The development officer will also introduce the member of the solicitation team who will tell the story or make the case for support.
3. *The case for support.* This is the time in the meeting for the president, dean, or faculty member to explain why the project is important to the institution. The

focus during this step should not be expressed in terms of the need, but rather in terms of the benefits offered by the project.

4. *The ask.* The member of the solicitation team tasked with making the ask should be direct in requesting a specific dollar amount and should explain that a gift can be paid over an extended period of time and can be paid using various gift instruments.

After the ask is made, the solicitation team should wait silently for a reaction from the donor before proceeding. Remaining silent at this point can be a difficult thing to do, but it is import to allow the donor to digest the ask and to respond in some way. In general, there are three typical donor responses: (1) a positive response, (2) a request for time to consider the ask, and (3) a no response. In the case of a positive response, the donor should sign a pledge commitment that outlines the total amount of the gift, the specific purpose for the gift, the term of payments (generally from three to no more than five years depending on the size of the gift), and a clear path to properly dispose of any excess or remaining gift proceeds should the original intended purpose be fulfilled or come into conflict with the institution's mission. Finally, a gift agreement, between the university and the donor, should state how the donor will pay the gift (monthly, quarterly, etc.), when payments will begin, and when the last payment is due.

It is likely that the response will be a request for more time to consider the gift solicitation proposal. Often a major gift prospect will want to consult with family,

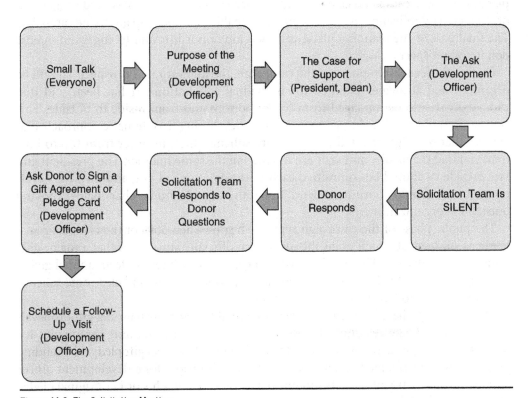

Figure 11.2 The Solicitation Meeting

legal, and/or financial advisors before committing to an amount. In these circumstances, it is important to schedule a set time for a follow-up visit. Completed gift agreements should be recorded immediately, and all parties who will benefit from the gift—from the president to a particular student—should communicate their thanks to the donor in writing.

FOUR PHASES OF A MAJOR GIFTS OR CAPITAL CAMPAIGN

Until now, the focus of this chapter has been on the building blocks of university fundraising. Now the chapter will move into a discussion of a comprehensive major gifts or capital campaign. As shown in Figure 11.3, there are four major phases of a campaign: (1) Planning, (2) Leadership, (3) Public, and (4) Follow-up.

During the planning phase, the foundation of the entire campaign is built. Infrastructure in the form of staffing, organization, and volunteer identification is established. A theme is usually developed to set the campaign apart from other solicitation efforts, and often campaign-specific logos, slogans, and printed materials are developed. Many institutions engage a fundraising consultant to conduct a feasibility study before launching a capital campaign. The feasibility study process is simply a set of interviews conducted with the top 100 to 150 prospects to gauge the potential participation of individuals with the ability to make major gifts. In addition, the process should be structured to identify projects and programs that have the most appeal to the widest number of prospects. Also in the planning phase, a campaign chair should be selected. This individual should be a person of affluence and influence who is committed to making a leadership gift to the campaign. The final part of the planning phase is to develop donor lists and to engage in intense donor and prospect rating.

During the leadership phase of the campaign, the highest rated prospects should be organized and strategies planned for individual solicitations. It has been said that campaigns should be managed from top to bottom and from inside to outside. This commonly used fundraising jargon refers to developing a systematic approach that ensures that the highest rated prospects are solicited first, in order from top to bottom, and that the faculty and staff are solicited in the same manner. The president and vice presidents should be committed early with some type of gift, and then the development staff should continue to work down the organizational chart before moving outside the organization.

The public phase of the campaign typically begins when 50% of the campaign goal has been pledged, at which point the institution officially announces that a major gifts campaign is underway. The public phase of a campaign will resemble an annual giving campaign because it will involve mass mailings, phone-a-thons, and electronic solicitations in addition to face-to-face major gift solicitations.

The follow-up phase is the time to attempt a final close on outstanding gift proposals as well as to publicly celebrate successes with events such as naming ceremonies for major gifts. The follow-up phase is also the critical time to collect gift pledges by sending pledge reminders. If a pledge is not paid on time, it is proper for a development officer to make an appointment with the donor to discuss amending his or her original pledge or payment schedule.

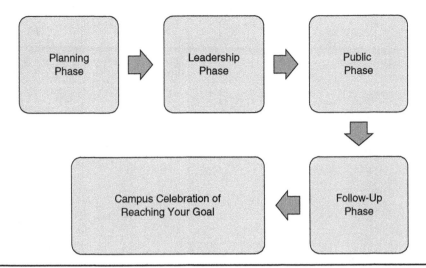

Figure 11.3 Phases of a Capital Campaign

CONCLUSION

This chapter explored the fundamental steps required to build a basic college or university fundraising operation. Office organization, data collection and maintenance, prospect identification and rating, writing an effective case statement, and planning the ask strategy are all components essential to the success both of annual giving campaigns and of major gift and capital campaigns. Each step in building a fundraising organization is critical to sustained philanthropic support for institutions of higher education, both private and public, now that the latter are increasingly dependent on such revenues.

REFERENCES

Caboni, T. C. (2010). The normative structure of college and university fundraising behavior. *The Journal of Higher Education, 81,* 339–365.

Hodson, J. B. (2010). Leading the way: The role of presidents and academic deans in fundraising. *New Directions for Higher Education, 149,* 39–49.

Kaufman, B. (2004). Juggling act: Today's college or university president must be a champion fundraiser and a strong internal leader. *University Business,* July. Retrieved May 10, 2011 from www.highbeam.com/publications/university-business-p1205/July-2004

Kozobarich, J. L. (2000). Institutional advancement. *New Directions for Higher Education, 111,* 25–34.

Nicoson, D. J. (2010). Prospect development systems: Empowering artful fundraising. *New Directions for Higher Education, 149,* 73–79.

Sevier, B. (2004). Enhance your annual fund response. *University Business,* June. Retrieved May 10, 2011 from www.highbeam.com/publications/university-business-p1205/june-2004

Stannard-Stockton, S. (2010). Probing questions all donors should ask before making a significant gift. *The Chronicle of Philanthropy On-line,* October 3. Retrieved May 10, 2011 from www.philanthropy.com.

Part III
Contingency Planning for Institutions

12

DEVELOPING CRISIS MANAGEMENT
AND EMERGENCY PLANS

Cyndy Caravelis Hughes and Thomas C. Johnson

INTRODUCTION

Residents of New Orleans have always known that they are vulnerable to natural disasters. New Orleans's elevation is as low as eight feet below sea level, making the city extremely vulnerable to the flooding that frequently accompanies hurricanes or the northern winter thaws that raise the level of the Mississippi River. According to the Independent Levee Investigation Team (2006), New Orleans flooded 25 times before the floods resulting from Hurricane Katrina. Officials at the University of New Orleans (UNO) recognized their institution's vulnerability and worked to address it.

In 2004, they obtained a disaster-resistant university grant from the Federal Emergency Management Agency (FEMA) (Kiefer, Farris, & Durel, 2006). With this grant, they formed an interdisciplinary team to plan how to protect their institution and its community. This team consisted of urban planning and policy faculty, environmental sociology faculty, civil engineering faculty, and facilities administrators. UNO also formed an advisory team consisting of key administrators. It obtained top-level support for its planning from senior university administrators. Further, the institution's collaborative approach drew broad stakeholder support for the plan. UNO completed its plan in 2005, but did not fully implement it.

When Hurricane Katrina struck, approximately one-third of the university flooded, resulting in massive damage to the residence halls. Indeed, almost all buildings incurred some form of damage. Significant looting and vandalism also occurred on campus. Further, university officials had difficulty communicating with faculty, staff, and students during and after the hurricane. However, UNO's plan, even though only partially implemented, allowed university officials to quickly begin the recovery phase. Despite all the difficulties, they made a sincere effort to establish communications (Kiefer et al., 2006). They established an off-campus base of operations, created an alternate e-mail server, motivated faculty and staff to assist with regional recovery efforts, established alternate class locations, and focused on business continuity (Kiefer et al., 2006). Within six weeks of the hurricane, UNO became the first university in New Orleans to begin fall classes, a testament to the importance of effective planning and preparation to protect an institution and its community from a disaster.

This chapter contains strategies that will help an institution of higher education formulate and implement a successful crisis management plan. As the example above illustrates, crises come in all shapes and sizes and with potentially thousands of students, faculty, staff, and visitors affected. Crisis management may therefore be one of the most important elements of college or university planning. While every institution hopes that it will never have need of emergency and disaster plans, a well-formulated plan for various types of emergencies may mean the difference between life and death.

This chapter is written to address crisis management in general. Many factors influence the size and dynamic of the crisis response structure, including the institution's size, location, budget, and place within the greater community. The following sections are meant to encourage higher education administrators to think about the various factors involved in creating a crisis management response team and implementing a plan of action for the different types of emergencies that could potentially threaten their campus.

TYPES OF EMERGENCIES AND LEVELS OF SERIOUSNESS

Table 12.1 lists natural and technological (man-made) disasters that could affect a college or university. Depending on the geographic location of the school, only a small percentage of the natural disasters may apply. Unfortunately, a larger percentage of the technological hazards may be applicable to almost every institution, regardless of size and location. With this in mind, a crisis management team should create a list of disasters that may potentially affect their area and plan for each one accordingly.

In formulating an "all hazards" plan, administrators must not only anticipate the types of disasters that may commonly occur, but also understand that no catastrophic event has boundaries. Even the most unlikely disaster scenario has the potential to materialize, and administrators must be prepared. For example, in 2004, Western Carolina University, the University of North Carolina—Asheville, and the surrounding mountainous area of western North Carolina and eastern Tennessee experienced massive flooding and strong wind gusts caused by the remnants of Hurricanes Frances and Ivan, which occurred within a week of one another. While the mountains of western North Carolina hardly seem a location where university officials should be concerned about hurricanes, the area nonetheless experienced up to 23 inches of rainfall and strong, gusty winds of between 40 and 60 miles per hour (National Weather Service, 2004; Roth, 2004). These two systems produced flooding, landslides, and road/bridge washouts. Additionally, the water supply, electricity, and transportation were adversely affected and several deaths were recorded.

It is important to rank the relative seriousness of each potential disaster. Different levels of seriousness will require different levels of response from the crisis management team. Seriousness scales are readily available for a number of natural disasters (see Table 12.2). For example, a thunderstorm is classified as severe if its winds reach or exceed 58 miles

Table 12.1 Examples of Natural and Technological Disasters

Natural Disasters

- Earthquake
- Sinkhole/land subsidence
- Flood
- Hurricane/tropical storm
- Storm surge
- Tornado
- Wildfire
- Landslide
- Tsunami
- Volcano
- Severe storm/thunderstorm
- Straight-line wind
- Blizzard/ice storm
- Drought
- Extreme heat
- Hail storm
- Avalanche

Technological Disasters

- Fire
- Hazardous materials, e.g., chemicals
- Nuclear accidents
- Terrorism
- Active shooter
- Hostage situation
- Crashes (motor vehicle, aircraft, boat/ship)
- Escaped prisoner
- Major crime (e.g., armed robbery)
- Riot/crowd control
- Bomb threat
- Explosion
- Computer hacker/IT failure
- Pandemic flu/mass illness
- Power failure
- Employee strike/unrest
- Structural collapse
- Traffic control
- Dam failure

Table 12.2 Examples of Seriousness Scales

Tornadoes	Enhanced Fujita–Pearson Scale
Hurricanes	Saffir–Simpson Scale
Earthquakes	Richter Scale and Modified Mercalli Intensity (MMI)
Severe winter storms	Northeast Snowfall Impact Scale (NESIS)

per hour, drops surface hail at least 0.75 inches in diameter, or produces a tornado (Haddow, Bullock, & Coppola, 2011). Pre-establishing various actions plans based on the level of seriousness will enable the crisis management team to respond to a disaster immediately upon recognition of the event.

Without a mitigation plan in place, smaller colleges and universities may be unable to successfully recover from a major disaster. Institutions with a comprehensive plan in place can resume regular operations more quickly, which helps them mitigate the effects on students, faculty, and staff (Brown, 2008). Additional mitigation activities that a number of institutions have adopted include obtaining flood insurance and improving building practices. A recent study reported that each dollar spent on mitigation activities saved society an average of $4 in return (MMC, 2005).

LOCAL COMMUNITY

Prior to establishing a crisis management planning committee, an institution must consider its position in the surrounding community. Based on that relationship, the institution may play an instrumental role in handling larger community disasters. For example, when a deadly F5 tornado struck Tuscaloosa, Alabama, on April 27, 2011, the University of Alabama took action to assist the community's recovery efforts. The school provided shelter during and after the tornado (Jones & Grayson, 2011) and coordinated a disaster relief fund entitled *Acts of Kindness* (Kausler, 2011). Moreover, faculty, staff, and students focused their service learning projects on helping the community to rebuild (Dialog, 2011; Pow, 2011). Adopting a role similar to that played by the University of Alabama, institutions in rural areas may provide shelter during certain disasters. By identifying whether the community at large considers campus buildings to be shelter points, the crisis management team can anticipate the number of evacuees they may be taking in during subsequent disasters.

Similarly, colleges and universities may have access to community resources and capabilities that can be utilized in emergency situations (Chachkes et al., 2007). Institutions should work with their local government partners to include mutual aid agreements in all areas of critical incident response and emergency management. While many colleges and universities may be prepared to respond to minor emergencies, large-scale disasters often overwhelm an institution's response capability. Their first responders frequently require augmented capabilities from the surrounding community's first responders to restore order, protect property, and save lives.

In its basic form, a mutual aid agreement is a compact among emergency responders across jurisdictional boundaries to assist one another during certain events. Generally, when the college or university is a state entity, the agreement must be made between the institution's chief executive officer and the head of the agency in the adjoining community. Many states have laws that establish the requirements for mutual aid agreements, including identifying who may enter into such agreements. The mutual agreement should specify information such as the type of events for which assistance may be requested, who may initiate the request on behalf of an agency, who may approve the response for the other agency, the duration for which the aid may be provided, and indemnification provisions (Commission on Accreditation for Law Enforcement

Agencies, 2006). After the mutual aid agreement is written, it should be signed by representatives of the parties in question.

For any event that involves multiple government entities, command structures can be confusing. It is important to have written agreements in place prior to a crisis that clarify command structure and coordination. By establishing intergovernmental agreements, public agencies will work together to develop operational plans and share resources, such as radio systems, information technologies, and facilities. Intergovernmental agreements may be particularly important for colleges and universities without sworn police officers. These agreements differ from mutual aid agreements in that they tend to define long-term relationships between organizations, while mutual aid agreements define the short-term provision of aid. Intergovernmental agreements are typically used for one of three purposes: the sharing of resources, the sharing of authority, or the sharing of services.

The complexity and expense of specialized equipment, coupled with budget restraints, makes it appropriate for organizations to share resources. For example, after the September 11 terrorist attacks, it became apparent that radio interoperability was a major issue. The State of North Carolina invested heavily in developing the Voice Interoperability Plan for Emergency Responders (VIPER), which provides an 800-megahertz infrastructure for public safety agencies. Currently, 9 municipalities, 58 counties, 26 state agencies, 6 universities, and 5 federal agencies have signed intergovernmental agreements to share this system (North Carolina Department of Crime Control & Public Safety, 2009).

Many colleges and universities are private institutions and therefore not covered by state laws that grant police authority to state institutions. An intergovernmental agreement may allow for a private institution to create its own police department. For example, the University of Miami has such an agreement with the Coral Gables (FL) Police Department. The agreement conveys authority to the university police officers and provides them with citywide jurisdiction. It further holds the City of Coral Gables harmless for the actions of the University of Miami police officers. Finally, it also serves as the mutual aid agreement between the university and city (Chief David Rivero, personal communication, March 11, 2011).

While many colleges and universities may desire to have a police force on campus, they may have neither the authority nor the resources to establish such a force. In this situation, the institution may enter into an intergovernmental agreement with a local law enforcement agency. Perhaps the largest arrangement of this type exists between the Los Angeles County Sheriff's Department and the Los Angeles Community College District, with the sheriff's department serving 9 campuses and over 130,000 students (Los Angeles County Sheriff's Department, 2009). Such agreements can be tailored to fit the needs of the institution. For example, Pensacola State College in Florida has its own police officers on duty from 7:00 a.m. to 11:00 p.m. during the week, while the Pensacola Police Department has agreed to respond to crime calls on campus outside those times (Coreen Goben, personal communication, March 11, 2011). This agreement saves the college the expense of providing 24-hour law enforcement coverage.

Colleges and universities that have intergovernmental agreements with community first responders generally have close working relationships and understandings with those who are responsible for emergency response. These agreements also ensure that the necessary rules are already in place with regard to responsibilities, liability, accountability, authority, training, and cost (Burdick, 2006). Additionally, institutions that have pre-existing arrangements for food, fuel, water, buses, and IT functions generally have a faster response time and smoother recovery operations (U.S. Department of Homeland Security, 2006).

STATE AND FEDERAL AGENCIES

In addition to coordinating with public agencies on the city or county level, colleges and universities must also coordinate with state and federal agencies that assist with funding planning, preparedness, response, and recovery initiatives (Brown, 2008). Based on the Disaster Mitigation Act of 2000, all communities are required to develop hazard mitigation plans in order to be eligible for funding related to disasters. Colleges and universities should make certain that they are included in any FEMA grant proposals, which can assist with the development of mitigation plans and programs to increase disaster awareness. Also, academic institutions should be mindful of ensuring that their buildings and property are included in the damage assessments conducted by FEMA after a disaster.

CRISIS MANAGEMENT PLANNING COMMITTEE

Depending on the size of the college or university, there are numerous functions that may be handled by a single committee or divided among multiple committees. Regardless of the committee type and size, certain elements of crisis management must be discussed: emergency preparedness, threat assessment, and crisis response. The purpose of each is discussed below, as are the recommended representatives from various departments who may serve a key role on the committee.

Emergency Preparedness Committee

The role of the emergency preparedness committee is twofold. First, the committee must anticipate the numerous crisis situations that could potentially impact the campus community. After identifying these potential threats, they must then formulate a plan of action in the event that a disaster materializes. Research findings consistently point to inadequate safety planning, ineffective management, poor training of crisis managers, and uncoordinated communication methods as primary areas of concern (Mak et al., 1999; Piotrowski et al., 1997; Reilly, 2008; Smith et al., 2001; Wang, 2008). All of these areas of concern can be anticipated and alleviated with proper planning.

Members

a. *Emergency Manager.* Seventy percent of larger institutions (15,000 students or more) have a dedicated emergency manager with sole responsibility for disaster planning, preparation, and response (National Association of College and University Business Officers, 2009).

b. *Head of campus police or security.* Many institutions that do not have an emergency manager do have a director of safety, security, or police, who generally assumes many of the same responsibilities. Further, campus safety, security, or police officers are typically present on campus 24 hours a day and are the first responders to any event. The response of these officers is typically dictated by policies, procedures, and training developed or mandated by the director of campus safety, security, or police. Further, the director of campus safety, security, or police is the individual to whom these officers first report the incident; therefore, the director must collect the initial information about any emergency or disaster and make the appropriate notifications to the institution's management team. The director is frequently the individual charged with ensuring that the campus community is notified of the emergency and that mutual aid is requested from adjacent jurisdictions.

c. *Provost/chancellor/president.* By virtue of their position, senior officials are the parties ultimately accountable for how the institution copes with the incident. They also have the latitude to commit resources, make policy decisions, and obtain any additional resources necessary to avert or respond to a crisis event. While they will delegate authority to the individual in charge of responding to the incident, they serve a vital role in planning and preparing for emergencies (FEMA, 2008).

d. *Representative from the business office.* The business office is typically responsible for implementing the institution's continuity-of-operations plan in the event of an emergency or disaster. The representative generally partners with other senior campus administrators to ensure that the institution's business continues as normally as possible. Additionally, he or she plays a key role in helping to make emergency purchases that aid in the response to a crisis.

e. *IT representative.* Information technology is critical to continuing the business of the institution and to disseminating information to the campus community. The IT representative is a key partner with the representative from the business office in implementing the institution's continuity-of-operations plan. Further, the IT representative is responsible for ensuring that sensitive data remain protected during an emergency or disaster, and that the institution continues complying with privacy and data protection laws.

f. *Faculty representative.* Faculty partner with other university administrators to support the institution in its response to and recovery from an emergency or disaster. Faculty can provide much-needed staffing for critical functions such as communications and transportation. Further, faculty play a key role in continuity of operations to ensure that classes continue and students are kept on track for completion of the semester.

g. *Student representative.* This individual is key to representing student interests in the institution's response to and recovery from an emergency or disaster. Further, the student representative can work with administrators to determine how students and student groups can assist the institution during and after the crisis. Finally, the student representative can keep the student body informed of the institution's plans for response and recovery.

Threat Assessment Team

One of the challenging features of dealing with many crisis events is that critical decisions with long-term impacts need to be made with limited, unofficial information in a relatively short period of time (Piotrowski & Guyette, 2009). The purpose of the threat assessment team is both to provide an analysis of the threat potential of any given situation and to recommend strategies to de-escalate the potentially threatening situation (Jaeger et al., 2003). For smaller institutions, the emergency preparedness committee and threat assessment team may consist of the same members and have overlapping responsibilities.

Members

a. *Head of campus police or security.* The institution's director of safety, security, or police is responsible for providing a first response to an active threat. When the potential threat is a person who is jeopardizing others with threats of violence, it may be necessary to remove the person from the campus or even arrest the person. The director of safety, security, or police coordinates these activities.

b. *Representative from human resources.* When the person posing the threat is an employee, the representative from human resources is responsible for interpreting institutional personnel policies and state and federal workplace violence laws as they relate to personnel actions. The human resources representative provides guidance for supervisors and other employees.

c. *Representatives from student affairs and academic affairs.* When the person posing the threat is a student, representatives from student affairs and academic affairs are important in helping to assess the individual and suggest a course of action. Student affairs representatives generally provide information regarding the student's out-of-classroom activities and behavior as well as enforce the student code of conduct. The academic affairs representatives provide information regarding the student's academic progress, classroom demeanor, and relationships with faculty and other students, as well as options for addressing the student's academic performance.

d. *Legal counsel.* The legal counsel assists with interpreting college or university policies and procedures, and state and federal laws. Further, the legal counsel assists in determining a lawful course of action for the institution's officials to pursue in addressing the threat.

e. *Representative from mental health services.* The mental health services representative is helpful in assessing the person of concern's behavior. Frequently, a mental health services representative can meet with the individual, conduct an assessment, and recommend a course of action to assist the individual. In extreme cases, the mental health services representative may recommend that a student be withdrawn from courses or an employee placed on leave due to an imminent threat.

Crisis Response Team

The crisis response team is the group of individuals that can be brought quickly together to initiate a response to an incident. On some campuses, the threat assessment team and the crisis response team serve the same role. The crisis response team's role may include managing potentially violent or dangerous situations, advising administrators and other appropriate personnel on critical incidents, facilitating the delivery of post-incident recovery needs, and disseminating information about the crisis event (Jaeger et al., 2003).

Members

a. *Head of campus police or security.* The director of safety, security, or police generally is responsible for coordinating the initial emergency response to an event. In addition to coordinating the activities of campus safety, security, or police, the director frequently serves as a liaison to local community first-responder agencies and is responsible for making requests for mutual aid. Further, the director keeps other team members and senior administrators informed of conditions or activities related to the incident.

b. *Representative from the provost's office.* The provost's office representative is responsible for assessing the impact of an event upon the academic mission of the institution and determining how academic resources can support the institution in responding to and recovering from that event. In the absence of the institution's president or chancellor, the provost is often the senior administrator for the institution and assumes responsibility for directing institutional activities.

c. *Representative from human resources.* The human resources representative is responsible for assessing the impact of an event upon the institution's employees and identifying resources that are available to support employees during an event and through its recovery. The representative is also helpful in interpreting institutional policies and procedures, and state and federal laws that affect employees and their presence during or in the wake of an event.

d. *Representative from the dean of students' office (student affairs).* The student affairs representative is responsible for determining the impact of an event upon students, and for coordinating or directing activities designed to enhance student safety. Further, the representative is responsible for identifying and implementing resources to help students recover from an event.

e. *Parent liaison.* The parent liaison is responsible for keeping fellow parents informed about an event, the effect of the event upon students, and the welfare of the students. This liaison provides timely updates to parents and helps them communicate with their children. Generally, the liaison is a member of the student affairs division.

f. *Representative from mental health services.* The use of a mental health services representative frequently depends upon the nature of the event. In situations where the threat results from an individual, the mental health services representative may be helpful in assessing that person's behavior. However, in all events, the mental health services representative can provide assistance to individuals who may be traumatized and identify ways in which an institution can help the campus community emotionally recover from an event.

Once the committee(s) have been established, it is important to determine an order of succession for each member, particularly with regard to the crisis response team. Generally, the members appointed to the crisis response team serve a critical function that must be addressed during any event. An order of succession defines the roles that must be staffed and who will staff them in the absence of the incumbent members (Perry & Lindell, 2007). The crisis response team will be discussed in greater detail later in the chapter.

PLACEMENT OF THE PLANNING COMMITTEES

Timely response to a crisis of any magnitude is of paramount importance. Virtually all responses to a crisis require the mobilization of resources. Therefore, the office of emergency and disaster management should be closely aligned to the institution's senior operations officer with decision-making authority (Thrower et al., 2008). At larger institutions, the emergency management function may be its own department and report directly to a vice president or vice chancellor for administration or business operations. At smaller institutions, the emergency management function may be placed under the police or security department, or the facilities management department, as these departments often have resources that can be quickly mobilized to respond to an emergency or disaster. It is important that the relationship between the campus public safety executive and the senior decision-makers be established in advance so that the emergency response team has direct access to an individual who can grant them the authority to mobilize resources in the event of an emergency.

BUDGET AND FUNDING

The mobilization of resources (such as personnel, equipment, and supplies) is critical to the successful implementation of the crisis management plan (FEMA, 2008). Regardless of the size of the budget set aside for crisis management, it is important to have a flexible plan that is adaptable to various situations. The ability to manage resources to adjust to changing conditions is particularly vital in light of increasing budget constraints.

Campus police, security, and safety officials are charged with protecting sensitive research projects and facilities (such as nuclear, biological, and chemical projects and areas), large-venue events (such as football games), and a vulnerable population consisting primarily of 18- to 22-year-old students; yet, they are frequently denied access to external grant and funding sources that are available to traditional law enforcement and public safety agencies (Greenberg, 2007). For example, when the Department of Homeland Security was created after the September 11 terrorist attacks and began issuing grants for emergency preparedness, colleges and universities were all but excluded. Grants were made available only to governmental entities, leaving private institutions ineligible to receive these funds (Greenberg, 2005). State-supported institutions had to compete with state highway patrols, police, and bureaus of investigation and frequently were denied access to funding. While many law enforcement and public safety agencies in communities that were home to institutions of higher education used these institutions for at least part of the justification for these grants, very little, if any grant funds actually made their way into the budgets of campus police, security, and safety departments. Although there have been calls for increased grant funding for colleges and universities (Greenberg, 2005), this funding has not substantially materialized.

Even when grants are available, campus police, safety, and security agencies are confronted with the challenge that many such grants require some level of matching funding. Additionally, many grants have use restrictions or require a continuing obligation that must be met within an agency's resources. For example, the Office of Community Oriented Police Services (COPS) Universal Hiring Program established a three-year grant to eligible law enforcement agencies, including campus agencies, for the employment of new officers. According to the terms of the grant, agencies must provide a match of at least 25% from funds that have not previously been budgeted for any law enforcement purpose, cannot use the position to supplant existing positions, and must retain the position for one year or one budget cycle after the grant expires (United States Department of Justice Office of Community Oriented Police Services, 2005). Agencies who fail to comply with the grant requirements are subject to an audit by COPS and may be required to repay the grant. The inability to provide the matching funding or otherwise comply with the conditions of a grant is a primary reason why many agencies do not avail themselves of these opportunities (Haddow et al., 2011).

THE CRISIS MANAGEMENT RESPONSE STRUCTURE

Once the crisis management team is in place and an "all hazards plan" has been formulated, the next crucial steps are implementing the plan through pre-disaster preparation and proper training. Part of pre-disaster preparedness is creating a Crisis Response Box (Williams, 2009), which contains directions that will facilitate a streamlined response to the crisis. A number of other elements are also included in the Crisis Response Box; below is a list of some common components:

1. *Map of campus and the surrounding areas.* Crisis planners should review traffic patterns and create an emergency traffic plan that will both accommodate traffic and allow emergency personnel direct access to the crisis location.
2. *Aerial photos of the campus.* Providing all critical response agencies (including police, paramedics, and fire personnel) with an aerial perspective of both the campus and its surrounding areas is very helpful in expediting their response to a disaster.
3. *Campus layout.* Beyond current and accurate blueprints of all campus buildings, this includes information about main leads for water, gas, electric, cable, telephone, sprinkler systems, alarm systems, elevators, and hazardous material locations.
4. *Keys.* A master key and an extra set of keys when the master key cannot be used should be made readily available.
5. *Fire alarm turn-off procedures.* The fire alarm can make it difficult for responders to communicate with each other and potential victims in a crisis.
6. *Sprinkler system turn-off procedures.* Water may make evacuations more difficult and could potentially lead to a secondary hazardous situation if it comes into contact with electrical outlets.
7. *Utility shut-off values.* There should be clear identification of the access points and shut-off points for all utilities (water, electricity, and gas) so that they can be quickly shut off.
8. *Layout of gas and utility lines.* A diagram that shows all of the utility lines on campus should be readily available.
9. *Telephone numbers for the key crisis response team members.* Include the names and telephone numbers of key individuals responsible for coordinating with the local emergency responders. Other helpful numbers to have available would include those of the public information officer, student affairs, grounds and maintenance (facilities management), and the coordinator for food, water, and supplies.
10. *Designated command post and staging areas.* Three distinct staging areas should be predetermined, one for each of the following groups: (1) emergency personnel and law enforcement, (2) media, and (3) parents and students.

11. *Emergency resource list.*

A list of organizations and individuals who may be called on to assist in an emergency should be compiled and readily available. This list might include the following, with complete contact information:

- American Red Cross
- Federal Aviation Authority (FAA) local office
- National Organization for Victim Assistance (NOVA)
- Local emergency radio channels
- County District Attorney's Victim/Witness Assistance
- Parent representatives (trained to help parents receive information and answer questions)
- Trained crisis intervention counselors

12. *Evacuation sites.* Several predetermined evacuation sites should be included based on the type and nature of the disaster. For example, the evacuation site designated for a school shooter may be different from the one designated for a large chemical spill.

13. *First-aid supplies location.* First-aid supplies should be located throughout the entire campus. The locations can be noted in the building blueprints and layouts.

Once all of the requisite plans and documents are in place, the necessary personnel must be trained to respond appropriately during an emergency. Colleges and universities must do more than just plan for all hazards; they must train on their plans. Plans without training are almost worthless. The rapid and fluid nature of emergencies and disasters does not allow time for campus officials to pull an emergency plan off of a shelf and read it. The time to read, understand, and prepare to implement a crisis management plan is *before* the crisis occurs.

Mississippi State University (MSU) has an aggressive training program for its emergency plans. MSU conducts quarterly training sessions that range from table-top exercises to full drills. The exercises and drills address a variety of scenarios, such as active shooter, inclement weather, or natural disaster, in a variety of settings, such as during an athletic event or on a typical class day. Key organizations that routinely participate in these training sessions include the university police department, a representative from the Faculty Senate, the Vice President for Student Affairs, Facilities Management representatives, representatives from all major student affairs offices, Athletic Department representatives if necessary, local emergency medical services representatives, Oktibbeha County Emergency Management representatives, and, if necessary, FEMA representatives. This frequency of training by so many key organizations ensures that MSU is well prepared for emergencies and disasters.

The most comprehensive and well-developed crisis management plan is only as good as the ability of campus officials to implement it. Therefore, campus officials should conduct regular training on the plan with all those who share responsibility for its implementation. Training exercises not only prepare campus officials for implementing the plan, they also expose flaws in the plan before an emergency or disaster occurs and allow campus officials the opportunity to correct or compensate for these flaws. Further, training enables campus officials to practice skills or use equipment and implements that do not figure into their in everyday duties, promoting a greater level of proficiency that will reduce their stress and anxiety during a crisis.

Even though campus administrators are generally not considered first responders, they should participate in crisis management plan training. This participation provides administrators with direct knowledge of the various components of the plan, the response capability of campus employees, and the level of cooperation that exists with community public safety officials. Such knowledge is important for campus administrators, who in times of crisis must frequently make critical decisions under time pressures and with limited information (Hale, Hale, & Dulek, 2006; Moats, Chermak, & Dooley, 2008).

The campus community must be informed of the crisis management plan so they understand how campus officials and public safety officials will respond. Additionally, the campus community shares responsibility for its own safety and should understand how they may contribute to the effectiveness of the plan. Many colleges and universities have posted this information online (http://www-bfs.ucsd.edu/emerg/ucsdemp.htm) or have developed presentations (http://www.police.vt.edu/VTPD_v2.1/emergencytraining.html) for training their campus community.

INCIDENT COMMAND GROUP FUNCTION AND RESPONSIBILITY

The Incident Command System (ICS) is a standardize, all-hazard, on-scene management approach that allows community responders and campus personnel to adopt an organizational structure that matches the demands of the crisis without being hindered by jurisdictional boundaries (FEMA, 2008). Based on the overlap between institutions of higher education and the greater community that was discussed earlier in the chapter, the ICS model allows all parties to know their assigned roles and work together in an effective manner. The flexibility of ICS makes it a cost-effective approach, as it can readily grow or shrink to meet the various institutional crises that may arise.

ICS is based on proven best practices and consists of procedures for managing personnel equipment, facilities, and communications. Its three primary purposes are (1) the safety of responders and others, (2) the achievement of tactical objectives, and (3) the efficient use of resources. Standard management and command features of ICS provide for the efficient direction of the operations, planning, logistic, and finance/administration functions. Other features include a common terminology, modular organization, use of position titles, unified command structure, incident action plans, manageable span of control, organizational facilities, integrated communications, accountability, and an emergency operations center.

While the features of ICS are consistent regardless of the application, FEMA recognizes the uniqueness of applying ICS within the higher education environment. To help campus administrators and first responders understand and implement ICS, FEMA has developed an ICS for Higher Education training course (http://training.fema.gov/EMIWeb /IS/is100HE.asp).

Just as they need to train on their crisis management plans, campus administrators and first responders must also train in the use of ICS. While ICS is flexible and can expand or contract to meet the size of the crisis, campus officials and first responders must practice this expansion and contraction. Further, campus employees who are seldom used in a crisis response except in the most serious situations must still be trained on how they would fit into an expanded ICS. To ensure familiarity with ICS, many campuses use it to manage major non-emergency events. For example, Appalachian State University uses ICS to manage its home football games (Norris, 2011).

It is critical to establish command before the onset of a crisis for a variety of reasons. First and foremost, decision-making is impossible without the presence of a command structure. Furthermore, lack of command can become a safety hazard in and of itself for first responders, students, and staff. Therefore, a designated Incident Commander is responsible for all management functions until he or she delegates the function to another party. The Incident Commander is, essentially, in charge of managing the scene and performing of the following functions:

- Establishing a command post
- Mobilizing personnel
- Requesting outside assistance
- Preparing a staging area
- Maintaining media relations.

Effective accountability of all personnel is essential during incident operations. All campus personnel, including students, must be informed that they should not go to the crisis location unless they have been mobilized by the Incident Commander. Uncontrolled and uncoordinated arrival of personnel at emergencies, coupled with curious spectators, can cause significant accountability issues (FEMA, 2008) along with crowd control problems. It also causes chaos at the scene and can unwittingly lead to blocked emergency access routes as well as safety risks to responders, civilians, and other personnel who are operating within the parameters of the crisis management plan.

Once an individual has been mobilized or activated, he or she should report to a designated staging area unless otherwise directed in order to receive further guidance and instructions that are in accordance with the established procedures. After the individual has checked in and been given an assignment, he or she will then locate the assigned incident supervisor to obtain the initial briefing and additional information. Other information that may be relayed to dispatched personnel includes the location of the work area, the identification of break areas, procedural instructions for obtaining needed resources, and the required safety procedures for assisting with the emergency (FEMA, 2008).

Besides the Incident Command function, there are other essential roles that need to be filled during a crisis situation, the first of which is the Operations function. The individual appointed to direct the Operations Section is responsible for all activities related to the tactical response to the event (FEMA, 2008). The Operations Section director is usually the person with the greatest experience and/or training in addressing the tactical response. He or she is responsible for organizing, supervising, and assigning resources for the tactical response.

The Operations Section is usually one of the first staff functions created and involves a bottom-up development starting with the first units on the scene (FEMA, 2008). As additional units become available for the tactical response, such as police, firefighters, or air units, these resources are fed into the Operations Section. If resources are available for a tactical response but are not immediately deployed, they are frequently assigned to a staging area, where the Operations Section director assigns a liaison (FEMA, 2008). The liaison organizes the units when they report to the staging area, assigns them to teams, if necessary, and then dispatches them as directed by the Operations Section director.

The individual appointed to direct the Planning Section is responsible for collecting and disseminating useful information to the responders (FEMA, 2008). For example, in an active shooter response in a class building, it may be helpful for responders to know how many classes are currently being conducted in the target building and how many students are enrolled in those classes. Additionally, the Planning Section can obtain campus maps, building floorplans, incident action plans, and other documents. Therefore, the Planning Section director should be a person who knows how to access resources that will provide useful information to the Incident Commander and other section directors.

In an expanded response, the Planning Section may be subdivided into four units: the resources unit, the situation unit, the documentation unit, and the demobilization unit (FEMA, 2008). The resources unit manages check-in activities, monitors the status of all event resources, and plays a significant role in writing the crisis management plan. The situation unit collects and analyzes data on the situation; prepares situation reports, displays, and summaries; and develops maps and overviews. The documentation unit provides duplication services, maintains the crisis management plan, and records and archives data relevant to the event. The demobilization unit works with the Incident Commander and section directors to ensure that resources are released from the incident in an orderly manner and also documents expenditure of resources to assist with resource replenishment.

The Logistics Section supports the response by managing service and support needs (FEMA, 2008). According to FEMA (2008), the duties of the Logistics Support function include:

- Ordering, obtaining, maintaining, and accounting for essential personnel, equipment, and supplies.
- Providing communication planning and resources.
- Setting up food services for responders.
- Setting up and maintaining incident facilities.
- Providing support transportation.
- Providing medical services to incident personnel (pp. 5–33).

In an expanded incident, the Logistics Section director has to work closely with the Finance/Administration Section (see below) director to purchase or otherwise acquire the services and supplies needed.

Depending upon the size of the event, the Logistics Section can be expanded to include a number of different units to support the response. The communications, medical, food, supplies, facilities, and ground support units are those most commonly included in the Logistics Section. The director of the Logistics Section must be someone who is adept at acquiring and coordinating the necessary resources to support the first responders.

The Finance/Administration Section addresses the primary issue of paying for the response. In minor responses, agencies typically fund their response from their operating budgets. However, for major events, such as when a formal disaster declaration is made, the Finance/Administration Section director must ensure meticulous record-keeping in order to apply for disaster funding or grants to pay for the response. Further, when assisting the Logistics Section in acquiring resources, the Finance/Administration Section ensures that purchase orders and contracts are issued and paid.

Personnel administration is also part of the Finance/Administration Section function. Employees must be tracked so that they can be paid for their services, particularly if they are paid at an overtime rate. In addition, the Finance/Administration Section administers workers' compensation and insurance claims for employees who are injured or killed in the response.

Given the overlapping responsibilities of the Finance/Administration Section, it is not uncommon to find administrators from different campus business functions involved in the section's operations. For example, the director may be the campus's chief business officer, assisted by the human resources director and purchasing agent. When the response is expanded and involves a higher authority, such as the county emergency manager, these employees may find themselves working on a team with their counterparts from local or state government.

Declaring a State of Emergency

Declaring a state of emergency allows for the suspension of some or all normal activities in response to or anticipation of a threat to personal safety, property, or both. This suspension of activities permits first responders and critical employees to respond to or prepare for the threatening event. A college of university can be affected by a declaration of emergency issued at the institutional, local, state, or federal level.

The president, chancellor, or board of trustees is usually allowed to declare an institutional state of emergency by virtue of legislative or other official action. As chief executive officers, these officials are responsible for the campus community and facilities, and are expected to take reasonable and prudent actions to protect them. Institutions may also use declarations of emergency to raise public awareness of the risks associated with the crisis and let people know what safety measures need to be taken. When conditions dictate, administrators may suspend normal operations and mobilize campus resources to respond to an actual or anticipated threat. When the institution has mutual aid agreements or memoranda of understanding with local public safety agencies, it may request assistance from these agencies even when there is no local declaration of emergency.

A local declaration of emergency is generally issued by the local city or county emergency manager authorized to do so by ordinance or statute. When a college or university is located within the jurisdiction of the declaring official, the institution is covered by this local declaration of emergency. State law, mutual aid agreements, and memoranda of understanding dictate how resources will be mobilized and shared between the institution and the local government. Communities with a college or university in their jurisdiction have a valuable asset, given that these institutions often have resources and capabilities that can be shared in emergency situations (Chachkes et al., 2007). Many communities avail themselves of these resources and capabilities and have incorporated them into their crisis management plan. For example, many local governments include their local college's or university's facilities as shelter locations in their local crisis management plan.

When the scope of the emergency or disaster is beyond the capabilities of local government, the emergency manager may request assistance or mutual aid from other municipalities and/or counties, or appeal to the state for aid. State laws usually allow for a local government to request aid from the state government. However, colleges and universities are generally excluded from these laws due to their status as either private or state-supported institutions rather than local governmental entities. Therefore, when an on-campus emergency or disaster exceeds the response capability of the institution and local government, it is the local emergency manager, rather than the institution's chief executive officer, who must request aid from the state (Oliver, 2011).

Generally, when a local emergency manager requests aid from the state, that request is made to the state emergency management office, which forwards the request to the governor's office (Oliver, 2011). If the request is approved, the governor's office may activate the state emergency plan and provide state resources to assist in response and recovery. In addition to providing state resources, governors frequently have the authority to suspend state laws or local ordinances if doing so will aid in the response to and recovery from the emergency (Oliver, 2011).

Major disasters, such as tornadoes or hurricanes, may affect a substantial portion of a state, prompting the governor to declare a state of emergency in the affected areas; this includes local colleges and universities. A state declaration of emergency allows the governor to suspend laws, establish economic controls over resources such as food and gasoline, issue emergency orders, and mobilize the National Guard (Oliver, 2011). Further, governors generally work with state legislators to release emergency funds and reallocate state agency budgets to benefit state-supported colleges and universities that expend resources in emergency response and need assistance in repairing or replacing facilities and equipment (Oliver, 2011).

When the scope of the emergency or disaster is beyond the capabilities of the state, the governor may request that the President of the United States declare a state emergency as allowed by the Robert T. Stafford Act (2007). A presidential declaration allows FEMA to coordinate the mobilization of federal resources to respond to the event. Depending upon the nature of the event, the President may issue either an emergency or disaster declaration (FEMA, 2010). An emergency declaration allows the President to appoint officials and agencies to address the emergency and use resources and override processes for the response effort. An example of a presidential emergency declaration occurred during Hurricane Katrina. A presidential disaster declaration allows FEMA to determine the type and amount of federal resources and aid that may be extended to an affected area. Hurricane Katrina devastated many colleges and universities along the Mississippi and Louisiana coast, making them eligible for aid from FEMA.

COMMUNICATION NETWORK

Incident responders rely heavily upon effective communications and information systems in order to coordinate disaster efforts. The National Incident Management System (NIMS) describes the requirements necessary to create a standardized communications framework (FEMA, 2008). Those requirements include the following:

1. *Interoperability.* Interoperable communications systems are those that allow for multiple agencies to exchange information directly, even if they are using disparate communication systems (Thrower et al., 2008). The National Governors Association Center for Best Practices has cited interoperable communications as one of the top issues with regard to homeland security. With interoperability, all on-scene personnel have the ability to communicate directly with each other to streamline emergency and rescue efforts. It is recommended that colleges and universities partner with law enforcement and other first responder agencies to ensure interoperability. Such coordination might include identifying alternative methods of communication, such as Voice-over-Internet protocol and digital radio systems.

2. *Reliability.* During an emergency or disaster, the sharing of information—whether it be between college or university officials, officials and the campus community, or officials and other government first responders and agencies—is critical. Technology and an information-demanding culture have produced first responders, government and campus officials, and campus communities who not only need but demand information (Haddow et al., 2011). The communication means and equipment must be resilient and capable of allowing continuous sharing of information to enable their operation for the duration of the emergency or disaster. Colleges and universities should have a contingency plan in the event that their normal communications network fails. For example, handheld radios or satellite telephones would still be operable if telephone lines and cellular telephones were disabled.

3. *Scalability.* This refers to the ability of a communications system to expand or contract as needed for an emergency or disaster response (DHS, 2008). The rapid increase in communication demands that accompany a major crisis means that communications equipment and capability must exist *before* the crisis occurs. Scalability does not simply refer to the number of radios, cellular telephones, or other communications devices that are available; it also refers to the capability of a system to accommodate a large number of these devices. Colleges and universities should plan for a "worst-case communications scenario" and ensure that their communications equipment and capability would be adequate under such circumstances.

4. *Portability.* This refers to the capability of communications equipment and protocols to be carried, available, or otherwise used by first responders and officials involved in an emergency or disaster (DHS, 2008). It also refers to the capability of communication systems to allow the assignment of radio frequencies across jurisdictions so that mutual aid responders can communicate with primary first responders (DHS, 2008). An advantage to allowing frequencies to be shared is that all responders can use their own equipment, with which they are already familiar.

5. *Redundancy.* This refers to the capability of accomplishing a task using alternative means and/or equipment. In communications, it refers to the ability of first responders and officials to sustain communications in the event that the primary communications system breaks down (DHS, 2008). Regarding radio communications, many agencies and organizations maintain alternative radio frequencies or even alternative radio systems that may be used if the primary frequency is lost. Another example is the use of text messaging when cellular telephone capability is overwhelmed or otherwise lost.

EMERGENCY NOTIFICATION

Depending on the nature and size of the crisis event, the Incident Commander may designate personnel to disseminate information about the disaster as well as provide safety information and liaison services (FEMA, 2008). Campus public safety officials should have the authority to send emergency messages both from campus and off of campus grounds. Prior to sending an emergency message, campus administrators should consider its timeliness and accuracy, and only relay information that is useful to recipients (Thrower et al., 2008). The Public Information Officer (PIO), or an individual in a similar role, typically serves as the conduit of information to the media, parents, and other interested parties. While the Incident Commander ultimately approves information released by the PIO, the PIO advises the Incident Commander about media relations and the necessary dissemination of information.

Institutions should employ a variety of means and methods to disseminate information about emergencies to the campus community. The campus mass-notification system should include both high-technology notification systems (i.e., cellphone texts, email communications, etc.) and low-technology solutions, such as the passing out of flyers and use of loud speakers (Thrower et al., 2008). The criticism surrounding Virginia Tech's failure to issue timely information about the campus shooting, coupled with the Clery Act, which requires colleges and universities to disclose information about crime on and around their campuses, has led many institutions to avail themselves of both high- and low-technology means of emergency communication. The use of high and low technology provides redundancy to ensure that information is disseminated through multiple channels. Colleges and universities should use the following criteria when selecting their emergency notification systems:

1. *Multi-point communication.* The system should have the capability of notifying the entire campus through multiple channels and points of contact, such as text messaging, voice messages, and email.
2. *Capacity.* The system should be proficient in delivering all messages reliably and quickly.
3. *Security.* In the event that a third-party vendor is used, access to private data should be limited to authorized personnel.
4. *24/7 service.* Training, customer support, and technical support should be included in services provided by a third-party vendor.

5. *Experience.* The vendor should have considerable experience in providing this service to institutions of all sizes.
6. *Assessment.* The service should provide the ability to create reports that allow institutions to monitor, measure, and manage the effectiveness of the system.

Although a large number of institutions report the use of multiple means of emergency notification, including email, Web pages, voice mail, text messages, and telephone trees, a number of these notification systems are based on an "opt-in for participation" approach where faculty, staff, and students must sign up to participate (Piotrowski & Guyette, 2009). Unfortunately, there is a major problem with text messaging as a means of emergency communication. Federal law forbids service providers from forcing this service upon students (CAN-SPAM Act of 2003). Rather, students must subscribe to the system, and therein lies the problem. Many students choose not to subscribe, thus depriving themselves of critical and timely notification and information in the event of an emergency. A survey administered by the National Association of College and University Business Officers (2009) found that 70% of the respondent institutions required students to "opt-in" or register for the system.

An alternative to the "opt-in" feature is to provide an "opt-out" feature. With the opt-out feature, students are automatically included in the emergency notification system and must choose to remove themselves from it. Research suggests that less than 8% of students remove themselves from opt-out systems, while less than 40% register when the system provides an opt-in feature (Staman et al., 2009). Nevertheless, an opt-out system still affords students the opportunity to deprive themselves of the benefits of receiving emergency notifications.

LEGAL IMPLICATIONS

When planning for campus disasters and emergencies, certain legal requirements set forth by federal, state, and local entities may need to be considered in the formulation and implementation of a crisis management plan. While virtually all businesses and organizations can benefit from the creation of such plans, colleges and universities are among the few institutions that are federally mandated to create and assess management plans for dangerous and emergency situations (Healy, 2010). For example, as mentioned earlier in the chapter, institutions of higher education must comply with the Clery Act. Also, federal law requires that institutions of higher education include an emergency response and evacuation policy statement in their annual security report. Based on the requirements set forth in the Higher Education Opportunity Act (HEOA), this statement must include the following:

- The procedures put in place to immediately notify the campus community about a significant crisis event that poses an immediate threat to their health and safety.
- A description of the process in place that will be used to confirm that a dangerous situation exists; determine the segments of the campus community to be notified; determine the content of the emergency notification; and activate the notification system.

- A list of the titles of the personnel responsible for initiating and implementing the crisis management plan.
- A description of procedures for disseminating information to the larger community.
- A description of processes put in place to conduct an annual test of the emergency response and evacuation procedures.

Another relevant federal law that could potentially impact crisis management plans is the Superfund Amendments and Reauthorization Act (SARA) of 1986, which established federal regulations for handling hazardous materials. Under this law, institutions that store large quantities of certain chemicals must provide regular reports to the Occupational Safety and Health Administration (OSHA) regarding the storage of these chemicals. One reason for this requirement is so that first responders will have rapid access to information regarding these chemicals and plan their response accordingly. However, what may be of greater importance to campus first responders is that OSHA rules require that campuses storing these chemicals and involved in a response to a hazardous material incident involving these chemicals use the Incident Command System for their response protocol (FEMA, 2008).

Federal laws also protect the privacy of education records under the Family Educational Rights and Privacy Act (FERPA). Under FERPA, any education records that contain specific student information cannot be released to an outside party without the prior written consent of the student. One exception of note, which allows the accessing and sharing of information for threat assessment inquiries, falls under the area of health and safety emergencies; FERPA states that schools many disclose information in order to protect the safety of the student or others. Under this exception, schools must explicitly define what qualifies as a "health or safety emergency" and can only disclose records to the individuals who need the information in order to prevent harm to the student or others. FERPA only covers information contained in education records and does not restrict the ability of school officials to share other information about a student, such as personal observations or interactions with the student.

In addition to federal laws that affect colleges and universities during emergencies and disasters, there are also state laws to consider. For example, in North Carolina, state law gives a county or municipal health director jurisdiction over a college or university in the event of an infectious or pandemic disease outbreak (North Carolina General Statutes §130A-41, 1999). The facilities of state-supported institutions are the property of the state, and there are generally state laws addressing their use, maintenance, and care. For example, Florida state statute mandates that state-supported universities shall make their facilities available to a local emergency manager upon request as a public hurricane evacuation shelter (Florida State Statute §252.385, 2006).

MEDICAL AID

The most important planning with regard to medical aid is developing a relationship with the local emergency medical service (EMS) as well as with the local hospitals. Whether it takes the form of a mutual aid agreement or a memorandum of understanding, a contract should be in place to specify how the local EMS will be used in the crisis management plan. Additionally, disaster drills should be held on an annual basis and should include the Incident Command Team, the EMS, local hospitals, and other appropriate public safety and state agencies. These training drills should be followed by a formal post-incident evaluation to assess the success of the drill and any problems that may have arisen.

Colleges and universities take a variety of approaches to providing EMS. The many small and private institutions that exist in the United States generally rely upon local community EMS. In areas where there are well-equipped, well-staffed, and well-trained EMS units, high-quality treatment and care of pre-hospital injuries and reliable transport are reasonably assured. However, in rural areas, particularly those that may be staffed by volunteer EMS units, the service can be problematic.

A study conducted by the North Carolina Rural Health & Research Policy Centers highlighted two major problems with volunteer EMS units: recruitment/retention and training (Freeman, Rutledge, Hamon, & Slifkin, 2010). According to the study, most volunteer EMS organizations only offer Basic Life Support services. Additionally, most of these organizations have difficulty recruiting and retaining trained volunteers, with approximately half of EMS organizations reporting that these problems are not improving or are worsening. Institutions located in areas that are serviced by volunteer EMS organizations will do well to partner with these organizations and support their training and recruitment/retention efforts.

More than 100 colleges and universities have their own EMS unit. Many of these organizations are partnered with an EMS training/degree program and provide a student with supervised practical experience. Other institutions have EMS units with a paid staff. The paid staff may work on their own, in conjunction with student employees or volunteers, or as a hybrid organization with police officer or firefighters cross-trained as emergency medical technicians or paramedics.

The organizational location of a college or university EMS unit varies and frequently depends upon how the unit is staffed. For example, EMS units that are staffed almost entirely with students and are funded from student fees will frequently be found within a student affairs division. Colleges and universities with medical schools, centers, or hospitals will frequently have the EMS unit reporting to one of these entities. Units with paid employees may report to the director of campus safety, security, or police.

The level of service provided by these units also varies. Given that many are staffed by students who are in training, most offer only basic emergency services. Because of this, the institution must still have a relationship with community EMS units that are capable of providing advance emergency services and rapid emergency transport, such as by helicopter. Colleges and universities with medical schools, centers, or hospitals may have EMS units that are capable of providing advanced services.

FIRE SUPPRESSION

While building codes having been steadily improving since the 1970s, the level of fire safety in older buildings is not equal to that of newer facilities. In older buildings, fires often result in a total loss due to a variety of factors including delay of discovery and alarm, lack of firewalls and/or compartmentation, lack of automated sprinkler systems, lack of draft stopping and combustible attacks, and inadequate water supplies for manual fire suppression (FEMA, 2004).

In order to protect older facilities, their levels of fire safety must be evaluated and solutions must be developed to protect both life and property. According to FEMA (2004), the evaluation comprises three categories: fire safety, means of egress, and general safety. The evaluation of fire safety includes automatic fire detection, structural fire safety, and fire alarm and fire suppression systems. The means of egress portion of the evaluation includes the configuration, characteristics, and support features of the means of egress. Finally, the general safety section includes an evaluation of various fire safety and means of egress parameters.

When facilities consider upgrading existing facilities, the most effective method of providing fire protection is to install automatic fire sprinklers, but more cost-effective methods might include installing automatic fire alarms and detection, draft stopping in combustible attic spaces, and smoke and fire compartmentation walls in occupied spaces.

Generally, the cost of fire suppression equipment and employing firefighters makes it cost prohibitive for colleges and universities to have their own fire departments. However, there are many examples of institutions that have partnered with their local community fire department to enhance their capability to respond to fire and other emergency calls on campus. For example, the University of New Hampshire has partnered with the City of Durham to jointly fund the area's paid fire department. In some areas, high-rise residence halls are the tallest structures, and institutions with these buildings have helped their local fire department acquire ladder or aerial platform trucks (Longwood University, 2005). Other colleges and universities have partnered with fire departments to either contract or reimburse the fire department for calls to the campus.

Colleges and universities can help decrease the response time for fire emergencies by having a fast-response vehicle on campus. A fast-response vehicle need not be a fully equipped pumper or ladder truck, but may consist of a pick-up truck with a small water tank, pump, and hose. Indeed, some manufacturers are producing miniature fire engines that are built on frames not much bigger than an oversized golf cart, but capable of carrying a foam container and firefighting equipment. In areas where the campus is served by a volunteer fire department, a fast-response vehicle can make up for some of the time it takes, after the alarm first sounds, for the first volunteers to arrive at the fire station, procure trucks, and respond to the scene. In situations where college or university employees are volunteer firefighters, their access to a fast-response vehicle can save precious minutes in knocking down a fire in its infancy.

SEARCH AND RESCUE

The search-and-rescue function of a crisis management plan most frequently deals with ensuring that the disaster areas have been successfully evacuated. In many jurisdictions, responsibility for the search-and-rescue function falls to the local fire department, although multiple public safety agencies may partner to ensure this function is addressed. In areas where there are actual search-and-rescue units, these units may specialize in urban, mountain, ground, water, or vertical search and rescues.

Urban search and rescue frequently occurs in populated areas where there is a danger of people being trapped in collapsed buildings. These teams tend to be multi-jurisdictional and consist of personnel from different public safety organizations. Mountain search and rescue occurs in mountainous or rugged terrain where accessibility is difficult, frequently requiring specialized equipment and techniques. Ground search-and-rescue operations assist people who are lost or in distress on land or certain inland waterways. Although traditionally associated with woods, forests, and wilderness areas, ground search-and-rescue units can be used to search for lost children or elderly individuals suffering from Alzheimer's disease.

Water rescue is used to search for lost individuals on lakes or other large bodies of water. For institutions located on or near the coast of an ocean, this type of search and rescue may be referred to as air-sea rescue. Aircraft and boats are frequently used to search for lost individuals or rescue those in distress. Vertical rescue involves the use of ropes to rescue individuals who may be in distress in a location accessible only by rappelling or climbing. Vertical rescues can occur on cliffs, in elevator shafts, in silos, in wells, on towers, and in a variety of industrial applications.

CONTINGENCY PLANS

An integral part of crisis management is the development of a continuity-of-operations plan, which is designed to return the campus to normal operations after a disaster. While many institutions have plans that provide for three days of self-sufficiency, the U.S. Department of Homeland Security (2006) recommends that a 7- to 10-day provision plan would be better. Having access to stored provisions is particularly important during natural disasters, such as hurricanes and earthquakes, when the surrounding community has also been heavily impacted. With regard to the acquisition of food and supplies, campuses with national or regional food service contractors fare better than those who relied on local resources.

Other considerations in the formation of contingency plans include anticipating equipment needs. In many cases, backup generators are designed to provide power only for short periods of time. Additional generators may be needed in the event of a sustained and prolonged power outage. All generators should be located well above ground level to account for the potential of rising water levels. Likewise, patrol vehicles should be located out of flood zones during weather incidents so that they do not become inoperable.

Colleges and universities rely heavily on wireless and online environments. Careful consideration should be given to the preservation of information technology functionality. One method of dealing with the potential loss of IT systems is to establish a "cold site" that is equipped with backup systems and where the IT personnel could relocate if the institutional site became inoperable. Alternatively, servers can be permanently located at an off-campus location to ensure the preservation of payroll operations, Web pages that can serve as sources of information, and other vital records.

In the event of an evacuation, key personnel and administrators should account for their whereabouts in order to be reachable when decisions need to be made regarding post-incident operations.

CONCLUSION

This chapter discussed strategies to help institutions of higher education formulate and implement a successful crisis management plan. While every institution hopes that it will never have need of such a plan, this chapter sought to highlight important considerations that must be taken into account before disaster strikes to help those colleges and universities that do face crises successfully respond to these events and resume normal operations in a timely manner.

REFERENCES

Brown, V. (2008). A campus plan for natural and man-made disasters. *The Police Chief,* 75(2), 66–71.

Burdick, C. (2006). The impact of governance, operations, and technology on critical emergency response: Lessons learned from Columbine. *Campus Law Enforcement Journal,* 36(6), 11–13.

CAN-SPAM Act of 2003. 15 USC 103 §7701—7713. (2003).

Chachkes, E., Nelson, L., Portelli, I., Woodrow, R., Bloch, R., & Goldfrank, L. (2007). An organisational safety net in an academic setting: An evaluation. *Journal of Business Continuity & Emergency Planning,* 2(4), 403–415.

Commission on Accreditation for Law Enforcement Agencies. (2006). *Standards for law enforcement agencies: The standards manual of the Law Enforcement Agency Accreditation Program.* Fairfax, VA: CALEA.

Department of Homeland Security. (2008). *National incident management system.* Washington DC: Department of Homeland Security.

Dialog. (2011). APR professor recognized for post-tornado volunteer service, August 29. Retrieved from http:// dialog.ua.edu/2011/08/accolades-for-aug-29-2011/

Disaster Mitigation Act of 2000. 42 USC §5121. (2000).

Federal Emergency Management Agency. (2004). *Design guide for improving school safety in earthquakes, floods, and high winds.* Retrieved February 8, 2011 from http://www.fema.gov/library/view Record.do?id=1986

Federal Emergency Management Agency. (2008). *IS-100.HE: Introduction to the Incident Command System, ICS-100 for higher education instructor guide.* Retrieved February 8, 2011 from http://training.fema.gov/EMIWeb/ IS/IS100HE/IG_PDF /ICS100 HigherEd_IG.pdf

Federal Emergency Management Agency. (2010). *Presidential Disaster Declaration.* Retrieved March 16, 2011 from http://www.fema.gov/government/grant/pa /pr_declaration.shtm

Florida State Statutes. (2006). Public shelter space. §252.385.

Freeman, V., Rutledge, S., Hamon, M., & Slifkin, R. (2010). *Rural volunteer EMS: Reports from the field.* Chapel Hill: North Carolina Rural Health Research & Policy Centers.

Greenberg, S. (2005). *National summit on campus public safety: Strategies for colleges and universities in a homeland security environment.* Washington, DC: Office of Community Oriented Policing Services, U.S. Department of Justice.

Greenberg, S. (2007). State of security at US colleges and universities: A national stakeholder assessment and recommendations. *Disaster Medicine and Public Health Preparedness,* 1(1), S47–S50.

Haddow, G., Bullock, J., & Coppola, D. (2011). *Introduction to Emergency Management* (4th Ed.). Boston: Elsevier.

Hale, J., Hale, D., & Dulek, R. (2006). Decision processes during crisis response: An exploratory investigation. *Journal of Managerial Issues,* 18, 301–320.

Healy, P. (2010). Sacred Heart University's online emergency plan boosts interagency cooperation. *Campus Law Enforcement Journal,* 40(1), 21–22.

Independent Levee Investigation Team. (2006). *Investigation of the performance of the New Orleans flood protection systems in Hurricane Katrina on August 29, 2005,* July 31. Retrieved from http://www.ce.berkeley.edu/ projects/neworleans/report /intro&summary.pdf

Jaeger, L., Deisinger, E., Houghton, D., & Cychosz, C. (2003). *A coordinated response to critical incidents.* Ames: Iowa State University.

Jones, A., & Grayson, W. (2011). Survivors emerge, fill up local shelters quickly. *Tuscaloosa News,* April 28. Retrieved from http://www.tuscaloosanews.com/article/20110428 /NEWS/110429648

Kausler Jr., D. (2011). UA Acts of Kindness fund gets $1 million donation from Alabama athletics department, May 6. Retrieved from http://www.al.com/sports/index.ssf/2011 /05/ua_acts_of_kindness_fun_gets_1.html

Kiefer, J., Farris, M., & Durel, N. (2006). *Building internal capacity for community disaster resiliency by using a collaborative approach: A case study of the University of New Orleans disaster resistant university project.* The University of New Orleans.

Longwood University (2005). Longwood University donates $100,000 to Town of Farmville for new ladder truck for Farmville Fire Department, August 5. Retrieved March 21, 2011 from http://www.longwood.edu/news/releases/laddertruck.html

Los Angeles County Sheriff's Department. (2009). *Contract law enforcement services.* Los Angeles: LASD.

Mak, H., Mallard, A., Bui, T., & Au, G. (1999). Building online crisis management support using work flow systems. *Decision Support Systems, 25,* 209–224.

Moats, J., Chermack, T., & Dooley, L. (2008). Using scenarios to develop crisis managers. *Advances in Developing Human Resources, 10,* 397–424.

Multihazard Mitigation Council. (2005). *Natural hazard mitigation saves: An independent study to assess the future savings from mitigation activities.* Washington, DC: National Institute of Building Sciences.

National Association of College and University Business Officers. (2009). *Results of the National Campus Safety and Security Project Survey.* Retrieved February 8, 2011 from http://www.nacubo.org/Documents/Initiatives/CSSPSurveyResults.pdf

National Weather Service. (2004, October 18). *Hurricane Frances.* Retrieved March 11, 2011 from http://www4.ncsu.edu/~nwsfo/storage/cases/20040908/

Norris, S. (2011). *University emergency operations plan—Basic plan.* Retrieved March 15, 2011 from http://epo.appstate.edu/emergency-operations-plan-basic-plan

North Carolina Department of Crime Control & Public Safety. (2009). *VIPER partnerships.* Retrieved March 11, 2011 from http://www.nccrimecontrol.org/Index2 .cfm?a =000001,001148,001151

North Carolina General Statutes. (1999). Powers and duties of local health director. §130A-41.

Oliver, C. (2011). *Catastrophic disaster planning and response.* Boca Raton, FL: CRC Press.

Perry, R., & Lindell, M. (2007). *Emergency planning.* Hoboken, NJ: Wiley.

Piotrowski, C., Armstrong, T., & Stopp, H. (1997). Stress factors in the aftermath of Hurricanes Erin and Opal: Data from small business owners. *Psychological Reports, 80,* 1387–1391.

Piotrowski, C., & Guyette, R. (2009). Lockdown: Reactions of university faculty and staff. *Organizational Development Journal, 27*(4), 93–99.

Pow, C. (2011). UA service projects to involve students in rebuilding Tuscaloosa, August 22. Retrieved from http://blog.al.com/tuscaloosa/2011/08/ua_service_projects_to _involve.html

Reilly, A. (2008). The role of human resource development competencies in facilitating effective crisis communication. *Advances in Developing Human Resources, 10,* 331–351.

Robert T. Stafford Disaster Relief and Emergency Assistance Act. 42 USC §5121–5207. (2007).

Roth, D. (2004). *Hurricane Frances rainfall.* Retrieved March 11, 2011 from http://www.hpc.ncep.noaa.gov/tropical/rain/frances2004.html

Smith, S., Kress, T., Fenstemaker, M., & Hyder, G. (2001). Crisis management preparedness of school districts in three southern states in the USA. *Safety Science, 39,* 83–92.

Staman, E., Katsouros, M., & Hach, R. (2009). The multi-dimension nature of emergency communications management. *EDUCAUSE Review, 44*(1), 48–62.

Thrower, R., Healy, S., Margolis, G., Lynch, M., Stafford, D., & Taylor, W. (2008). *Overview of the Virginia Tech tragedy and implications for campus safety: The IACLEA blueprint for safer campuses.* Retrieved February 8, 2011 from http://www.iaclea.org/visitors /PDFs/VT-taskforce-report_ Virginia-Tech.pdf

United States Department of Homeland Security, the Federal Bureau of Investigation, and the International Association of Chiefs of Police. (2006). *Campus public safety preparedness for catastrophic events: Lessons learned from hurricanes and explosives,* June. Retrieved February 8, 2011 from http://www.iaclea.org/visitors / PDFs /Hurricane2.pdf

United States Department of Justice Office of Community Oriented Policing Services. (2005). Universal hiring program: adding officers to the street. Washington, DC: Office of Community Oriented Policing Services, U.S. Department of Justice.

Wang, J. (2008). Developing organizational learning capacity in crisis management. *Advances in Developing Human Resources, 10,* 425–445.

Williams, J. (2009). *Active shooter: School safety considerations.* Retrieved February 8, 2011 from http://info.publicintelligence.net/laactive shootertactics.pdf

13

KEY LEGAL ASPECTS FOR HIGHER EDUCATION ADMINISTRATORS

Janet Park Balanoff and Monoka Venters

INTRODUCTION

The laws governing higher education are like a blanket: multifaceted and flexible. Although a blanket appears to be one cohesive color or texture, in reality it is multifaceted, consisting of numerous threads. The threads in the blanket of higher education law consist of statutes passed by Congress, laws passed by state legislatures, and policies adopted by colleges and universities. Each thread may have a different purpose, but they all combine to serve a common goal: providing a protective shield that is flexible enough to protect student and institution, employee and employer.

Despite the reservation of control to the states over educational issues contained in the 10th Amendment of the U.S. Constitution, the federal government has imposed numerous statutory restraints on higher education through "valid exercises of congressional power, such as the authority to regulate matters that affect interstate commerce and the national economy" (Hutchens, 2011, p. 35). In addition, the federal government has encouraged postsecondary institutions to conform to various practices by utilizing the spending clause of the U.S. Constitution to condition receipt of federal funding, in particular federal student financial aid, on adherence to certain standards. For instance, institutions must agree to protect student educational records in accordance with the Family Educational Rights and Privacy Act (FERPA) in exchange for receiving federal funding (Hutchens, 2011).

Among the most important federal laws that institutions of higher education must be aware of are FERPA, the Higher Education Opportunity Act of 2008, the Copyright Act of 1976, the Technology Education and Copyright Harmonization Act of 2002 (TEACH Act), the Civil Rights Act of 1964, the Americans with Disabilities Act of 1990, Title IX of the Education Amendments of 1972, the Family and Medical Leave Act of 1993, and the Age Discrimination in Employment Act of 1967. This chapter discusses how each of these federal laws applies to institutions of higher education.

FAMILY EDUCATIONAL RIGHTS AND PRIVACY ACT

The Family Educational Rights and Privacy Act (2011) was enacted by Congress and signed into law in 1974 to serve the dual purpose of protecting rights and preserving privacy. On the rights side, FERPA (2011) ensures access to educational records by appropriate parties; on the privacy side, FERPA (2011) protects unwarranted access to educational records by others. To protect those rights, federal law provides that no funds will be made available to an institution that has a policy or practice of denying or effectively preventing a student who is or has been in attendance at the institution the right to review and inspect educational records. To preserve privacy, federal law provides that no funds will be made available to an institution that has a policy or practice of permitting the release of educational records of students unless the institution has written permission to release such information or federal law provides a specific exception for the release. Both public and private postsecondary institutions typically receive federal funding and are therefore subject to FERPA (2011).

Rights of Eligible Students Under FERPA

In the postsecondary context, the rights of access to and privacy for educational records belong to the student. Federal regulations refer to postsecondary students as eligible students (Family Educational Rights and Privacy Rule [FERPR], 2011). Institutions must notify eligible students about FERPA rights on an annual basis. An eligible student has the right to inspect and review his or her educational records. Such access must be granted within a reasonable period not to exceed 45 days from the date of the request. If an eligible student would like to obtain copies of educational records, the institution may charge a reasonable fee for the copies unless doing so would effectively prevent the student from inspecting and reviewing the records.

If the eligible student finds information in an educational record that he or she feels is inaccurate or misleading, the student has the right to request that the institution correct the record. The institution is not required to make the requested correction to the educational record, but must provide the student the right to request a formal hearing in cases where it decides not to make the requested correction. If the institution does not make the requested correction after the formal hearing, it must allow the student to place a statement outlining his or her position in the educational record (FERPA, 2011; FERPR, 2011). None of these rights may be used to challenge a grade, an opinion, or a substantive decision made by an institution.

When an institution receives a request for information about a student, the first question to address is whether the request is being made by an eligible student. Even eligible students do not have access to all records. For instance, students do not have access to their parents' financial records. Students also do not have access to letters of recommendation for admission, employment, or honorary recognition if the student signed a voluntary waiver of such rights (FERPA, 2011).

Rights of Others Under FERPA

Regardless of the postsecondary student's age (even if he or she is under the age of 18), the right to access educational records does not extend to the student's parents except in limited circumstances. For instance, an institution may disclose educational records to parents if the student is a dependent for federal income tax purposes. An institution may also inform parents or legal guardians about any violation of a law, rule, or policy if the institution determines that a student under the age of 21 committed a disciplinary violation related to the use or possession of alcohol or a controlled substance. Finally, an institution may disclose educational records to parents in connection with an emergency if such knowledge is necessary to protect the health or safety of the student or other persons. The institution may share information only during the time of the emergency; moreover, the institution must note in the student's educational record the articulable and significant threat that formed the basis of the disclosure (FERPA, 2011; FERPR, 2011).

In addition, an eligible student may provide written consent to the institution to allow third parties, including his or her parents, access to educational records (FERPR, 2011). Higher education institutions routinely receive requests from parents for information contained in a protected educational record. Parents who pay tuition and fees to a college or university often feel that the institution has no right to refuse to provide requested information. Unless the parents fall into one of the specified exceptions, FERPA prohibits the institution from disclosing educational records. Establishing policies and providing training to institutional employees outlining how to respond to requests from parents are key components of the institution's strategy for dealing with such requests. During orientation or at the beginning of each academic year, some institutions ask eligible students to sign a written authorization allowing the institution to provide educational records to the students' parents. Even if the institution has signed authorization, it should confirm that the student still wants the institution to release his or her educational records to the parent at the time of any request because the student has the right to withdraw consent at will.

Education Records Under FERPA

If the request comes from an eligible student, the first question to address is whether the material is an educational record. Educational records are defined as materials that contain information directly related to a student and are maintained by the educational institution (FERPA, 2011). Once a document has been defined as an educational record, an institution must provide access to the record for appropriate parties while protecting the record from being disclosed to others unless a specific exception applies. Federal law provides certain exclusions from the definition of educational records. For instance, educational records do not include documents made by an employee for the employee's use that are not accessible or revealed to any other person (FERPA, 2011). Personal notes that an instructor maintains about a student would fall under this exclusion and would not be considered an educational record; therefore, a student cannot review and inspect such notes.

Records created and maintained by a law enforcement unit of the institution for law enforcement purposes are also not considered educational records (FERPA, 2011). Therefore, law enforcement units may choose whether to disclose their records to eligible students and others (even without consent of the eligible student). If a law enforcement unit receives educational records from other campus representatives, those records are protected under FERPA. The best course of action for law enforcement units is to keep records created for law enforcement purposes separate from educational records received from other campus representatives.

Records relating to the treatment of a postsecondary student by a physician, psychiatrist, psychologist, or other recognized professional are excluded from educational records if the records are made, maintained, and used only in connection with the student's treatment and are disclosed only to treatment providers (FERPA, 2011). To be classified as a treatment record, the record must be shared only with health professionals and cannot be provided to the student or anyone else. If an institution chooses to provide the record to the student, the record is then classified as an educational record rather than as a treatment record, meaning that the protections of FERPA apply. The records may be shared with others if the student consents in writing or the situation falls into one of the exceptions outlined in FERPA. For instance, the records may be shared with the parents if the parents claim the student as a dependent for federal income tax purposes.

Directory Information Under FERPA

If the institution receives a request from someone other than an eligible student, the first question to consider is whether the information is an educational record or directory information. Directory information is not considered an educational record; therefore, such information is not protected under FERPA and may be made public. Directory information is not generally considered harmful or an invasion of privacy if disclosed (FERPR, 2011). Specifically, directory information includes the student's name, address, telephone listing, email address, photograph, date and place of birth, major field of study, enrollment status, dates of attendance, and degrees and awards received; the most recent previous educational agency or institution attended by the student; the student's participation in officially recognized activities and sports; and weight and height of members of athletic teams. Directory information includes unique personal identifiers such as student ID numbers if the identifier cannot be used to gain access to educational records unless used in combination with another authentication source such as a password. Directory information does not include the student's Social Security number (FERPA, 2011; FERPR, 2011).

The institution must provide public notice to the eligible student if it intends to make directory information public, and allow the student to opt out of public disclosures. The public notice must inform the eligible student of the period of time in which the student has to notify the institution in writing that the student does not want such information released as directory information. Such notification does not have to be directed to the eligible student individually and may be made in numerous ways, such as in a student handbook or a newsletter. Recent changes to FERPA rules allow institutions to adopt limited directory information policies that allow disclosure of directory information only for specific purposes (such as publishing a graduation program or yearbook), to specific parties, or both (FERPA, 2011; FERPR, 2011). Such policies allow institutions to restrict disclosure of directory information to protect students from becoming targets of marketing campaigns or criminal activity.

Exclusions from FERPA

If the information is an educational record but is being requested by someone other than the eligible student, the second question is whether an applicable exclusion exists.

FERPA provides numerous exclusions that allow disclosure of otherwise protected educational records. The following list outlines the permitted exclusions from the privacy protections of FERPA:

- Written consent of eligible student
- School officials who have legitimate educational interests
- Officials from other schools in which the student seeks or intends to enroll
- Authorized representatives of the Comptroller General, the Secretary of the U.S. Department of Education, or State educational authorities for audit, evaluation, or required enforcement activities provided there is a written agreement that

  - designates an individual or entity as an authorized representative;
  - specifies the personally identifiable information to be disclosed;
  - specifies the purpose as being in furtherance of an audit, evaluation, or enforcement activity;
  - describes the activity;
  - specifies that personally identifiable data will be destroyed when no longer needed;
  - specifies the time period in which the personally identifiable information must be destroyed; and
  - protects the education records from further disclosure

- Authorized representatives of the Attorney General for law enforcement purposes provided that personally identifiable data will be destroyed when no longer needed
- In connection with a student's application for or receipt of financial aid
- State and local officials pursuant to state statute if disclosure relates to the juvenile justice system
- Organizations conducting studies for, or on behalf of, educational agencies or institutions for the purpose of developing, validating, or administering predictive tests, administering student aid programs, and improving instruction provided that the organization enters into an agreement that

  - specifies the purpose, scope, and duration of the study;
  - specifies the information to be disclosed;
  - requires the organization to use the information only for the purposes identified in the agreement;
  - requires the organization to conduct the study without identifying students or parents;
  - requires the organization to destroy personally identifiable data when it is no longer needed for the purpose of the study; and
  - specifies the time period in which the information must be destroyed

- Accrediting organizations to the extent necessary to carry out accrediting functions
- Parents if the student is defined as a dependent in the Internal Revenue Code of 1982
- Appropriate persons in connection with an emergency if such knowledge is necessary to protect the health or safety of the student or other persons
- In response to a judicial order or lawfully issued subpoena provided the eligible student is notified in advance

- Authorized persons conducting program monitoring, evaluations, and performance measurements of agencies and institutions receiving or providing benefits under the Richard B. Russell National School Lunch Act or the Child Nutrition Act of 1996 provided that such aggregate de-identified data will be destroyed when no longer needed
- Alleged victims of any crime of violence or non-forcible sex offense may be provided the final results of any disciplinary proceeding conducted by the institution against the alleged perpetrator with respect to such offense
- The final results of any disciplinary proceeding in which a student is found to have committed a violation of the institution's policy for any crime of violence or non-forcible sex offense
- Information provided under the Violent Crime Control and Law Enforcement Act of 1994 concerning registered sex offenders
- Parents or legal guardians of students under the age of 21 may receive information regarding the violation of a law, rule, or policy if the institution determines that the student committed a disciplinary violation with respect to the use or possession of alcohol or a controlled substance
- Designated federal representatives of the Attorney General who are investigating and prosecuting acts of domestic or international terrorism and who have obtained a court order (FERPA, 2011; FERPR, 2011)

If the request falls within one of the exclusions outlined in the list above, the institution may release the educational record but is not required to do so.

Records Under FERPA

Institutions must maintain a record of all individuals (other than school officials with a legitimate educational interest) who have requested and obtained access to educational records. The record must indicate the legitimate interest of each person or organization in requesting or obtaining access to educational records (FERPA, 2011). If personally identifiable information is released during a health or safety emergency, this record must also include "the articulable and significant threat to the health or safety of a student or other individuals that formed the basis for the disclosure" (FERPR, 2011, §99.32). This record must be maintained with the student's educational record and is accessible only by the eligible student, officials responsible for the custody of educational records, and authorized representatives of the Comptroller General, the Secretary of the U.S. Department of Education, or State educational authorities auditing the system (FERPA, 2011).

Complaints Under FERPA

An eligible student may file a complaint with the U.S. Department of Education Family Policy Compliance Office (FPCO) if the student feels that a violation of the student's rights under FERPA has occurred. Such complaints must be submitted within 180 days of the alleged violation or within 180 days of the date that the student knew or reasonably should have known about the alleged violation. FCPO may extend the filing deadline for good cause. FCPO notifies institutions if it institutes an investigation and may direct the institution to submit a written response within a specified period of time. FCPO must provide written notice of its findings and the basis for the findings to the eligible student and the institution. If FCPO finds that an institution has not complied with FERPA, FCPO must provide a statement of the specific steps that the institution must take to comply and a reasonable time period within which the institution may comply voluntarily. If the institution does not comply during the established time period, the Secretary of Education may withhold or terminate federal funding (FERPR, 2011). To date, the Secretary has not terminated federal funding for any institution based on failure to comply with FERPA.

HIGHER EDUCATION OPPORTUNITY ACT OF 2008

In 2008, Congress reauthorized the Higher Education Act of 1965 by passing the Higher Education Opportunity Act ([HEOA], Pub. L. No. 110-315, 122 Stat. 3078). The text of HEOA is more than 400 pages long and contains hundreds of amendments to the Higher Education Act. Of necessity, our summary will cover only select changes.

Transparency in College Tuition for Consumers in HEOA

Many of the changes contained in HEOA are intended to assist students and parents in determining the costs of college by increasing the availability of information. For instance, the Transparency in College Tuition for Consumers section of HEOA requires the U.S. Department of Education (U.S. DOE) to publish information on the College Navigator website such as college affordability lists and consumer information including, among other things, descriptions of institutional mission, admissions statistics, and demographic composition of the student body (HEOA, 2008, §111). As of July 1, 2011, the college affordability lists must be published annually for public, private non-profit, and private for-profit institutions at the four-year, two-year, and less than two-year levels and must include the following categories: (1) institutions with the highest tuition and fees, (2) institutions with the lowest tuition and fees, (3) institutions with the highest net price (tuition and fees minus grant aid), (4) institutions with the lowest net price, (5) institutions with the largest increase in tuition and fees, and (6) institutions with the largest increase in net price.

In addition, the Transparency in College Tuition for Consumers section of HEOA required the U.S. DOE to publish a net price calculator showing the cost of tuition and fees minus grant aid for each institution of higher education no later than August 14, 2009. By October 29, 2011, each institution of higher education that received federal financial aid funds was required to publish its own net price calculator showing the cost of tuition and fees minus grant aid using institutional data and allowing students to base the calculation on their family circumstances. HEOA allowed institutions to link to the net price calculator on College Navigator (HEOA, 2008, §111).

Textbook Information in HEOA

The Textbook Information section of HEOA requires institutions of higher education receiving federal financial aid to ensure timely access to affordable course materials to students (HEOA, 2008, §112). As of July 1, 2010, institutions must provide information about the costs of availability of required textbooks, recommended textbooks, and supplemental material to students. Each institution must include on its Internet course schedule either (1) the International Standard Book Number (ISBN) and retail price of required textbooks, recommended textbooks, and supplemental material; (2) the author, title, publisher, and copyright date of the material; or (3) a statement that the information is "To Be Determined." Institutions are encouraged to provide information about renting textbooks, purchasing used textbooks, textbook buy-back programs, and alternative content delivery programs. In addition, the Textbook Information section of HEOA requires textbook publishers to provide faculty with the following information about textbooks and supplemental materials: (1) the price of the textbook, (2) the copyright dates of the three previous editions of the textbook, (3) a description of substantial revisions from the prior edition, (4) the availability and price of other formats, and (5) the price of the textbook without supplemental material (HEOA, 2008, §112).

Copyrighted Material in HEOA

HEOA also amended the Copyrighted Material section of the Program Participation Agreement (HEOA, 2008, §488). Each institution of higher education must certify that it has policies in place addressing the unauthorized distribution of copyrighted material, including unauthorized peer-to-peer file sharing. Such policies must be made available to prospective and enrolled students and must list not only institutional sanctions but also civil and criminal penalties for unauthorized distribution of copyrighted material. In addition, each institution must, to the extent practicable, offer alternatives to illegal downloading or unauthorized peer-to-peer file sharing (HEOA, 2008, §488).

COPYRIGHT ACT OF 1976

The Copyright Act of 1976 protects original works of authorship fixed in any tangible medium of expression including literary works, musical works, dramatic works, motion pictures, and sound recordings. The Act does not protect ideas, procedures, processes, systems, methods of operation, concepts, or principles (Copyrights Act, 2011).

The owner of a copyright has the exclusive right to reproduce the work; to prepare derivative works; to distribute copies for sale, rental, lease, or lending; to perform or display literary, musical, dramatic, choreographic, or cinematographic works publicly; and to transmit sound recordings digitally. The author or authors of a work own the copyright unless the work is considered a work made for hire. The employer or the person for whom the work was prepared own the copyright of a work made for hire (Copyrights Act, 2011).

The protections provided by the Copyright Act exist from the moment that the work is fixed in tangible form. Neither publication of the work nor registration of the work is necessary to secure protection under the Copyright Act. Although notice of the copyright was originally required under the Copyright Act of 1976, notice has not been required to achieve protection since March 1, 1989. However, providing notice of copyright is important because it alerts the public to the protections and eliminates the use of the innocent infringement defense in a copyright infringement lawsuit. Notice of copyright should contain three elements: (1) the © symbol or the word "copyright,"

(2) the year of first publication, and (3) the name of the owner of the copyright (Copyrights Act, 2011).

Typically, a person who wishes to make use of copyrighted material must obtain permission from the owner. If a person makes use of copyrighted material without permission from the owner, he or she may be sued for copyright infringement. Relief for copyright infringement may include an injunction to prevent or restrain further use of the copyrighted work, a judgment for damages and profits made by the infringer, and costs and attorney's fees. In addition, a person who willfully infringes a copyright for commercial advantage or private financial gain may be found guilty of criminal infringement (Copyrights Act, 2011).

However, a number of exceptions exist that allow someone other than the owner of a copyright to use copyrighted material without obtaining permission. Perhaps the most common exception is fair use, which allows reproduction for purposes such as criticism, comment, news reporting, teaching (including multiple copies for classroom use), scholarship, or research. To determine whether a particular use falls within the fair use exception, a four-factor test is used. First, consider the purpose and character of the use, including whether the use is commercial or educational. Second, consider the nature of the copyrighted work. Third, consider the amount and substantiality of the portion used in relationship to the entire copyrighted work. Fourth, consider the effect of the use upon the potential market for or value of the copyrighted work (Copyrights Act, 2011).

Another exception to the copyright protection that is particularly relevant in the higher education context is the exception for face-to-face teaching activities. This exception allows a faculty member or a student to display or perform copyrighted materials during a face-to-face class. If the faculty member or student is using a copy of a motion picture or other audiovisual work, the copy must have been obtained within the parameters of the Copyright Act (Copyrights Act, 2011).

TECHNOLOGY EDUCATION AND COPYRIGHT HARMONIZATION ACT OF 2002

Because instruction is no longer limited to face-to-face courses, Congress passed in 2002 the Technology Education and Copyright Harmonization Act ([TEACH Act], Pub. L. No. §13301, 116 Stat., 1910). The TEACH Act allows faculty and students in distance learning or online classes to perform or display non-dramatic literary works, musical works, and reasonable and limited portions of other works in an amount comparable to what is typically displayed in a live classroom under the circumstances specified in the following paragraph.

To qualify under the TEACH Act, the performance or display must be made by, at the direction of, or under the actual supervision of the instructor as an integral part of a class session at an accredited non-profit educational institution. In addition, the performance or display must be directly related and of material assistance to the teaching content. The transmission must be made solely for and, to the extent technologically feasible, limited to students officially enrolled in the course. The institution must take the following additional steps:

- adopt policies related to copyright;
- provide information to students, faculty, and other relevant staff that describe and promote compliance with copyright laws;
- provide notice to students that materials used in connection with the course may be subject to copyright protection; and
- apply technological measures that reasonably prevent the retention of the work for longer than the class session or unauthorized further dissemination of the work.

The institution also must not engage in conduct that could reasonably be expected to interfere with technological measures used by copyright owners to prevent retention or unauthorized further dissemination (TEACH Act, 2002).

The TEACH Act does not cover certain materials. For instance, copyrighted materials produced or marketed primarily for distance learning or online courses are not covered (TEACH Act, 2002). Students must still obtain these materials in compliance with copyright laws.

Institutions and faculty should not confuse the TEACH Act with the fair use exception to the copyright laws. The TEACH Act does not replace the fair use exception; instead, both provisions are exceptions to the copyright protections. Therefore, faculty members teaching distance learning courses should analyze whether either provision allows distribution of otherwise protected material. If material is not allowed to be distributed to students in a distance learning course under the TEACH Act, the faculty member should evaluate whether the material could be distributed to students under the fair use exception.

When considering whether to utilize the benefits provided by the TEACH Act, an institution must evaluate the costs of compliance with the law. Ashley (2004) recommends that the analysis address three questions:

1. What is the role of distance or online learning in the overall delivery of instruction?
2. What is the likelihood of successfully coordinating faculty, administration, and IT staff to ensure that procedures are in the place to meet the requirements?
3. What is the feasibility of implementing the necessary technological controls?

Ashley (2004) suggests that institutions that are replacing face-to-face instruction with distance or online learning should invest the time and resources into complying with the provisions of the TEACH Act.

CIVIL RIGHTS ACT OF 1964: TITLE VI AND VII

In 1964, Congress passed the Civil Rights Act (Pub. L. No. 88-52, 78 Stat. 241), covering several types of employers in its prohibition of unlawful discrimination. Title VI of the Civil Rights Act pertains only to programs receiving federal financial assistance, while Title VII pertains to all employers with a workforce of 15 or more. The Civil Rights Act of 1991 (Pub. L. No. 102-166, 105 Stat. 1071) amended this law to change the legal avenues available to plaintiffs. It added jury trials as an option, and it opened the door for punitive as well as compensatory damages in cases of intentional discrimination.

Title VI

Congress limited Title VI to prohibiting discrimination on the bases of race, color, and national origin (Civil Rights Act, 1964). Only in 1972 did they address sex discrimination in federally funded programs, passing Title IX of the Education Amendments (Pub. L. No. 92-318, 86 Stat. 373). The ultimate penalty for employers violating Title VI (or Title IX) is termination of federal funds to the program. The law provides for extensive administrative processing to achieve voluntary compliance prior to that action. The precise wording of the law prohibits intentional discrimination. Federal funding agencies have extended protection by implementing regulations that address the functional effects of discrimination based on race, color, or national origin.

The law prohibits an employer from preferring candidates of one race over another or advertising such hints as a preference for U.S.-born applicants. Each of those practices represents disparate treatment—basic discrimination. The regulations for the U.S. Department of Education (one agency offering federal funding) also prohibit the recipient (employer) from practices that create disparate impact—patterns and practices that have the effect of discriminating based on race, color, or national origin. The U.S. Department of Justice investigates complaints of discrimination under Title VI.

The U.S. Department of Education would ask an employer responding to a complaint involving a hiring decision to identify the steps taken to make the decision. The complaint could have come from an external applicant or a current employee seeking a promotion. In the following example, Candidate is an external applicant alleging that the employer's practices had the effect of discriminating based on race. Candidate is Hispanic and indicated on her application several employment experiences and one educational degree obtained in Mexico.

As the Respondent, the employer (a small public institution of higher education) first outlined the criteria for employment and identified them as neutral. They included: filing an application by the posted deadline; possessing the required degree; documenting the required years of experience; obtaining at least some of that experience in a small public institution of higher education; experience with the legacy computer system of that employer; successful completion of an interview; and a reference check. Candidate met the first four criteria. She had never worked for the employer, so current and former employees advanced to the interview stage and her candidacy ended before step 5. She based her complaint on information that the interview pool included former employees whose experience with the legacy computer system was more than 10 years ago, while her computer experience was current.

Each interviewee was white. The composition of the IT function at the employer was 90% white, 5% African-American, and 5% Asian/Pacific Islander. Census data indicated that local workforce representation of IT specialists is 66% white, 9% African-American, 10% Hispanic, and 15% Asian/Pacific Islander.

Candidate based her case on patterns and practices that had the effect of discriminating against Hispanic applicants. The employer's representation in the career field fell significantly short of the local qualified applicant pool. The employer used a criterion of past or present employment in the career field with the employer, thereby eliminating Hispanic representation from the applicant pool. The criterion was not job-related:

experience with a computer system 10 years prior was an invalid predictor of future success in the position.

Candidate would likely win this pattern and practice case. The criteria seemed neutral on their face, but close examination indicated that they were not the only methods to screen for computer expertise with the current system. Since there were less-discriminatory ways of screening, the hiring criterion would be considered to have the effect of discriminating.

Originally, the federal agencies bound by Title VI interpreted their regulations supporting Title VI quite broadly, especially in the area of a federally funded program or activity. They used the term to mean that acceptance of federal assistance resulted in coverage of the entity. After 20 years of such interpretations, a Supreme Court case sharply narrowed the definition. The case actually addressed Title IX, the companion language that prohibited sex discrimination in federally funded programs. It also applied to Title VI and two other statutes that used Title VI as a model: the Age Discrimination Act and Section 504 of the Rehabilitation Act, focused on individuals with disabilities.

Grove City College v. Bell (1984) restricted coverage of Title IX to the actual office receiving federal funds: the student financial aid office. The *Grove City* decision (1984) held that applicants or employees could challenge the employment practices within the financial aid office, but in no other area of the university. See the Title IX section of this chapter for a detailed discussion of the impact on intercollegiate athletics.

For four years, employers who were recipients of federal funds functioned as if the only requirement involved in accepting all those dollars was to maintain non-discriminatory practices in the financial aid workforce. By 1988, Congress asserted its original intent, passing the Civil Rights Restoration Act (Pub. L. No. 100-259, 102 Stat. 28). Agencies returned to interpreting enforcement regulations as covering the entire recipient: all of its programs and activities.

Title VII

Title VII prohibits an employer from taking an adverse employment action based on race, color, religion, national origin, or sex (Civil Rights Act, 1964). Congress amended the law in 1978 to add pregnancy as a protected class and a basis for discrimination, as part of the definition of sex discrimination (Pregnancy Discrimination Act of 1978, Pub. L. No. 95-555, 92 Stat. 2076). Within each basis, employers also are liable if their representatives take adverse action against participants in the process to resolve discrimination. Retaliation against the party who complains of discrimination or files a charge is prohibited. Witnesses are also protected; the language covers individuals who participate in an employment discrimination investigation, complaint, or lawsuit and then experience an adverse action based on that participation. The Equal Employment Opportunity Commission investigates complaints of discrimination under all areas of Title VII.

This prohibition of retaliation accompanied the Pregnancy Discrimination Act in 1978. In 2010, retaliation became the most frequent basis for civil rights complaints filed with the agency responsible for investigation. The Equal Employment Opportunity Commission (EEOC) reported that, in 2010, retaliation topped race for the first time in the 50-year history of the agency.

In 2009, the Lily Ledbetter Fair Pay Act (Pub. L. No. 111-2, 123 Stat. 5) redefined the standards for pursuing sex discrimination claims related to wages. Congress authorized EEOC to pursue the method it had long embraced: to trace the discrimination back in time to its inception and calculate the damages from the date of discrimination. This resolved the Supreme Court case in which Goodyear claimed as the defendant that plaintiff Ledbetter could sue only for the difference in pay with male counterparts for the previous two years.

Title VII covers two types of actions. The first is refusing to hire someone, discharging someone, or discriminating in compensation or terms of employment. The second type of action is when an employer limits or classifies employees to deprive them of opportunities. Each requires a showing that the employer took the adverse action based on race, color, religion, national origin, or sex. Congress spoke to such practices by employment agencies, labor organizations, and training programs, as well: they must avoid actions that an employer must avoid (Civil Rights Act, 1964).

The case records of EEOC contain many examples of each type of prohibited action. Since Congress created the Civil Rights Act of 1964, it has issued regulations, guidelines, and Memos of Understanding. Prohibited actions include printing employment notices that specify or indicate a preference or refusal to hire, such as advertising for a "girl Friday" or a "Christian trainee." Another prohibited action is describing opportunities with less structure in contrast to more arduous or time-consuming roles, such as "Partner- and Mommy-track opportunities available."

EEOC will consider an employer's argument that a posting specification was a bona fide occupational qualification (BFOQ). Employers must be aware that BFOQs must be defined very narrowly, by specific circumstance, and in functional terms rather than by sex or other protected class. A classic example includes "sperm donor," in which an individual is hired to provide that substance from within the body. A requirement for a female or male actor is considered a BFOQ when the face and/or body must convey the role. Costumed and masked characters likely would not support sex as a BFOQ.

Title VII—Race

Until 2010, EEOC most frequently received complaints of discrimination based on race. Race discrimination includes adverse employment actions based on the identification of an individual as belonging to a particular race. The person taking the discriminatory action does not have to be correct in identifying the race. Even if the perception was mistaken, a hiring official's refusal to hire an applicant perceived to be African-American would constitute race discrimination.

One of the leading race discrimination cases, *Griggs v. Duke Power Company* (1971), forever changed employers' understanding of the term "job-related criterion." Prior to the Civil Rights Act, Duke Power hired African-Americans only in the Labor division. Thirteen African-American employees challenged the company's new criteria of possessing a high-school diploma and passing two general aptitude tests for transfer from Labor to other divisions. The employees cited a disparate impact on African-Americans with a claim that the diploma and the two tests were unrelated to the jobs in the inside divisions with starting salaries above the highest salary in Labor. As evidence, they cited the continued successful performance of white colleagues who transferred among other divisions without having a high-school diploma or taking either test. Those colleagues continued to be promoted within the company. The Supreme Court ruled that tests producing an adverse impact by race must be job-related. Employers also must document whether instruments with lower adverse impact are available and reasonable (*Griggs v. Duke Power Company*, 1971).

Adverse actions extend beyond failure to hire and include demotions, failure to promote, layoffs, or other negative terms or conditions of employment. An employee may bring a viable charge if he is discriminated against because he is affiliated with an individual who brought a charge based on race. As an example, if an employer feels prejudice against employees involved in biracial relationships or marriage, it would be unlawful for the employer to terminate the employee on that basis. Adverse action based on affiliation with an individual of another race can support a charge of race discrimination.

Title VII—Color

This section within Title VII addresses the skin tone of an individual. This element was intended to halt the onerous "paper bag" test employed with African-Americans: if his skin tone was lighter than a paper bag, he might be employed in front-desk or customer service positions. The alleged discriminating official may be of the same or similar skin tone as the target of discrimination; a complaint would still be viable. Harassment based on color might include the display of racially offensive symbols such as a noose, references such as the paper bag test, or slurs, if they create a hostile or offensive work environment or result in an adverse employment action (Civil Rights Act, 1964).

Title VII—Religion

Religion includes a good-faith statement by the employee regarding the religious practices that might be discussed with the employer. A small or relatively unknown sect or group of individuals might practice the religious beliefs, but EEOC has held that the popularity of the beliefs is irrelevant (Civil Rights Act, 1964). The employer may challenge the nature of the beliefs in highly limited circumstances. If an applicant's or employee's religious beliefs are sincerely held, the employer must provide reasonable accommodation unless doing so would impose an undue hardship on the operation of the employer's business. When the employer considers the applicant's or employee's religious observance or practice, it is important to solicit specific information from the individual. The requestor is responsible for explaining the functional impact on the employer, but has no requirement to explain or defend the tenets of the faith.

As an example, an employee may request authorization to pray at noon each workday. She may cite her sincerely held religious belief without identifying the name of the religion. An employer faced with that vague request may open a dialogue that pinpoints the request in business terms, so the employer can make a decision. That inquiry might include when the employee will need to leave the workplace, when she will return to the workplace, and on what pay status she will take this time. After receiving those specifics, the employer will also consider her assigned position. Is she in charge of small children who require adult supervision at the time she requests? Is her lunch break normally at noon? If the absence coincides with her scheduled midday meal break, which she may use in any way she seems fit, this solution represents coordination and communication, but involves no accommodation to religious observance. Religious accommodation occurs when the employer assigns another employee to supervise the children from 11:55 to 12:25 and releases the employee for a 30-minute break.

In a more complex case, employers will face situations in which an employee's responsibilities place him or her in a singular situation. An example might be a police officer, who must continue responding to a crisis no matter what time of day it occurs. These situations call for employers to discuss options with the employee. It is critical to ensure the employee's participation in developing the list of options. The employer then chooses the accommodation(s) offered.

Title VII—National Origin

National origin discrimination differs from race discrimination. National origin refers to the country of birth, the part of the world from which an individual comes to the United States jurisdiction, ethnicity from within a country, or even accent. As with other types of discrimination, the alleged discriminating official could be wrong about the national origin, but if that was the basis for an adverse action, it can be the basis for a charge. As with race, sex, and other categories, the national origin of the alleged discriminating official might be the same as that of the person discriminated against. Title VII covers hiring, termination, pay, benefits, and other terms and conditions of employment (Civil Rights Act, 1964).

One of the most common violations of Title VII relating to national origin is the requirement to speak only English in the workplace. A broad statement to that effect, if not job-related and necessary to the operation of the business, is unlawful. Broad, unlawful statements would include language such as, "When this office is open, all employees will speak only English."

An employer may require employees executing work functions to speak only English if it promotes the safety and well-being of all employees (a non-discriminatory reason). This may be needed when the unit's mission is health care, and each member of the team must communicate clearly to all other members in the shortest possible time. However, it is not job-related to regulate an individual's conversation in a language other than English while that person is on a meal break, taking a trip to the restroom, or passing a friend on the way from one building to another, which could lead to a complaint.

A related complaint may be filed when an individual's accent is used as the basis for an adverse action. This still must relate to national origin; a Southern United States accent considered by some to represent a slow cadence or a New York accent considered by some to be brusque would not qualify. The employer may take an action based on the employee's ability to communicate in English in the situations experienced on the job, but not on the accent itself.

The third most common area of complaint under this section is citizenship discrimination. An individual is eligible to work in the United States with appropriate documentation. Employers may not tell an applicant that he or she must present a driver's license and U.S. passport, just so they are doubly sure that individual is eligible to work. Unless the job requirements call for U.S. citizenship as a qualification, an

Table 13.1 Title VII Remedies and Avenues

Administrative	Judicial
• EEOC complaint substantiated • EEOC negotiation with employer • EEOC notification that conciliation has been filed, with time for recipient to reply • Civil action by U.S. Department of Justice, if recommended by EEOC	• Federal district court, regardless of EEOC finding • Declaratory relief • Injunctive relief • Attorney's fees and costs • Reinstatement with back pay up to two years (if discrimination was intentional)

employer may not impose it. Jobs requiring security clearances may support such a requirement, for example.

Title VII—Pregnancy Discrimination

Pregnancy is defined more broadly than the physical status of currently carrying a fetus (Pregnancy Discrimination Act, 1978). The Pregnancy Discrimination Act (1978) includes pregnancy, childbirth, or a medical condition related to pregnancy or childbirth in its definition. Females experiencing these conditions must be treated the same as other employees for all purposes related to employment. If an employer considers males in staff positions for unpaid leaves of absence following exhaustion of all sick, annual, and compensatory time, the employer must consider females for such leaves of absence related to pregnancy.

Each provision in the Pregnancy Discrimination Act (1978) addresses the right of the employee to continue working when she is able or to be treated similarly to any other employee who is unable to work. That involves sick leave authorizations based on inability to work, without regard to the cause, and continuation of benefits during authorized leave, to the extent provided to other individuals on authorized leave.

AMERICANS WITH DISABILITIES ACT OF 1990

Disability discrimination by non-governmental employers was only loosely constrained prior to the Americans with Disabilities Act of 1990 (ADA). This Act (Pub. L. No. 101-336, 104 Stat. 327) was a landmark because it covered employers with 25 or more employees, thereby including for the first time a large segment of private-sector employers. That threshold is 15 employees now. Prior to the ADA, governmental employers responded to Sections 503 and 504 of the Rehabilitation Act of 1973 (Pub. L. No. 93-112, 87 Stat. 355). That pertained to employment and enrollment in institutions that accepted federal contracts. No other employers were prohibited from discriminating based on disability. The Equal Employment Opportunity Commission investigates complaints of discrimination under all areas of the ADA.

The ADA prohibits employers from discriminating against qualified individuals with a disability (Pub. L. No. 101-336, 104 Stat. 327, 1990). Table 13.2 summarizes the components of the Americans with Disabilities Act of 1990.

There are many aspects to determining if an individual is covered by the ADA. The basic definition speaks to a physical or mental impairment that substantially limits a

Table 13.2 Components of the Americans with Disabilities Act of 1990

Section Description	Implementation Tips
Title I Employment—prohibits discrimination against qualified employees in the private sector and in state and local government; prohibits retaliation	Plan to offer reasonable accommodation to the known physical or mental limitations of an otherwise qualified applicant or employee with a disability
Title II Public Entities and Transportation—programs, activities, services of public entities	Ensure both physical access and program access. The educational program includes such learning strategies as readers, interpreters, technological assistance, extended time on tests, among others
Title III Public Accommodations (commercial facilities)	Consider accessibility of the institution's public retail outlets, lodging, recreation, transportation, dining, places of public display. If the public can access it without an institutional ID or registration, Title III covers it. Institutions must remove architectural barriers and observe barrier-free building standards
Title IV Telecommunications	Led to wide use of Telecommunications Device for the Deaf (TDD) installations. Established foundation for dual-party relay systems in all 50 states, where deaf individuals call an operator on a TDD and the operator voices information over a telephone and vice versa
Title V Miscellaneous provisions	Specifies the non-retaliation provisions

major life activity. After the status determination, the employer proceeds to determine a reasonable accommodation.

The status determination assumed a much lower threshold in 2008, when Congress passed the ADA Amendments Act (Pub. L. No. 110-325, 122 Stat. 3553). Now, an employer may assume that any substantial limitation of a major life activity or major bodily function will trigger the ADA coverage. The life activity may be unrelated to the job. Examples of major life activities include sleeping and lifting; examples of newly covered "major bodily functions" include circulatory or reproductive functions. It is irrelevant that the job does not require the employee to lift, or to reproduce. The status of a substantial limitation in lifting or reproducing makes the employee an individual with a disability (ADA Amendments Act, 2008).

An employer also may trigger coverage with an action that implies belief that the individual has a disability, even if that is not the case (ADA Amendments Act, 2008). If the employer does not promote the employee to a position involving public presentations because of a fear that clients will not respond well to an individual with a prominent scar, the employer has discriminated based on the belief that the individual has a substantial limitation.

In addition, if an employer receives a report that an applicant attended a school known for addressing a particular health condition or status and refuses to hire on that basis, the employer has regarded the applicant as an individual with a disability. The employer may speculate that a graduate of Gallaudet University is an individual with a disability and decide not to hire graduates of that institution. An applicant with a degree from that institution can take action under the ADA Amendments Act because of the discriminatory refusal to hire based on perception, no matter whether he or she actually is deaf.

There are transitory and minor conditions that do not trigger ADA protection. Generally, transitory conditions are those that a physician expects to heal or resolve within six months (ADA Amendments Act, 2008). The ADA requires no accommodation. The employer may provide strategies for success, but these are not accommodations required by the ADA.

The employer is responsible for screening against the definition of an otherwise qualified individual. A qualified individual can perform the essential functions of the position with or without reasonable accommodation (ADA Amendments Act, 2008). Examples of individuals not qualified would include employees terminated for violating conduct rules or applicants who do not possess the minimum posted qualifications. In those cases, the individual is not otherwise qualified no matter what his or her physical or mental condition might be. The employer defines the essential functions. Employers who define those functions prior to filling the job present a defensible rationale for applying those decisions later, because they made the decisions without knowing the applicants in the pool.

Pre-employment skill tests are essential elements of the hiring process and must be offered to all applicants. Employers must offer applicants reasonable accommodations such as speech-to-text or text-to-speech versions of tests, adjustments in time, or use of specific equipment. On the job, reasonable accommodations might include readers, sign language interpreters, speech-to-text or text-to-speech technology, or modified work schedules.

An employer must offer a reasonable accommodation unless doing so would pose an undue hardship on the operation of that employer's business (ADA Amendments Act, 2008). EEOC regards employers in large systems (public universities, state or community colleges, school districts) as single employers with access to substantial resources. EEOC is likely to compare the cost of an accommodation with the total institutional budget to test the assertion that the cost was an unreasonable burden.

The ADA Amendments Act clarified several definitions left vague in competing federal district court cases. Most pertinent to educational administrators, the ADA Amendments Act (2008) specified that employers must consider applicants and employees without mitigating measures such as medicine or technological support. If their physical or mental condition produces a disability without medication, therapy, or accommodation, they are individuals with disabilities (ADA Amendments Act, 2008).

Examples include individuals who control diabetes with insulin, regulating their blood sugar to acceptable levels each day, and individuals with multiple sclerosis, who may have intermittent days on which they experience mobility impairments. Substantially limiting conditions (even when helped with medication) or conditions that produce limitations only intermittently are disabilities.

The definitions of discrimination within the ADA include two types: limiting or classifying employees to deprive them of opportunities, or a failure to accommodate (ADA, 1990). There are specific exemptions to the ADA, such as current illegal use of drugs, status as an individual with a communicable disease when no reasonable accommodation will achieve safety for the food supply, near-sightedness corrected with corrective lenses, and compulsive gambling.

TITLE IX OF THE EDUCATION AMENDMENTS OF 1972

Intending to extend the race-discrimination protections of Title VI to complaints of sex discrimination, Congress passed Title IX (Pub. L. No. 92-318, 86 Stat. 373, 1972). This statute extends to federally funded educational programs or activities. A recipient of federal funds may not exclude someone from participation in a program, deny someone the benefits of a program, or subject someone to discrimination in a program (Title IX, 1972).

Supporters brokered numerous exemptions from Title IX to ensure its passage. Traditional single-sex institutions, social fraternities or sororities, the membership practices of the Boy Scouts and Girl Scouts, and scholarship assistance awarded in a pageant based on personal appearance, poise, and talent are exempt from coverage. Recipients may maintain single-sex living facilities (such as campus residence halls).

Title IX (1972) differs from other statutes in that it prohibits the consideration of population statistics in determining a gender imbalance in a program. This clause satisfied original opponents of Title IX by defusing any argument that girls constituted approximately 50% of the population and should represent 50% of the athletic participation opportunities. In fact, Title IX regulations neither permit nor impose quotas for athletic or academic participation.

Athletics turned into the primary focus of Title IX conversation, but the statute clearly applies to every program or activity of a school, college, university, or educational training program. An overview of the total coverage of Title IX will thus precede a detailed examination of athletics. Major topic headings and guidelines of Title IX are presented in Table 13.3.

Much of the Title IX literature relates to athletics and the requirement to achieve proportionality. That term has been redefined over the years, starting from the early days when high schools and universities informally excluded football from assessment and then compared opportunities in all other sports. From 2000, when federal agencies joined to promulgate the common regulations for all agencies enforcing Title IX, recipients (schools and universities) concentrated on two types of measures: (1) factors to assess equity, and (2) the three-prong test of equity (Nondiscrimination, 2011).

The regulations call for use of 10 factors in assessing athletic equity; these are shown in Table 13.4 (Nondiscrimination, 2011).

Using the three-prong test, a recipient institution must confirm annually that it is in compliance with Title IX. Failing that, it must demonstrate that it has prepared an effective plan for achieving equity. The three prongs are accommodation of interests and abilities, substantial proportionality, and history and practice of expansion of sports (Nondiscrimination, 2011).

To analyze accommodation of interest and abilities, institutions should use the first of the 10 factors in Table 13.4. The recipient institution may consider its program equitable even with a proportionate difference exceeding approximately 3%. This may occur if participation in intramural and club sports shows no overwhelming participation by the underrepresented gender, and surveys of area or state high-school participation show little if any unmet need. However, if the club and intramural levels of crew show an excellent participation rate for women, and women are underrepresented in the

Table 13.3 Title IX Coverage

Topic	Guidelines
Admission; recruitment	Commingle applicant lists (no male list/female list of applicants); no quotas for male/female proportions to be admitted; eliminate choice of "Miss" and "Mrs." from applications to avoid decisions based on marital status of females but not males
Education programs, activities	In addition to primary academic program, includes research opportunities and other enhancements of academic success
Housing	Same-sex housing permitted. Facilities must be similar for each sex (quality and cost)
Comparable facilities	Same-sex restroom, locker, shower facilities permitted if comparable for male and female participants
Access to course offerings	Physical education contact sports: male and female groupings permitted. Choruses featuring a specific vocal range are permitted, even if they result in participation predominantly by one sex
Counseling; appraisal materials	Guidance or career counseling must be gender-neutral, without steering men and women into gender-traditional careers or majors
Financial assistance	Permits administration of donor-designated scholarships for one sex, if the overall program of assistance is proportionate
Employment assistance to students	Listings for external positions and referral for internal employment of students must be non-discriminatory
Health and insurance benefits and services	Equivalent benefits, even if one sex may use them more (i.e. birth control). Full-service coverage must include gynecological care
Marital or parental status	Pregnant and parenting students must be included in the main program unless they request separation. Pregnancy and related conditions justify a leave of absence while medically necessary
Athletics	Covers interscholastic, intercollegiate, club, or intramural programs. If competitive skill is required, separate male and female teams are permitted
Employment: criteria, compensation, benefits, pre-employment inquiries	Criteria and benefits must not discriminate. Examples of discriminatory criteria: preferring graduates of a known single-sex institution; classifying similar jobs for males and females with different pay levels. Discriminatory benefits: obstetrical coverage to female employees but not the female spouses of male employees

intercollegiate program, there would appear to be a clear opportunity to correct the representation by transitioning to an intercollegiate women's crew team.

To evaluate substantial proportionality, institutions should compare the proportions of male and female undergraduates to male and female intercollegiate athletes. If the comparison results in a difference of less than approximately 3%, the program may be regarded as equitable.

Assessing history and practice of expansion of sports was more popular during the 1980s than it is now. Institutions with disproportionate participation ratios used this prong. Those institutions may have been blessed with an abundance of female high-school, intramural, and club lacrosse players, bowlers, and equestrians in the area, just waiting for an intercollegiate team to form. If the institution could show that it had added and/or planned to add each women's sport, one every three years, to achieve proportionality, it could claim equity in the report.

The regulations also require each recipient organization to notify all students and employees of the Title IX Coordinator's name and contact information

Table 13.4 Ten Factors to Assess Athletic Equity

Factor	Guidelines and strategies
1. Accommodation of interest	If the male/female proportions involved in intercollegiate athletics differ from the undergraduate enrollment proportions by less than approximately three percent, the program is balanced. If not, institutions must assess the situation and address it. They may survey the feeder schools in various sports; survey current students, and/or assess interest in intramural sports
2. Provision of equipment and supplies	The recipient institution must check quality as well as inventory. If the women's tennis team must hit practice tennis balls against a backboard and retrieve them, but the men's tennis team has a ball machine and assistants to retrieve the balls, the equipment may be found inequitable
3. Scheduling of games and practice times	Some schools schedule the men's soccer team at 7AM for half the season and the women's for the second half, moving the men to the 3PM practice. Each team likes one and dislikes the other, but practice times are equitable
4. Travel and per diem allowance	Institutions must offer teams equivalent arrangements (two to a double room, or bus travel only under three hours) and payments (a certain amount for food, or a requirement to attend the team lunch provided at no charge)
5. Opportunity to receive coaching and tutoring	Addresses the availability of coaches (three assistants for Men's Basketball, three for Women's Basketball, as an example) and tutoring access, if tutoring is offered specifically for athletes
6. Assignment and compensation of coaches and tutors	Measured through salaries at equitable levels or percentiles. It might be inequitable to provide Men's Golf with an experienced coach earning in the 75th percentile in their NCAA division while providing Women's Golf with a part-time graduate student coach earning in the 10th percentile
7. Provision of locker rooms, practice, and competitive facilities	The focus is less on appearance than functionality. If Women's Soccer shares lockers with Women's Volleyball and must vacate them in November for Women's Basketball, it might be inequitable if Men's Soccer has private lockers accessible year-round
8. Provision of medical and training facilities and services	Assignment of full-time trainers who travel with the team and attend practices; services such as first attention to injuries
9. Provision of housing and dining facilities and services	There is no requirement to provide housing. If male athletes are given early priority to sign up for campus housing, female athletes should be accorded the same priority
10. Publicity	Media guides, weekly announcements on campus, special nights welcoming sport alumni that increase attendance and support must be equitable

(Nondiscrimination, 2011). This designee often wears other hats at the institution but is responsible for annual updates to the self-evaluation all recipient organizations had to complete in 2000. The Title IX Coordinator also publicizes the recipient's internal complaint policy. The Coordinator might be the primary investigator under the policy, but that is not required by regulation.

The U.S. Department of Education's Office for Civil Rights investigates complaints of sex discrimination under all areas of Title IX in educational institutions. Other federal agencies investigate complaints of sex discrimination in educational programs receiving funding. As an example, the U.S. Department of Energy's Office of Civil Rights may investigate Title IX compliance in higher education disciplines in which it funds faculty members' research grants.

FAMILY AND MEDICAL LEAVE ACT OF 1993

The Family and Medical Leave Act of 1993 ([FMLA], Pub. L. No. 103-3, 107 Stat. 6) provides a safety net for parents, caregivers, and employees who experience a serious illness. This law protects the individual's job during his or her absence, without guaranteeing paid leave status. The U.S. Department of Labor investigates FMLA claims. The employer must consider whether the employee is eligible, whether the purpose meets the definition in the law, and how the employee must document the authorized leave.

After all these steps are taken, what does the employee actually receive? The employee's absence is authorized, and he or she may return to the same or a similar position. The leave is limited to 12 workweeks in any 12-month period (FMLA, 1993). Some employers fix that period, starting the calculation over on July 1 or January 1 of each year. Others follow the definition of the 12-month period, floating the period from the current date to 12 months ago to determine the remaining authorization for leave.

The authorization under the law relates to unpaid leave. Employers may grant paid leave in accordance with their policies. Common types of paid leave include sick, annual, and accrued compensatory time. Employers determine eligibility first by considering the size of their workforce; smaller employers may be exempt from this law. They then look to the employee's work history to confirm that the employee has worked there for at least 12 months, and in that time has worked at least 1,250 hours. The 12 months need not be consecutive. Military service and collective bargaining agreements impact these calculations, as well.

FMLA leave is provided for specific purposes, which have been enhanced since the 1993 passage of the law. These purposes are (1) birth and care of a newborn child of the employee, (2) placement with the employee of a child for adoption or foster care, (3) care for a one-degree relative (spouse, parent, sibling, or child) with a serious health condition, (4) inability of the employee to work due to a serious health condition, and (5) circumstances relating to the employee's one-degree relative who is on active military duty or call to active duty from reserve or National Guard status. A 2009 enhancement expanded the leave period to 26 weeks for an employee to care for a one-degree relative or next-of-kin who is a member of the Armed Forces.

The employer may collect documentation to support the use of leave under the FMLA. Certain illnesses might occur on an emergency basis, providing no opportunity to notify the employer until the next day. In situations when notice is possible, the employee is required to provide it. When medical treatments are pre-scheduled, the employee must show reasonable care to avoid disrupting the business functions. The employee may utilize intermittent leave for medical care, such as chemotherapy or physical therapy. This may involve reducing the normal work schedule and taking FMLA leave for part of a day or a week. The employer may choose whether to approve intermittent leave related to birth and care of a child, or placement of a child for adoption or foster care.

The definitions of a serious health condition differ from medical concepts within the Americans with Disabilities Act, which deals with "substantial limitations to a major life activity or major bodily function" (ADA Amendments, 2008). For the FMLA, one definition of a serious health condition is a physical or mental condition that calls for inpatient care (an overnight stay) in a treatment facility and an associated period of incapacity. As an example, an employee reports that he experienced suicidal behaviors, was admitted by a psychiatrist to a residential care facility for two days, and was then prescribed strong drugs to regulate his mood and behaviors. During the drugs' adjustment period, he was unable to work or perform other daily activities. The physician cleared him for return to work on the seventh workday following the admission date. The employer checks the employment record: the date of hire was two years ago and the employee has taken no leaves of absence or other significant interruptions, just vacations. The employee meets the test of 12 months of employment with that employer as well as 1,250 working hours in the past 12 months. He meets the test of a serious health condition: it required inpatient care. He reported incapacity: the physician documented that he could not work while the drugs were taking effect, and the dosage was regulated. In this example, all seven workdays of absence (date of admission plus six more) would be authorized under the FMLA.

To go further: this employer offers sick and annual leave accrual to employees. The employee has 17 hours of sick leave and three hours of annual leave accrued. The employee may choose to use all 20 leave hours to place him in pay status within the 56 hours of leave. The employer may withhold pay for the balance, 36 hours of absence. However, the employer may not take any adverse action because of that 36-hour leave without pay status. This employer has a policy that leave without pay represents lack of productivity and generates a Conditional rating on Attendance in the annual performance appraisal. The employer may enforce that for employees who utilized leave without pay to extend vacations, attend to unexpected personal business, or other non-covered matters. The employer may not use this 36-hour leave without pay period to rate this employee as Conditional in Attendance on the annual appraisal; that would be an adverse action against an employee authorized for FMLA leave.

The FMLA also protects employees requiring intermittent leave. The provisions related to intermittent care are extensive, and the summary in Table 13.5 omits certain qualifiers or exceptions.

Educational administrators may authorize leave in complex situations involving two or more laws. The following example illustrates a balance of the Family and Medical Leave Act and the Americans with Disabilities Act. The employee developed a serious health condition (cancer). Over the past two years of employment, she has taken extensive periods of leave without pay. The employer measures FMLA entitlement by fiscal year starting July 1. The employee provided a physician's statement that includes all the elements the employer needed: her name, treating physician's full contact information, duration of the condition, prognosis, functional limitations, ability to perform certain job tasks, and expected date of recovery or return to work. She requests intermittent leave and preservation of the same job. She is a faculty member with an active research program involving live cell cultures and experiments.

Table 13.5 Summary of Eligible Leave Circumstances for Continuing Care

FMLA Provision	Guidelines and Strategies
Incapacity lasting more than three days, including certain treatment schedules	The employer may require documentation related to the specific definitions involving dates of treatment and continuing treatment regimens
Prenatal care or incapacity related to pregnancy	The employee is not required to visit a health care provider for each episode
Treatment for or incapacity based on a chronic serious health condition which continues over an extended period of time	The employee is not required to visit a health care provider for each episode
Permanent or long-term incapacity for a condition for which treatment may not be effective	The employer may require documentation of supervision of a health care provider, but active treatment is not required
Multiple treatments for restorative surgery or a condition that would result in more than three days' incapacity if not treated	The employer may require documentation related to the specific definitions involving the condition and the dates of treatment

To determine her FMLA eligibility, conduct the following analysis using the flow chart in Figure 13.1: If the employee worked for this employer at least one year, then proceed. If the employee worked 1,250 hours this eligibility year, then proceed. If the illness is serious, then proceed. If the employee meets at least one test of eligibility based on continuing care, then proceed. The employee is eligible for FMLA if she provides clarification for intermittent leave.

For ADA eligibility, conduct the following analysis using the flow chart in Figure 13.1: If the employee is currently employed, then proceed. If the employee is a person with a disability, then proceed. If other options are possible in addition to intermittent leave, then discuss those options with the employee. The options must be reasonable. It would not be reasonable to eliminate research from her assignments or to pay her full time for research and eliminate all her teaching duties. If intermittent leave is not approvable, the employer has to offer something else. The employer and employee negotiate over offered accommodation.

AGE DISCRIMINATION IN EMPLOYMENT ACT OF 1967

Under the Age Discrimination in Employment Act ([ADEA], Pub. L. No. 90-202, 81 Stat. 602, 1967), the protected class starts at age 40 and continues without limit. No employer may take an adverse employment action based on age. Once again, this law echoes other civil rights laws in prohibiting retaliation for having complained or participated in a complaint. Congress intended the ADEA to prohibit artificial barriers to employment such as arbitrary age limits or requirements for retirement. It encourages employers to base decisions on the potential for full job performance. Similar to Title VII, it prohibits two types of actions by employers: refusing to hire, discharging, or discriminating in compensation or terms of employment based on age. The Equal Employment Opportunity Commission investigates complaints of discrimination under all areas of the ADEA.

FMLA

ADA

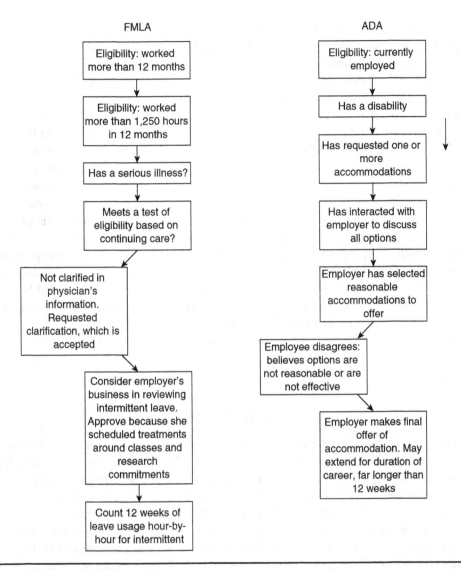

Figure 13.1 Flow Chart for FMLA and ADA

Congress recognized that age may be a BFOQ, but EEOC has limited the application of this possibility. Employers may set a minimum age for employment consistent with state and federal labor restrictions, including higher age standards for individuals working with certain machinery, for instance. Congress also authorized the payment of pension benefits that differ based on the age of the recipient as well as the decision of an employer to offer an early retirement incentive plan if based on employer needs.

One of the most common complaint situations results from a reduction in force (RIF) following economic trends. Employers may select the smallest number of higher-paid employees necessary to balance the budget in a RIF, unintentionally selecting the oldest employees in the workforce. When they are the only individuals laid off, it creates an adverse impact for those in the protected age category of 40 and older.

The employer might justify the adverse impact, but EEOC recommends instead that employers use appropriate prevention strategies. Such analyses begin with data to determine which employees are similarly situated. That term refers to individuals with identical compensation, position, date of hire, work history, and other relevant factors, such as performance appraisals and lead-worker status.

If any employees in the decisional unit are 40 or older, employers should take all precautions to ensure that they base their actions on permissible factors. Since EEOC would conduct similar analyses of RIFs for any protected-class member, these points are applicable when units are heterogeneous in other ways. In a diverse unit with men and women of various races and ages under and over 40, the employer will appreciate having conducted a non-discriminatory process with a detailed record of the decisions.

Some RIFs involve an incentive payment for voluntary resignation. This pertains more to the private sector than to public employers. The ADEA contains a specific requirement for ample notice and time to consider all settlements. This notice provision differs from other civil rights laws. An applicant or employee may accept an incentive payment or settlement by waiving the right to sue only if the offer specifies rights under the ADEA; the offer does not involve waiver of future causes of action; and the right to consult an attorney is spelled out clearly. The applicant or employee must have 21 days to consider the offer and seven days to rescind a signed offer. A court would weigh all these factors in any later dispute over whether the waiver of rights was knowing and voluntary.

CONCLUSION

This chapter discussed how the Family Educational Rights and Privacy Act, the Higher Education Opportunity Act of 2008, the Copyright Act of 1976, the Technology Education and Copyright Harmonization Act of 2002, the Civil Rights Act of 1964, the Americans with Disabilities Act of 1990, Title IX of the Education Amendments of 1972, the Family and Medical Leave Act of 1993, and the Age Discrimination in Employment Act of 1967 apply to institutions of higher education. Each of these laws has complexities and provisions outside the limits of this chapter, whose purpose was to acquaint higher education administrators with important points to consider when implementing policies. This information should also be useful when administrators inevitably encounter issues; however, administrators should seek legal counsel if involved in a lawsuit. Each law may have a different purpose, but, like the threads of a blanket, they all combine to provide a flexible yet protective shield.

REFERENCES

ADA Amendments Act of 2008, Pub. L. No. 110–325, 122 Stat. 3553 (2008).
Age Discrimination in Employment Act, Pub. L. No. 90–202, 81 Stat. 602 (1967).
Americans with Disabilities Act of 1990, Pub. L. No. 101–336, 104 Stat. 327 (1990).
Ashley, C. L. (2004). The TEACH Act: Higher education challenges for compliance. *Educause Center for Applied Research—Research Bulletin, 2004*(13), 1–11. Retrieved December 10, 2011, from http://net.educause.edu/ir/library/pdf/ERB0413.pdf
Civil Rights Act of 1964, Pub. L. No. 88-52, 78 Stat. 241 (1964).

Civil Rights Act of 1991, Pub. L. No. 102–166, 105 Stat. 1071 (1991).

Civil Rights Restoration Act of 1987, Pub. L. No. 100–259, 102 Stat. 28 (1988).

Copyrights Act, 17 U.S.C. §101 *et seq.* (2011).

Family and Medical Leave Act of 1993, Pub. L. No. 103-3, 107 Stat. 6 (1993).

Family Educational Rights and Privacy Act, 20 U.S.C. § 1232g (2011).

Family Educational Rights and Privacy Rule, 34 C. F.R. § 99 (2011).

Griggs v. Duke Power Company, 401 U.S. 424 (1971).

Grove City College v. Bell, 465 U.S. 555, (1984).

Higher Education Opportunity Act of 2008, Pub. L. No. 110–315, 122 Stat. 3078 (2008).

Hutchens, N. H. (2011). Systems governance. In R. Fossey, K. B. Melear, & J. B. Beckham (Eds.), *Contemporary issues in higher education law* (2nd ed.) (pp. 19–36). Dayton, OH: Education Law Association.

Lily Ledbetter Fair Pay Act of 2009, Pub. L. No. 111–12, 123 Stat. 5 (2009).

Nondiscrimination on the Basis of Sex in Education Programs or Activities Receiving FederalFinancial Assistance Rule, 34 C. F.R. §106 (2011).

Pregnancy Discrimination Act of 1978, Pub. L. No. 95–555, 92 Stat. 2076 (1978).

Rehabilitation Act of 1973, Pub. L. No. 93–112, 87 Stat. 355 (1973).

Technology Education and Copyright Harmonization Act, Pub. L. No. §13301, 116 Stat., 1910 (2002).

Title IX of the Education Amendments of 1972, Pub. L. No. 92–318, 86 Stat. 373 (1972).

BIOGRAPHIES

EDITORS

Patrick J. Schloss served as the eighth president of Valdosta State University from 2008 to 2011. He was born in Harvey, Illinois on October 1, 1953. President Schloss' academic career includes appointments as a tenured Professor and Chair at Penn State and the University of Missouri. He is among the most prolific and influential scholars in special education, having authored 20 books and over 100 research publications. Prior to serving at VSU, Dr. Schloss was provost at Bloomsburg University of Pennsylvania from 1994 to 2004, and President at Northern State University in Aberdeen, South Dakota from 2004 to 2008.

Kristina M. Cragg is Associate Vice President of Institutional Research at Ashford University where she provides leadership for federal and state reporting, surveys, and special data-analysis reports. Dr. Cragg earned her doctorate from Florida State University in Educational Leadership and Policy Studies with an emphasis in Higher Education Policy. She publishes in the area of student success with a focus on retention and graduation rates using national databases and institutional data. Dr. Cragg is an active member in the Association for Institutional Research. She also serves as a national trainer for IPEDS.

CONTRIBUTORS

Hana Addam El-Ghali is the Senior Program Coordinator for the Research, Advocacy and Public Policy-making (RAPP) program at the Issam Fares Institute for Public Policy and International Affairs at the American University of Beirut (AUB). Dr. El-Ghali is also a Consultant with the World Bank's Center for Mediterranean Integration (CMI) looking at pressing issues in higher education policy in the Middle East and North Africa (MENA). She received her Ph.D. in Administrative and Policy Studies with a focus on Social and Comparative Analysis in Education from the University of Pittsburgh. Dr. El-Ghali also serves as the MENA region co-editor for *Comparative and*

International Higher Education, the journal for the Higher Education Special Interest Group of the Comparative and International Education Society.

Janet Park Balanoff is the Director of Equal Opportunity and Affirmative Action (EO/AA) Programs, University of Central Florida. EO/AA designs and implements programs encouraging faculty, staff, and students to practice affirmative action and end discrimination in programs, personnel actions, and facilities. Ms. Balanoff served as the founding Chair of the Council on Equal Opportunity and Diversity, working with the equity officers in the Florida state university system before passing the gavel after five years. Ms. Balanoff holds a Master of Science in Public Administration from Florida State University and a bachelor's degree in journalism from the University of Florida.

Steven T. Breslawski is Associate Professor of Management and MIS and former Head of the Business Degree Programs at the College at Brockport, State University of New York. He is perennially immersed in the strategic planning, curriculum development, accreditation, and assessment activities of the school. Recipient of the SUNY Chancellor's Award for Excellence in Teaching, Dr. Breslawski's research pursuits include topical research in business as well as business education research in the areas of student motivation, student quality metrics, and analysis of assessment outcomes.

Cyndy Caravelis Hughes is an Assistant Professor of Criminology and Criminal Justice at Western Carolina University. She received her doctorate from Florida State University. Her research interests include the relationship between social threat and social control, the effect of inequality on crime, theoretical criminology and the death penalty. She is the former Managing Editor of the journal *Social Problems* and her field experience includes working as a legislative analyst for Florida's Commission on Capital Cases, as a crime intelligence analyst for the Florida Department of Law Enforcement and as an academic instructor in both male and female correctional institutions.

Julie Carpenter-Hubin is Assistant Vice President for Institutional Research and Planning at The Ohio State University. She was elected Vice-President of the Association for Institutional Research for 2011–12, and will serve as its President for 2012–13. She represents Ohio State to the Association of American Universities Data Exchange, and is a past chair of the Exchange's governing council. She served on the National Research Council's Data Panel, which advised the NRC's Committee on an Assessment of Research-Doctorate Programs on the questionnaires used in the assessment. Her research interests include higher education performance measurement and its use in developing improvement strategies.

John D. Crawford is Vice President for University Advancement at Valdosta State University and the CEO of the VSU Foundation, Inc. He was instrumental in the planning and execution of The University of West Alabama's *The University We Will Be* capital campaign while serving as Associate Vice President for University Advancement. He has significant experience in identifying, cultivating, and soliciting major gift prospects and has negotiated and closed several six- and seven-figure gifts. He is an active member of the Council for the Advancement and Support of Education (CASE), as well as the Georgia Education Advancement Council (GEAC).

Barrie D. Fitzgerald is an institutional research analyst at Valdosta State University in Valdosta, Georgia. His research interests include retention, graduation, and institutional effectiveness. Mr. Fitzgerald is an active member of and presenter at the Southern Association of Institutional Research (SAIR) and the Association for Institutional Research (AIR).

Ross A. Griffith has been Director of Institutional Research and Academic Administration at Wake Forest University since 1993. He has served as President of the Southern Association for Institutional Research, President of the North Carolina Association for Institutional Research and as Board Member of the Society for College and University Planning. He has participated on accreditation committees for the Southern Association of Colleges and Schools (SACS), has successfully directed Wake Forest's most recent Self-Study, and continues to serves as Liaison to SACS. Griffith has published his work on the Wake Forest strategic plan and its assessment in books and journals.

Angela E. Henderson is Associate Vice Chancellor of Institutional Research, Planning, and Assessment at Keiser University. She has co-presented sessions on organizing assessment and compliance processes at conferences including the Association for Institutional Research, the Southern Association of Colleges and Schools, and the Southern Association for Institutional Research. Her areas of expertise and interest include data-driven analyses, assessment, data visualization, and development of tools to facilitate institutional research and assessment processes.

Carrie E. Henderson serves as Coordinator of Student Success in Florida Department of Education's Division of Florida Colleges. Her professional experience includes state policy analysis, program evaluation, strategic planning, and grant writing. Henderson is a doctoral student in the Higher Education Administration program at Florida State University, and her research interests include the intersection of higher education and state government.

Shouping Hu is a Professor of Higher Education at Florida State University. His research interests examine issues related to college access and success, student engagement, and higher education policy. Dr. Hu currently serves as an editorial/advisory board member of the *Journal of Higher Education, Educational Researcher, Research in Higher Education, ASHE Higher Education Report Series*, and has previously served for six years on the editorial board of the *Journal of College Student Development.*

Jennifer Iacino serves as Dean of Student Development and Campus Life at Berkeley College, and previously served the Student Affairs divisions of Florida State University and Johnson & Wales University. Her professional experience includes areas of student organization advising, campus event planning, women in STEM programs, leadership development, civic engagement, and program evaluation. Additionally, her research interests include issues related to faculty development, student engagement via online technologies and social media, institutional culture, and student perceptions of race and diversity. Dr. Iacino recently developed a model, Faculty Development for Interdisciplinary Team-Teaching, to support innovations in sustainability curriculum.

Thomas C. Johnson is an Assistant Professor in the Emergency and Disaster Management Program in the Criminology and Criminal Justice Department at Western Carolina University. Dr. Johnson previously served for 35 years in the municipal and campus law enforcement profession including 15 years as a police chief for the Marshall University, Mississippi State University, and Western Carolina University police departments. Dr. Johnson's research interests are in emergency management technology including the integration of emergency management technology into the curriculum.

Shruti Kumar is a freelance Consultant in the area of Higher Education Management. She earned her master's degree in Higher Education Management—Master of Education (M.Ed.) from the University of Pittsburgh. Prior to starting her consulting work she worked at University of Pittsburgh and McGill University for over four years in areas like student affairs, curriculum development and international admissions. She also has more than six years of work experience in Corporate Communications and Human Resource Management across various industries in India. Her areas of interest include strategic planning, instructional technology, curriculum development, managing diversity at American campuses, and human resource management.

Valerie Martin Conley is the Director of the Center for Higher Education and Associate Professor of Higher Education and Student Affairs at Ohio University. Dr. Conley is the principal investigator for a National Science Foundation funded research project: "Academic Career Success in Science and Engineering-Related Fields for Female Faculty at Public Two-Year Institutions." She is a TIAA-CREF Institute Research Fellow, received the Ohio University Outstanding Graduate Faculty Award in 2007, and served on the Association for Institutional Research Board of Directors. Dr. Conley has published widely on faculty issues and is nationally recognized for her expertise on faculty retirement.

Kerry Brian Melear is an Associate Professor of Higher Education at the University of Mississippi, and his areas of expertise include college and university legal, financial, and public policy concerns. He is a member of the Board of Directors of the Education Law Association, the Author's Committee of *West's Education Law Reporter*, the editorial board of the *Journal of Cases in Educational Leadership*, and serves as the Book Review Editor for the *Journal of Law and Education*. He was selected as the University of Mississippi School of Education's Researcher of the Year in 2007 and 2010.

Kent J. Smith, Jr. currently serves as President and full Professor with tenure at Langston University. Dr. Smith has co-authored multiple publications. The topics of his most recent publications include cyberbullying in higher education, and managing human resources at colleges and universities. Dr. Smith received his Bachelor of Science and

Master of Education from Southern University. His Doctor of Philosophy degree was conferred from Colorado State University in Education and Human Resource Studies. Dr. Smith resides in Langston, OK with his wife Tiffany and has four children: Morgan, Trey, Tyler, and Trent.

Lydia Snover is the Director of Institutional Research at the Massachusetts Institute of Technology. Her research interests include developing measures of faculty productivity and doctoral outcomes and developing metrics for inter-institutional comparisons of research activity. She has presented findings and has served on panels at meetings of the Association of Institutional Research, European Association of Institutional Research, Northeast Association of Research, the Consortium on the Financing of Higher Education Institutional Research Meetings, the Association of American Universities Data Exchange and various other institutional research groups. She holds a BA in Philosophy and an MBA, both from Boston University.

Monoka Venters is the Corporate Secretary for the State University System of the Florida Board of Governors. She is a Doctoral Candidate in the Department of Educational Leadership and Policy Studies at The Florida State University. Her research concentrates on the legal aspects of higher education and understanding the factors behind the development of education policy. Her dissertation is a historical analysis of the evolution of federal policies designed to assist low-income students prepare for and enroll in college. She received a B.A. in English from Furman University and a J.D. from Washington and Lee University School of Law.

John L. Yeager has served at the University of Pittsburgh since 1966. Dr. Yeager has held a number of senior management positions such as University Vice President for Administration and Vice President for Planning and Budget. Currently he serves on the faculty in the Department of Administration and Policy Studies where he is responsible for teaching higher education management courses. He has consulted both nationally and internationally, and presented and published numerous papers, journal articles and book chapters. He has been active in professional societies such as the Society of College and University Planning where he served as President.

INDEX